COMPOSERS ON
MODERN
MUSICAL
CULTURE

COMPOSERS ON MODERN MUSICAL CULTURE

An Anthology of Readings on Twentieth-Century Music

Compiled and edited by
Bryan R. Simms

SCHIRMER BOOKS
New York

Copyright © 1999 by Schirmer Books

Schirmer Books
1633 Broadway
New York, NY 10019

Library of Congress Catalog Card Number 98-14757

Printed in the United States of America

Printing Number

1   2   3   4   5   6   7   8   9   10

Library of Congress Cataloging–in–Publication Data

Composers on modern musical culture : an anthology of readings on
    twentieth-century music / compiled and edited by Bryan R. Simms.
        p.   cm
    Includes bibliograhical references and index.
    ISBN 0–02–864751–3 (alk. paper)
    1. Musical—20th century—History and criticism. I. Simms, Bryan R.
ML197.C748   1999
780' .9'04—dc21   98-14757
                                                           CIP
                                                           MN

This paper meets the requirements of ANSI/NISO Z39.48–1992 (Permanence of Paper).

*This book is
dedicated to my daughter
Martha Randolph Simms*

CONTENTS

PREFACE

This volume contains thirty essays, each written by a major composer of the twentieth century and each dealing with cultural and aesthetic questions that have shaped music in the modern period. Each is presented in its entirety, prefaced by notes that underscore its relevance to the history of modern music. Essays by Charles Koechlin, Arnold Schoenberg, Luigi Nono, and Elliott Carter are found here for the first time in English, and others by Béla Bartók, Kurt Weill, and Darius Milhaud are presented in new English translations. Many of the other essays have until now not been reprinted and have become difficult to find.

The essays were selected for their clear and concise discussions of shaping forces that underlie the evolution of modern musical style. Writings that are limited to descriptions of individual composers' own works, specific compositions, interviews, or special compositional methods have been bypassed in favor of those that deal with broader cultural and artistic issues. Essays by critics are avoided in favor of the more authoritative and relevant essays of the composers themselves. Since the articles address underlying formative elements in modern music, they will complement the study of many different selections of musical works.

The essays are presented in rough chronological order under six headings, corresponding to the issues that they address. In the first group are statements concerning the late romantic aesthetic in music and impulses leading to new treatments of musical elements. The second group of essays originated mainly between the world wars, when bitter artistic feuds erupted concerning neoclassicism, objectivity in music, national idioms, and the relevance of earlier musical styles. A group of articles originating during the Cold War contains discussions of such issues as formalism in music, political and social responsibilities, expressivity, and a tendency toward depersonalization in music of that time. The most recent articles touch on the return to established musical values during the last quarter of the century. Essays by American composers addressing issues distinctive of their own country follow, and the anthology ends with articles on jazz, reflecting the viewpoint of composers on a largely improvisational art.

A selected list of the composer's writings follows each of the editor's introductory remarks, and the editor's notes are placed in brackets with the endnotes.

The editor wishes to acknowledge the generosity of all authors, their heirs, and their publishers who have allowed their materials to appear in this volume. I am especially grateful to my wife, Charlotte Erwin, who has assisted with translations and made valuable improvements in the entire volume. I am indebted to Professor Walter B. Bailey of Rice University, who provided me with important information concerning Maurice Ravel's lecture "Contemporary Music" and to Professor Jonathan W. Bernard of the University of Washington for making it possible to include Elliott Carter's "France-America Ltd." in this volume.

INTRODUCTION

The twentieth century is unique in the number and importance of writings by major composers on their own musical culture. As musical styles in this century have changed with ever greater swiftness to embrace unprecedented and often conflicting ideas, composers have resorted to the written word to explain their music and its underlying intentions, to criticize rival movements, and to underscore the social and artistic issues that their music addresses. The writings of composers have often imparted unique information on the motivation for and content of important works, giving primary evidence for an accurate critical interpretation of these compositions and their placement within the broad currents of modern art.

Composers began to write important cultural essays concerning music only in the nineteenth century. Before that time, those musicians who were inclined to write professionally usually limited their efforts to theoretical or pedagogical treatises. In the eighteenth century, music critics, like Joseph Addison, were often nonmusicians, or like Friedrich Marpurg, scholars with no claim to the rank of major composer. This situation changed early in the nineteenth century when outstanding composers with literary interests—Hector Berlioz and Robert Schumann among others—turned to musical journalism as a profession. There was a considerable demand for their services. The early nineteenth century was just the time when major daily newspapers began to run regular concert reviews, and when many music publishers founded specialized music periodicals to advertise new publications. Musical journalism became an important avenue for composers to supplement their income and to fulfill their desire to write.

But the reviews written by the major composers at this time were hard to distinguish from the critical writings of far lesser musicians; all aspired to formulate engaging and authoritative judgments on new compositions or on recent musical performances. There was little evidence of self-consciousness among the early composer-critics as to their personal role in shaping the development of music, an awareness that would have given special status to their writings and artistic ideology. The genre of the musical essay or review remained a place for opinion and expert judgment only, not for the exposition of ideas that were relevant to the future of music itself.

This broader and more important role for the composer-critic emerged strikingly in the career of Richard Wagner. His earliest essays—mainly critiques of German opera of his day—began to appear sporadically in periodicals in 1834, and during his years in Paris from 1839 to 1842, he wrote regularly on contemporary

French and German music for the *Revue et gazette musicale* and produced lighter essays for other periodicals and newspapers. The beginning of a new direction for his critical and aesthetic oeuvre coincided with the revolutionary uprisings throughout Europe in 1848. Stimulated apparently by these political and social events, his thoughts about music turned from judgments on contemporary musical life to an enunciation of an ideal of art in a revolutionary society, a vision that was closely connected with his own development as a composer and hence with the future of music itself. No longer did the readers of his books and essays encounter mere opinion about music, however authoritative and visionary. They had to grapple instead with his ideas as they clarified and complemented his own highly original musical works, ideas that stood alongside a musical oeuvre that became central to the artistic culture of his own time and beyond.

This was the new image of the composer-essayist that was carried into the twentieth century and which has distinguished the writings of leading modern musicians from their pre-Wagnerian counterparts or from those of non-composer critics. The writings of critics, however important in their own genre, almost never stimulate new works or shape and clarify the future of music. Even the ideas of a critic of lasting importance such as Theodor Adorno, whose ideas have become established in modern musical aesthetics, have not been a major force in shaping the development of musical style. The reader of essays by John Cage, Arnold Schoenberg, and Paul Hindemith, on the contrary, encounters ideas that are indispensable to a firsthand understanding of how and why music of the twentieth century became what it did.

As composer-critics relinquished their role as mere journalists intent upon issuing authoritative opinion, their judgments concerning music and musicians took on a new meaning that is often in need of careful analysis and interpretation. In his lecture "New and Outmoded Music, Style and Idea," for example, Arnold Schoenberg dismisses the importance of Handel, whose music he describes as stylish but empty in substance. Few musicians will find Schoenberg's statements on Handel to be convincing or even accurate as an objective assessment. But his observations are important for an understanding of his own conception of music—its historical development, how musical space was used, and how thematic material could be expanded. These were all considerations that had led Schoenberg to his twelve-tone method of composition and thus reshaped music for much of the century. A similar evaluation of Handel by a noncomposer critic, even if supported by an elaborate rationale, has no comparable significance.

Composers in the twentieth century have been most ready to write about their art during periods of social anxiety, when conflicting musical styles followed major changes of taste. The years after World War I are an example, as social unrest swept Germany and Russia and as the neoclassical movement emerged as a vigorous rebellion against prewar music and its underlying aesthetic. Almost all of the major composers of the 1920s and 1930s were provoked to speak out in the form of essays and lectures about the conflicts apparent in their own musical culture. Arnold Schoenberg, Alban Berg, Charles Koechlin, and Ernst Krenek vociferously held out for the older aesthetic, while Igor Stravinsky, Kurt Weill, and Paul Hindemith spoke for the new taste. By contrast, composers since the mid-1970s have been less inclined to write about the issues implicit in their new music, in part because of the current nondogmatic, live-and-let-live spirit that is evident in contemporary musical styles.

Twentieth-century composers have been widely encouraged to write essays. The Charles Eliot Norton lectures at Harvard University have produced some of the most important statements by major modern composers on their art. Stravinsky's *Poetics of Music* was only the first book to result from the Harvard lectures, and it was followed by important books by Paul Hindemith, Aaron Copland, Roger Sessions, Leonard Bernstein, Carlos Chavez, and John Cage. Journals specializing in modern music—especially *Modern Music, Melos, Score,* and *Perspectives of New Music*—have provided a significant outlet for composers' words.

But what will the twenty-first century hold for the composer-essayist? Will musicians in the future continue to write as importantly on their art as they did in the past? The answer depends on the future of serious musical culture. Will it remain as engaging and filled with conflict as in the twentieth century? Will there be journals in the next century that deal with important issues, journals like *Modern Music* and *Score,* now both defunct? Will universities of the future find it appropriate to establish lectures with the high standards of the Norton lectures at Harvard? Will music of the future engage in important ideas, and will these ideas be found relevant in a new century that begins firmly in the grip of material values and popular culture? If so, then composers will continue to speak out on their art, and their words will have authority and importance for readers of the future.

PART I

THE ORIGINS OF MODERNISM, 1900–1930

DURING THE EARLY DECADES OF THE TWENTIETH CENTURY, European composers extended the styles of the late romantic period. Like romantic music in general, early twentieth-century works tended to be supremely expressive. Composers experimented ever more audaciously with new elements and forms, finding in them a way to evoke unfamiliar ideas, to intensify emotions, and to create a sense of freedom from existing restraints. The most important outcome of this spirit of liberation was the freeing of harmony and melody from the strict control of key, a phenomenon that went hand in hand with an ever greater enrichment of harmony by dissonance. This trend, which began much earlier in the nineteenth century, led composers in the first decade of the twentieth to write atonal music, in which key was essentially abandoned as a principle of syntax.

It is not surprising that the most prominent theme throughout the following groups of essays concerns the nature and availability of new musical resources. Ferruccio Busoni proposes new modes and microtonal scales, Arnold Schoenberg writes with fascination about tone color melodies, and Alban Berg and Béla Bartók describe the greatly expanded palette of dissonant chords newly opened to the composer. Several of the writers explore the origins and characteristics of atonal music. They assure their readers that hitherto unknown musical elements and unexplained styles will help to create new levels of expressivity, the unquestioned goal of music.

As in the romantic period, Germany and Austria continued to exert a near hegemony throughout the world of music, remaining the sources of most of the new ideas in music as well as producing the world's leaders in musical scholarship and pedagogy. Only the works of Claude Debussy could rival those of the German modernists in their lasting importance and brilliant originality. The German primacy in music was an absolute for most of the German writers on music at this time, including Schoenberg and Berg. Understandably, composers living in other countries, especially Debussy and Bartók, expressed more than a touch of annoyance with the style of German works—too complex and pretentious for Debussy, and for Bartók, too distant from the natural element of peasant music.

But for virtually all, modernism remained as the dominant force in music until after World War I. Its main distinguishing features were unremitting innovation in elements and forms, an originality in language that tended toward atonality and pervasive dissonance, and a sense that art should be directed more at an idealized future audience than at the limited understanding of the present one. Indeed, "music of the future," a slogan associated with Richard Wagner, could well serve to designate much of the important music composed in the decades before World War I. Wagner had speculated that music in the future would be part of a "total work of art," and this ideal proved influential upon progressive composers after the turn of the century although in a somewhat different way from Wagner's prediction. The early twentieth-century modernists created works that integrated the most diverse elements of form and medium, and they brought into their music highly complex ideas, all suggesting universal rather than regional or limited significance. It was in this spirit of the universal and integrated artwork that Gustav Mahler in 1907 described the symphonic genre to Jean Sibelius: "The symphony must be like the world," Mahler remarked, "it must embrace everything." The futuristic stance of these composers is strongly implied in the essays that follow. On one hand it is seen in the elitist thinking of Debussy, who was greatly annoyed by the insensitivity and lack of understanding for new music shown by contemporary audiences. For Busoni the entire art of music was like a child whose maturity and greatness lay entirely in the future. Similarly, Schoenberg wrote in his *Harmonielehre*:

> I do believe in the new; I believe it is that *Good* and that *Beauty* toward which we strive with our innermost being, just as involuntarily and persistently as we strive toward the future. There must be, somewhere in our future, a *magnificent fulfillment* as yet hidden from us, since all our striving forever pins its hopes on it.

The writings of composers also make it clear that the modernity and futuristic posture of this time contained no strong impulse of rebellion against the immediate past. In fact, the important composers of this period—Richard Strauss, Gustav Mahler, Arnold Schoenberg, Claude Debussy, and Giacomo Puccini among many others—were inspired and stimulated precisely by what had come before. Schoenberg was a great admirer of the late romantic composers, especially Wagner and Brahms; Debussy was much influenced by Fauré among other recent French predecessors; Puccini looked to Verdi for guidance; and Richard Strauss enjoyed being called "Richard the Second," a reference to his similarities with Wagner, the "first" Richard. The modernist idiom of the years before World War I was formed not by rebellion but by a relentless expansion and reinterpretation of the ideas of the late romantic period.

This underlying continuity between the modernist revolution and its immediate past was a major theme addressed by composers in essays written early in the century. It was a firmly established viewpoint in the writings of Schoenberg and those of his students, primarily Alban Berg. The principal theme of Berg's interview-essay "What Is Atonality?" is that atonal music differs from late romantic music only in its harmonic language. Similarly, Béla Bartók observes in his essay "The Problem of the New Music" that atonality was a gradual development, taking its origin in romantic harmony and treatment of key. His discussion is drawn to a considerable extent directly from Schoenberg's *Harmonielehre*, which had appeared a decade before.

I

CLAUDE DEBUSSY

(1862 – 1918)

In 1901, Debussy began to write music criticism, which he first published in the Parisian art journal *La revue blanche*. He had then many friends who were writers, and he had long maintained his own aspirations as an author. Earlier he had tried his hand at writing poetry in the symbolist vein, which he then set to music in his *Proses lyriques*. But the life of the music critic did not long agree with him, although he continued to deliver short reviews and essays to several different journals until 1915. In these articles Debussy concisely reveals his musical tastes, and his writing style effectively holds a mirror to his own music, which tended to be brief, understated, and light in tone. He made his point without bombast or unnecessary show of technique, and he was always sensitive to subtleties of feeling and nuance.

In his final years Debussy compiled an anthology of his writings, which appeared posthumously in 1921 under the title *Monsieur Croche antidilettante*. M. Croche, "a spare, wizened man whose gestures were obviously suited to the conduct of metaphysical discussion," was Debussy's alter ego, his imaginary interlocutor in several of the early reviews. With little elaboration Croche proclaims Debussy's views on what music should be: simple, innovative, as expressive as a painting, and always close to nature. His profession is that of "antidilettante"—one who disdains the public for its insensitivity, its tendency to boredom, and its resistance to the new. Croche also shares Debussy's ambiguity concerning German music. The detailed programmaticism and musical onomatopoeia of Beethoven's *Pastoral* Symphony are disdained. "To see the sun rise is more profitable than to hear the *Pastoral* Symphony," says Croche. But in later reviews Debussy found much to praise in Beethoven's revolutionary treatment of musical forms. His attitude toward Wagner—only touched on in the following essay—was equally divided. Debussy could never escape the power of Wagner's imagination and passion, but he was repelled by Wagner's apparatus—the leitmotifs, bombast, and complication.

Croche most revealingly enunciates Debussy's aesthetic when he tells of his favorite music: not Beethoven, Wagner, or Schumann, not even Debussy's beloved Chopin, but instead "the simple notes of an Egyptian shepherd's pipe; for he collaborates with the landscape and hears harmonies unknown to your treatises."

Debussy's Writings: A Selective Bibliography

Debussy on Music. Translated by Richard Langham Smith. New York: Alfred A. Knopf, 1977. Contains all of Debussy's published writings about music, essentially translating *Monsieur Croche et autres écrits*, ed.

François Lesure (Paris: Editions Gallimard, 1971). Smith's translations are more literal than earlier English translations of Debussy's essays by Maire O'Brien and B. N. Langdon Davies.

— ɯ —

CONVERSATION WITH M. CROCHE

(L'entretien avec M. Croche, 1901)

It was a lovely evening. I had decided to idle. I mean, of course, that I was dreaming. I do not want to imply that anything of great emotional value was happening or that I was laying the foundations of the future, I was just enjoying that occasional carefree mood which brings peace with all the world.

And of what was I dreaming? What were my limits? What was the goal of my work? Questions, I fear, prompted by a somewhat childish egotism and the craving to escape from an ideal with which one has lived too long! Questions, moreover, that are but a thin disguise for the foolish yearning to be regarded as superior to others! The struggle to surpass others has never been really great if dissociated from the noble idea of surpassing oneself—though this, involving as it does the sacrifice of one's cherished personality, implies a very special kind of alchemy. Besides, superiority over others is difficult to maintain and gives in the end but a barren victory. The pursuit of universal approbation means the waste of a great deal of time in continual demonstration and sedulous self-advertisement. These things may win one the honor of inclusion in a collection of distinguished persons whose names are used as the sauce for insipid conversations on art. But I will not labor the point. I should not like to check ambition.

The evening was as lovely as ever, but, as must already be obvious, I was out of humor with myself—I had lost grip and found that I was drifting into the most irritating generalizations.

At this precise moment my doorbell rang and I made the acquaintance of Monsieur Croche. It is unnecessary to check the flow of this narrative with the obvious or trifling incidents of his first visit.

Monsieur Croche was a spare, wizened man and his gestures were obviously suited to the conduct of metaphysical discussions; his features are best pictured by recalling those of Tom Lane, the jockey, and M. Thiers.[1] He spoke almost in a whisper and never laughed, occasionally enforcing his remarks with a quiet smile which, beginning at his nose, wrinkled his whole face, like a pebble flung into still waters, and lasted for an intolerably long time.

He aroused my curiosity at once by his peculiar views on music. He spoke of an orchestral score as if it were a picture. He seldom used technical words, but the dimmed and slightly worn elegance of his rather unusual vocabulary seemed to ring like old coins. I remember a parallel he drew between Beethoven's orchestration— which he visualized as a black-and-white formula resulting in an exquisite gradation of greys—and that of Wagner, a sort of many-colored "makeup" spread almost uniformly, in which, he said, he could no longer distinguish the tone of a violin from that of a trombone.

Since his intolerable smile was especially evident when he talked of music, I suddenly decided to ask him what his profession might be. He replied in a voice which checked any attempt at comment: "Dilettante Hater." Then he went on monotonously and irritably:

"Have you noticed the hostility of a concert-room audience? Have you studied their almost drugged expression of boredom, indifference, and even stupidity? They never grasp the noble dramas woven into the symphonic conflict in which one is conscious of the possibility of reaching the summit of the structure of harmony and breathing there an atmosphere of perfect beauty. Such people always seem like guests who are more or less well-bred; they endure the tedium of their position with patience, and they remain only because they wish to be seen taking their leave at the end; otherwise, why come? You must admit that this is a good reason for an eternal hatred of music."

I argued that I had observed and had even shared in highly commendable displays of enthusiasm. To which he answered:

"You are greatly in error; for, if you showed so much enthusiasm, it was with the secret hope that some day a similar honor would be paid to you. Surely you know that a genuine appreciation of beauty can only result in silence? Tell me, when you see the daily wonder of the sunset have you ever thought of applauding? Yet you will admit that it is a rather more unrehearsed effect than all your musical trifles. Moreover, face to face with the sunset you feel so mean a thing that you cannot become a part of it. But before a so-called work of art you are yourself and you have a classical jargon which gives you an opportunity for eloquence."

I dared not confess how nearly I agreed with him, since nothing withers conversation like agreement. I preferred to ask if he himself played any instrument. He raised his head sharply and replied:

"I dislike specialists. Specialization is for me the narrowing of my universe. It reminds me of those old horses who, in bygone days, worked the roundabouts and died to the well-known strains of the Marche Lorraine! Nevertheless, I know all music and it has only given me a special pride in being safe from every kind of surprise. Two bars suffice to give me the clue to a symphony, or to any other musical incident.

"Though we may be certain that some great men have a stubborn determination always to break fresh ground, it is not so with many others, who do nothing but repeat the thing in which they have once succeeded. Their skill leaves me cold. They have been hailed as Masters. Beware lest this be not a polite method of getting rid of them or of excusing the sameness of their performances. In short, I try to forget music because it obscures my perception of what I do not know or shall only know tomorrow. Why cling to something one knows too well?"

I mentioned the most famous of our contemporaries and Monsieur Croche was more aggressive than ever.

"I am much more interested in sincere and honestly felt impressions than in criticism, which often enough resembles brilliant variations on the theme: 'Since you do not agree with me, you are mistaken'; or else: 'You have talent, I have none; it is useless to go any further.' In all compositions I endeavor to fathom the diverse impulses inspiring them and their inner life. Is not this much more interesting than the game of pulling them to pieces, like curious watches?

"People forget that, as children, they were forbidden to pull their jumping jacks to pieces—even when such behavior was treason against the mysteries—and they continue to want to poke their aesthetic noses where they have no business to be. Though they no longer rip open puppets, yet they explain, pull to pieces and in cold blood slay the mysteries; it is comparatively easy; moreover you can chat about it. Well, well! An obvious lack of understanding excuses some of them; but others act with greater ferocity and premeditation, for they must of necessity protect their cherished little talents. These last have a loyal following.

"I am only slightly concerned with works hallowed either by success or tradition: once and for all, [Giacomo] Meyerbeer, [Sigismond] Thalberg, and [Ernest] Reyer are men of genius; otherwise they are of no importance.

"On Sundays, when God is kind, I hear no music: please accept my apologies. Finally, be so good as to note the word 'impressions' which is applicable, since it leaves me free to preserve my emotion from all superfluous aestheticism.

"You are inclined to exaggerate events which, in Bach's day, would have appeared natural. You talk to me about Dukas's [Piano] Sonata. He is probably one of your friends and even a musical critic. Good reasons for speaking well of him. Your praise, however, has been surpassed; for Pierre Lalo, in an article in *Le temps*, devoted exclusively to this sonata, made simultaneous sacrifice to Dukas of the sonatas written by Schumann and Chopin. As a matter of fact, Chopin's nervous temperament was ill-adapted to the endurance needed for the construction of a sonata: he made elaborate 'first drafts.' Yet we may say that Chopin inaugurated a special method of treating this form, not to mention the charming artistry which he devised in this connection. He was fertile in ideas, which he often invested without demanding that hundred per cent on the transaction which is the brightest halo of some of our Masters.

"Lalo, of course, evokes the noble shade of Beethoven in reference to the sonata of your friend Dukas. Personally, I should have been only mildly flattered! Beethoven's sonatas are very badly written for the piano; they are, particularly those that came later, more accurately described as orchestral transcriptions. There seems often to be lacking a third hand which I am sure Beethoven heard; at least I hope so. It would have been safer to leave Schumann and Chopin alone; undoubtedly they wrote for the piano; and if that is not enough for Lalo, he ought at least to be grateful to them for having opened a way towards the perfection represented by a Dukas—and incidentally some others."

Monsieur Croche uttered these last words with an imperturbable detachment: a challenge to be taken up or ignored. I was too much interested to take it up and left him to continue. There was a long silence, during which there came from him no sign of life save for the smoke ascending in blue spirals from his cigar which he watched curiously as if he were contemplating strange distortions—perhaps bold systems. His silence became disconcerting and rather alarming. At length he resumed:

"Music is a sum total of scattered forces. You make an abstract ballad of them! I prefer the simple notes of an Egyptian shepherd's pipe; for he collaborates with the landscape and hears harmonies unknown to your treatises. Musicians listen only to the music written by cunning hands, never to that which is in nature's script. To see the sun rise is more profitable than to hear the *Pastoral* Symphony. What is the use of your almost incomprehensible art? Ought you not to suppress all the parasitical complexities which make music as ingenious as the lock of a strongbox? You paw the ground because you only know music and submit to strange and barbarous laws. You are hailed with high-sounding praises, but you are merely cunning! Something between a monkey and a lackey."

I ventured to say that some had tried in poetry, others in painting—I added with some trepidation one or two musicians—to shake off the ancient dust of tradition and it had only resulted in their being treated as symbolists or impressionists—convenient terms for pouring scorn on one's fellows.

"It is only journalists and hucksters who treat them so," Monsieur Croche continued without a falter, "and it is of no importance. A beautiful idea in embryo has in it something absurd for fools. There is a surer hope of beauty in such derided men than in those poor sheep who flock docilely to the slaughter houses which a discerning fate has prepared for them.

"To be unique, faultless! The enthusiasm of society spoils an artist for me, such is my fear that, as a result, he will become merely an expression of society.

"Discipline must be sought in freedom, and not within the formulas of an outworn philosophy only fit for the feebleminded. Give ear to no man's counsel; but listen to the wind which tells in passing the history of the world."

As he spoke Monsieur Croche appeared to be lit up from within. I seemed to see into him and his words came to me like some strange music. I cannot adequately convey his peculiar eloquence. Something like this, perhaps:

"Do you know anything more splendid than to discover by chance a genius who has been unrecognized through the ages? But to have been such a genius oneself—can any glory equal it?"

Day was breaking; Monsieur Croche was visibly fatigued and went away. I accompanied him as far as the landing door; he no more thought of shaking my hand than I of thanking him. For a considerable time, I listened to the sound of his steps dying away flight by flight. I dared not hope that I should ever see him again.

Notes

[Text: Debussy, "L'entretien avec M. Croche," *La revue blanche* 25 (July 1901): 384–87. Translated by B. N. Langdon Davies.]

[1. Adolphe Thiers (1797–1877) was a French statesman and historian.]

2

FERRUCCIO BUSONI

(1 8 6 6 – 1 9 2 4)

In his *Sketch of a New Esthetic of Music* Ferruccio Busoni expresses a utopian vision that captured the imagination and aspirations of the modernists of his day. He speaks of music as an art whose growth is threatened by a tendency, in his contemporary musical culture, to restrain it with rules, established forms, and hidebound traditions. These, Busoni concludes, are always ignored by the great masters, who break rules rather than conform to them, create new forms rather than reuse existing ones, and chafe against the limitations of existing tonal elements. Busoni theorizes about new scales and, most original of all, microtonal tunings as examples of new pitch resources for the future.

The history of the *Sketch of a New Esthetic of Music* is complex. It was written in 1906, while Busoni was living in Berlin, and published in Trieste in 1907 by a friend, Carlo Schmidl. Before this time Busoni was known mainly as a virtuoso pianist who also composed, conducted, and taught music. He was not thought to be an important or original essayist, having written relatively few articles for a variety of German newspapers and journals. But the *Sketch* vaulted him to a position of preeminence among modernists in their bitter struggle against the overwhelmingly conservative outlook of music critics of the day. The *Sketch* was itself a compilation of brief statements and aphorisms on a variety of musical topics, without a strongly unifying thread. Its focus on music's future and its appearance just at the time that major European composers were approaching a freely dissonant and atonal style brought to it an added measure of attention. The young French modernist Edgard Varèse is said to have traveled to Berlin to meet Busoni out of his enthusiasm for the article's progressive ideology, and Arnold Schoenberg found it bold.

In 1911 an English translation was published by G. Schirmer in New York, for which Busoni expanded a few passages and added an addendum. This is the version of the *Sketch* that is reprinted here. Finally, in 1916, a second German edition was prepared for the Insel-Verlag in Leipzig, and for this version Busoni integrated the addendum from the English edition into the text, rewrote a few paragraphs, and added a small amount of new material. One of the new passages in the 1916 edition considerably sharpened the work's futuristic tone. Here Busoni declared that an era in music was at an end, its traditional materials exhausted in their expressive power. Where would composers now turn?

> *All our efforts must strive in that direction [toward abstract sounds, toward unlimited techniques, toward tonal unrestrictedness] so that an uncorrupted new beginning will arise.*

> *The born creators will have the great but negative responsibility of first freeing themselves from all that they have learned and heard, all that is ostensibly musical. Then, after they are fully cleansed, they will invoke a fervent, ascetic state of mind that will allow them to hear the inner chord, then take further steps and communicate to the masses. These Giottos of this musical renaissance will be crowned as holy figures in an ordination. After this first revelation will follow a period of religious musical zealousness in which guilds will play no role because those called and initiated will be unmistakable and alone empowered. At this time we will see the fullest and perhaps the first flowering of mankind within the history of music. I can also foresee the beginning of a decline, when the purity of their commandments will be sullied and the holy order desecrated.*

The timing of the appearance of the 1916 edition of the *Sketch*—at the height of World War I—was destined to make Busoni's modernistic ideology all the more controversial, since it was couched in distinctly anti-German language. Not only does Busoni question the importance of German composers after Beethoven, he also loses no opportunity to criticize German thinking about the subject. German scholars of music—considered leaders in the fields of musicology and musical theory in the nineteenth century—are caricatured as mere "lawgivers," and the German emphasis on "musicality" and "depth" is parodied. These remarks by an Italian living in Germany in wartime were certain to produce a caustic backlash. Among the many attacks upon Busoni that followed publication of the 1916 edition was a pamphlet written in 1917 by the composer Hans Pfitzner, titled *Futuristengefahr* (The Danger of Futurism). Pfitzner goes virtually sentence-by-sentence through Busoni's *Sketch* to attack its every thought. Busoni himself is portrayed as a deluded Moses leading his followers to an unknown destination in the future and as a jaded "bohemian who sits at noon in a coffee house, with his cognac and cigarettes." The only music that interests him, says Pfitzner, is the "futuristic kitsch" of the last few years.

Ironically, it was left to Busoni himself to recant most strikingly the utopian viewpoint of his *Sketch of a New Esthetic of Music*. In an open letter to the critic Paul Bekker, first published in February 1920 and widely reprinted, Busoni speaks of the preceding fifteen years of music history as a time of exaggeration, satire, rebellion, defiance, and foolishness. The future, he says, will be dominated by a "Young Classicism" in music, objective in outlook rather than subjective, that will return to clear melody, "strong and beautiful forms," and a mixing of old and new. Just as the *Sketch of a New Esthetic of Music* anticipated the unprecedented innovations in music in the years just before World War I, the concept of Young Classicism forecast the spirit of the 1920s, when freedom and futurism seemed largely irrelevant to new music.

Busoni Writings: A Selective Bibliography

The Essence of Music and Other Papers. Translated by Rosamond Ley. London: Rockliff Publishing, 1957. Reprinted, New York: Dover, 1965 and 1987. This is a translation of essays first appearing under the title *Von der Einheit der Musik: Verstreute Aufzeichnungen* (Berlin: Max Hesses Verlag, 1922).

Ferruccio Busoni: Selected Letters. Edited and translated by Antony Beaumont. New York: Columbia University Press, 1987. Contains, among other important letter exchanges, the complete correspondence between Busoni and Arnold Schoenberg.

—ᨡ—

SKETCH OF A NEW ESTHETIC OF MUSIC

(*Entwurf einer neuen Aesthetik der Tonkunst*, 1906, revised 1911)

What seek you? Say! And what do you expect?—

I know not what; the Unknown I would have!

What's known to me, is endless; I would go

Beyond the end: The last word still is wanting.

[FROM BUSONI'S *DER MÄCHTIGE ZAUBERER*]

1

Loosely joined together as regards literary form, the following notes are, in reality, the outcome of convictions long held and slowly matured. In them a problem of the first magnitude is formulated with apparent simplicity, without giving the key to its final solution; for the problem cannot be solved for generations—if at all. But it involves an innumerable series of lesser problems, which I present to the consideration of those whom they may concern. For it is a long time since any one has devoted himself to earnest musical research. It is true, that admirable works of genius arise in every period, and I have always taken my stand in the front rank of those who joyfully acclaimed the passing standard-bearers; and still it seems to me that of all these beautiful paths leading so far afield—none lead *upward*.

The spirit of an artwork, the measure of emotion, of humanity, that is in it—these remain unchanged in value though changing years; the form which these three assumed, the manner of their expression, and the flavor of the epoch which gave them birth, are transient, and age rapidly.

Spirit and emotion retain their essence, in the artwork as in man himself; we admire technical achievements, yet they are outstripped, or cloy the taste and are discarded.

Its ephemeral qualities give a work the stamp of "modernity"; its unchangeable essence hinders it from becoming "obsolete." Among both "modern" and "old" works we find good and bad, genuine and spurious. There is nothing properly modern—only things which have come into being earlier or later; longer in bloom, or sooner withered. The modern and the old have always been.

Art forms are the more lasting, the more closely they adhere to the nature of their individual species of art, the purer they keep their essential means and ends.

Sculpture relinquishes the expression of the human pupil, and effects of color; painting degenerates, when it forsakes the flat surface in depiction and takes on complexity in theatrical decoration or panoramic portrayal.

Architecture has its fundamental form, growth from below upward, prescribed by static necessity; window and roof necessarily provide the intermediate and finishing configuration; these are eternal and inviolable requirements of the art.

Poetry commands the abstract thought, which it clothes in words. More independent than the others, it reaches the furthest bounds.

But all arts, resources and forms ever aim at the one end, namely, the imitation of nature and the interpretation of human feelings.

Architecture, sculpture, poetry, and painting are old and mature arts; their conceptions are established and their objects assured; they have found the way through uncounted centuries, and, like the planets, describe their regular orbits.[1]

Music, compared with them, is a child that has learned to walk, but must still be led. It is a virgin art, without experience in life and suffering.

It is all unconscious as yet of what garb is becoming, of its own advantages, its unawakened capacities. And again, it is a child-marvel that is already able to dispense much of beauty, that has already brought joy to many, and whose gifts are commonly held to have attained full maturity.

Music as an art, our so-called occidental music, is hardly four hundred years old; its state is one of development, perhaps the very first stage of a development beyond present conception, and we—we talk of "classics" and "hallowed traditions!" And we have talked of them for a long time.[2] We have formulated rules, stated principles, laid down laws; we apply laws made for maturity to a child that knows nothing of responsibility!

Young as it is, this child, we already recognize that it possesses one radiant attribute which signalizes it beyond all its elder sisters. And the lawgivers will not see this marvelous attribute, lest their laws should be thrown to the winds. This child— it *floats on air!* It touches not the earth with its feet. It knows no law of gravitation. It is well nigh incorporeal. Its material is transparent. It is sonorous air. It is almost Nature herself. It is—free.

But freedom is something that mankind have never wholly comprehended, never realized to the full. They can neither recognize nor acknowledge it.

They disavow the mission of this child; they hang weights upon it. This buoyant creature must walk decently, like anybody else. It may scarcely be allowed to leap—when it were its joy to follow the line of the rainbow, and to break sunbeams with the clouds.

Music was born free; and to win freedom is its destiny. It will become the most complete of all reflexes of nature by reason of its untrammeled immateriality. Even the poetic word ranks lower in point of incorporealness. It can gather together and disperse, can be motionless repose or wildest tempestuosity; it has the extremest heights perceptible to man—what other art has these?—and its emotion seizes the human heart with that intensity which is independent of the "idea."

It realizes a temperament, *without* describing it, with the mobility of the soul, with the swiftness of consecutive moments; and this, where painter or sculptor can represent only one side or one moment, and the poet tardily *communicates* a temperament and its manifestations by words.

Therefore, representation and description are not the nature of music; herewith we declare the invalidity of program music and arrive at the question: What are the aims of music?

2

Absolute music! What the lawgivers mean by this, is perhaps remotest of all from the absolute in music. "Absolute music" is a form-play without poetic program, in which the form is intended to have the leading part. But form, in itself, is the opposite pole of absolute music, on which was bestowed the divine prerogative of buoyancy, of freedom from the limitations of matter. In a picture, the illustration of a sunset ends with the frame; the limitless natural phenomenon is enclosed in quadrilateral bounds; the cloud-form chosen for depiction remains unchanging forever. Music can grow brighter or darker, shift hither or yon, and finally fade away like the sunset glow itself; and instinct leads the creative musician to employ the tones that press the same key within the human breast, and awaken the same response, as the processes in nature.

Per contra, "absolute music" is something very sober, which reminds one of music desks in orderly rows, of the relation of tonic to dominant, of developments and codas.

Methinks I hear the second violin struggling, a fourth below, to emulate the more dexterous first, and contending in needless contest merely to arrive at the starting point. This sort of music ought rather to be called the "architectonic," or "symmetric," or "sectional," and derives from the circumstance that certain composers poured *their* spirit and *their* emotion into just this mould as lying nearest them or their time. Our lawgivers have identified the spirit and emotion, the individuality of these composers and their time, with "symmetric" music, and finally, being powerless to recreate either the spirit, or the emotion, or the time, have retained the form as a symbol, and made it into a fetish, a religion. The composers sought and found this form as the aptest vehicle for communicating *their* ideas; their souls took flight—and the lawgivers discover and cherish the garments Euphorion left behind on earth.

> A lucky find! 'Twas now or never;
> The flame is gone, it's true—however,
> No need to pity mankind now.

> Enough is left for many a poet's tiring,
> Or to breed envy high and low;
> And though I have no talents here for hiring,
> I'll hire the robe out, anyhow.

Is it not singular, to demand of a composer originality in all things, and to forbid it as regards form? No wonder that, once he becomes original, he is accused of "formlessness." Mozart! the seeker and the finder, the great man with the childlike heart—it is he we marvel at, to whom we are devoted; but not his tonic and dominant, his developments and codas.

Such lust of liberation filled Beethoven, the romantic revolutionary, that he ascended one short step on the way leading music back to its loftier self: a short step in the great task, a wide step in his own path. He did not quite reach absolute music, but in certain moments he divined it, as in the introduction to the fugue of the Sonata [Op. 106, in B-flat] for Hammerklavier. Indeed, all composers have drawn nearest the true nature of music in preparatory and intermediary passages (preludes and transitions), where they felt at liberty to disregard symmetrical proportions, and unconsciously drew free breath. Even a Schumann (of so much lower stature) is seized, in such passages, by some feeling of the boundlessness of this pan-art (recall the transition to the last movement of the D Minor Symphony); and the same may be asserted of Brahms in the introduction to the finale of his First Symphony.

But, the moment they cross the threshold of the *principal subject*, their attitude becomes stiff and conventional, like that of a man entering some bureau of high officialdom.

Next to Beethoven, Bach bears closest affinity to "infinite music."[3] His Organ fantasias (but not the fugues) have indubitably a strong dash of what might be overwritten "Man and Nature."[4] In him it appears most ingenuous because he had no reverence for his predecessors (although he esteemed and made use of them), and because the still novel acquisition of equal temperament opened a vista of—for the time being—endless new possibilities.

Therefore, Bach and Beethoven[5] are to be conceived as a *beginning*, and not as unsurpassable finalities. In spirit and emotion they will probably remain unexcelled; and this, again, confirms the remark at the beginning of these lines: That spirit and emotion remain unchanged in value through changing years, and that he who mounts to their uttermost heights will always tower above the crowd.

What still remains to be surpassed, is their form of expression and their freedom. Wagner, a Germanic Titan, who touched our earthly horizon in orchestral tone-effect, who intensified the form of expression, but fashioned it into a *system* (music drama, declamation, leading motive), is on this account incapable of further intensification. His category begins and ends with himself; first, because he carried it to the highest perfection and finish; secondly, because his self-imposed task was of such a nature, that it could be achieved by one man alone.[6] The paths opened by Beethoven can be followed to their ends only through generations. They—like all things in creation—may form only a circle; but a circle of such dimensions, that the portion visible to us seems like a straight line. Wagner's circle we can view in its entirety—a circle within the great circle.

3

The name of Wagner leads to program music. This has been set up as a contrast to so-called "absolute" music, and these concepts have become so petrified that even persons of intelligence hold one or the other dogma, without recognition for a third possibility beyond and above the other two. In reality, program music is precisely as one-sided and limited as that which is called absolute. In place of architectonic and symmetric formulas, instead of the relation of tonic to dominant, it has bound itself in the stays of a connecting poetic—sometimes even philosophic—program.

Every motive—so it seems to me—contains, like a seed, its life-germ within itself. From the different plant seeds grow different families of plants, dissimilar in form, foliage, blossom, fruit, growth and color.[7] Even each individual plant belonging to one and the same species assumes, in size, form and strength, a growth peculiar to itself. And so, in each motive, there lies the embryo of its fully developed form; each one must unfold itself differently, yet each obediently follows the law of eternal harmony. *This form is imperishable, though each be unlike every other.*

The motive in a composition with program bears within itself the same natural necessity; but it must, even in its earliest phase of development, renounce *its own proper mode of growth* to mold—or, rather, twist—itself to fit the needs of the program. Thus turned aside, at the outset, from the path traced by nature, it finally arrives at a wholly unexpected climax, whither it has been led, not by its own organization, but by the way laid down in the program, or the action, or the philosophical idea.

And how primitive must this art remain! True, there are unequivocal descriptive effects of tone-painting (from these the entire principle took its rise), but these means of expression are few and trivial, covering but a very small section of musical art. Begin with the most self-evident of all, the debasement of tone to noise in imitating the sounds of nature—the rolling of thunder, the roar of forests, the cries of animals; then those somewhat less evident, symbolic—imitations of visual impressions, like the lightning flash, springing movement, the flight of birds; again, those intelligible only through the mediation of the reflective brain, such as the trumpet call as a warlike symbol, the shawm to betoken ruralism, march rhythm to signify measured strides, the chorale as vehicle for religious feeling. Add to the above the characterization of nationalities—national instruments and airs—and we have a complete inventory of the arsenal of program music. Movement and repose, minor and major, high and low, in their customary significance, round out the list. These are auxiliaries, of which good use can be made upon a broad canvas, but which, taken by themselves, are no more to be called music than wax figures may pass for monuments.

And after all, what can the presentation of a little happening upon this earth, the report concerning an annoying neighbor—no matter whether in the next room or in an adjoining quarter of the globe—have in common with that music which pervades the universe?

To music, indeed, it is given to set in vibration our human moods: dread (Leporello), oppression of soul, invigoration, lassitude (Beethoven's last quartets), decision (Wotan), hesitation, despondency, encouragement, harshness, tenderness, excitement, tranquilization, the feeling of surprise or expectancy, and still others; likewise the inner echo of external occurrences which is bound up in these moods of the soul. But not the moving cause itself of these spiritual affections; not the joy over an avoided danger, not the danger itself, or the kind of danger which caused the dread; an emotional state, yes, but not the psychic species of this emotion, such as envy, or jealousy; and it is equally futile to attempt the expression, through music, of moral characteristics (vanity, cleverness), or abstract ideas like truth and justice. Is it possible to imagine how a poor, but contented man could be represented by music? The contentment, the soul-state, can be interpreted by music; but where does the poverty appear, or the important ethic problem stated in the words "poor, but contented"? This is due to the fact that "poor" connotes a phase of terrestrial and social conditions not to be found in the eternal harmony. And music is a part of the vibrating universe.

I may be allowed to subjoin a few subsidiary reflections: The greater part of modern theater music suffers from the mistake of seeking to repeat the scenes passing on the stage, instead of fulfilling its own proper mission of interpreting the soul-states of the persons represented. When the scene presents the illusion of a thunderstorm, this is exhaustively apprehended by the eye. Nevertheless, nearly all composers strive to depict the storm in tones—which is not only a needless and feebler repetition, but likewise a failure to perform their true function. The person on the stage is either psychically influenced by the thunderstorm, or his mood, being absorbed in a train of thought of stronger influence, remains unaffected. The storm is visible and audible without aid from music; it is the invisible and inaudible, the spiritual processes of the personages portrayed, which music should render intelligible.

Again, there are "obvious" psychic conditions on the stage, whereof music need take no account. Suppose a theatrical situation in which a convivial company is passing at night and disappears from view, while in the foreground a silent, envenomed duel is in progress. Here the music, by means of continuing song, should keep in mind the jovial company now lost to sight; the acts and feelings of the pair in the foreground may be understood without further commentary, and the music—dramatically speaking—ought not to participate in their action and break the tragic silence.

Measurably justified, in my opinion, is the plan of the old opera, which concentrated and musically rounded out the passions aroused by a moving dramatic scene in a piece of set form (the aria). *Word* and stage play conveyed the dramatic progress of the action, followed more or less meagerly by musical recitative; arrived at the point of rest, music resumed the reins. This is less extrinsic than some would now have us believe. On the other hand, it was the ossified form of the "aria" itself which led to inveracity of expression and decadence.

4

The audible presentation, the "performance," of music, its *emotional interpretation*, derives from those free heights whence descended the art itself. Where the art is threatened by earthliness, it is the part of interpretation to raise it and reendow it with its primordial essence.

Notation, the writing out of compositions, is primarily an ingenious expedient for catching an inspiration, with the purpose of exploiting it later. But notation is to improvisation as the portrait to the living model. It is for the interpreter to *resolve the rigidity of the signs* into the primitive emotion.

But the lawgivers require the interpreter to reproduce the rigidity of the signs; they consider his reproduction the nearer to perfection, the more closely it clings to the signs.—

What the composer's inspiration *necessarily* loses[8] through notation, his interpreter should restore by his own.

To the lawgivers, the signs themselves are the most important matter, and are continually growing in their estimation; the new art of music is derived from the old signs—*and these now stand for musical art itself*.

If the lawgivers had their way, any given composition would always be reproduced in precisely the same tempo, whensoever, by whomsoever, and under whatsoever conditions it might be performed.

But, it *is* not possible; the buoyant, expansive nature of the divine child rebels— it demands the opposite.—Each day begins differently from the preceding, yet always with the flush of dawn. Great artists play their own works differently at each repetition, remodel them on the spur of the moment, accelerate and retard, in a way which they could not indicate by signs—and always according to the given conditions of that "eternal harmony."

And then the lawgiver chafes, and refers the creator to his own handwriting. As matters stand today, the lawgiver has the best of the argument. "Notation" ("writing down") brings up the subject of transcription, nowadays a term much misunderstood, almost discreditable. The frequent antagonism which I have excited with "transcriptions," and the opposition to which an ofttimes irrational criticism has provoked me, caused me to seek a clear understanding of this point. My final conclusion concerning it is this: Every notation is, in itself, the transcription of an abstract idea. The instant the pen seizes it, the idea loses its original form. The very intention to write down the idea, compels a choice of measure and key. The form, and the musical agency, which the composer must decide upon, still more closely define the way and the limits.

It is much the same as with man himself. Born naked, and as yet without definite aspirations, he decides, or at a given moment is made to decide, upon a career. From the moment of these decisions, although much that is original and imperishable in the [abstract musical] idea or the man may live on, either is depressed to the type of a class. The musical idea becomes a sonata or a concerto; the man, a soldier or a priest. That is an arrangement of the original. From this first transcription to a second the step is comparatively short and unimportant. And yet it is only the second, in general, of which any notice is taken; overlooking the fact, that a transcription does not destroy the archetype, which is, therefore, not lost through transcription.

Again, the performance of a work is also a transcription, and still, whatever liberties it may take, it can never annihilate the original.

For the musical artwork exists, before its tones resound and after they die away, *complete and intact*. It exists both within and outside of time, and through its nature we can obtain a definite conception of the otherwise intangible notion of the ideality of time.

For the rest, most of Beethoven's piano compositions sound like transcriptions of orchestral works; most of Schumann's orchestral compositions, like arrangements from pieces for the piano—and they are so, in a way.

Strangely enough, the variation form is highly esteemed by the "worshippers of the letter." That is singular; for the variation form—when built up on a borrowed theme—produces a *whole series of "arrangements"* which, besides, are least respectful when most ingenious.

So the arrangement is *not* good, because it *varies* the original; and the variation *is* good, although it *"arranges"* the original.

5
———

The term *musikalisch* (musical) is used by the Germans in a sense foreign to that in which any other language employs it.[9] It is a conception belonging to the Germans, and not to culture in general; the expression is incorrect and untranslatable. "Musical" is derived from *music*, like "poetical" from *poetry*, or "physical" from *physic(s)*. When I say, "Schubert was one of the most musical among men," it is the same as if I should say, "Helmholtz was one of the most physical among men." That is musical, which *sounds* in rhythms and intervals. A cupboard can be "musical," if "music-works" be enclosed in it.[10] In a comparative sense, "musical" may have the further signification of "euphonious." "My verses are too musical to bear setting to music," a noted poet once remarked to me.

> "Spirits moving musically
>
> To a lute's well-tuned law,"

writes Edgar Allan Poe. Lastly, one may speak quite correctly of "musical laughter," because it *sounds* like music.

Taking the signification in which the term is applied and almost exclusively employed in German, a musical person is one who manifests an inclination for music by a nice discrimination and sensitiveness with regard to the *technical aspects* of the art. By "technics" I mean rhythm, harmony, intonation, part-leading, and the treatment of themes. The more subtleties he is capable of hearing or reproducing in these, the more "musical" he is held to be.

In view of the great importance attached to these elements of the art, this "musical" temperament has naturally become of the highest consequence. And so an artist who plays with perfect technical finish should be deemed the most musical player. But as we mean by "technics" only the mechanical mastery of the instrument, the terms "technical" and "musical" have been turned into opposites.

The matter has been carried so far as to call a composition itself "musical,"[11] or even to assert of a great composer like Berlioz that he was not sufficiently musical.[12] "Unmusical" conveys the strongest reproach; branded thus, its object becomes an outlaw.[13]

In a country like Italy, where all participate in the delights of music, this differentiation becomes superfluous, and the term corresponding is not found in the language. In France, where a living sense of music does not permeate the people, there are musicians and non-musicians; of the rest, some "are very fond of music," and others "do not care for it." Only in Germany is it made a point of honor to be "musical," that is to say, not merely to love music, but more especially to understand it as regards its technical means of expression, and to obey its rules.

A thousand hands support the buoyant child and solicitously attend its footsteps, that it may not soar aloft where there might he risk of a serious fall. But it is still so young, and is eternal; the day of its freedom will come. When it shall cease to be "musical."

6
___

The creator should take over no traditional law in blind belief, which would make him view his own creative endeavor, from the outset, as an exception contrasting with that law. For his individual case he should seek out and formulate a fitting individual law, which, after the first complete realization, he should annul, that he himself may not be drawn into repetitions when his next work shall be in the making.

The function of the creative artist consists in making laws, not in following laws ready made. He who follows such laws, ceases to be a creator.

Creative power may be the more readily recognized, the more it shakes itself loose from tradition. But an intentional avoidance of the rules cannot masquerade as creative power, and still less engender it.

The true creator strives, in reality, after *perfection* only. And through bringing this into harmony with *his own* individuality, a new law arises without premeditation.

So narrow has our tonal range become, so stereotyped its form of expression, that nowadays there is not one familiar motive that cannot be fitted with some other familiar motive so that the two may be played simultaneously. Not to lose my way in trifling,[14] I shall refrain from giving examples.

These things which, within our present-day music, most nearly approach the essential nature of the art, are the rest and the hold (pause). Consummate players, improvisers, know how to employ these instruments of expression in loftier and ampler measure. The tense silence between two movements—*in itself music,* in this environment—leaves wider scope for divination than the more determinate, but therefore less elastic, sound.

What we now call our tonal system is nothing more than a set of "signs"; an ingenious device to grasp somewhat of that eternal harmony; a meager pocket edition of that encyclopedic work; artificial light instead of the sun. Have you ever noticed how people gaze open-mouthed at the brilliant illumination of a hall? They never do so at the millionfold brighter sunshine of noonday.

And so, in music, the signs have assumed greater consequence than that which they ought to stand for, and can only suggest.

How important, indeed, are "third," "fifth," and "octave"! How strictly we divide "consonances" from "dissonances"—*in a sphere where no dissonances can possibly exist!*

We have divided the octave into twelve equidistant degrees, because we had to manage somehow, and have constructed our instruments in such a way that we can never get in above or below or between them. Keyboard instruments, in particular, have so thoroughly schooled our ears that we are no longer capable of hearing anything else—incapable of hearing except through this impure medium. Yet nature created an *infinite gradation—infinite!* Who still knows it nowadays?[15] And within this duodecimal octave we have marked out a series of fixed intervals, seven in number, and founded thereon our entire art of music. What do I say—*one* series? Two such series, one for each leg: The major and minor scales. When we start this series of intervals on some other degree of our semitonic ladder, we obtain a *new key,* and a "foreign" one, at that! How violently contracted a system arose from this initial confusion,[16] may be read in the law books; we will not repeat it here.

We teach four-and-twenty keys, twelve times the two series of seven; but, in point of fact, we have at our command only two, the major key and the minor key. *The rest are merely transpositions.* By means of the several transpositions we are supposed to get different shades of harmony; but this is an illusion. In England, under the reign of the high "concert pitch," the most familiar works may be played a semitone higher than they are written, without changing their effect. Singers transpose an aria to suit their convenience, leaving untransposed what precedes and follows. Songwriters not infrequently publish their own compositions in three different pitches; in all three editions the pieces are precisely alike.

When a well-known face looks out of a window, it matters not whether it gazes down from the first story or the third.

Were it feasible to elevate or depress a landscape, far as eye can reach, by several hundred yards, the pictorial impression would neither gain nor lose by it.

Upon the two series of seven, the major key and the minor key, the whole art of music has been established; one limitation brings on the other.

To each of these a definite character has been attributed; we have learned and have taught that they should be heard as contrasts, and they have gradually acquired the significance of symbols: major and minor—*maggiore e minore*—contentment and discontent—joy and sorrow—light and shade. The harmonic symbols have fenced in the expression of music, from Bach to Wagner, and yet further on until today and the day after tomorrow. *Minor* is employed with the same intention, and has the same effect upon us now, as two hundred years ago. Nowadays it is no longer possible to *compose* a funeral march, for it already exists, once for all. Even the least informed nonprofessional knows what to expect when a funeral march—whichever you please—is to be played. Even such a one can anticipate the difference between a symphony in major and one in minor. We are tyrannized by major and minor—by the bifurcated garment.

Strange, that one should feel major and minor as opposites. They both present the same face, now more joyous, now more serious; and a mere touch of the brush suffices to turn the one into the other. The passage from either to the other is easy and imperceptible; when it occurs frequently and swiftly, the two begin to shimmer and coalesce indistinguishably. But when we recognize that major and minor form one whole with a double meaning, and that the "four-and-twenty keys" are simply an elevenfold transposition of the original twain, we arrive unconstrainedly at a perception of the UNITY *of our system of keys* [tonality]. The conceptions of "related" and "foreign" keys vanish, and with them the entire intricate theory of degrees and relations. *We possess one single key*. But it is of most meager sort.

"Unity of the key system."

"I suppose you mean that 'key' and 'key system' are the sunbeam and its diffraction into colors?"

No—that I cannot mean. For our whole system of tone, key, and tonality, taken in its entirety, is only a part of a fraction of one diffracted ray from that sun, "Music," in the empyrean of the "eternal harmony."

However deeply rooted the attachment to the habitual, and inertia, may be in the ways and nature of humankind, in equal measure are energy, and opposition to the existing order, characteristic of all that has life. Nature has her wiles, and persuades man, obstinately opposed though he be to progress and change; nature progresses continually and changes unremittingly, but with so even and unnoticeable movement that men perceive only quiescence. Only on looking backward from a distance do they note with astonishment that they have been deceived.

The reformer of any given period excites irritation for the reason that his changes find men unprepared, and, above all, because these changes are appreciable. The reformer, in comparison with nature, is undiplomatic; and as a wholly logical consequence, his changes do not win general acceptance until time, with subtle, imperceptible advance, has bridged over the leap of the self-assured leader. Yet we find cases in which the reformer marched abreast of the times, while the rest fell behind. And then they have to be forced and lashed to take the leap across the passage they have missed. I believe that the major-and-minor key with its transpositional relations, our "twelve-semitone system," exhibits such a case of falling behind.

That some few have already felt how the intervals of the series of seven might be differently arranged (graduated) is manifested in isolated passages by Liszt, and recently by Debussy and his following, and even by Richard Strauss. Strong impulse, longing, gifted instinct, all speak from these strains. Yet it does not appear to me that a conscious and orderly conception of this intensified means of expression had been formed by these composers.

I have made an attempt to exhaust the possibilities of the arrangement of degrees within the seven-tone scale, and succeeded, by raising and lowering the intervals, in establishing *one hundred and thirteen different scales*. These 113 scales (within the octave C–C) comprise the greater part of our familiar twenty-four keys, and, furthermore, a series of new keys of peculiar character. But with these the mine is not exhausted, for we are at liberty to *transpose* each one of these 113, besides the blending of two such keys in harmony and melody.

There is a significant difference between the sound of the scale C-Db-Eb-Fb-Gb-Ab-Bb-C when C is taken as tonic, and the scale of Db minor. By giving it the customary C-major triad as a fundamental harmony, a novel harmonic sensation is obtained. But now listen to this same scale supported alternately by the A-minor, Eb-major, and C-major triads, and you cannot avoid a feeling of delightful surprise at the strangely unfamiliar euphony.

But how would a lawgiver classify the tone-series C-Db-Eb-Fb-G-A-B-C, C-Db-Eb-F-Gb-A-B-C, C-D-Eb-Fb-Gb-A-B-C, C-Db-E-F-Gb-A-Bb-C? Or these, forsooth: C-D-Eb-Fb-G-A♯-B-C, C-D-Eb-Fb-G♯-A-B-C, C-Db-Eb-F♯-G♯-A-Bb-C?

One cannot estimate at a glance what wealth of melodic and harmonic expression would thus be opened up to the hearing, but a great many novel possibilities may be accepted as certain, and are perceptible at a glance.

With this presentation, the unity of all keys may be considered as finally pronounced and justified. A kaleidoscopic blending and interchanging of twelve semitones within the three-mirror tube of taste, emotion, and intention—the essential feature of the harmony of today.

The harmony of *today*, and not for long; for all signs presage a revolution, and a next step toward that "eternal harmony." Let us once again call to mind that in this latter the gradation of the octave is *infinite*, and let us strive to draw a little nearer to infinitude. The tripartite tone (third of a tone) has for some time been demanding admittance, and we have left the call unheeded. Whoever has experimented, like myself (in a modest way), with this interval and introduced (either with voice or with violin) two equidistant intermediate tones between the extremes of a whole tone, schooling his ear and his precision of attack, will not have failed to discern that tripartite tones are wholly independent intervals with a pronounced character, and not to be confounded with ill-tuned semitones. They form a refinement in chromatics based, as at present appears, on the whole-tone scale. Were we to adopt them without further preparation, we should have to give up the semitones and lose our "minor third" and "perfect fifth"; and this loss would be felt more keenly than the relative gain of a system of eighteen one-third tones.

But there is no apparent reason for giving up the semitones for the sake of this new system. By retaining, for each whole tone, a semitone, we obtain a second series of whole tones lying a semitone higher than the original series. Then, by dividing this second series of whole tones into third-tones, each third-tone in the lower series will be matched by a semitone in the higher series.

Thus we have really arrived at a system of whole tones divided into sixths of a tone; and we may be sure that even sixth-tones will sometime be adopted into musical speech. But the tonal system above sketched must first of all train the hearing to thirds of a tone, without giving up the semitones.

To summarize: We may set up either two series of third-tones, with an interval of a semitone between the series; or the usual semitonic series *thrice repeated* at the interval of one-third of a tone.

Merely for the sake of distinction, let us call the first tone C, and the next third-tones C♯, and D♭; the first semitone (small) c, and its following thirds c♯ and d♭; the result is fully explained by the table below:

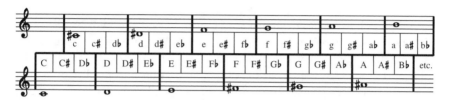

C	C♯	D♭	D	D♯	E♭	E	E♯	F♭	F	F♯	G♭	G	G♯	A♭	A	A♯	B♭	etc.

A preliminary expedient for notation might be, to draw six lines for the staff, using the lines for the whole tones and the spaces for the semitones:

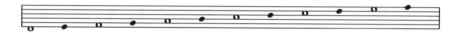

then indicating the third-tones by sharps and flats:

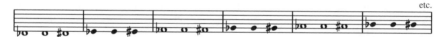

etc.

The question of notation seems to me subordinate. On the other hand, the question is important and imperious, how and on what these tones are to be produced. Fortunately, while busied with this essay, I received from America direct and authentic intelligence which solves the problem in a simple manner. I refer to an invention by Dr. Thaddeus Cahill.[17] He has constructed a comprehensive apparatus which makes it possible to transform an electric current into a fixed and mathematically exact number of vibrations. As pitch depends on the number of vibrations, and the apparatus may be "set" on any number desired, the infinite gradation of the octave may be accomplished by merely moving a lever corresponding to the pointer of a quadrant.

Only a long and careful series of experiments, and a continued training of the ear, can render this unfamiliar material approachable and plastic for the coming generation, and for art.

And what a vista of fair hopes and dreamlike fancies is thus opened for them both! Who has not dreamt that he could float on air? And firmly believed his dream to be reality? Let us take thought, how music may be restored to its primitive, natural essence; let us free it from architectonic, acoustic and esthetic dogmas; let it be pure invention and sentiment, in harmonies, in forms, in tone colors (for invention and sentiment are not the prerogative of melody alone); let it follow the line of the rainbow and vie with the clouds in breaking sunbeams; *let music be naught else than nature mirrored by and reflected from the human breast;* for it is sounding air and floats above and beyond the air; within man himself as universally and absolutely as in creation entire; for it can gather together and disperse without losing in intensity.

7

In his book *Jenseits von Gut und Böse* (Beyond Good and Evil) Nietzsche says: "With regard to German music I consider precaution necessary in various ways. Assuming that a person loves the South (as I love it) as a great training school for health of soul and sense in their highest potency, as an uncontrollable flood and glamour of sunshine spreading over a race of independent and self-reliant beings; well, such an one will learn to be more or less on his guard against German music, because while spoiling his taste anew, it undermines his health.

"Such a Southlander (not by descent, but by belief) must, should he dream of the future of music, likewise dream of a redemption of music from the North, while in his ears there rings the prelude to a deeper, mightier, perchance a more evil and more mysterious music, a super-German music, which does not fade, wither and die away in view of the blue, sensuous sea and the splendor of Mediterranean skies, as all German music does; a super-European music, that asserts itself even amid the tawny sunsets of the desert, whose soul is allied with the palm tree, and can consort and prowl with great, beautiful, lonely beasts of prey.

"I could imagine a music whose rarest charm should consist in its complete divorce from the Good and the Bad[18], only that its surface might be ruffled, as it were, by a longing as of a sailor for home, by variable golden shadows and tender frailties: an art which should see fleeing toward it, from afar off, the hues of a perishing moral world become wellnigh incomprehensible, and which should be hospitable and profound enough to harbor such belated fugitives."

And Tolstoy transmutes a landscape impression into a musical impression when he writes, in "Lucerne": "Neither on the lake, nor on the mountains, nor in the skies, a single straight line, a single unmixed color, a single point of repose; everywhere movement, irregularity, caprice, variety, an incessant interplay of shades and lines, and in it all the reposefulness, softness, harmony and inevitableness of beauty."

Will this music ever be attained?

"Not all reach Nirvana; but he who, gifted from the beginning, learns everything that one ought to learn, experiences all that one should experience, renounces what one should renounce, develops what one should develop, realizes what one should realize—he shall reach Nirvana"[19] ([Hendrik] Kern, *Der Buddhismus und Geschichte in Indien*).

If Nirvana be the realm "beyond the Good and the Bad," *one* way leading thither is here pointed out. A way to the very portal. To the bars that divide man from 'eternity'—or that open to admit that which was temporal. Beyond that portal sounds *music*. Not the strains of "musical art."[20] It may be, that we must leave Earth to find that music. But only to the pilgrim who has succeeded on the way in freeing himself from earthly shackles, shall the bars open.

Addenda

8

Feeling—like honesty—is a moral point of honor, an attribute of whose possession no one will permit denial, which claims a place in life and art alike. But while, in life, a want of feeling may be forgiven to the possessor of a more brilliant attribute, such as bravery or impartial justice, in art feeling is held to be the highest moral qualification.

In music, however, feeling requires two consorts, taste and style. Now, in life, one encounters real taste as seldom as deep and true feeling; as for style, it is a province of art. What remains, is a species of pseudoemotion which must be characterized as lachrymose hysteria or turgidity. And above all, people insist upon having it plainly paraded before their eyes! It must be underscored, so that everybody shall stop, look, and listen. The audience sees it, greatly magnified, thrown on the screen, so that it dances before the vision in vague, importunate vastness; it is cried on the streets, to summon them that dwell remote from art; it is gilded, to make the destitute stare in amaze.

For in life, too, the *expressions* of feeling, by mien and words, are oftenest employed; rarer, and more genuine, is that feeling which acts without talk; and most precious is the feeling which hides itself.

"Feeling" is generally understood to mean tenderness, pathos, and extravagance, of expression. But how much more does the marvelous flower "emotion" enfold! Restraint and forbearance, renunciation, power, activity, patience, magnanimity, joyousness, and that all-controlling intelligence wherein feeling actually takes its rise.

It is not otherwise in art, which holds the mirror up to life; and still more outspokenly in music, which repeats the emotions of life—though for this, as I have said, taste and style must be added; style, which distinguishes art from life.

What the amateur and the mediocre artist attempt to express, is feeling in little, in detail, for a short stretch.

Feeling on a grand scale is mistaken by the amateur, the semi-artist, the public (and the critics too, unhappily!), for a want of emotion, because they all are unable to hear the longer reaches as parts of a yet more extended whole. Feeling, therefore, is likewise economy.

Hence, I distinguish feeling as taste, as style, as economy. Each a whole in itself, and each one-third of the whole. Within and over them rules a subjective trinity: temperament, intelligence, and the instinct of equipoise.

These six carry on a dance of such subtlety in the choice of partners and intertwining of figures, in the bearing and the being borne, in advancing and curtseying, in motion and repose, that no loftier height of artistry is conceivable.

When the chords of the two triads are in perfect tune, fantasy may—nay, must—associate with feeling; supported by the six, she will not degenerate, and out of this combination of all the elements arises individuality. The individuality catches, like a lens, the light-impressions, reflects them, according to its nature, as a negative, and the hearer perceives the true picture.

In so far as taste participates in feeling, the latter—like all else—alters its forms of expression with the period. That is, one aspect or another of feeling will be favored at one time or another, onesidedly cultivated, especially developed. Thus, with and after Wagner, voluptuous sensuality came to the fore; the form of *intensification of passion* is still unsurmounted by contemporary composers. On every tranquil beginning followed a swift upward surge. Wagner, in this point insatiable, but not inexhaustible, turned from sheer necessity to the expedient, after reaching a climax, of starting afresh softly, to soar to a sudden new intensification.

Modern French writers exhibit a revulsion; their feeling is a reflective chastity, or perhaps rather a restrained sensualism; the upstriving mountain paths of Wagner are succeeded by monotonous plains of twilight uniformity.

Thus "style" forms itself out of feeling, when led by taste.

The "Apostles of the Ninth Symphony" have devised the notion of "depth" in music. It is still current at face value, especially in Germanic lands.

There is a depth of feeling, and a depth of thought; the latter is literary, and can have no application to tones. Depth of feeling, by contrast, is psychical, and thoroughly germane to the nature of music. The Apostles of the Ninth Symphony have a peculiar and not quite clearly defined estimate of "depth" in music. *Depth* becomes *breadth*, and the attempt is made to attain it through *weight*; it then discovers itself (through an association of ideas) by a preference for a *deep register*, and (as I have had opportunity to observe) by the insinuation of a second, mysterious notion, usually of a literary sort. If these are not the sole specific signs, they are the most important ones.

To every disciple of philosophy, however, depth of feeling would seem to imply exhaustiveness in feeling, a complete absorption in the given mood.

Whoever, surrounded by the full tide of a genuine carnival crowd, slinks about morosely or even indifferently, neither affected nor carried away by the tremendous self-satire of mask and motley, by the might of misrule over law, by the vengeful feeling of wit running riot, shows himself incapable of sounding the depths of feeling. This gives further confirmation of the fact, that depth of feeling roots in a complete absorption in the given mood, however frivolous, and blossoms in the interpretation of that mood; whereas the current conception of deep feeling singles out only one aspect of feeling in man, and specializes that.

In the so-called "Champagne Aria" ["Finch'han dal vino," Act 1] in *Don Giovanni* there lies more "depth" than in many a funeral march or nocturne: Depth of feeling also shows in not wasting it on subordinate or unimportant matters.

9

Routine is highly esteemed and frequently required; in musical "officialdom" it is a *sine qua non*. That routine in music should exist at all, and, furthermore, that it can be nominated as a condition in the musician's bond, is another proof of the narrow confines of our musical art. Routine signifies the acquisition of a modicum of experience and artcraft, and their application to all cases which may occur; hence, there must be an astounding number of analogous cases. Now, I like to imagine a species of art-praxis wherein each case should be a new one, an exception! How helpless and impotent would the army of practical musicians stand before it! In the end they would surely beat a retreat, and disappear. Routine transforms the temple of art into a factory. It destroys creativeness. For creation means, the bringing of form out of the void; whereas routine flourishes on imitation. It is "poetry made to order." It rules because it suits the generality: in the theatre, in the orchestra, in virtuosi, in instruction. One longs to exclaim: "Avoid routine! Let each beginning be, as had none been before! Know nothing, but rather think and feel! For, behold, the myriad strains that once shall sound have existed since the beginning, ready, afloat in the aether, and together with them other myriads that shall never be heard. Only stretch forth your hands, and ye shall grasp a blossom, a breath of the sea-breeze, a sunbeam; avoid routine, for it strives to grasp only that wherewith your four walls are filled, and the same over and over again; the spirit of ease so infects you, that you will scarcely leave your armchairs, and will lay hold only of what is nearest to hand. And myriad strains are there since the beginning, still waiting for manifestation!"

"It is my misfortune, to possess no routine," Wagner once wrote Liszt, when the composition of *Tristan* was making no progress. Thus Wagner deceived himself, and wore a mask for others. He had too much routine, and his composing machinery was thrown out of gear, just when a tangle formed in the mesh which only inspiration could unloose. True, Wagner found the clue when he succeeded in throwing off routine; but had he really never possessed it, he would have declared the fact without bitterness. And after all, this sentence in Wagner's letter expresses the true artist-contempt for routine, inasmuch as he waives all claim to a qualification which he thinks meanly of, and takes care that others may not invest him with it. This self-praise he utters with a mien of ironic desperation. He is, in very truth, unhappy that composition is at a standstill, but finds rich consolation in the consciousness that his genius is above the cheap expedients of routine; at the same time, with an air of modesty, he sorrowfully confesses that he has not acquired a training belonging to the craft.

The sentence is a masterpiece of the native cunning of the instinct of self-preservation; but equally proves—and that is our point—the pettiness of routine in creative work.

10

Respect the pianoforte! Its disadvantages are evident, decided, and unquestionable: the lack of sustained tone, and the pitiless, unyielding adjustment of the inalterable semitonic scale.

But its advantages and prerogatives approach the marvelous.

It gives a single man command over something complete; in its potentialities from softest to loudest in one and the same register it excels all other instruments. The trumpet can blare, but not sigh; contrariwise the flute; the pianoforte can do both. Its range embraces the highest and deepest practicable tones. Respect the pianoforte!

Let doubters consider how the pianoforte was esteemed by Bach, Mozart, Beethoven, Liszt, who dedicated their choicest thoughts to it.

And the pianoforte has one possession wholly peculiar to itself, an inimitable device, a photograph of the sky, a ray of moonlight—the pedal.

The effects of the pedal are unexhausted, because they have remained even to this day the drudges of a narrow-souled and senseless harmonic theory; the treatment accorded them is like trying to mold air or water into geometric forms. Beethoven, who incontestably achieved the greatest progress on and for the pianoforte, divined the mysteries of the pedal, and to him we owe the first liberties.

The pedal is in ill repute. For this, absurd irregularities must bear the blame. Let us experiment with *sensible* irregularities.

11

"I felt . . . that the book I shall write will be neither in English nor in Latin; and this for the one reason . . . namely, that the language in which it may be given me not only to write, but also to think, will not be Latin, or English, or Italian, or Spanish, but a language not even one of whose words I know, a language in which dumb things speak to me, and in which, it may be, I shall at last have to respond in my grave to an Unknown Judge."
(Hugo von Hofmannsthal, *Letter of Lord Chandos*)

Notes
[Text: Busoni, *Sketch of a New Esthetic of Music*, translated by Theodore Baker (New York: G. Schirmer, 1911).]

1. Nonetheless, in these arts, taste and individuality can and will unceasingly find refreshment and rejuvenation.

2. Tradition is a plaster mask taken from life, which, in the course of many years and after passing through the hands of innumerable artisans, leaves its resemblance to the original largely a matter of imagination.

3. *Die Ur-Musik,* is the author's happy phrase. But as this music *never has been*, our English terms like "primitive," "original," etc., would involve a nonsequitur which is avoided, at least, by "infinite" [translator's note].

4. In the recitatives of his Passions we hear "human speech"; *not* "correct declamation."

5. As characteristic traits of Beethoven's individuality I would mention the poetic fire, the strong human feeling (whence springs his revolutionary temper), and a portent of modern nervousness. These traits are certainly opposed to those of a "classic." Moreover, Beethoven is no "master," as the term applies to Mozart or the later Wagner, just because his art foreshadows a greater [one that is] as yet incomplete. (Compare the section next-following.)

6. "Together with the problem, it gives us the solution," as I once said of Mozart.

7. ". . . Beethoven, dont les esquisses *thématiques ou élémentaires* sont innombrables, mais qui, sitôt les thèmes trouvés, semble par cela même en avoir établi tout le développement . . ." [Vincent d'Indy, in *César Franck*].

8. How strongly notation influences style in music, and fetters imagination, how "form" grew up out of it and from form arose "conventionalism" in expression, is shown very convincingly and avenges itself in tragic wise in E. T. A. Hoffmann, who occurs to me here as a typical example.

   This remarkable man's mental conceptions, lost in visionary moods and reveling in transcendentalism, as his writings set forth in often inimitable fashion, must naturally—so one would infer—have found in the dreamlike and transcendental art of tones a language and mode of expression peculiarly congenial.

   The veil of mysticism, the secret harmonies of nature, the thrill of the supernatural, the twilight vagueness of the borderland of dreams, everything, in fact, which he so effectively limned with the precision of *words*—all this, one would suppose, he could have interpreted to fullest effect by the aid of music. And yet, comparing Hoffmann's best musical work with the weakest of his literary productions, you will discover to your sorrow how a conventional system of measures, periods and keys—whereto the hackneyed opera-style of the time adds its share—could turn a poet into a Philistine. But that his fancy cherished another ideal of music, we learn from many, and frequently admirable, observations of Hoffmann the *littérateur*.

9. The author probably had in mind the languages of southern Europe; the word is employed in English, and in the tongues of the Scandinavian group, with precisely the same meaning as in German [translator's note].

10. The only kind of people one might properly call *musical* are the singers; for they themselves can sound. Similarly, a clown who by some trick produces tones when he is touched might be called a *pseudomusical* person.

11. "But these pieces are so musical," a violinist once remarked to me of a four-hand worklet which I had characterized as trivial.

12. "My dog is *very* musical," I have heard said in all seriousness. Should the dog take precedence of Berlioz?

13. Such has been my own fate.

14. With a friend I once indulged in such trifling in order to ascertain how many commonly known compositions were written according to the scheme of the second theme in the Adagio of the Ninth Symphony. In a few moments we had collected some fifteen analogues of the most different kinds, among them specimens of the lowest type of art. And Beethoven himself: —Is the theme of the Finale in the Fifth [Symphony] any other than the one wherewith the Second introduces its Allegro?—or than the principal theme of the Third Piano Concerto, only in minor?

15. "The equal temperament of 12 degrees, which was discussed theoretically as early as about 1500, but not established as a principle until shortly before 1700 (by Andreas Werkmeister), divides the octave into twelve equal portions (semitones, hence 'twelve-semitone system') through which mean values are obtained; no interval is perfectly pure, but all are fairly serviceable" (Riemann, *Musik-Lexikon*). Thus, through Andreas Werkmeister, this master workman in art, we have gained the "twelve-semitone" system with intervals which are all impure, but fairly serviceable. But what is "pure," and what "impure?" We hear a piano "gone out of tune," and it sounds impure to us. The diplo-

matic "twelve-semitone system" is an invention mothered by necessity; yet none the less do we sedulously guard its imperfections.

16. It is termed "the science of harmony."

17. "New Music for an Old World." Dr. Thaddeus Cahill's Dynamophone, an extraordinary electrical invention for producing scientifically perfect music. Article in *McClure's Magazine* for July, 1906, by Ray Stannard Baker. Readers interested in the details of this invention are referred to the above-mentioned magazine article. [In his translation Theodore Baker omitted a lengthy extension to this footnote: "Concerning this transcendental music machine, Mr. [Ray Stannard] Baker reports further: a realization of the imperfection in tone production on all instruments set Dr. Cahill to thinking. The material from which they are made, design, temperament, and the climatic conditions can spoil their dependability. The pianist loses control of the decay of the sound the moment that he strikes the key. On the organ the quality of a sustained tone cannot be changed. Dr. Cahill conceived of an instrument with which the player would have total control over each note and its expressivity. He used the theories of Helmholtz as his model, which taught him that the number of and energy in overtones of the fundamental were decisive for the tone color of the various instruments. Accordingly, he constructed, in addition to a device that sounds the fundamental, a number of supplemental devices each of which produces a certain overtone. The gradation of energy in each of these can be manipulated so that each sound is susceptible to the most diverse of characteristics. Its production can be controlled dynamically in the most sensitive manner, producing a range of volume from the nearly inaudible pianissimo to an unbearable loudness. And since the instrument is manipulated from a keyboard, it can be made to conform to the wishes of the artist. A number of such keyboards played by several performers can be put together into an orchestra.

The construction of the instrument is extraordinarily large and costly, and its practical value must, in truth, be questioned. The inventor chose the telephone diaphragm as the medium that transmits vibrations from electrical current to air. Through this happy inspiration it became possible to send the sound of the device from a central point out to other positions connected by wire, even to those a great distance off. Experiments conducted so far prove that in this way neither the quality nor strength of tone is lost. The surrounding space is magically filled with sound—invisibly, effortlessly, and continually—a sound that is scientifically perfect and unfailing. The report from which I drew this description is provided with authentic photographs, which remove any doubt as to the authenticity of this almost incredible creation. The device looks like an engine room."]

[18. In his translation Baker omits the following footnote: "Here Nietzsche contradicts himself. Earlier he spoke of a 'worse' music; now he imagines a music 'completely divorced from the Good and the Bad'."]

19. As if anticipating my thoughts, M. Vincent d'Indy has just written me: ". . . laissant de côté les contingences et les petitesses de la vie pour regarder constamment vers un idéal qu'on ne pourra jamais atteindre, mais dont il est permis de se rapprocher" ["leaving behind the limitations and pettiness of life to look incessantly toward an ideal that one can never attain but which we are allowed to approach"].

20. I think I have read, somewhere, that Liszt confined his *Dante* Symphony to the two movements, *Inferno* and *Purgatorio*, "because our tone-speech is inadequate to express the felicities of Paradise."

3

ARNOLD SCHOENBERG

(1 8 7 4 – 1 9 5 1)

Arnold Schoenberg's *Theory of Harmony*, published in 1911, was the composer's first major writing on music, undertaken primarily to support his burgeoning career as a teacher of composition. The book, in Schoenberg's own estimation, was divided into certain "practical" parts and other parts that were speculative, less crucial for the student of basic harmony but more in tune with Schoenberg's reputation as an original thinker. The practical matters outline a theory of tonal harmony much indebted to earlier doctrines on the subject, especially to Simon Sechter's *Die Grundsätze der musikalischen Komposition* (Fundamentals of Musical Composition, 1853–54) and to the famous lectures on harmony at the University of Vienna given by Anton Bruckner. Schoenberg's practical treatise, he says, is purely a "system for the presentation" of harmonic elements—not a compilation of hard and fast rules that could deter new musical ideas.

In the final sections of the *Theory of Harmony*, Schoenberg goes beyond traditional thinking on the subject to touch upon resources more characteristic of music since the turn of the century. These topics include "fluctuating" and "suspended" tonality, chromatic pitch resources, whole-tone scales and chords that derive from them, and fourth chords, all of which he relates to an expanded treatment of key. In the final section of the book, subtitled "Aesthetic Evaluation of Chords With Six or More Tones," Schoenberg turns at last to aspects of harmony characteristic of his own recent music, which others would soon call "atonal," in which chords had no tonal functions at all. This passage is decidedly speculative, and it has the character of an independent essay. Indeed, it was published separately as an article in the journal *Der Merker* shortly before the harmony treatise appeared in December 1911.

Schoenberg begins this final passage by returning to thoughts that he had broached at the beginning of the treatise. Strict rules, he says, are contrary to great music, which flows instead from the instinctive powers of true artists, provoked by their urge for self-expression. The role of the unconscious or instinctual mind is stressed as the primary faculty by which great composers see into the future of music and bypass such mundane and misleading considerations as beauty or hidebound forms. The power of instinct was much on Schoenberg's mind just at the time that he wrote the *Theory of Harmony*. In a letter of 1909 to Ferruccio Busoni he said that he intended in his recent music "to place nothing inhibiting in the stream of my unconscious sensations, not to allow anything to infiltrate that may be invoked either by intelligence or consciousness."

Schoenberg then turns to the new harmonies themselves, whose tones, he says, are chosen not according to any laws but only from an unconscious feeling for their correctness. Some of these large, dissonant harmonies arise from voice leading, others are spaced so as to diminish their dissonant sonority, and still others have component parts that resemble traditional chords. Neighboring chords, he says, are often mutually exclusive in pitch content, thus contributing to a greater chromatic saturation, a tendency also enhanced by the avoidance of octave doublings.

Schoenberg ends his book with a futuristic speculation upon the expressive power of tone color, a resource that someday may lead even to "tone color melodies" in which a melodylike line is constructed from changing colors rather than from different pitches and rhythms. This resource, he says, would be purely expressive, far beyond the grasp of any theory or rule. As a composer Schoenberg experimented with a heightened application of tone color in his music just before writing the harmony book—especially in passages from his *Five Orchestral Pieces, Op. 16*, and in his opera *Erwartung*.

Soon after completing the *Theory of Harmony*, Schoenberg's idealistic fascination for instinctive musical expression began to wane. From about 1912 it was steadily displaced in his oeuvre by procedures ensuring rational and conscious control over musical elements, techniques that crystallized in the early 1920s in his twelve-tone method of composition. His later writings clearly reflect this change of compositional viewpoint. Compare, for example, the final sentences of "Aesthetic Evaluation," where Schoenberg speaks of tone color melodies as "the illusory stuff of our dreams," with his discussion of tone color in the 1941 lecture "Composition With Twelve Tones": "More mature minds," he wrote, "resist the temptation to become intoxicated by colors and prefer to be coldly convinced by the transparency of clear-cut ideas."

Schoenberg's *Theory of Harmony* was a great success, certainly one of the most widely used harmony treatises of the early twentieth century. The author revised and expanded it in 1921, although he made no significant changes at that time in the concluding section.

Schoenberg's Pedagogical Writings: a Selective Bibliography (see also the bibliography concerning Schoenberg with essay no. 10)

Fundamentals of Musical Composition. Edited by Gerald Strang and Leonard Stein. New York: St. Martin's Press, 1967. A study of musical forms based on classical models.

Structural Functions of Harmony. London: Williams & Norgate, 1946; revised edition, edited by Leonard Stein, New York: Norton, 1969.

Theory of Harmony. Translated by Roy E. Carter. Berkeley and Los Angeles: University of California Press, 1978. A complete translation of Schoenberg's *Harmonielehre* from its revised and expanded edition of 1922.

—m—

"AESTHETIC EVALUATION OF CHORDS WITH SIX OR MORE TONES" FROM *THEORY OF HARMONY*

("Ästhetische Bewertung sechs und mehrtöniger Klänge" from *Harmonielehre*, 1911, revised 1921)

I do not recommend that the pupil use the harmonies presented here in his attempts to compose, so far as they do not also appear in other, older texts. His efforts, regardless of whether he uses modern or unmodern means, will be good or bad depending on how his innate talent for having something to express relates to his ability to express it. The teacher has influence only on one component of this relation, on the ability to express. Perhaps not even on that; I doubt whether even this ability can be increased by imparting technical devices. The pupil does not learn to express *himself* when he imitates the techniques of models. Actually, the real artist is unteachable in the first place. If we show him "how he must do it," and base what we say on the fact that others have also done it that way, then that may be instruction in art, but it is not instruction of the artist. Ability to express oneself certainly does not depend on the kind and number of means placed at one's command. But inability depends on that. Inability can develop only by way of techniques; for it does not exist through what it produces of itself but thrives on what others have produced. The work of the truly gifted, however, ultimately manifests very little external relationship with the literature that was once his model. Because he esteems himself; because, through this self-esteem, he evolves away from his preliminary conditions, from his models which perhaps at the beginning did serve as props, crutches he used in his first efforts to walk. Because ultimately he will not write what is *artistically acceptable*, but rather what is *acceptable to him, the artist.*

The following consideration seems to contradict this view: That there are essential distinctions between Mozart's style and that of Beethoven, for example, is today still clear to everyone; nevertheless, the distinctions are not so great as to justify a contention that the laws applicable to the one do not hold for the other. On the contrary, there are passages, even movements, by Mozart that could almost be by Beethoven, and some by Beethoven that could almost be by Mozart. If we go even farther back, say into the sixteenth or seventeenth century, then the distinctions become so subtle to our eyes that we can easily mistake the music of one composer for that of another. Distance from a group of objects equalizes them to such a great extent that it erases the individual distinctions. Stylistically, perhaps even in content, one artist can hardly be distinguished clearly from the other; we only perceive common traits, from which we can abstract the artistically acceptable. There is a certain distance, however, from which we can really detect only the spirit of the century. He who can set himself far enough apart will detect the spirit of mankind. Individualities disappear at this distance, but what they express—mankind, the best that is in it—becomes visible. The highest pinnacles, which are most accessible to the observer, into which the capillaries lift the finest and best from the depths, these alone set forth the spirit of mankind. Thus, increasing distance, initially reductive, once again magnifies: the individuals, the pinnacles, become visible again, even if in a different way. One sees that they are related and how they are related, that they are coherent among themselves; one no longer sees what proximity revealed, one no longer sees that they were sharply separate; *but the relationships are not those of art, not those of the techniques of art; they are rather deeper ones.*

Naturally, observing from a moderate distance, we can, as I said, even find a line revealing the path of the techniques and of the artistically acceptable. And if we admit that the smallest part of a curve may be viewed as an infinitely small straight line, then such an optical illusion is surely also allowed with the vascular network that designates the way the techniques of art developed. Discounting the little deviations, that can surely be a line. Even must be, perhaps, for the ultimate goal is common to all. And something else is common to all: our ultimate limits.

The eye that will occupy itself with the contemplation of art must be able to focus on all these distances. The images revealed by distance are as important as those seen close at hand. But from a distance we can only contemplate the past. If we could look at the present from afar, then all our struggles would be over. But the struggle will not release us, even though its outcome is predetermined. Its goal we know. We know who will be victorious. As with maneuvers, where in fact the victor is determined in advance. The struggle must be carried on, nevertheless, just as seriously as if one could change the outcome. We must fight just as passionately as if we did not know which idea would conquer. Although this idea would conquer anyway, even if we did not fight, since its victory is predestined. Perhaps our struggle itself is predestined; anyway, the passion is justified.

Proximity, the present, which we do indeed sense most strongly, most directly, reveals the living personality poised for the struggle, in vigorous conflict with its environment. The personalities differ sharply from each other; it looks almost as if they had nothing in common, as if they would fall completely out of the line of evolution, as if nothing connected them with the rest of mankind. And, as in maneuvers, the one marked for defeat must try to turn every previously known situation to his advantage, so the idea that will succumb struggles for every inch of its property. And as the predestined conqueror in maneuvers may not simply fold his hands in his lap, but must operate as if he could otherwise be defeated, so the conquering idea acts with the same vigor, even though it would win anyway, even if it did nothing. Battle position, all muscles taut, every movement has a reason and a goal. This is the state, as we see it up close, of the personality that is striving.

If proximity teaches us diversity, so distance teaches us the general. If the present shows us the divergencies of individuals, so the median distance shows the similarity of means; but the great distance in turn cancels out both, shows the individuals as different, but even so also shows what really connects them. It shows what is most important about the individual, that most profound introspection into and absorption with his own nature, that which leads him to express: the nature of mankind.

What really matters, the ability to listen to oneself, to look deep into oneself, that can hardly be acquired; certainly it cannot be taught. The average person seems to possess this ability only in a few sublime moments, and to live the rest of the time, not according to his own inclinations, but according to principles. He who really has principles, principles of humanity, lives according to his own inclinations. These correspond of course to the principles of humanity, without his knowing it; but perhaps he senses it is so.

And that which is considered the means of art, which is considered style, all those characteristics of which the mediocre believe it is only necessary that they imitate them and they too will become artists—all these things turn out to be secondary matters, whose value is at most that of symptoms. True, the stylistic similarity of masterworks of a time already remote from us can be explained by our external distance from them, and that similarity disappears whenever we draw nearer. And the straight line of the evolution of means shows, upon closer inspection, manifold complexity. Everything that makes up style, however, is at most characteristic for the time in which the person is still alive and struggling with his contemporaries. It is merely a symptom by which the contemporaries are supposed to recognize which are the significant individuals. But it is inconsequential in relation to what distance reveals.

Thus, instruction that is supposed to educate an artist could consist at most in helping him to listen to himself. Technique, the means of art, will not help him. This ought to be, wherever possible, occult knowledge, to which he alone has access who finds the way himself. He who listens to himself acquires this technique, by a route different from that of the curriculum, by roundabout ways perhaps, but with unerring certainty. For he hears that which is common to all, and what it is that sets him apart from the others is perhaps not how he hears it, but *that* he does in fact hear it. And the *how* of the means is more likely to separate one from the *what* of art than to bring one closer.

Therefore, I do not recommend to the pupil that he use modern techniques. Of course he should practice them so that he will have the ability to accomplish whatever the spirit should eventually demand. The older means will also do here. The newer will of course cause no harm. But there is perhaps still a copyright on them, a quite arrogant right of ownership, that refuses to open the road to those who will not make the effort themselves. Those who themselves make the effort find it anyway, find it in a way that gives them the right of use. To them the road is open; to the others, who only want to try their hand at it, may it remain closed. Ultimately, the newer techniques will be in the public domain; but then those who use them will at least no longer be wanting to learn "how to represent a personal style."

Precisely because I am not recommending these harmonies, it is not necessary for me to give an aesthetic evaluation of them. Besides, whoever comes to them on his own will have no need for a guide. His ear and his sense of integrity will lead him more dependably than any law of art could ever do. There is yet another reason, however, why I may easily omit such an evaluation, without hiding behind a procedure like that in other textbooks. The older theories give a system, and in it appears that which experience can designate as beautiful. But other things also appear in it, other things that are not recommended, that are even forbidden. The method is as follows: one sets up a number of possible combinations and excludes as exceptions those one considers unfit. A system with exceptions, however, is no system, or at least an inadequate one. Besides, I have proved that the arguments for these exceptions are mostly wrong and—this would be to me the most important thing anyone could learn from this book—that these exceptions are solely the expression of a certain taste in art, which relates to what is natural only in that the taste lags behind what is natural. [I have proved] that these exceptions are only imperfect adaptations to the natural, whereas a more adequate adaptation has to lead to what this book has set as its goal. Yet certainly to more than that, certainly beyond that. [I have proved] then that the rules indicate at best only the degree of penetration into what is naturally given, hence, that they are not eternal laws, but only such that the next achievement always flushes them away. And now, should I also give laws, myself carry out an evaluation of that kind and make exceptions? No one could require that of me, no one who has followed and agreed with what I have said.

I suspect the following question will be put to me: how does one distinguish between the skillful and the bungler, if there is nothing to establish what is good and what is bad? First, I have to say, I do not consider it very important to make any essential distinction between this skill that is meant and bungling. There is little that is impressive about this skill that really consists only in carefully noting and obeying all laws. It is truly difficult to distinguish from bungling, but [to make that distinction is] just as superfluous. The skill of the artist, however, has nothing to do with that. The artist does nothing [so] that others will consider [it] beautiful; he does, rather, only what is necessary for him to do. If others want to apply aesthetic laws to his works, then it is their affair—if they just cannot live without aesthetic laws—to find such as are applicable. But are they really necessary? Can one really not enjoy works of art without aesthetic laws? And then, what about the artistic sensitivity of the layman, who knows nothing of the code? Schopenhauer explains the respect of the mediocre for the great work of art as belief in authority. Certainly, as far as the respect shown by the broad masses is concerned. But among laymen I have found people whose organs of perception were much more sensitive than those of most professionals. And I know for sure that there are musicians who are more receptive to painting than many painters, and painters who are more receptive to music than most musicians. Whoever does not agree will still at least have to see that—if there is any sense at all in disseminating art—the receptiveness, the sensitivity, the powers of discrimination of the layman are absolutely prerequisite. If he responds sensitively to art, then he must surely be able to evaluate it also—if that is necessary! And if he can evaluate for himself, then for him the aesthetic laws are superfluous. For whom, then, do they exist? For the critic? He who can distinguish a good fruit from a bad with his palate does not have to be able to express the distinction through the chemical formula and does not need the formula to recognize the distinction. But should someone who has no palate pass judgment on foods? And would the chemical formula then be of use to him? Moreover: would he understand how to apply it, and if so: for what purposes would he apply it? Does the pupil have need for the laws, so that he can know how far he may go? I have indeed just said how far he may go: as far as his nature drives him; and he must strive to hear his nature precisely if he wants to be an artist! If he only wants to be a craftsman, then a barrier will appear somewhere all of its own accord; the same barrier that keeps him from artistry will also keep him from going all too far. And suppose a young man should err and go farther than his talent pushes him! Whether he does not become anything special because he went too far or because he did not go far enough, let that be as it may. But fools are always afraid that they will be taken for fools, that is: recognized. They fear they will be duped. This, their uncertainty, is what demands protection. Since the aesthetic laws, in this form at least, cannot be ends in themselves, it seems to me almost as if their sole purpose were to protect the inferior from being taken for fools. Or, perhaps also, secretly, to protect the inferior against being overwhelmed by a new beauty. The mediocre person fears nothing else so much as he fears being compelled to change his view, his philosophy, of life. And he has also set up an ideal for himself, which expresses this fear: character. The man of character, that's the one (to paraphrase a saying of Karl Kraus) whose hardening of the arteries comes from his view of the world.

In another form, however, the aesthetic laws could be an end in themselves: as precise description of those effects that are common to the greatest possible number of works; as attempts to reduce the greatest possible number of effects to the fewest possible common causes; as attempts to organize the phenomena to give perspective. That could be an end in itself, but one would have to be content with it so; and above all, one should never draw the conclusion: "that is true of most works of art, hence it must be true of all others." Enough would have been accomplished, more than one dares require, but the utmost that may be allowed.

Someone will ask why I am writing a textbook of harmony, if I wish technique to be occult knowledge. I could answer: people want to study, to learn, and I want to teach, to disseminate what I hold to be good; thus, I teach. But I think that a person should study. The artist, perhaps, only so that he will get into errors from which he must free himself. The surge of energy that washes away the error then cleanses him also of whatever other inhibitions were soiling him. A catarrh of the eye is healed by provoking inflammation of the eye. The healing process heals not only this inflammation but also the actual illness. But the artist should also study because not everyone has to begin at the beginning, not everyone has to experience first-hand all the errors that accompany the progress of human knowledge. One must and may to a certain degree depend upon one's predecessors. Their experiences and observations they have recorded in part in the [literature of the various] sciences; but another part—I do not know whether it is the most dependable or not—lies in the unconscious, in instinct. It is our right and duty to doubt. But to make ourselves independent of instinct is as difficult as it is dangerous. For alongside [the knowledge of] what is right and what is wrong, alongside the inherited experiences and observations of our ancestors, alongside that which we owe to their and our past, there is in the instinct perhaps a faculty that is only now being developed: a knowledge of the future; perhaps also other faculties, which man will one day consciously possess, but which at present he can at most only sense and yearn for but cannot translate into action. The artist's creative activity is instinctive. Consciousness has little influence on it. He feels as if what he does were dictated to him. As if he did it only according to the will of some power or other within him, whose laws he does not know. He is merely the instrument of a will hidden from him, of instinct, of his unconscious. Whether it is new or old, good or bad, beautiful or ugly, he does not know. He feels only the instinctual compulsion, which he must obey. And in this instinct the old may find expression, and the new. Such as depends on the past, and such as points out paths to the future. Old truths or new errors. [It is] his musical nature, as he inherited it from a musical ancestor or acquired it through the literature, but [it is] also the outflow of an energy that is seeking new paths. Right or wrong, new or old, beautiful or ugly—how does one know who only senses the instinctual urge? Who would dare to differentiate right from wrong in the instinct, in the unconscious, to keep separate the knowledge inherited from predecessors and the intuitive power granted by the spirit? The artist must study, must learn, whether he wants to or not; for he has learned already, before he became capable of wanting to. In his instinct, in his unconscious lies a wealth of old knowledge, which he will resurrect whether he wants to or not. The true artist will be as little harmed by what he learns from the teacher as by what he learned this way prior to his time of awareness.

And the person of ordinary talents, who is not actually productive in that high-est sense—he, above all, should study. For him study and learning is an end in itself. His task is to take for knowledge what is in reality only belief. Knowledge makes him strong; for the others, belief is enough. He does not discover for himself from the beginning, nor would he know how to advance on his own beyond the middle. If he will really remain the ordinary person, as he was born, then he must always keep equal the distance above and below himself; and since those above him push forward, he must move along at a suitable interval behind. What he does not have to discover because it was already discovered, and is not able to discover because otherwise he would be superior, that he must learn. To protect him from errors is just as little nec-essary as it is possible. But instruction can lead him as far as he must go if he wants to be a good average. Since he cannot himself produce something of value, he can at least be made capable of appreciating properly the values others create; and that is an end that would make teaching worthwhile. "There are relatively enough people who know how to produce, but relatively few who know how to be consumers," says Adolf Loos. It could indeed even be the purpose of teaching to cultivate consumers. Not through aesthetic rules, of course, but through enlargement of their field of vision.

But there is yet another reason [for my writing this book], perhaps the most com-pelling: the formulation of a course of study can be an end in itself. Without being directed at an actual pupil it can speak to an imaginary one. Perhaps the pupil is only an outward projection of the teacher. The teacher speaks to himself when he speaks to that pupil. "Mit mir nur rat ich, red ich zu dir" ("I am only deliberating with myself when I speak to you").[1] He instructs himself, is his own teacher, his own pupil. That he allows the public to listen in, when his intention is actually to make things clear to himself, by removing the rubble of old errors and setting up in their place new errors, perhaps, but at least more farsighted ones—that here he allows the public to listen in is analogous to the work of art that he creates and turns over to the public. He comes to terms with himself, and the public listens; for the people know: it concerns them.

Hence, I can just as well abstain from giving an aesthetic evaluation of these new harmonies. It will come sometime; perhaps it will not. Perhaps it will be good, though probably not. I hope it will be intelligent enough to affirm: these are the things that up to now are considered good; the others have for the time being still not found favor, but probably sometime later they, too, will be accepted. I should not fail to mention, however, a few little experiences and observations that have come to me from the contemplation of actual compositions. Obviously, I can do that only by intuition; this intuition, moreover, is dependent upon preconditions, upon the influence of my inborn and acquired *Kultur*. Therefore, I do not exclude what I do not happen to mention. Possibly, I have not noticed it yet; probably, I do not know it yet. And if I do not write everything that must be considered possible by association or inference, perhaps it is because inhibitions of my earlier education stand in my way. In composition I make decisions only according to feeling, according to the feeling for form. This tells me what I must write; everything else is excluded. Every chord I put down corresponds to a necessity, to a necessity of my urge to expression; perhaps, however, also to the necessity of an inexorable but unconscious logic in the harmonic structure. I am firmly convinced that logic is present here, too, at least as much so as in the previously cultivated fields of harmony. And as proof of this I can cite the fact that corrections of the inspiration, the idea, out of external formal considerations, to which the alert consciousness is only too often disposed, have generally spoiled the idea. This proves to me that the idea was obligatory, that it had necessity, that the harmonies present in it are components of the idea, in which one may change nothing.

Generally, in the use of chords with six or more tones, there will appear the tendency to soften the dissonances through wide spacing of the individual chord tones. That such is a softening is obvious. For the image of what the dissonances actually are, more remote overtones, is imitated in a satisfying way. It is in this sense that the following quotation from my monodrama, *Erwartung* [mm. 382–83], is to be understood.

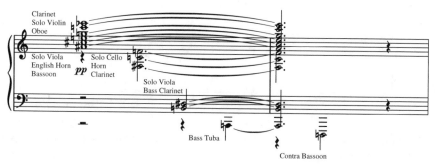

Example 3.1

Eleven different tones appear in this chord. But the gentle instrumentation and the fact that the dissonances are widely spaced make this sound quite delicate. Perhaps there is something else besides: the individual groups of tones are so arranged that one could easily refer them to previously known forms. For example, in the first group I believe the ear expects the following resolution:

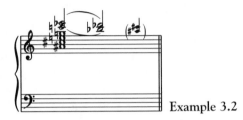

Example 3.2

That it does not come can do no more damage here than when the resolution is omitted in simple harmonies. The second chord may be resolved as in Example 3.3a; this resolution may be combined (Example 3.3b) with that of the first chord (Example 3.2), and this combination may be interpreted as in Example 3.3c. [It is] an addition of two chords that have a diminished seventh chord in common; by virtue of two different bass tones this diminished seventh chord is turned into two different ninth chords.

Example 3.3

Such a derivation, however, will not always apply; the reference to older forms will not always work, or if so, only by very broad interpretation. For on a different occasion I write such a chord in much closer position. And in a string quartet by my pupil Anton von Webern [Five Movements for String Quartet Op. 5, No. 1, m. 5] there is the following:

Example 3.4

Franz Schreker, in his opera, *Der ferne Klang*, writes, among many other things, the following [Act 1, scene 7, m. 36]:

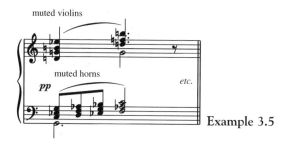

Example 3.5

where, although of course many of the individual sonorities are to be attributed to moving voices, the similarity with the samples previously given still holds: namely, that the chord-building capacity of dissonances does not depend on possibilities of or tendencies toward resolution. The Hungarian composer Béla Bartók also comes close in some of his piano pieces to these acoustical sensations, as the following passage [from Fourteen Bagatelles Op. 6, No. 10, mm. 36–37] demonstrates:

Example 3.6

The following, from a composition by my pupil Alban Berg ["Warm die Lüfte," Op. 2, No. 4, m. 22] is also an interesting example:

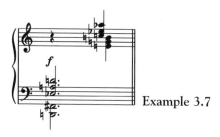

Example 3.7

Why it is that way and why it is correct, I cannot yet explain in any detail. In general, it is self-evident to those who accept my view concerning the nature of dissonance. But that it is correct, I firmly believe, and a number of others believe it too. It seems that the progression of such chords can be justified by the chromatic scale. The chord progression seems to be regulated by the tendency to include in the second chord tones that were missing in the first, generally those a half step higher or lower. Nevertheless, the voices seldom move by half step. Then, I have noticed that tone doublings, octaves, seldom appear. The explanation for that is, perhaps, that the tone doubled would acquire a predominance over the others and would thereby turn into a kind of root, which it should scarcely be. There is perhaps also an instinctive (possibly exaggerated) aversion to recalling even remotely the traditional chords. For the same reason, apparently, the simple chords of the earlier harmony do not appear successfully in this environment. I believe, however, that there is another reason for their absence here. I believe they would sound too cold, too dry, expressionless. Or, perhaps, what I mentioned on an earlier occasion applies here. Namely, that these simple chords, which are imperfect imitations of nature, seem to us too primitive. That they lack something, which, for example, Japanese painting lacks when compared with ours: perspective, depth. Perspective and depth of sound could be what we find wanting in the simple three- and four-part harmonies. And as in a picture one section can hardly show regard for perspective while another disregards it, without impairing the effect, so perhaps, analogously, these somewhat empty sounds cannot appear alongside those full, sumptuous sounds; whereas the exclusive use of the one *or* the other assures coherence, hence the right effect.

It is striking, and suggestive of conclusions, that I and those who write in a similar vein distinguish precisely when a five- or six-part chord should appear, when a chord of yet more parts. It would not be possible without impairing the effect to omit a tone in an eight-part chord, or to add one to a five-part chord. Even the spacing is obligatory; as soon as a tone is misplaced the meaning changes, the logic and utility are lost, coherence seems destroyed. Laws apparently prevail here. What they are, I do not know. Perhaps I shall know in a few years. Perhaps someone after me will find them. For the present the most we can do is describe.

I will forgo any further description in favor of yet another idea I want to mention in closing. In a musical sound three characteristics are recognized: its pitch, color, and volume. Up to now it has been measured in only one of the three dimensions in which it operates, in the one we call "pitch." Attempts at measurement in the other dimensions have scarcely been attempted at all. The evaluation of tone color, the second dimension of tone, is thus in a still much less cultivated, much less organized state than is the aesthetic evaluation of these last-named harmonies. Nevertheless, we go right on boldly connecting the sounds with one another, contrasting them with one another, simply by feeling; and it has never yet occurred to anyone to require here of a theory that it should determine laws by which one may do that sort of thing. Such just cannot be done at present. And, as is evident, we can also get along without such laws. Perhaps we should differentiate still more precisely, if attempts at measurement in this second dimension had already achieved a palpable result. Again, perhaps not. Anyway, our attention to tone colors is becoming more and more active, is moving closer and closer to the possibility of describing and organizing them. At the same time, probably, to restrictive theories, as well. For the present we judge the artistic effect of these relationships only by feeling. How all that relates to the essence of natural sound we do not know, perhaps we can hardly guess at it yet; but we do write progressions of tone colors without a worry, and they do somehow satisfy the sense of beauty. What system underlies these progressions?

The distinction between tone color and pitch, as it is usually expressed, I cannot accept without reservations. I think the tone becomes perceptible by virtue of tone color, of which one dimension is pitch. Tone color is, thus, the main topic, pitch a subdivision. Pitch is nothing else but tone color measured in one direction. Now, if it is possible to create patterns out of tone colors that are differentiated according to pitch, patterns we call "melodies," progressions whose coherence evokes an effect analogous to thought processes, then it must also be possible to make such progressions out of the tone colors of the other dimension, out of that which we call simply "tone color," progressions whose relations with one another work with a kind of logic entirely equivalent to that logic which satisfies us in the melody of pitches. That has the appearance of a futuristic fantasy and is probably just that. But it is one which, I firmly believe, will be realized. I firmly believe it is capable of heightening in an unprecedented manner the sensory, intellectual, and spiritual pleasures offered by art. I firmly believe that it will bring us closer to the illusory stuff of our dreams; that it will expand our relationships to that which seems to us today inanimate as we give life from our life to that which is temporarily dead for us, but dead only by virtue of the slight connection we have with it.

Tone-color melodies! How acute the senses that would be able to perceive them! How high the development of spirit that could find pleasure in such subtle things!

In such a domain, who dares ask for theory!

Notes

[Text: Schoenberg, "Ästhetische Bewertung sechs- und mehrtöniger Klänge," from *Harmonielehre,* third edition, revised and expanded (Vienna: Universal Edition, 1922). Translated by Roy E. Carter in Schoenberg, *Theory of Harmony* (Berkeley and Los Angeles: University of California Press, 1978): 411–22. © 1978 Faber and Faber. Reprinted by permission.]

[1. Wotan's statement to Brünnhilde in Act 2, scene 2, of Wagner's *Die Walküre.*]

4

BÉLA BARTÓK

(1 8 8 1 – 1 9 4 5)

Bartók's "The Problem of the New Music" contains a discussion of the origins and essential features of atonal music. Published in 1920, it is one of the earliest technical treatments of the concept of atonality, a term that Bartók uses to depict the harmonic language of modern music. The word *atonal* had begun to appear in German music criticism only shortly before, where it had a generally pejorative connotation. It was also used by the Viennese composer Josef Matthias Hauer in 1920 in his book *Vom Wesen des Musikalischen* (On the Essence of Music), although Hauer's application of it is highly specialized. Certainly, in the early 1920s the meaning of atonality and the music to which it could be applied were still unclear to most people.

Bartók's characterization of atonal music emphasized its close connections with traditional music. Atonality gradually emerged from tonality, he says, as composers more frequently altered diatonic chords, connected them by ever freer linear motions, and most importantly, used the twelve tones more and more equally so that no pitch could be interpreted as having the function of a tonic, a dominant, a leading tone, or any other such effect. The equalization of the twelve pitch classes spelled the end of traditional tonality. Although Bartók is not specific about what music can be considered fully atonal, he leaves the impression that the term adequately described his own recent works—his Piano Etudes, Op. 18, are good examples—as well as compositions by Arnold Schoenberg and other leading progressive musicians. Later, Bartók joined Schoenberg, Berg, and Stravinsky in rejecting the term *atonal* as both misleading and illogical.

Ideas from Schoenberg's *Harmonielehre* were highly influential upon Bartók's description of atonality. In this book—which appeared in 1911, well before the term *atonal* became current—Schoenberg describes modern developments in harmony by referring to "fluctuating" and "suspended" tonality (see essay no. 3). He maintains, as does Bartók, that nontonal music evolved gradually from tonal music, beginning with the instability of key found in the development sections of classical instrumental movements and continuing with an ever freer and more prominent treatment of dissonance. Both writers also emphasize the expressive capacity of dissonant chords and the importance of compositional instinct in their regulation and use.

In several important observations, however, Bartók differs distinctly from Schoenberg in his description of nontonal music. Bartók recommends a mixed style of atonality, in which homophony can coexist with polyphony and traditional chords can be brought in beside larger, unfamiliar dissonant formations. For Schoenberg such eclecticism was illogical. "There is perhaps also an instinctive aversion," wrote Schoenberg in his *Harmonielehre*, "to recalling even remotely the traditional chords." Bartók's own atonal music is characterized by just this mixing of elements. His choice of harmonies juxtaposes triadic shapes with other chords unfamiliar in earlier music, a mixture that speaks to the "unlimited and complete exploitation of the entirety of tonal elements" cited in the essay.

Throughout his life Bartók was an active, if sometimes reluctant, essay-ist. Taciturn by nature, he tended to write in an unusually concise manner. His "Autobiography" of 1921, for example, covered fewer than four pages. He most often wrote analytic essays concerning peasant music, the collecting and study of which was a lifelong passion for him. He also expressed his views on the artistic music of his time, especially its relationship to folk idioms. An impor-tant example of the latter, "The Relationship of Folk-Song to the Development of the Art Music of Our Time" is found as essay no. 5 in this anthology.

Bartók's Writings: A Selective Bibliography

Béla Bartók Essays. Selected and edited by Benjamin Suchoff. New York: St. Martin's Press, 1976. Reprint-ed, Lincoln and London: University of Nebraska Press, 1992. An important collection of eighty-nine essays, translated into English.

Béla Bartók Letters. Edited by János Demény. Translated by Péter Balabán. New York: St. Martin's Press, 1971. Bartók's early letters are expansive, revealing important aspects of the composer's outlook on life and art; the later letters are guarded.

Béla Bartók Studies in Ethnomusicology. Selected and edited by Benjamin Suchoff. Lincoln and London: University of Nebraska Press, 1997. Fifteen writings stemming from Bartók's folk song research.

—◊◊◊—

THE PROBLEM OF THE NEW MUSIC

(*Das Problem der neuen Musik*, 1920)

Music of the present day tends decisively toward atonality. But it is not correct to con-clude that the tonal principle is completely the opposite of the atonal principle. The latter is instead the outcome of a gradual development that took its departure from the former. It occurred in steps with no gaping omissions or sudden leaps forward.

In his *Harmonielehre* Schoenberg said that the "development section" in a sonata form could in some respects be considered the model for atonality. This is because in the development there is neither the exclusive use of two keys (as in the exposition) nor one (as in the recapitulation) but instead a relatively free succession of different tonalities of which any one could be temporarily felt as primary. In other words, in the development section there exists a degree of *equalization* of the twelve keys.

The amassing of altered chords in the period after Beethoven (Wagner, Liszt) and the ever freer use of cambiata and passing-note figures (Strauss, Debussy) amid otherwise tonal harmonies were two important transitional stages between tonality and atonality. In works by Strauss and his successors there are isolated passages in which tonality is clearly suspended within pieces still having a tonal character (e.g., "The Hero's Adversaries" from *Ein Heldenleben*). The penultimate step toward atonality appears in works that are atonal despite the presence of tonal starting and ending passages. These passages produce a unified effect, as in older models, by establishing a firm framework.

The complete adoption of atonality began only after these preliminary stages, when the necessity was first felt for an equalization of the twelve different tones of our twelve-tone system, that is, when composers first attempted to use the twelve tones both vertically and horizontally in any configuration whatever, not deployed according to an established scale system in which some tones were always accorded greater or lesser weight. In this new procedure some tones may still have a greater weight in a composition, but the differences in weight no longer result from a preestablished scalar hierarchy; instead, they occur as a feature of one particular configuration. Similarly, in groups of such configurations some members have a different value and intensity compared to the others. The potential for expressivity from the free and equal treatment of the twelve individual tones is increased to a distinctly higher level.

Previously, four-note chords were the primary ones, and among these there were only a few admissible types. Now, chords made from a simultaneous sounding even of all twelve tones, in the most diverse arrangements, may be used. The peculiar emptiness of a trichord as in Example 4.1, or the resonant tenderness of a chord as in Example 4.2, or the shrill force of the chord in Example 4.3 can all confer an unprecedented richness of shadings and nuances. Three or more neighbor tones in close position will evoke a "stylized" noise of greater or lesser density depending on whether they are in the lower or upper register. The same noiselike effect can be approximated by placing tones in the lower register in a more open position, as in Example 4.4. If this chord were taken up two octaves, its character would change, making it more ethereal. Its effect would then be more similar to that of the chord in Example 4.2.

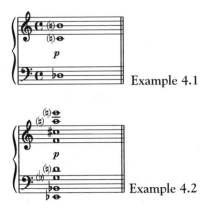

Example 4.1

Example 4.2

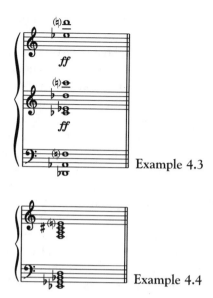

Example 4.3

Example 4.4

In homophonic music the composer works with sound masses whose notes are either simultaneously heard or given rapidly one note after the other. The effect of these tone columns will be dense or airy, massive or thin, according to how many notes are used, their particular register, the position of the notes relative to one another (i.e., close or open), and so forth. These tone columns will have differing degrees of intensity according to how they are disposed, and their individual tones will have different functions according to their vertical positioning. This allows in atonal music for the adumbration of a "line," as a result precisely of this diversity. To what extent the rise and fall of such a line creates a harmonious entity will depend purely on the formal perfection of each work.

The power of content (which is hard to nail down with words), the freshness of what Schoenberg calls the "first inspiration," the harmonic implications of voice leading—these three factors produce the artwork. But weren't all these factors also present in older musical artworks? The main prerequisites [for artistic music] have not changed at all; a change has only occurred in the way that materials are used. In the past the composer worked with limited means, now he works with expanded ones. Only the future will tell if the free access to richer possibilities will lead to artworks as great as those produced by musicians of the past.

There is much confusion in the study of atonal music over the apparent lack of rules or written guidelines for the harmonic element in voice leading or for other emancipated materials. In this respect both composers and listeners are guided only by their instinct. We have not yet arrived at the time for the establishment of a system for our atonal music (on page 49 of his *Harmonielehre*, Schoenberg made an effort, although a tentative one).[1] This newest period in music history has only just begun, and there are still too few works in the new style to allow for the creation of a theory. When a theory is at last constructed, it will play the same role for later generations as each older theory did for its own time, that is, it will be at most a basis upon which more can be built, until finally something entirely new is achieved and will itself be the stimulus for yet another theory.

Concerning homophony and polyphony, I favor a mixing of both, and I also favor a procedure that provides more variety than by limiting oneself to only one of the two textures. For similar reasons, it also seems to me that a carefully considered use (not excessive) of chords of the older tonal type within atonal music is not stylistically incongruous, especially since it is not a question of two entirely opposite principles. An isolated triad drawn from a diatonic scale, or a third, perfect fifth, or octave placed within a larger atonal chord—when these are used at special and appropriate places—arouse no sense of tonality. These chords—which have long become banal on account of their use and misuse—maintain in their new circumstances a fresh and quite powerful effect, which arises from their capacity to provide contrast. Indeed, we can imagine whole successions of such triads and intervals—provided only that they do not create a tonality—as entirely consistent with the new style. The radical exclusion of these older chords would amount to a renunciation of a not insignificant resource for our art. Bear in mind that the overarching intention of our work is the unlimited and complete exploitation of the entirety of tonal materials that are at our disposal. At the same time it is obvious that certain progressions—for example, one that is reminiscent of a tonic alternating with a dominant—are entirely out of keeping with today's music. (One finds these wrapped up in a pompously dissonant cloak in many works that are trying hard to be modern; such pieces have essentially little in common with the new movement.)

There should be no fear that atonal music that has renounced the symmetrical structures of the tonal system will turn into a formless mass. First, architectonic or similar forms are not always necessary; they can be fully compensated for by a linearity that comes from the ordering of tone groups having inherently differentiated levels of intensity. (This sort of form has a distant analogy with the form of written prose works.) Second, atonal music does not exclude certain external means of formal articulation, certain repetitions (occurring in a different register, varied, etc.) of things already presented, sequences, refrainlike recurrences of ideas, or the return at the conclusion of an opening passage. All of these have less similarity to architectonic symmetry than to the verse structure of poetry.

The attempt to base the essence of atonal music on the overtone system seems to me to be futile. The differences in the character and effect of intervals may well be explainable by the phenomenon of the overtone, but this does not satisfyingly answer the question of free use of the twelve tones.

We can conceive of the development leading to atonality in this way: all possible musical materials consist of an infinite number of tones of differing pitch, ranging from the lowest to the highest audible frequencies. (We will ignore rhythm, tone color, and dynamics as secondary elements in this development.) Our abstract goal is to use more and more of these materials in artworks. Originally, only a small number of tones suggested by the overtone system were selected from this infinite gamut as usable. Thus the diatonic scale was created, recurring in twelve different transpositions, and, again based on the overtone system, the diatonic system emerged. Soon, however, the tendency toward further development (through free modulations) made this system inadequate. Nature was forcefully attacked and a twelve-fold division of the octave was wrenched from her. The artificial, tempered twelve-tone scale arose, and it was adopted and propagated by keyboard instruments with artificial intonations. But despite this violent alienation from nature, musical thought remained on diatonic soil for centuries, until finally, following the development already described, music was awakened to the equal treatment of the twelve half tones, all equal among themselves. This new stage contained within it immeasurably new possibilities, so many that Busoni's desire for a third- or quarter-tone system seemed premature. (The works of Schoenberg and Stravinsky that have appeared since the time of his *Sketch of a New Esthetic of Music* [1907] show that the half-tone system still has not spoken its last word.) The day for a further division of the half tone (perhaps infinitely divisible?) will surely come, although not in our time, but in decades or centuries in the future. This will require the solving of such huge technical problems as the new construction of keyboard and keyed instruments, not to mention overcoming the intonational difficulties of the human voice and all those instruments whose pitches are determined by exact placement of the fingers. These problems will most likely extend the life of the half-tone system, as a technical necessity, far into the future.

Let me say in closing a word about our notation. It is based on the diatonic system and as such is an entirely inadequate tool for the written preservation of atonal music. Accidental signs, for example, indicate an alteration of diatonic degrees; in atonal music, however, there is no question of altered or natural diatonic degrees, instead of twelve equal half tones. Moreover, it is quite difficult to maintain consistency in note spelling. One is often in doubt, for example, how to produce a simpler reading of a vertical or horizontal motion.

It would be desirable to have a notation with twelve equal signs in which each of the twelve tones had its own symbol, equivalent to that of the others, so that some notes would not have to be rendered as alterations. Such an innovation, however, is still awaiting its inventor.

Notes

[Text: Bartók, "Das Problem der neuen Musik." *Melos* 1 (1920): 107–10. Translated by Bryan R. Simms.]

[1. Bartók's reference to p. 49 of Schoenberg's *Harmonielehre* is probably in error. Although Schoenberg does not advance a system for atonal music anywhere in this treatise, Bartók may be alluding to the discussion found as essay no. 3 in this volume.]

5

BÉLA BARTÓK

(1 8 8 1 – 1 9 4 5)

Bartók was inclined to exaggerate the influence of folk song upon his own highly advanced musical language. He attributed virtually all of his innovations to
peasant music, but he remained silent on his relationship to progressive aspects
of the music of his contemporaries, especially to those of the modern German
and Austrian school. It was perhaps inevitable that a patriotic Hungarian—living
in an empire ruled by an Austrian-German king and amid influential Germans all
too ready to show disdain for their Hungarian neighbors—should have asserted his isolation from the new ideas in music that poured from Germany and
Austria during the early years of the twentieth century.

In his essay "The Relation of Folk-Song to the Development of the Art
Music of Our Time" Bartók makes connections between peasant music and the
seemingly remote language of atonality. He finds the origin for the equalization
of tones that characterizes atonality (see essay no. 4) not in Wagner, Strauss, and
Schoenberg, but in old Hungarian peasant songs in which familiar tonic, dominant, and leading tone functions are absent. In lectures given at Harvard University in 1943 he even devised an explanation for the chromaticism of his own
atonal music in terms of the diatonicism of folk music. The former, he says, is
simply a compounding of the modes that characterize folk melody—a simultaneous statement, for example, of the pitch content of two modes. Even atonality itself, a movement connected in most minds with German and Austrian modernism, was ultimately denied by Bartók as a phenomenon in his own works.

Although his tendency to link modernism with peasant art was often over-
stated, even untenable, Bartók was a great authority on folk music and an expert
at finding its traces in the works of classical and modern composers. In this essay
he enunciates an important insight to which he often later returned: Peasant
music—the only true folk music in his view—was different both in style and origin
from "popular art music." The latter, which was unwittingly accepted as folk music
even by such musicians as Chopin and Liszt, originated in the city, and it had no
inherent artistic value. The former, preserved by isolated peasant cultures around
the world, could be a model of concise and unsentimental artistry for music in the
twentieth century. Bartók suggests that it was known to and imitated by Debussy
and Ravel, and he found peasant music clearly exploited by Stravinsky in *The Rite
of Spring* and by the Hungarian composer Zoltán Kodály. Not only could true folk
music be a font of technical resources for new music, he says, but more importantly, it provides a way for bringing nature and life into the modern idiom.

But Bartók has only criticism for both Stravinsky and Schoenberg in this
respect. The former uses folk song in *The Rite of Spring*, but he misunderstands
his source, contorting it with mosaiclike discontinuities of form and excessive rep-

etitions. Schoenberg is untouched by the folk idiom, Bartók concludes, which alienates him from nature and explains the lack of acceptance of his music.

"The Relation of Folk-Song to the Development of the Art Music of Our Time" was one of a large number of essays written by Bartók in 1920 and 1921, the result of his need to increase his income at a time of devastating inflation in Hungary. It was written in German for the English journal *The Sackbut*, where it appeared in 1921 in an English translation. The editor of this periodical, Philip Heseltine (also known as Peter Warlock), was one of Bartók's most important early supporters in England.

A bibliography concerning Bartók is found with essay no. 4.

—ᴍ—

THE RELATION OF FOLK-SONG TO THE DEVELOPMENT OF THE ART MUSIC OF OUR TIME

(*Das Verhältniss der Volksmusik zur Entwicklung der Kunstmusik unserer Tage*, 1921)

1

This essay makes no attempt at being a systematic description of all the various manifestations in the art music of our day which can be traced back to the influence of some folk music or other. It will only refer to some of these manifestations, with the special objects of calling attention to the significance of folk music to the creative artist, and of throwing light on the part each plays or can play in the growth of the music of the present day—and for that matter of the future also.

At first sight it seems that the influence of folk music only began to make itself felt to any considerable extent in the nineteenth century, on the one hand in the works of Chopin and Liszt, on the other in those of representatives of the various nationalistic movements (Grieg, Smetana, Dvořák, Tchaikovsky, etc.). This view is not altogether correct, since in the first place the works of the composers just mentioned have had their roots in the popular art music of their native countries rather than in folk music proper—and in the second place, even in those composers who stand nearer to true folk music (the so-called Slav school) this relationship has not set an unmistakable seal upon their whole output but is revealed only here and there in their work.

We must, therefore, before all realize the essential difference between popular art music and real folk music in the strict sense of the term.

True folk music consists of those melodies which grow up as representatives of a more or less uniform musical style among the peasant classes of a nation.[1] From this point, for brevity's sake, we shall call it simply peasant music.

But how does this music grow up? For a long time it was generally supposed that it was made in some mysterious way by "the folk" considered as a homogeneous mass; this notion is of course impossible to accept, more especially as it leaves the question "How?" entirely unanswered.

On the other hand it has been maintained that particular melodies were invented by particular peasants, although this view has never been substantiated by a single observed instance, and, besides, is scarcely acceptable on psychological grounds. As the result of researches into the new peasant music which has been developed in Hungary, during the last half century or so, evidence was discovered of fresh styles of peasant music, in accordance with which its origin may be explained in the following manner: Every nation possesses an individual musical style in a certain stage of culture and development. Through various causes foreign melodies of a higher level of culture—either "art melodies" or folk melodies of a neighboring people—are disseminated among the people in question, and in the process of their dissemination, local variants arise—first through small changes, later from an accumulation of more important deviations from the original form. By reason of the peasants' innate conservatism the foreign melodies are ornamented with the idiosyncrasies of the existing musical style of the country into which they have been imported, or they may be completely transformed by the same means.

This process of transformation, which of course is effected in different ways in different districts and countries, is influenced to a considerable extent by the peculiarities of language and intonation, etc. Eventually there grows up a body of melodies which reveal a certain uniformity in their structure and which differ very considerably from their imported originals. The gradual development of these differences may very well be attributed to the impulses of individual peasants, or of small or larger groups of peasants. It may, then, be taken for granted that the older *original* musical style of this peasant class has been evolved by a similar process, although it consists of elements whose origin is unknown to us. Indeed the problem of the origin of the primitive music of a people is as insoluble as that of the origin of root languages or of the human race itself. Many countries show an extraordinary propensity to cling to the peculiarities of their own traditional musical style. In spite of the most revolutionary movements which bring to birth a style of music which is in spirit entirely new, there yet appear, even in their newest melodies, many gleams of the old primitive characteristics. This is the case with the neo-Hungarian peasant music style which has sprung up during the last ten years or so, for in its melodies the influence of the pentatonic scale, reminding one of the Asiatic origin of the Hungarian race, is still unmistakable.

Peasant music, in the strict sense of the word, must be regarded as a natural phenomenon; the forms in which it manifests itself are due to the instinctive *transforming power* of a community entirely devoid of erudition. It is just as much a natural phenomenon as, for instance, the various manifestations of nature in fauna and flora. Correspondingly it has, in its individual parts, an absolute artistic perfection—a perfection in miniature forms which—one might almost say—is equal to the perfection of a musical masterpiece of the largest form, with the greatest simplicity of means, with freshness and life, briefly yet completely and properly proportioned. This is quite sufficient to account for the fact that peasant music, in the strict sense of the word, is not generally understood by the average musician. He finds it empty and inexpressive; popular art music suits his tastes much better. This latter derives from individual composers, known or unknown, who possess a certain musical erudition. With us in East Europe, it comes from amateurs of gentle birth who satisfy the creative impulse of their slender musical talents by the composition of more or less simple tunes. Their music is partly made up of elements of Western European art music—a jumble of commonplaces in this respect—but it also bears traces of the peasant music of their own country. This is what lends their music a certain exotic flavor by which even men like Liszt, Brahms, and Chopin felt themselves attracted. Nevertheless the outcome of this mixture of exoticism and banality is something imperfect, inartistic, in marked contrast to the clarity of real peasant music with which it compares most unfavorably. At all events it is a noteworthy fact that artistic perfection can only be achieved by one of the two extremes: on the one hand by peasant folk in the mass, completely devoid of the culture of the town dweller; on the other hand by creative power of an individual genius. The creative impulse of anyone who has the misfortune to be born somewhere between these two extremes leads only to barren, pointless, and misshapen works. When peasants or the peasant classes lose their naïveté and their artless ignorance, as a result of the conventional culture, or more accurately half-culture, of the town dwelling folk, they lose at the same time all their artistic transforming power. So that in Western countries it is a long while since there was any real peasant music in the strict sense of the word.

In Eastern Europe about a hundred years ago or even earlier many popular art melodies were appropriated by the peasant classes, who, by means of alterations, in a greater or lesser degree, have given them a new lease of life in a new milieu; but these tunes have not led to the formation of a new style of peasant music, nor indeed have they contributed anything towards it. The greater the alteration or rather the more complete the process of perfection that they have undergone at the hands of their peasant appropriators has been, the more nearly do they approximate to the true style of peasant music; at the same time it is impossible to regard them as representative peasant melodies.

2

At the beginning of the nineteenth century, when the strengthening of national feeling in the, politically speaking, most oppressed of the smaller nations (as for example the Poles, Czechs, and Hungarians) increased the demand for a national art, intellectual circles in these countries were, generally speaking, familiar only with the popular art music which, thanks to its exotic qualities, was not lacking in a certain charm. No attention was paid to the real peasant music. It was looked down upon as something rather common. No wonder, then, that composers like Chopin and Liszt who could not go round collecting these tunes themselves probably had no opportunity of hearing the genuine peasant music at any time. Perhaps they never came into contact with the peasant classes or, if they did on occasions, they only heard from the mouths of the peasants those popular art songs which had been appropriated by them. For the peasants feel instinctively—many know from practical experience— that most of the gentlefolk look upon their "simple" art products with scant respect.

They are, therefore, chary of exhibiting them to the townsfolk and the most they will do is to take the opportunity of showing off the products that they have taken over from the townsfolk themselves, of which they are proud as they feel they have accomplished an achievement in mastering them.

Chopin was to a certain extent influenced by the Polish and Liszt by the Hungarian popular art music. Liszt however as an international, was especially interested in the similar products of Italy, Spain, and other countries. Yet so much that was banal was incorporated by them, with much that was exotic, that the works concerned were not benefited thereby. That is why it is not the nationalistic polonaises that rank highest amongst Chopin's works, and the same applies to Liszt's Hungarian Rhapsodies and to his tarantellas and polonaises. In any case it is only these slighter works that have received what is after all only a nationalistic whitewash; the principal works of both composers are happily for the most part exempt from this influence.

It is only recently, that is, at the beginning of the twentieth century that the influence of genuine peasant music has again become noticeable. I say again, because in the Viennese classical epoch a similar manifestation occurred, of which more anon.

The vein of exoticism in the popular art music was worked out; its insipidity had become disagreeable, the early researches, modest though they were, into the youngest of the sciences, namely musical folklore, drew the attention of certain musicians to the genuine peasant music, and with astonishment they found that they had come upon a natural treasure store of surpassing abundance.

This exploration of the natural treasures of music seems to have been the inevitable result of a reaction against the ultrachromaticism of the Wagner-Strauss period. The genuine folk music of Eastern Europe is almost completely diatonic and in some parts, such as Hungary, even pentatonic. Curiously enough at the same time an apparently opposite tendency became apparent, a tendency towards the emancipation of the twelve sounds comprised within our octave from any system of tonality. (This has nothing to do with the ultrachromaticism referred to, for there chromatic notes are only chromatic in so far as they are based upon the underlying diatonic scale.) The diatonic element in eastern European folk music does not in any way conflict with the tendency to equalize the value of semitones. This tendency can be realized in melody as well as in harmony; whether the foundation of the folk melodies is diatonic or even pentatonic, there is still plenty of room in the harmonization for equalizing the value of the semitones.

So whether under the influence of peasant music in the formation of the melody, diatonic or pentatonic prevails, the harmony still gives sufficient play to admit of an equalizing treatment of the semitones. (The melody of exotic peasant music as for instance that of the Arabs is not even diatonic.) In fact such newer compositions derive from the diatonic simplicity of peasant music an element of refreshing contrast: the opposition of the two tendencies reveals the more clearly the individual properties of each, while the effect of the whole becomes all the more powerful. Moreover the influence of peasant music saves such works from the danger of falling into the wearying or surfeiting extreme.

When I speak of the influence of peasant music, I do not mean as it were a mere whitewash of it, nor the mere adaptation of peasant melodies or snatches of melodies and their piecemeal incorporation in musical works, but rather the expression of the real spirit of the music of any particular people which is so hard to render in words. The manner in which the spirit is interpreted in the compositions is closely dependent upon the personality and musical talent of the particular composer so that it is of little use for a blockhead or a man with no musical talent to run to "the people" in order to get inspiration for his thin ideas.

Although every comparison between painting and music tends to break down, it is possible to illustrate from the art of painting the relation between peasant music and art music. Peasant music itself plays the part in composition that natural objects play in painting. Real folk music can be regarded as a natural phenomenon from the point of view of higher art music just as well as the properties of bodies as perceived by the eye are so regarded by the painter, or again, in order to illustrate this point from the art of writing, popular music is to the composer what nature herself is to the writer,[2] but just as the poet cannot come to understand nature from written descriptions, so the composer cannot hope to learn the nature of peasant music from dead collections of musical preserves. In the process of notation that very essence of peasant music is lost, which enables it to awake the emotions in the soul of the composer. The harsh characters cannot possibly render the subtler shades of rhythm, of intonation, of sound transitions, in a word all the pulsing life of peasant music. The [written] record of peasant music is as it were the picture of its corpse. He who has never heard the actual melodies or similar ones from the mouths of the peasant themselves will never obtain a true idea of them by the mere reading of the score.

It is essential therefore to seek out the peasants and to become acquainted with them, not only for the sake of their music in their truest type. The effect of the experience is incomparably enhanced by the accessory elements such as the surroundings, the ceremonial customs, etc., that accompany the music.

The invention of such instruments as the gramophone has fortunately enabled us to preserve peasant music and more or less to dispense with the necessity for those visits to the peasants themselves which would often be difficult and sometimes impossible. It is admitted that individual peculiarities and the spirit of songs or of music are rendered to incomparably greater perfection by means of the most primitive phonograph record than, for instance, the most accurate photograph of the scene. Through listening to phonograph records, we obtain a perfect tone picture of peasant music. All that is necessary is that musicians or musical investigators who wish to possess this should have access to as large a collection of records as possible.

3

The purpose of this essay is not to discover which of the modern composers have been influenced by the folk music of one country or another and in what form the influence has manifested itself. So I shall not raise the question as to whether Debussy acquired certain characteristics through the medium of Musorgsky or from direct contact with Russian folk music, nor shall I speculate upon the sources of the pentatonic element in the work of Ravel.

I shall invite your attention only to the most remarkable manifestations of those that owe their origin to the influence of peasant music. The first in this category is undoubtedly Musorgsky, some scores of years before any other. It did not fall to him to achieve perfection—he should be regarded rather as a forerunner of this tendency.

Stravinsky's *Rite of Spring* is one of the best examples of the intensive permeation of art music by genuine peasant music. The work, in spite of its extraordinary verve and power, fails to be completely satisfying. Under the influence of the short-winded structure of the Russian peasant melodies Stravinsky did not escape the danger of yielding to a broken mosaiclike construction which is sometimes disturbing and of which the effect is enhanced by his peculiar technique, monotonous as it becomes by repetition and by its practice of, as it were, automatically superimposing several chord sequences of varying length, in constant repetition, without regard to their consonances.

It is not the Russian peasant music that we must blame for this, but the composer's lack of grasp and power of organization.

The majority of the works of the Hungarian Zoltán Kodály, which may be called the apotheosis of the old Hungarian folk music, furnish a second and moreover a satisfactory example. As a young Hungarian critic[3] aptly remarks: "Kodály, having discovered in the peasant music of the Hungarians, that is of the Seklers, the Transylvanian Hungarians, a language appropriate to his specifically Hungarian thoughts, he did not apply himself to it as to a scientific proposition but learnt the language and spoke it as one speaks one's mother tongue." Kodály's technique lacks any striking sensational novelty, but he is a master of form and has something thoroughly individual to say—two factors which always ensure perfection in creative work.

Finally, as a negative example of what I mean, the works of Schoenberg may be mentioned. He is free from all peasant influence and his complete alienation to nature, which of course I do not regard as a blemish, is no doubt the reason why many find his work so difficult to understand.

The two composers [Stravinsky and Kodály] who furnish the examples quoted above gave themselves up to the folk music of a particular country but I wish especially to emphasize that this exclusiveness is not important. The personality of the composer must be strong enough to synthesize the results of his reactions to most widely divergent types of folk music. He will, for course, probably react only to a folk music in harmony with his personality. It would be stupid to force a selection for exterior reasons such as a wrongly conceived patriotism.

Naturally a composer will be most influenced by the music he hears most of— the music of his home. This circumstance ensures a certain geographical difference in style—at least superficially.

4

As I have already indicated, the practice of employing peasant music in the attempt to put life into works of art music is not entirely new, but appears merely to have disappeared for a certain time during the nineteenth century. In fact, many symphonic themes—especially in last movements—of the Viennese classics, Haydn, Mozart, and Beethoven, suggest peasant music; in their case it would seem to be a matter of

Slavonic peasant instrumental music. We shall probably never arrive at a clear solution of this question as the material in the form of contemporary peasant music necessary for a thorough comparative analysis is lacking. In many cases the Croatian melodies, which were preserved until the second half of the nineteenth century, and were then actually committed to writing, give us grounds for supposing that peasant music exercised a considerable influence at that time. For certain melodies which had quite accidentally escaped oblivion appear in a collection[4] published between the years 1878–81; and these were made use of in Haydn's and Beethoven's works. In order to make some of these interesting cases known more widely in musical circles, I will quote three melodies out of the collection.[5]

Oj Je - le - na, Je - le - na, ja - bu - ka ze - le - na, - le - na.

Example 5.1

Ri - sa pa - da, tra - va ___ ra - ste, bor se ze - le -

ni, Ri - sa pa - da, ___ tra va ra - ste

bor se ___ ze - li - ni. _____

Example 5.2

Šir - vo - nja do šir - vo - nja, Bo ___ žon ___ ja,

Bo - žur ___ ti, Bo - žu - ri - ca skoj - la ___

le - pa Ju - la, ___ le - pa Ju - la, ___ Bo - žu - ri - ca

skoj - la ___ le - pa ___ Ju - la ___ iz - ko - la.

Example 5.3

The first melody [Example 5.1] is identical with the main theme of Haydn's D Major Symphony [No. 104] (finale). The second and third melodies [Examples 5.2 and 5.3] (two variations) constitute the main theme of the first passage of the *Pastoral* Symphony. The possible theory that this was Beethoven's own theme and penetrated to the Croatian peasantry with the popularization of the symphony is quite untenable. The peasantry is capable of taking up only such melodies as it hears repeated to the point of satiety at village dances or other meetings. Nobody can imagine that Beethoven's symphonies achieved such widespread popularity in the villages of the east of Europe. One has only to consider that in the country districts of the east of Europe the very name of Beethoven is unknown even to the gentry, these circles in fact lack the slightest acquaintance with the higher art music of any period. It is much nearer the truth to say that Beethoven heard this melody from a bagpipe player in West Hungary, where Croats also are settlers and where he often stayed. Before strangers peasants play on an instrument much more naturally than they sing melodies from a text. The tune appealed to Beethoven and as it just seemed to give a picture of rural life he used it in his symphony without acknowledgment—as was in fact usual at the time. Bars 16 to 25, which constantly repeat the selfsame one-bar motif, are in fact a very faithful imitation of the bagpipe interlude passages as they can still be heard in our day. Thus for instance the interlude occurs as the eight- or ten-fold repetition of the motif in a melody which I heard played on the bagpipes by a Hungarian peasant. My theory is strengthened by the bagpipelike accompaniment of the theme. As I have already said, there are scarcely eight, or at the most, ten examples of this kind. How many such melodies may have perished amongst the peasantry before they could be written down!

An examination of the part played by the chorale melodies in the art music of the seventeenth century will furnish still older analogy. I cannot say for certain whether or not these melodies may be counted as peasant music, as I have not investigated this question, but their simple and uniform character agrees fairly generally with that of all genuine peasant music. As chorale melodies have been used to serve as the basis of instruction in composition, more especially in the study of counterpoint, up to the present day, peasant melodies might to still greater advantage be made to serve an academic purpose in the future. One of the most difficult tasks is to find such accompaniments to peasant melodies as will not obscure but will emphasize and bring into relief their characteristic features. In the hands of a good teacher these melodies could exercise an extraordinarily beneficent effect. Students of composition and in fact musical students generally would be well advised to study peasant melodies thoroughly, where possible from phonograph records, or if they can, in their natural form—not that a person of medium talent can thereby be transformed into a creator of note, but it is a study which will refine the budding musician's taste and considerably enlarge his horizon.

5

I have endeavored so far to show the significance for art and the wide scope of the study of peasant music. Its scope in research is, I believe, already admitted beyond all question. It has attempted to throw light upon the stages in the development of the art of music, an art the high cultural significance of which is more and more generally recognized even by the nonmusical. Yet in spite of its wide range in two directions, incredibly little attention has as yet been devoted to the study of musical folklore in comparison with other scientific researches. That this should have been so up to the end of the nineteenth century can be readily understood as the apparatus essential for research work was lacking. But now that there is nothing to prevent the collection of phonograph records such indifference, nay, every neglect is an unpardonable sin. The three most important requirements are:

(1) The foundation of systematic collections which should constantly be enriched by expert investigation.

(2) The galvano-plastic fixation of the records—first to avoid the disadvantage of the ephemeral duration of the originals, and secondly so that any number of copies may be taken.

(3) Institutions which possess such collections should enter into relation with those of other countries for mutual exchange so that the results of these researches might become universally accessible.

Indeed this research work should be carried out in each country according to a uniform plan, the main features of which should be common to all countries. So far as I am aware no institute fulfilling all these requirements exists. The Paris Institute, for example, has no music folklore collection.

The Berlin University possesses a fairly rich one which owes its existence to the labor of Professor Erich von Hornbostel and is being fixed by the galvano-plastic process; yet the material even for this collection is acquired casually and at hazard. No systematically organized expeditions by musical experts to explore new territory have been carried out. The Hungarian National Museum in Budapest certainly possesses a collection that is fairly rich for the resources of what was Greater Hungary; its material is drawn almost entirely from the country districts; but unhappily nothing has been done hitherto to effect the fixation of these most valuable specimens, so that they must gradually perish. There has not been and, of course, there is not now any suggestion for mutual exchange or a common scheme of work with other institutions.

Meanwhile the ancient peasant music of each people is disappearing day by day, submerged beneath the waves of new cultures, so that the neglect of each day causes an irretrievable treasure for music to vanish forever.

It is quite possible that in the future peasant music will have to play a far more important part than it does today. A future generation might conceivably discover and embody in their art music properties of the peasant music which have altogether escaped us. We in the meantime, through sheer indifference, do practically nothing to preserve this perishable treasure.

Notes

[Text: Bartók, "The Relation of Folk-Song to the Development of the Art Music of Our Time," translated by Brian Lunn, *The Sackbut* 2/1 (June 1921): 5–11. Bartók's original text, in German, is published in László Somfai, "Vierzehn Bartók-Schriften aus den Jahren 1920/21:

Aufsätze über die zeitgenössische Musik und Konzertberichte aus Budapest," *Documenta bartókiana* 5 (1977): 92–100.]

1. Or in any class of an even lower level of culture.

2. As it might be supposed that poetry can draw upon a similar source in popular songs and ballads it should be explained that folk songs appear to lack the significance for poetry that folk music has for art-music. Folk [poetry] lacks more especially the infinite variety that we musicians find in folk music.

3. Aládar Tóth in the periodical *Nyugat*, July 1920.

4. Franjo Šaver Kuhač, ed., *Južno-slovjenske narodne popievke* [South Slavic Folksongs], 4 volumes (Zagreb, 1878–81). The collection contains about sixteen hundred Croatian, Slovenian, and Serbian melodies.

[5. These musical examples were omitted in the first edition in *The Sackbut*. They are returned here as they appeared in Bartók's original German text.]

6

ALBAN BERG

(1 8 8 5 – 1 9 3 5)

Alban Berg's "What Is Atonality?" originated as an interview given on Radio Vienna (called RAVAG) on 23 April 1930. The opportunity for the talk was arranged by Berg's friend Anton Webern, who was then working as a program supervisor for the radio, and it was intended to create publicity for and explain aspects of the musical language of Berg's opera *Wozzeck*, which would have its Viennese premiere a month later. The interview was conducted by the conservative critic Julius Bistron, to whom Berg gave in advance a preliminary version of his ideas to guide the formulation of questions. Following the broadcast, Berg turned over a transcript of the interview to his student Willi Reich, for use in Reich's journal *23: Eine Wiener Zeitschrift*, where it was published in 1936. Shortly thereafter an abbreviated English translation was published in the appendix of Nicolas Slonimsky's *Music Since 1900*. It appears here for the first time in a complete English translation.

Berg's subject in this talk is a style of music, then commonly called *atonal,* with which he and others from his circle had been associated for more than two decades. His purpose is twofold: to assert the similarities of this type of music to traditional musical styles and to reject decisively the term itself. The word *atonal* had gained a foothold in German journalistic writing around the end of World War I in 1918, and, as Berg notes, it took on a broad meaning and a strongly pejorative connotation—any music that used nontraditional harmonic, melodic, or rhythmic elements was often dismissed as atonal, suggesting that it was irregular, arbitrary, and devoid of beauty in any traditional sense. For these reasons Berg dismisses the term as "diabolical."

Composers outside of Schoenberg's circle were more inclined to accept the term as a suitable designation for their new music. In his 1920 essay "The Problem of the New Music" (essay no. 4), Béla Bartók used the term approvingly, finding atonal music to be characterized by an equality of all twelve tones and to be the outcome of a long historical evolution. The Viennese composer Josef Matthias Hauer used the term from 1920 to describe his own music, which utilized a rudimentary form of twelve-tone composition.

Neither Berg nor his teacher, Arnold Schoenberg, ever agreed upon a satisfactory term for their own music that others called atonal. For Schoenberg such works exhibited a style characterized by a free and pevasive use of dissonant chords, which ruled out the traditional triadic harmonic progressions that established a keynote. In a 1941 lecture entitled "Composition With Twelve Tones," Schoenberg characterized the style as one that "treats dissonances like consonances and renounces a tonal center." In his radio interview, Berg followed the ideas of his teacher. Atonal music, he says, differs from traditional music only in a new harmonic language. Its other salient features—counterpoint, irregular phrasing, traditional forms, proselike rhythms, and lyrical melody—are all apparent in the music of such esteemed composers as Brahms.

Music that exemplifies Berg's discussion is readily found in his own works, as well as in those of Schoenberg and Webern, written between roughly 1908 and 1922. Berg's opera *Wozzeck* is especially apposite, since it is his best-known "atonal" work, and, since it was soon to be premiered in Vienna, it was no doubt on his mind during his interview. In the first scene of Act 3, for example, the counterpoint that he sees as typical of new music is prominent, there in the strict and traditional form of the fugue. Other traditional forms derived from instrumental music are located in every scene, although the application of conventional forms is not as pronounced in Schoenberg's atonal music. Berg's opera is highly melodious, virtually bel canto in such passages as Marie's lullaby in scene 3 of Act 1.

Berg's other writings show his skill as a musical analyst, his strict adherence to the aesthetic positions enunciated by Schoenberg, and a keen awareness of his own place in the history of modern music. His longest essays are technical analyses of works by Schoenberg, including *Gurrelieder*, *Pelleas und Melisande*, Chamber Symphony No. 1, and First String Quartet. Berg also wrote frequently about his own opera *Wozzeck*.

Berg's Writings: A Selective Bibliography

"To the Teacher," "The Musical Impotence of Hans Pfitzner's 'New Aesthetic'," "Why Is Schönberg's Music So Hard to Understand?," "Chamber Concerto for Piano and Violin with Thirteen Wind Instruments," "The Problem of Opera," [To Karl Kraus], "Commemorative Address for Emil Hertzka," and "Two Feuilletons" appear in Willi Reich's *Alban Berg*, translated by Cornelius Cardew (New York: Vienna House, 1965).

"Arnold Schoenberg: *Gurrelieder* Guide." Translated by Mark DeVoto, *Journal of the Arnold Schoenberg Institute* 16 (1993): 24–133. This issue also includes DeVoto's translations of Berg's guides to Schoenberg's Chamber Symphony No. 1 and *Pelleas und Melisande*.

"Berg's Lecture on *Wozzeck*." In: Hans Redlich, *Alban Berg: The Man and His Music*, pp. 261–85. London: John Calder, 1957. Reprinted in Douglas Jarman, *Alban Berg "Wozzeck,"* pp. 154–70, Cambridge Opera Handbooks (Cambridge: Cambridge University Press, 1989).

Écrits. Edited by Henri Pousseur. Monaco: Éditions du Rocher, 1957. Second edition, enlarged, edited by Dominique Jameux. Paris: Christian Bourgois, 1985. A collection of Berg's major writings, in French.

Glaube, Hoffnung und Liebe: Schriften zur Musik. Edited by Frank Schneider. Leipzig: Verlag Philipp Reclam jun., 1981. Berg's complete literary oeuvre, in German.

"The Musical Forms in My Opera *Wozzeck*." In: *Alban Berg: "Wozzeck,"* edited by Douglas Jarman, pp. 149–52. Cambridge Opera Handbooks. Cambridge: Cambridge University Press, 1989.

—ᵐ—

WHAT IS ATONALITY?

(Was Ist Atonal?, 1930)

Interlocutor: Well, my dear Herr Berg, let's begin!

Alban Berg: You begin, then. I'd rather have the last word.

Int.: Are you so sure of your ground?

Berg: As sure as anyone can be who for a quarter-century has taken part in the development of a new art—sure, that is, not only through understanding and experience, but—what is more—through faith.

Int.: Fine! It will be simplest, then, to start at once with the title of our dialogue: What is atonality?

Berg: It is not so easy to answer that question with a formula that would also serve as a definition. When this expression was used for the first time—probably in some newspaper criticism—it could naturally only have been, as the word plainly says, to describe a kind of music the harmonic course of which did not correspond to the laws of tonality previously recognized.

Int.: Which means: In the beginning was the Word, or rather, a word, which should compensate for the helplessness with which people faced a new phenomenon.

Berg: Yes, that, but more too: This designation of *atonal* was doubtless intended to disparage, as were words like *arhythmic, amelodic, asymmetric,* which came up at the same time. But while these words were merely convenient designations for specific cases, the word *atonal*—I must add, unfortunately—came to stand collectively for music of which it was assumed not only that it had no harmonic center (to use tonality in Rameau's sense), but was also devoid of all other musical attributes such as melos, rhythm, form in part and whole; so that today the designation as good as signifies a music that is no music, and is used to imply the exact opposite of what has heretofore been considered music.

Int.: Aha, a reproach! And a fair one, I confess. But now tell me yourself, Herr Berg, does not such a distinction indeed exist, and does not the negation of relationship to a given tonic lead in fact to the collapse of the whole edifice of music?

Berg: Before I answer that, I would like to say this: Even if this so-called "atonal" music cannot, harmonically speaking, be brought into relation with a major-minor harmonic system—still, surely, there was music even before that system in its turn came into existence. . .

Int.: . . . and what a beautiful and imaginative music!

Berg: . . . so it doesn't follow that there may not, at least considering the chromatic scale and the new chord-forms arising out of it, be discovered in the "atonal" compositions of the last quarter-century a harmonic center which would naturally not be identical with the old tonic. . . . We already have today in the "composition in twelve tones related only to each other" which Schoenberg has been the first to practice, a system that yields nothing in organization and control of material to the old harmonic order.

Int.: You mean the so-called twelve-tone rows? Won't you tell us something more about them in this connection?

Berg: Not now; it would lead too far afield. Let us confine ourselves to this notion of "atonality."

Int.: Agreed. But you have not yet answered my question whether there does not indeed exist a distinction such as that implied in the word between earlier music and that of today, and so whether the giving up of relationship to a keynote, a tonic, has not indeed unsettled the whole structure of music?

Berg: Now that we have agreed that the negation of major and minor tonality does not necessarily bring about harmonic anarchy, I can answer that question much more easily. Even if certain harmonic possibilities are lost through abandonment of major and minor, all the other qualities we demand of a true and genuine music still remain.

Int.: Which, for instance?

Berg: They are not to be so quickly listed, and I would like to go into that more closely—indeed, I must do so, because the point in question is to show that this idea of atonality, which originally related quite exclusively to the harmonic aspect, has now become, as aforesaid, a collective expression for music that is no music.

Int.: No music? I find that expression too strong; nor have I heard it before. I believe that what the opponents of atonal music are most concerned with is to emphasize the implied antithesis to so-called "beautiful" music.

Berg: That view you take from me. Anyhow, this collective term "atonality" is intended to repudiate everything that has heretofore made up the content of music. I have already mentioned such words as *arhythmic, amelodic, asymmetric,* and could name a dozen more expressions derogatory of modern music: like *cacophony* and *manufactured music,* which are already half forgotten, or the more recent ones like *linear music, constructivism,* the *new factuality* [Neue Sachlichkeit], *polytonality, machine music,* etc. These terms, which may perhaps properly apply in individual special instances, have all been brought under one hat to give today the illusory concept of an "atonal" music, to which those who admit no justification for this music cling with great persistence, purposing in this single word to deny to the new music everything that, as we said, has heretofore constituted music, and hence its right to exist at all.

Int.: You take too black a view, Herr Berg! You might have been entirely justified in that statement of the case of a while ago. But today people know that atonal music for its own sake can be fascinating, inevitably in some cases—where there is true art! Our problem is only to show whether atonal music may really be called musical in the same sense as all earlier music. That is, to show, as you have said, whether if only the harmonic foundation has changed, all the other elements of former music are still present in the new.

Berg: That I declare they are, and I could prove it to you in every measure of a modern score. Prove above all—to begin with the most important—that in this music, as in any other, the melody, the principal voice, the theme, is fundamental, that the course of the music is in a sense determined by it.

Int.: But is melody in the traditional sense at all possible in atonal music?

Berg: Yes, of course, even vocal melody.

Int.: Well, so far as song is concerned, Herr Berg, atonal music surely does follow a new path. There is certainly something in it that has never been heard before,
I would almost like to say, something temporarily shocking.

Berg: Only as concerns harmony: on that we agree. But it is quite wrong to
regard this new melodic line as taking a path entirely new, as you declare, in comparison with the usual characteristics of melodic procedure, or even as never before
heard and shocking. Nor is this true of a vocal line, even if it is marked with what
someone recently described as intervals of an instrumental chromaticism, distorted,
jagged, wide-spaced; nor that it thereby totally disregards the requirements of the
human voice.

Int.: I never said that, but I cannot help feeling that vocal melody and melody
in general does seem never to have been treated like that before.

Berg: That is just what I am objecting to. I maintain on the contrary that vocal
melody, even as described, yes, caricatured, in these terms, has always existed, especially in German music; and I further maintain that this so-called "atonal" music,
at least in so far as it has emanated from Vienna, has also in this respect naturally
adhered to the masterworks of German music and not—with all due respect—to
Italian bel canto opera. Melody that is linked with harmony rich in progressions,
which is almost the same thing as being bold, may naturally, so long as one doesn't
understand the harmonic implications, seem "distorted"—which is no less the case
with a thoroughly chromatic style of writing, and for which there are hundreds of
examples in Wagner. But take rather a melody of Schubert, from the famous song
"Letzte Hoffnung." Is that distorted enough for you? And to remain with Schubert,
that melodist par excellence, what do you say to his treatment of the voice in the
song "Der stürmische Morgen" [from *Winterreise*] (mm. 4–8)? Isn't this a typical
example of an amply jagged vocal line? And here is an example of something
"wide-spaced" (mm. 15–18). You will find similar things, like instrumental parts, in
Mozart vocal lines. A mere glance at the score of *Don Giovanni* will suffice. We
have an example in Donna Elvira's aria [probably "Mi tradì" in Act 2] (m. 1),
which sounds as though it were written for strings, or the hidden imitation of a clarinet in the same aria (m. 5), or the instrumental-like passage in the duet of Leporello and Zerlina ["Per queste tue manine," Act 2] (mm. 30–31), or the entire part
for Donna Anna, or—to point to an especially clear example of a jagged, wide-
spaced melody covering more than two octaves—this vocal excerpt from *Così fan
tutte* (Act 1, Fiordiligi's aria ["Come scoglio immoto resta"], mm. 9–13)! You see
that there is a way of handling the voice differently from what is always held out to
us as a model, which arose fundamentally only through the frequent use of long-
held notes in the high register of the prevailing vocal line. As the classicists have
shown, the voice can in some cases represent an instrument that is quite lively,
expressive in all registers, soulful, and still capable of declamation. But you will also
see by these examples from the classics that it has nothing to do with atonality if a
melody, even in opera music, departs from the voluptuous tenderness of Italian

cantilena—an element you will furthermore seek in vain in Bach, whose melodic potency nobody will deny.

Int.: Granted. But there seems to be another point in which the melody of this so-called "atonal" music differs from that of earlier music. I mean the asymmetrical structure of melodic periods.

Berg: You probably miss in our music the two- and four-bar periodicity as we know it in the Viennese classicists and all the romantics, including Wagner. Your observation is correct, but you perhaps overlook the fact that such metrical symmetry is peculiar to this epoch, whereas in Bach, for example, it is only to be found in his more homophonic works and the suites that derive from dance-music. But even in the Viennese classics, and especially in Mozart and Schubert, we observe again and again—and quite particularly in their most masterly works—efforts to break away from the restraints of this square symmetry.

For the sake of simplicity I will cite only a few famous passages from *Figaro*. One is in Cherubino's aria "Non so più cosa son," in which the first two four-measure phrases are immediately followed by four three-measure phrases, then again two two-measure phrases, and finally two five-measure units. Similarly, in the march from the wedding procession from Act 3 ["Ecco la marcia"], two three-measure phrases are suddenly interpolated [mm. 9–14] into the normal four-measure units, quite contrary to the nature of the march. Finally, in the "Rose Aria" [Susanna's "Deh vieni, non tardar" from Act 4] the phrasing entirely deviates from the symmetrical framework of period form. In a succession of three-measure phrases, the sixth one [mm. 16–20] is freely expanded to five measures. This art of asymmetric melodic construction developed still further in the course of the nineteenth century (just think of Brahms . . . "Vergebliches Ständchen," "Am Sonntagmorgen," or "Immer leiser wird mein Schlummer"), and while the four-bar period preponderates in Wagner and his followers (they clung to this earlier style-factor in favor of other innovations, notably in the harmonic field), even at this time there is a very clear tendency to give up the two- and four-bar form. A direct line runs here from Mozart through Schubert and Brahms to Reger and Schoenberg. And it is perhaps not without interest to point out that both Reger and Schoenberg, when they discussed the asymmetry of their melodic periods, pointed out that these follow the prose of the spoken word, while strictly square-rhythmed melody follows, rather, metrical speech, verse-form. Yet, as with prose itself, unsymmetrical melodies may be no less logically constructed than symmetrical melodies. They too have their half and full cadences, rest and high points, caesuras and bridges, introductory and concluding moments which, because of their directional character, may be compared with modulations and cadences. To recognize all this is to feel in them melody in the truest sense of the word.

Int.: . . . and perhaps even find them beautiful.

Berg: Quite right! But let us go on: This freedom of melodic construction is naturally accompanied by freedom of rhythmic organization. Because the rhythm of this music has undergone a loosening process—let us say through contraction, extension, overlapping of note-values, shifting of strong beats as we see it quite particularly in Brahms—does not mean that the laws of rhythm are dispensed with; and the term *arhythmic* for this treatment, which after all represents just another refinement of the artist's means, is just as silly as *amelodic*. This rhythmic treatment is particularly conditioned too by the multilinearity of the new music; we seem, indeed, to be finding ourselves in a time which very much resembles Bach's. For as that period, through Bach himself, wrought a change from pure polyphony and the imitative style (and the concept of the church modes), to a style of writing built on major-minor harmony, so now we are passing out of the harmonic era, which really dominated the whole Viennese classic period and the nineteenth century, slowly but incessantly into an era of preponderantly polyphonic character. This tendency to polyphony in so-called "atonal" music is a further mark of all true music and is not to be dismissed just because it has been nicknamed "linear structure."

Int.: Now I think we have arrived at a most important point.

Berg: Yes, at counterpoint!

Int.: Right! The essence of polyphony of course consists in the interordination and subordination of voices, voices, that is, which have a life of their own. Here again we are dealing with the harmonic aspect; I mean, the individual lives of all the voices give rise to a second, a new life, that of the collective sound . . .

Berg: . . . which is of course not accidental, but consciously built and heard.

Int.: Now that is just what surprises me. Then is that elemental interplay of atonal voices, which seem to me to lack any such essential contrast as would give rise to a strong internal life, also achieved by conscious construction, or is it the play of some admittedly highly inspired chance?

Berg: That question—to be brief and not too theoretical—I can answer with a truth won from experience, an experience that springs not only from my own creative work but from that of other artists to whom their art is as sacred as it is to me (so anachronistic are we of the "atonal" Viennese school!). Not a measure in this music of ours—no matter how complicated its harmonic, rhythmic, and contrapuntal texture—but has been subjected to the sharpest control of the outer and the inner ear, and for the meaning of which in itself and in its place in the whole, we do not take the artistic responsibility quite as much as in the case of some very simple form—as a simple motive or a simple harmonic progression—the logic of which is at once clear to the layman.

Int.: That explanation seems to me to make sense. But if so, it almost seems as though the word *atonal* must be a misnomer for this whole tendency in music.

Berg: Why, that's what I've been saying the whole time, trying to make it clear to you.

Int.: But then you, that is, your music, must somehow have some relation to the *formal* elements of earlier music too? If my guess is correct, this very music—the word "atonal" doesn't sound right after what we've said—strives to keep in close touch with older forms?

Berg: With form itself; and is it any wonder then that we should turn back to the older forms as well? Is this not a further proof of how conscious contemporary practice is of the entire wealth of music's resources? We have just seen that this is the case in all serious music. And since this wealth of resources is apparent in every branch of our music simultaneously—I mean, in its harmonic development, in its free melodic construction, in its rhythmic variety, in its preference for polyphony and the contrapuntal style, and finally in its use of all the formal possibilities established through centuries of musical development— . . . no one can reproach us with our art and tag it as "atonal," a name that has become almost a byword of abuse.

Int.: Now you have made an important declaration, Herr Berg. I am somewhat relieved, for even I thought that the word "atonal," whencesoever it came, had given rise to a passing theory foreign to the natural course of musical development.

Berg: That would suit the opponents of this new music of ours, for then they would be right about the implications which really lie in the word "atonal," which is equivalent to antimusical, ugly, uninspired, ill-sounding and destructive; and they would furthermore be justified in bemoaning such anarchy in tones, such ruination of music's heritage, our helpless state of deracination. I tell you, this whole hue and cry for tonality comes not so much from a yearning for a keynote relationship as from a yearning for familiar concords—let us say it frankly, for the common triads. And I believe it is fair to state that no music, provided only it contains enough of these triads, will ever arouse opposition even if it breaks all the old commandments of tonality.

Int.: So it is still sacred to you, after all, good old tonality?

Berg: Were it not, how could such as we—despite the skepticism of our generation—maintain faith in a new art for which Antichrist himself could not have thought up a more diabolical appellation than the word "atonal"!

Notes

[Text: Alban Berg, "Was ist atonal?," *23: Eine Wiener Zeitschrift* 26/27 (June 1936): 1–11. Translated by M. D. Herter Norton with additions by Bryan R. Simms.]

PART II

REBELLION AGAINST ROMANTICISM, 1920–1950

THE YEARS IMMEDIATELY FOLLOWING WORLD WAR I WITNESSED as sudden and profound a change of taste in music as ever in history. By the early 1920s a new style had emerged that embodied a far-reaching rebellion against virtually every aspect of romantic music. Pronounced expressivity was replaced by cool and detached objectivity, a concern for construction displaced free-formed emotionality, and the search for new musical resources came to an end in favor of the enshrinement of an eclectic mixture of tonal and atonal elements. The sense of freedom from restraint and rule at the turn of the century gave way to strictness of form and a willing acceptance of limitation. Debussy's earlier disdain for the audiences of his day yielded to a more democratic attitude in works often addressed to a whole community, many times flavored by popular styles, and almost never having the rigid highbrow aestheticism of the romantic period. Few musicians still spoke of music of the future; more typical was the epithet with which Igor Stravinsky closed his *Autobiography*: "It would be a great mistake to regard me as an adherent of *Zukunftsmusik*—the music of the future. Nothing could be more ridiculous. I live neither in the past nor in the future. I am in the present."

But new music of the 1920s became highly fractured by competing and conflicting directions, and for this reason no single term has ever successfully designated the breadth of the new style. "Neoclassicism" comes the closest, although terms such as "New Objectivity" (coined by art critics) and "New Music" were used prominently in German critical writing. Even the term *neoclassicism*, which suggests a return to eighteenth-century musical styles, is misleading, since the postwar movement was at first a rebellion against the immediate past, not a "back to . . ." style. Stravinsky, the leading neoclassical composer of the interwar period, made this distinction clear. In his earliest statements concerning the new style—short articles titled "Some Ideas About

My Octuor" (1924) and "Avertissement" (1927)—he emphasized that his recent works were nonemotive, strictly constructed, nonrepresentational, and objective, in other words quite the opposite of romantic or impressionistic music. In the latter essay he warned explicitly against attributing these features to a reversion to classicism. The idea that the new style was motivated by a revival of baroque or classical music came instead from critics of the 1920s, who found a model for Stravinsky's innovations most readily in the music of J. S. Bach. Only in the 1930s, when Stravinsky allowed his lectures and essays to be ghostwritten by these same critics, did the concept of neoclassicism per se appear in his aesthetic.

Divisions and bitter conflicts continued to arise in international musical circles even after the 1920s. Musicians faithful to the high art of prewar romanticism and impressionism were still very much alive; among them, Schoenberg and Charles Koechlin spoke out to denounce the new movement (see essays nos. 10 and 7). Their opponents included Stravinsky, Paul Hindemith, and Kurt Weill, who wrote just as trenchantly to attack the older order. Hindemith, for example, reduced the followers of l'art pour l'art to the level of "emotional imps, monsters, or snobs." Other musicians, such as Ravel, tried to remain above the fray, although Ravel himself made many concessions to neoclassicism in his own postwar music.

A separate branch of the neoclassical rebellion emerged in the 1930s, notably in the United States and England. It was both regionalist and populist in objective, making it easily distinguishable from Stravinsky's neoclassical language of the 1920s, which critics had come to call an "International Neoclassical Style." The regionalist-populist manner was thoroughly traditional and simplified in its musical language, plainly different from the residual modernism that characterized neoclassicism per se. It was parochial and folkloric while neoclassicism was international and abstractly cosmopolitan. The aesthetic of the regionalist-populist idiom is stated in a straightforward manner by Ralph Vaughan Williams (essay no. 11) and, among American composers, by Aaron Copland (essay no. 23). The music of Aaron Copland contains examples of both styles. His much admired Piano Variations embodies the International Neoclassical Style, and the three ballets (Appalachian Spring, Billy the Kid, and Rodeo) are distinguished examples of the regionalist-populist idiom.

The nationalistic element that existed in this branch of interwar music became a controversial theme among composers at this time. Stravinsky and his followers strictly avoided folklorism in their music after 1920, rejecting its associations with romantic music in Russia, which tended to be strongly national in character. In his Autobiography Stravinsky condemned folklorism in music as a "sterile tendency and an evil from which many talented artists suffer." Several prominent folkloristic composers from before World War I, such as the Spaniard Manuel de Falla, now followed Stravinsky by suppressing their earlier regionalist impulse. In this outlook—if in nothing else—they were joined by German composers who continued to represent the late romantic aesthetic. Schoenberg, for example, drew a strict distinction between folk and art music, and he denied the possibility that the two could ever be successfully mixed. In the essay "Folkloristic Symphonies" he wrote that "the discrepancy between the requirements of larger forms and the simple construction of folk tunes has never been solved and cannot be solved. A simple idea must not use the language of profundity, or it can never become popular." Compare this conclusion with that of Ralph Vaughan Williams from essay no. 11: "There is no difference in kind but only in degree between Beethoven and the humblest singer of a folk-song."

Béla Bartók represented yet another branch of the controversy. In essay no. 5, as in many other writings, he calls for just the mixing of folk and artistic elements that Schoenberg and Stravinsky rejected, but he did not share the populist outlook or simplified musical language of Vaughan Williams and Copland. Like many of the greatest composers, he rose above doctrinaire considerations and composed music that drew freely from so many sources that it cannot easily be located in any of the established trends of his day. So too Ravel. In essay no. 9 he declares a national element to be unavoidable in new music but does not equate this with the use of musical folklore, and he holds that great music will result from a synthesis of individualistic and nationalistic influences.

7

CHARLES KOECHLIN

(1867–1950)

Charles Koechlin's article "Back to Bach" is filled with irony and sarcasm directed at the emerging neoclassical movement in France of the 1920s, which he attacked repeatedly in his voluminous critical writings. In this essay Koechlin clearly separates the two faces of neoclassicism—its spirit of return to baroque or classical musical styles (especially those associated with Bach) and its antiromantic manner, in which intense expressivity is replaced by cool and abstract modernism. Koechlin had no argument with the former ideal, since the modern composers whom he most admired—Fauré and Debussy at their head— had always gone back to Bach for models of effective musical organization and content. But he had no tolerance for the antiromantic spirit of the 1920s, especially its suppression of the emotive dimension of French music composed prior to World War I.

It is no wonder that comparisons between Bach and French neoclassicists of the 1920s raised Koechlin's ire. He was widely respected as an authority on Bach's music, and time and again he addressed strict contrapuntal composition in his pedagogical writings and used it in his own compositions. In French music criticism from early in the 1920s, comparisons between Bach and neoclassicists—Stravinsky, for example—had become common. In 1924 Stravinsky himself was quoted in the Parisian press naming Bach as "the imperishable model for us all." Reviewing the 1925 festival of the International Society for Contemporary Music in *La revue musicale*, Henry Prunières found the "Back to Bach" movement in full swing. "More than ever," wrote Prunières, "Bach seems to be the god who will restore peace and light." Stravinsky's Piano Sonata, performed by its composer at this festival in Venice, was interpreted by Prunières as a "follow-up to *The Well-Tempered Clavier*." "This work is written in the contrapuntal style of J. S. Bach, treated with the greatest strictness," Prunières concluded.

It was such talk that caused Koechlin's eruption in the article "Back to Bach." Bach, he said, was a supremely emotional and expressive artist, quite foreign in spirit to an age when composers were all too willing to suppress the emotionality of their works.

Although Koechlin does not enumerate the composers who were guilty of a false return to Bach, he points an accusing finger at the International Society for Contemporary Music (ISCM). He suggests that the recent music of Stravinsky is suspect, as well as works by Georges Auric, Darius Milhaud, Francis Poulenc, and Arthur Honegger, all of which were heard in the early festivals of the Society. Much of Koechlin's ill humor is also directed toward his fellow critics—Prunières, Boris de Schloezer, Roland-Manuel, André Schaeffner among them—for whom the "back to Bach" phrase had become a handy, if largely misleading, critics' term.

Koechlin's own music was attuned to the romantic sentiments that he expressed so forcefully in his writings. His musical oeuvre was immense, channeled into all of the major romantic musical genres with the exception of opera. Like other French composers of the 1930s, he was involved with music for film, and his skill and authority in the craft of orchestration brought him important commissions. His music is highly melodious and evocative in a manner reminiscent of French impressionism, although following World War I, he adopted a more dissonant harmonic vocabulary, cautiously extending the harmonic modernisms implicit in Debussy and overtly present in works by younger French contemporaries.

But in the 1920s, as his music increasingly appeared to be a romantic atavism, Koechlin's importance as a critic and pedagogue superseded his importance as a composer. He was the author of over 125 published articles and reviews, which appeared throughout the first half of the century in most of the major French and in some international musical journals. Very few of these have appeared in English. He wrote widely used textbooks on harmony, orchestration, counterpoint, and fugue; and general studies of the life and works of his teacher, Fauré, and of Debussy. Koechlin also taught privately—among his students in orchestration was Cole Porter—although a permanent institutional appointment always eluded him.

Koechlin's Writings: A Selective Bibliography

"Atonal Music." In *Music Today: Journal of the International Society for Contemporary Music*, 1 (1949): 26–35. This is a summary of a longer article in French, "Quelques réflexions au sujet de la musique atonale," printed in the same place.

"On the Part Played by Sensibility in Music," *Pro-Musica Quarterly*, 6/1 (1927): 4–18; 6/2 (1927): 4–18.

"Time and Music," *Pro-Musica Quarterly* 5/3 (1926): 16–30.

—⁓⁓—

BACK TO BACH

(*Le "Retour à Bach"*, 1926)

You know this expression—it's the order of the day. Future historians will probably use it to characterize festivals of the ISCM. Just like people, some expressions don't always ring true. However apocryphal some famous saying by a king of France may be, it is still quoted by everyone. So too in our art—all the clichés live on. Gounod's music is sensual and mawkish; Fauré's is undulating; Debussy's is impressionistic, hazy, iridescent, faint. Bach's is austere and academic; Mozart's "exquisite." Vincent d'Indy's is finely calculated but devoid of feeling. As bad luck would have it, not a one of these fine-sounding generalizations can stand up to a study of the music itself. So I would like to explore this new phrase in its reference to the works of Bach.

Here is Roland-Manuel, with his knowing smile: "Bach is so multifaceted! Almost everything is found there. So can't it always be said that we endlessly return to him?" But I won't adopt this line of thought. His idiosyncrasies should be what guide us; let's examine the distinctive aspects of Johann Sebastian!

The "back to. . ." that is spoken of regarding contemporary music comes clearly enough from the character of an art that aims to be clear, robust, nondescriptive, even nonexpressive.[1] It was aptly defined in André Schaeffner's article, "Jacques Rivière et ses *Études sur la musique*."[2] He lists the commandments of this new cult, which supplants the dangerous religion of Debussyism.[3] It is an austere cult: only musical flagellation will atone for the sins that produced [Debussy's] *Nocturnes* or *Chansons de Bilitis*. The art of Bach—entirely a "remonstrance"—provides a hair shirt. It evokes the chastising rods used to batter the little heroines of the *Comédies et proverbes* by Madame de Ségur, née Rostopchine. Because its sturdy, "precise," and clearly etched forms have replaced the supple undulations, the impressionism, the "delightful vagueness" of the sorcerer of *Pelléas*, we are spared the rickets spread by Claude Debussy's followers.

André George and sometimes Georges Auric have told us in the *Nouvelles littéraires* that the health, even the very life of our art must be bought at the expense of this cruel but necessary indifference, leading us ultimately to stop our ears with wax to overcome the danger of hearing the fatal voices of the sirens. "Full steam ahead and hold the course toward Johann Sebastian!" seems to be the order, just as Phileas Fogg would have done.[4]

Now I won't question the merits of this point of view even though there is much to be said, especially about the *faintness* of the first theme of Claude Debussy's String Quartet, or about the *impressionism* of Golaud's curses hurled at Mélisande as he slings her about by her hair (or the rather Franck-like interlude that follows this scene), or the *undulating* construction of "Fêtes," or the *iridescence* of the Andante of the Quartet, or the *halos* in the Finale of *Saint-Sébastian*, or the *haziness* of the Toccata and "Jardins sous la pluie."[5] There is equally much to say on the influence of *Pelléas*. But in general I can list the principles of this brand of neoclassicism, whether disputable or not, without misrepresenting it: clear themes as in the allegros of Bach (again a *remonstrance*!); no pathos as in Beethoven, Franck, or Wagner; no *expressionism* as in Fauré or Debussy (I certainly can't call it *impressionism*!); a "pure music" which lays no claim to any meaning. And always with fugues, or, better, outlines of fugues, adapted to the needs of an epoch in which time is money.

Now if Bach in some pieces reveals this type of clarity in his squareness of rhythm, if we sometimes find in him a "pure music" which seems to be inexpressive, he is just doing what most of his contemporaries did. Even earlier, our French organists of the seventeenth century provided similar examples. Just look at the works of Marchand, Nicolas de Grigny, [François] Roberday. This was the *common practice of the period* from 1650 to 1750. Bach used it now and then.[6] But, born as he was in 1685, he was not its inventor. He found it fully formed in all its main features. *No part of it* was distinctively his alone.[7]

But what is distinctively Bach's? First of all is emotion [*sensibilité*]. This is often overlooked. People think that pure music cannot in principle be expressionist. Furthermore, they hold Bach up as a type, tidying up the facts concerning this master of expression by disguising him as a well-behaved academician free from the poison of emotion.

I don't need to cite the authority of Albert Schweitzer, who has used the term "musician-poet."[8] His erudition definitely upholds his use of the term. Here I only wish to talk about emotion. Now it would be odd to talk about abstraction in a composer who has left to us the "Crucifixus" from the B Minor Mass! It is impossible that such a figure should lead to or represent a "revolt against emotion."[9] This would be like making Fra Angelico into the head of a school of nonexpressive painting. A good joke perhaps, original certainly, but not showing much taste.

Bach is pure emotion.[10] He is almost always so, even when writing fugues whose lines are always so singable! Look again at *The Well-Tempered Clavier*. To grasp its charm is to go truly back to Bach, not just to make him into a remonstrance.

I won't hide the fact that Saint-Saëns has cited some passages from *The Well-Tempered Clavier* as examples of unexpressive music. But he has perhaps broadened the term *expression*, using it in a special way to refer to a harmonic expressivity that tends to degenerate toward sentimentality.[11] Still, by examining the pieces that he cites (Prelude and Fugue in C major from Book 1) and adding to them, if you wish, some large organ fugue (the G minor), one might conclude that such nonprogrammatic works—untranslatable into words, pure music—are only a play of tones whose unaffectedly plastic beauty (coming from their fluency and order) is unrelated to any movements of human emotion.

There is plenty of music—pure to be sure—that has nothing to say, absolutely nothing, precisely because of its vacuity, its emptiness. But never with Bach. Even the *subjects* of his fugues, each one of them, have their own character. In their musical language they speak, indeed they "sing," as Paul Valéry has said concerning expressive architecture in his *Eupalinos*.[12] But precisely in *The Well-Tempered Clavier* the nuances and diversity of emotion depart from the serenity of the Fugue in C and move on toward both joy and pain. The pieces in C-sharp major, cheerful and youthful; the fugues in F minor and B-flat minor, filled with anguish.

And there is still more in Bach (I choose from among a thousand examples): the radiant gentleness of the famous aria from the Pentecost Cantata [probably "Mein gläubiges Herze" from *Also hat Gott die Welt geliebt*, BWV 68] with its abundance of pure joy; the exaltation of the "[Et] resurrexit" from the B Minor Mass, or from the aforementioned organ chorale "Hier ist die Freude" ["In dir ist Freude," BWV 615?]; the extreme tenderness of the adagios from the organ sonatas, orchestral concertos, and so forth; the incomparable organ chorales (see volumes 5 and 6 of the Peters edition, especially the admirable prelude in E-flat); the serious and joyful expression of faith, irresistible and sweet, arising in another organ chorale[13] in volume 9; the sadness of "Aus tiefer Noth" [BWV 686 or 687] and of the "Crucifixus"; the mystery of the "Incarnatus," the plea for forgiveness of the "Qui tollis" [from the B Minor Mass]; the infinite mercy of the final chorus of the St. John Passion; the mystical promise that ends the *Actus tragicus* [BWV 106] ("Heute, wirst du mit mir im Paradies sein," "Today you will be with me in paradise"), with its magical commentary provided by the hymn tune in the contraltos.

Indeed, from the very beginning (the *Actus tragicus* is one of the earliest cantatas), Bach's music is invariably human, and also Christian. Profound, exalted, sometimes casual and even comic, but never vulgar. An emotionalism that is *truly his own* governs the music's character and the materials which grow from it.[14] In this way Bach reveals himself as an impressionist (despite the absence of subtitles), but different from those musicians who play with sounds for pleasure or for new materials, just to come up with new chordal combinations.[15] The effects produced by these new chords—"interesting," sometimes also coming from polytonal counterpoint where they arise in part by chance—seem to me quite contrary to Johann Sebastian's harmony, which today is still new, unexpected, and youthful. His chords and their progressions were not invented by him, to be sure. But in their relation to the melody, to the feeling of the musical phrase, together these phenomena reveal the sensitive being who has expressed himself through them. The deep basses of some chorales emanate from an inner gravity of which Bach himself, in his humble daily life, was surely unaware, but which lay at his very heart. And his faith, the steadfastness of his soul, was the source of his unwavering tonality, so clearly asserted.

His style of fugal composition, his incomparably skillful use of passing notes and points of imitation,[16] were all carried out with a beauty of harmony that we today perhaps do not stress enough. This too was his alone. Modern contrapuntal styles (I refer to those musicians of the ISCM in connection with whom the name Bach was mentioned) cannot compare to the flexibility—so fluent, so perfect, so *pleasant*—of their incomparable model. This achieved a perfection that is difficult even to approach (even an excellent fugal exposition or a good four-part "strict counterpoint" is something rare). In general among our contemporaries, composition has become much more independent of harmony.[17] The refinement, the subtlety, and the solidity that are joined in Bach's harmonizations seem now scarcely to be an inspiration, neither in astringent and complex polytonal works nor in the simplified style, the new hedonism that has already been indicated, as in works by G[eorges] Auric. I do not contend that this simplification nor this complexity lacks value, at least as practiced by some. But it is certainly not Bach, not in harmony, not in counterpoint, not in emotion.

His forms, although not lacking in reason, are not based on a dry intellectualism. They are not geometrical, instead highly diversified. Often they derive from the character of a theme. They are not built on any preestablished frames but resemble instead orderly improvisations.[18] Nothing could be more irregular, nothing less academic in the unexpectedness of their plans than the fugues of *The Well-Tempered Clavier*. Sometimes a stretto occurs at the beginning; in some there is no counterexposition, even no countersubject. I could easily cite pieces of free construction, nearly fantasies, such as the Organ Suite in G Major [BWV 530?] (found in the volume with the Passacaglia). In the truly improvisatory and lengthy recitatives in the Chromatic Fantasy, we ask anxiously when we will ever come to a "strict form" such as we find in the Toccata of Claude Debussy!

In Bach, finally, there is a moral character to the work and to the man. It is not just an elevated religious spirit, but a sense—deep and steadfast—of good and evil. Now it is undeniable that many of our contemporaries have chosen to place their art outside of this moralistic domain. Their affirmation of pitilessness seems to me to be utterly anti-Bach. With only a few exceptions, our contemporaries look for their themes outside of the story of Christ, outside of the promise of an afterlife. They are satisfied with faith as it now exists—a dance of humanity that supersedes the idea of angels. They have this right, but so much the less can they be said to occupy a place next to Bach.

To be sure, it cannot be denied that many moderns have a knack for adjusting to the spirit of their age, whether by a natural affinity between their outlook and the modern "sensibility" or by a violation of their natural inclinations in their calculated show of respect for "what the people want." Bach was just the opposite of this. He was no theoretician; he was cultured, but he was not ready to accept ideas a priori. He was not in the least inclined toward the "modern esthetics" of his day. This new esthetic position underlay a reaction against the art to which Bach remained faithful. It was a reaction from a theatrical viewpoint, one that suggested simplified accompaniments and a disdain for counterpoint, even a counterpoint so rich and expressive as that of J. S. Bach. All in all, he was judged to be a throwback due to his counterpoint and a revolutionary due to the profound innovation of his harmonic language and also because of his musical ideology.[19] He looked both to the past and to the future more than to the present, and because of this he was misunderstood by his own century.

Emotion, style, freedom and flexibility of form, the moral character of the man and his work—these are the true characteristics of this forerunner. Compare him with the proponents of a "return to Bach" as defined above and draw your own conclusion!

I would leave it there, but I must note that composers well before the present day—many of them—also went back to Bach. An even greater and more genuine intimacy with this master of the fugue has been a characteristic of the French school of composition during the last sixty years. Many names come to mind. Berlioz ignored Bach (or nearly so) until his late but decisive conversion at the hands of Saint-Saëns. But in his youth Gounod was initiated into the Bach cult by Mendelssohn's sister.[20] To see the influence one need look only at the first page of *Faust*, or note the epithet "academic" attached to the opera in contemporary reviews, or look at his carefully annotated edition of the 150 chorales of the "great cantor."

There can be no doubt that César Franck was nourished by this "lion's marrow" (to use Gounod's culinary metaphor).[21] It is equally certain that the well-informed Massenet—despite the tendencies present at the Conservatoire around 1860—understood the beauty of Bach's contrapuntal style. We can see traces of it in his fugue of 1863 that won the first prize.[22] With Bizet passages from the Prelude to *L'arlésienne*[23] and *Carmen*[24] were plainly inspired by the Bach tradition in its purest and boldest form. The influence of Bach on Camille Saint-Saëns is undeniable. There are many examples in addition to the fugues in *Le déluge*, *La lyre et la harpe*, or the Finale of the Third Symphony: The scene where Samson turns the millstone [in *Samson et Dalila*] takes its origins from the first chorus of the St. John Passion; the baritone quartet ("Justiciae domini rectae") from the psalm *Coeli enarrant*; the opening of *Samson et Dalila*; many passages from *La lyre et la harpe* (not to mention his chamber music). It is plain that this master, so expert in the art of counterpoint, thoroughly knows Johann Sebastian Bach.[25] I have already noted that in some respects Saint-Saëns is a precursor of our young nonexpressive composers, this through his theory of a purely plastic music (see, on this subject, his letters to Camille Bellaigue, published in the *Revue des deux-mondes*).[26] Think what you will of his work (it is quite possible that the present negative opinion about him is unjust), he did not wait for an anti-Debussy backlash to arrive at the "precise form" upon which he has strictly insisted.

If the best thing about the revival of the French school since 1860 is our symphonic art,[27] this was in large measure due to the influence of Bach. Much more so than the influence of Beethoven, it furnished our artists with the finest technique and it gave impetus to this movement, born from a revival of the past and channeled toward the future. It was set in motion shortly before 1870 and sustained by the multifaceted flowering of a trend toward expressive music during the thirty years from 1885 to 1915.[28] It is certain, however, that what was discovered in that venerable tradition is not at all what we see now in the present day. But it was no less a return to Bach—to his ideas, to the spirit of his style, sometimes even to certain salient traits of his emotionality.

I shall return momentarily to the theme of this essay, but the mention of style lures me into a parenthesis. We can't forget about fugue, strictly speaking. Where was it during this period of renovation? People in general would certainly think of César Franck, d'Indy, Albéric Magnard. I have already cited Saint-Saëns,[29] and let me also mention fugues from the Psalms of Guy Ropartz and Florent Schmitt—that from *Mârouf* (in the merchants' scene in Act 2 and the last scene of the last act) as also in "La fille de Roland," the beautiful meditation by Charlemagne and one of the best passages of the whole work. Also [Henri] Rabaud, a Bach devotee from his youth. See the cantata *Daphné*, with which he won the Rome Prize. Apollo's aria "Ne repousse point" uses a theme and bass rhythms that distinctively recall an andante from Bach's Violin Sonata as transcribed by Saint-Saëns.

Is it necessary to mention the teaching of André Gedalge? Among my many happy memories of him, his way of leading us to Bach is not the least! He left behind a book of Preludes and Fugues, perfect in style, as was his collection of Canons, his last work. Those of Paul Dupin are rather different—the influence of *The Well-Tempered Clavier* is not so evident in them. But the Three Fugal Pieces for piano by the same composer represent a sincere and indisputable homage to the author of the Magnificat.

With Gabriel Fauré one constantly finds evidence of this musical heritage, from the Offertory of the Requiem to the use of passing notes in *La bonne chanson* or "Mandoline," from there decidedly to *Prométhée*, *Pénélope*, and the Second [Piano] Quintet.[30] His classic equilibrium between emotion and reason shows the influence of Bach as does the inner power of the "life force" of his themes and their harmonizations. These never contain an empty gesture; each note says more than it seems to have in it. This influence is seen ultimately in the moral quality of an art created by the artist for himself and for music, without any concessions to the fashion of the day or to the pride of the composer.

Debussy himself—the composer whom they now want to escape by going back to the allegros of the eighteenth century—gave ample evidence of his profound admiration for Johann Sebastian,[31] so we must not be deceived by first appearances. I will not speak only of his Toccata or the "Jardins sous la pluie," or the String Quartet, whose first measures [m. 13] contain a chromatic movement in the cello, where an F-sharp is sustained against a G-minor harmony. How could he have dared this without a knowledge of and love for Bach?[32] Finally Ravel. If he had not felt these same sentiments, if he had not discovered this contrapuntal technique, how could he have written those lines from the Andante of his String Quartet, the Pavane, and the "Jardin féerique" from *Ma mère l'oye*, not to mention the Sonata for Violin and Cello? Except for Verdi's *Falstaff* [see note no. 29] I have drawn examples from the French school. But it is clear that others can be found elsewhere, and not only in *Die Meistersinger*! But it's not necessary.[33]

With all of these examples at hand, I am a bit hesitant to mention some of my own works. But I'll do so all the same because my religion is long-standing and because critics have wanted to count me among the "grandchildren of Bach." I was so labelled in connection with the Sonatine [Op. 59, 1916] or possibly after the more recent Clarinet Sonata No. 2 [Op. 86, 1923]. To these works allow me to add my *Les vendages* [Op. 30, No. 1] (heard at the third orchestral concert of the S.M.I. in 1910), about whose value I won't speak but whose contrapuntal style was certainly inspired by Johann Sebastian and by the teaching of my master, André Gedalge.

We see from this discussion that if our predecessors all remained *expressionists* (even in their pure music), they did not cease to know, love, and use the style of J. S. Bach.[34] We see also that there are different ways of returning to him and that in all cases musicians have not waited for the current fashion to do so. What can we make of this? Should we dismiss the current movement, blaming the trends of the day? Not at all, at least not a priori. Let us keep our focus on one thing: conditions which will lead to musical culture and to beauty. Such an outcome is not incompatible with current developments, even though one would wish that these were more flexible and less dogmatic. Should I discuss the idea of plastic music? I could do so at the end of the article, but the question is not one that could be dispatched in a few lines. The essential issue is that we should not restrict ourselves to a single approach, that we must be allowed to compose, now and in the future, expressive music without incurring the unjust reproach that we have fallen into "romantic femininity."[35] Moreover, those who have ideas *about life* should always imbue their music with humanity, voluntarily or not, explicitly or implicitly. See [Igor Stravinsky's] *Les noces*.

I only dispute that my contemporaries have a monopoly on a return to Bach. I dispute that they are truly returning to him—indeed, there are many other ways of rendering homage to him. I dispute finally and positively the right of anyone to mention his great name to support a "revolt against emotion."

Notes

[Text: Koechlin, "Le 'Retour à Bach'," *La revue musicale*, 8 (1926): 1–12. Translation by Bryan R. Simms. Used by permission of Yves Koechlin.]

1 It will not be very useful (because it is off the subject) to include in this movement the boldness of polytonal music or the contrapuntal style based on "free passing tones." These may well stem from Bach, but they were also used by others before him, including H[einrich] Schütz, Buxtehude, Marchand, Frescobaldi, Monteverdi (see *Orfeo* in Malipiero's edition, especially where a G-natural scrapes against a G-sharp). Even Anthoine de Bertrand, who in the sixteenth century did not shy away from the subversive simultaneity of a B-flat and B-natural. Furthermore, the independence [of lines] in contrapuntal polytonality often leads far away from Bach. I will speak on this subject again shortly.

2. *La revue musicale*, 6 (1 May 1925): 152–72.

3. Even before *Pelléas* Pierre Lalo, ahead of his time, used the term "diabolic" to describe Debussy's magic. I recall this from memory, not having Lalo's text in front of me, but I remember his term "devil" or "diabolic" to describe Claude-Achille.

[4. Phileas Fogg is the hero of Jules Verne's *Around the World in Eighty Days*.]

[5. Koechlin refers to works by Claude Debussy: *Pelléas et Mélisande*, "Fêtes" from *Nocturnes*, *Le martyre de Saint Sébastien*, the Toccata from *Pour le piano*, and "Jardins sous la pluie" from *Estampes*.]

6. In his own way, not without some spicy harmonies.

7. I don't insist on going "back to Rossini"—to harmonies swollen hedonistically, as Boris de Schloezer has described them. This is quite different from Bach despite the great tonal simplicity of the organ chorale in G, "Hier ist die Freude" ["In dir ist Freude," BWV 615?].

8. He used this term to describe Bach, about whom he wrote a well-known work.

9. See the article by Jean-R. Bloch that appeared under this title in the review *Europe*, important excerpts from which are quoted in the *Revue musicale*. [In the article by Jean-Richard Bloch, "Une insurrection contre la sensibilitée," *Europe: Revue mensuelle* 21 (15 September 1924): 109–12, the author praises contemporary composers such as Stravinsky for rejecting the romantic expressive cult, which, he says, approaches "musical hysteria." The new objective, he writes, is "to obtain the same creative, penetrating and convincing power with none of the [romantic] demand for emotion, stimulation of the feelings, and devoid of association with any ideas except for purely musical ones."]

10. I do not ignore what is often said about him (like Pliny's description of God at the beginning of his *Historia naturalis*). Bach is also pure reason, pure harmony, and so forth. But his harmony is based on his emotionality, and the latter is much more his own than his "reason." [At the beginning of his *Natural History*, Pliny the Elder explains his own lofty view of God, but he also gives due consideration to conceptions of God from other cultures on this subject, although these are made to appear ludicrously primitive.]

11. From whence his theory that expressive art is decadent art. You would think you were hearing the talk of a *neoclassicist*. [Koechlin refers here to the texts of letters from Saint-Saëns to the critic Camille Bellaigue. In a letter dated 4 February 1907 Saint-Saëns wrote: "The quest for expression, however legitimate and inevitable, is the seed of decadence, which enters at the moment when a search for expression goes beyond the search for formal perfection." In a letter of 3 March 1907 Saint-Saëns cites the opening of the C-Major Fugue from Book 1 of *The Well-Tempered Clavier*, about which he says: "There is no emotion here, but it is art at its greatest." See Saint-Saëns, "Lettres à un critique musical: A M. Camille Bellaigue," *Revue des deux mondes*, period 7, volume 16 (1 August 1923): 650–63.]

12. I understand this as referring in some way to internal expression, created by the charm of design and beauty of proportion. So too in music. There is architecture which can only speak (often of nothing). But Bach's *sings*, precisely because of its emotion.

13. The theme comes from a chorale, but the way that it is used in relation to the harmonies and phrase cadences gives the impression of an unfathomable mystery.

14. It could be argued that this emotionalism pertains so exclusively to Bach that it cannot be rightfully demanded in the "back to Bach" movement that is the subject of this article. Still, the closer one comes to this emotionalism, the more it can exert a positive influence, without any danger of epigonism, indeed, without any damage to the personality.

15. It is true that some artists have a genuine need for new sonorities to express their fantasies truly and sincerely. But this is not "playing with sounds."

16. Which are not found to the same degree or with the same variety in Handel.

17. Except in *Pulcinella* (as well as in other works by Igor Stravinsky). But the principle of free passing motion, as used by Bach, is always controlled by the solid consonant chords that occur on the downbeats of measures. Between chordal tones other notes occur, in conjunct motion, truly as "passing" notes. Today it is all different. The lines move completely freely, in counterpoint as well as in harmony. *This can still be musical*, but in a sense that is quite contrary to Bach.

18. It is well known that Bach was a wonderful improvisor. A number of his compositions were clearly written, so to speak, *currente calamo* [with a running hand].

19. It may be baffling that I underscore Bach's harmonic innovation at the same time that I say he used only the chords familiar in his own day. But Fauré's example has shown us that a composer can be innovative even with familiar materials. The originality of a collection of tones is ultimately much less important than is commonly thought.

20. During his sojourn in Rome.

21. See the Preface to his edition of the chorales.

22. This is seen also in the way that he corrected the counterpoint and fugues of his students.

23. See the variation passage, so bold in style, having triplets in the bass.

24. See the fugue from the first act, the entr'actes before the second and third, etc.

25. And he still applies lessons from Bach now at the age of more than fifty as in his student days. See the admirable choral writing for the girls in the second act of *Proserpine*. This, if I am not mistaken, is in eight real parts.

[26. Saint-Saëns, "Lettres à un critique musical." See note no. 11.]

27. I use this term broadly to refer to sonatas, symphonies, and other music in the grand style (even in some cases music for the theater).

28. This period of flowering in fact spans a somewhat longer time. Some fine works by Fauré and Franck appeared before 1885, and Fauré continued to compose until 1924. There were influences other than Bach—harmonic evolution, chant, and so forth.

29. To shorten the text of this article I will use this note to mention the fugues in Charles Gounod's *Mors et vita* and those in the last entr'acte of Ernest Guiraud's *Piccolino*; the final scene from Verdi's *Fastaff*, a wager masterfully won from the old "primer" *La traviata*; the fugue in Gabriel Dupont's *La farce du cuvier*, which has a similar character; and so forth. Finally, *L'apprenti sorcier*, which is a type of fugue, as is the middle of the Scherzo of Paul Dukas's Piano Sonata.

30. From this style came that of his later songs, with their beautiful and extremely supple and subtle motions. Elsewhere in his oeuvre, let me cite these examples: the canons from *Dolly*, those from *Pénélope* (at the end of the first and second acts), from *Prométhée* (beginning of the last scene), and all the broad passages from the prelude and first chorus of this same *Prométhée*, the scenes for Bia and Kratos, Pandora's funeral procession, and the like. In my view these all reveal the deep and genuine tradition of Bach and much more so than the lively and foursquare (but no more robust) themes of the current school.

31. On this subject let me recall the lines written by Claude Debussy in an article from the journal *La revue musicale de la S.I.M.* on 15 January 1913: "The beauty of the Andante of Bach's Violin Concerto is such that one does not know how to begin nor how to contain oneself so that one is able to listen to it properly. It haunts us long after it has ended, so that on coming out into the street one cannot fail to be astonished that the sky is not bluer and that the Parthenon does not rise out of the ground. But the blaring horns of the buses quickly bring us down to earth again."

32. Properly understood, this is only one example among many that could be found in the Quartet or in other works by a musician who is basically more of a contrapuntist than is generally thought.

33. Aside from *Die Meistersinger*, it may be that in France musicians have best rediscovered the contrapuntal tradition of Bach.

34. With the occasional exception of Saint-Saëns. His experiments with a plastic music have not been successful. It is found, here and there, in his sonatas. I like him infinitely better when he speaks with emotion and when he doesn't aim for the grandiose. The charming finale of Act 2 of *Proserpine*, many a seductive page from *Ascanio, La lyre et la harpe*, the Andante from the String Quartet are worthy of being preserved, but perhaps this could not be said of the second Trio [Op. 92] or the Sonatas for Violin and Piano [Opp. 75, 102]. [Saint-Saëns wrote two String Quartets, Opp. 112 and 153, but neither of them has an andante movement.]

35. I heard this epithet used a few years ago regarding Gabriel Fauré's classic Trio [Op. 120]. The foreign conductor who used it, with a scornful nuance, proved once more that our great Fauré is only understood in France. But we must be on guard. The tendency toward excess of motion and of vigor, the love for rhythm for its own sake—these constitute dangerous tendencies in those who have no natural sense of vigor. They arise only because of pride and pride is the most deadly of all human sins.

8

KURT WEILL
(1900–1950)

Shortly after the opening of his *Threepenny Opera* in Berlin in November 1928, Kurt Weill was asked by a Berlin newspaper to write a short explanation of his music, as though he were addressing a class of intelligent twelve-year-olds. The result, "The Musician Kurt Weill," was brash and puckish. Weill adopts the persona of a strict schoolmaster, imperiously commanding his students to write down the realities of music of the 1920s as he sees them.

Weill's article—filled with mordant humor—went directly to the central musical issues of the day. The late romantic period, the age of Wagner through Strauss, is gone, he declares, as is the society that had sustained it. Now music has to address the general public of the 1920s, not an elite few. It has to be relevant to a society that is intellectually shallow and materialistic, and accessible to listeners who demand music that is simple, tuneful, and lively. Weill's depiction of the new German society is accomplished in large part by his parody of the older society as represented by the Prussian schoolmaster. By extension, his authoritarian and self-assertive tone parodies musical criticism that is old, authoritarian, and self-assertive. Composers of the 1920s, he concludes, are faced with no less a challenge than to remake their musical culture from bottom to top.

Weill was an important writer on music and an outspoken supporter of the antiromantic, objectivist trend in German music during the Weimar Republic. He was the chief music critic for the weekly journal *Der deutsche Rundfunk* from 1925 to 1929, and he wrote longer essays for many of the important musical journals of his day.

Weill's Writings: A Selective Bibliography

Kowalke, Kim H. *Kurt Weill in Europe*. Ann Arbor: UMI Research Press, 1979. Appendix II contains English translations of twenty-seven articles by Weill written from 1925 to 1932.

Weill, Kurt. *Musik und Theater: Gesammelte Schriften*. Edited by Stephen Hinton and Jürgen Schebera. Berlin: Henschel, 1990. In German.

———. *Ausgewählte Schriften*. Edited by David Drew. In German.

—⟋⟍—

THE MUSICIAN WEILL
(*Der Musiker Weill*, 1928)

Stand up! Sit down! Stand up! Sit down! Stand up! Sit down!
We talked in our last class about the transformation of opera into music drama, and
I explained to you the concept of the total work of art. I'll write these names on the
board once more, so no one will have an excuse:

<blockquote>
Richard Wagner

    "   Strauss.
</blockquote>

Now we come to a new subject. You will recall that I read to you from Wagner's
texts. They were all about gods and heroes and notable topics like forest murmurs,
magic fire, knights of the grail, etc., which seemed quite strange to you. And there
were difficult thought processes that you couldn't follow, and other things that you
still don't understand and that still don't seem relevant to you. You just weren't interested in them. You would rather occupy yourselves with technology, airplanes, autos,
radios, bridge building; and the lectures you prefer are the sports news.

Write this down! The age of gods and heroes is past.

I also played for you the music of Wagner and his followers. You saw that it had
so many notes that I couldn't play them all. You tried to sing along with the melody,
but it didn't work. You sensed that this music was soporific or intoxicating, affecting
you like alcohol or other drugs. But you didn't want to go to sleep, you wanted to
hear music that you could understand without explanation, that you could readily
absorb with tunes that you could quickly learn. Apparently you're not aware that
your parents sometimes go to concerts. This is a custom that came from the social
conditions of the preceding century, conditions that are irrelevant to your generation. There are again today great issues that are of concern to everyone, and if music
cannot be placed in the service of the general public then it has lost its reason for
being.

Write this down! Music is no longer something for the few.

Modern musicians have taken this sentence to heart. Their music is simpler,
clearer, and more transparent. They no longer wish it to embody a philosophy, depict
external processes, or produce certain moods, but they still want it to fulfill its original purpose and have its original meaning. Look at it this way: When musicians had
achieved everything in their greatest of dreams, then they began again from scratch.

Write this down! Kurt Weill is attempting to begin from scratch in the area of
musical theater.

He has realized that opera can no longer continue as in its romantic manifestation, divorced from the atmosphere of the present. He wants opera that will conform
to the trends in theater of the day, opera characters who are again living people

speaking a language understood by everyone. For this reason he has joined up with the theatrical movement that most strictly fulfills the artistic demands of our time— the one founded by Bertolt Brecht—open parenthesis—Bertolt Brecht, the founder of epic drama—close parenthesis. Weill recognized in this movement a richness of new and astonishing challenges for the musician. Brecht and Weill have investigated the question of music's role in theater. They have concluded that music cannot further the action of a play or create its background. Instead, it achieves its proper value when it interrupts the action at the right moments.

Write down the term "gestic character of music"—it is the most important outcome of Weill's work so far.[1] We'll talk about it in detail in the specialized course next year, when those of you who want to be critics have left us.

Stand up! Let's sing No. 16:

Der Mensch lebt durch den Kopf, der Kopf reicht ihm nicht aus, versuch' es nur, von dei-nem Kopf lebt hoech-stens ei-ne Maus.

[Man lives off of his head, but his head isn't enough. Just try it; all that could live off your head is a mouse!][2]

Notes

[Text: Weill, "Der Musiker Kurt Weill," *Berliner Tageblatt*, 25 December 1928. Translated by Bryan R. Simms.]

[1. Weill elaborates upon his notion of a "gestic" character in his music in an article, "Die gestische Character der Musik," *Die Musik* 21 (March 1929). He says that the term refers to a musical style that could represent and establish the personal relations among the characters in a play, a style that was close in both rhythm and sense to the texts that the characters sing and that was capable of making the meaning of the drama crystal clear.]

[2. This is the first verse of Peachum's "Das Lied von der Unzulänglichkeit," from Weill's *Die Dreigroschenoper* (The Threepenny Opera). There the last word is "louse," not "mouse."]

9

M A U R I C E   R A V E L

(1 8 7 5 – 1 9 3 7)

The text of Ravel's "Contemporary Music" originated as a lecture given at The Rice Institute (now Rice University) in Houston in April 1928. It was read during a two-day festival honoring the French composer, at which time Ravel also performed his own music. He was in Houston toward the end of a grueling four-month tour of the United States, during which he performed and conducted in over twenty cities. His success in America was virtually complete, a gratifying tribute to a composer who at this time stood somewhat above the modern music fray, carefully avoiding the partisan strife that marked musical culture of the 1920s.

The main subject addressed in his lecture at Rice was influence in music, although he also touched upon other matters concerning his own works and outlook. His main thesis is that all great works are shaped by two types of influence—the national and the individual. The composer has no control over the former. The successful French composer, for example, can only conform to the longstanding French taste for clarity of design and refinement of expression. The German national consciousness, on the contrary, is by comparison expansive. But these common features are reshaped in the works of great composers by the distinctive language of the individual genius, which comes from many sources, some innate and others drawn from culture and history.

Ravel's thesis is related to an idea expressed by Béla Bartók in "The Relation of Folk-Song to the Development of the Art Music of Our Time" (essay no. 5 in this anthology). In this article Bartók wrote, "Artistic perfection can only be achieved by one of the two extremes: on the one hand by peasant folk in the mass, completely devoid of the culture of the town-dweller, on the other by creative power of an individual genius. The creative impulse of anyone who has the misfortune to be born somewhere between these two extremes leads only to barren, pointless and misshapen works." Unlike Bartók, however, Ravel does not equate nationalism with folklorism per se. In fact, he is skeptical of those who act as though "folklore is the only requisite to national music." Ravel argues that great music results when the two consciousnesses are merged so that neither one calls attention exclusively to itself.

Ravel was not a major essayist or music critic, although in the years just before his service in World War I he wrote concert reviews for two Parisian journals, *La revue musicale de la S. I. M.* and *Comoedia illustré*. As in his lecture at The Rice Institute he shows in these writings a great generosity toward almost all of his contemporaries, only occasionally revealing his own personal tastes. "Ravel was never heard to slander anybody," recalled his student Roland-Manuel. Ravel seemed intent instead upon remaining uncommitted in the bitter divisions in musical culture of his day—impressionism versus neoclassicism, atonality versus polytonality, Schoenberg versus Stravinsky. All, he says, can be influential in modern music, but all must be leavened by nationalism and individualism.

There remain areas of uncertainty concerning the authoritative text of the lecture "Contemporary Music." On his ocean journey to America he wrote to Roland-Manuel: "Write to me—and don't forget the lecture." Roland-Manuel, a professional critic, may well have been involved in writing it, as he was a decade later in ghostwriting Stravinsky's Charles Eliot Norton lectures given at Harvard University. Ravel read the lecture in French, since he knew virtually no English, but the original version is now apparently lost. The text was published in an English translation in the *Rice Institute Pamphlet* shortly after Ravel's lecture. Marcel Moreau, a French professor at Rice who was Ravel's interpreter while in Houston, later wrote about the English version: "Maurice Ravel, whom I knew well and with whom I had pleasant relations, had it translated by someone whom he met on the boat, whose name I have forgotten."

Ravel's Writings: A Selective Bibliography

A Ravel Reader: Correspondence, Articles, Interviews. Edited by Arbie Orenstein. New York: Columbia University Press, 1990. Contains letters and all of Ravel's published reviews and essays on music.

—ɯ—

CONTEMPORARY MUSIC
(1928)

It is of course impossible to offer any adequate survey of contemporary music or even of one of its phases within the space of a single lecture; moreover, I hasten to admit that there is only one thing which I should find still more difficult, and that would be to explain my own music or comment upon it; indeed, were I in position fully to explain my music I should then be inclined to doubt its worth and value. The reasons which lead me to this conclusion are, perhaps, different from those generally cited by lecturers on art. For instance, it is often said that music defies analysis, whereas other fine arts, such as painting, sculpture, and architecture have not a medium of manifestation so intangible, elusive, and evanescent as the vibration of sound. On this point I differ somewhat, because I am under the impression that current progress in acoustical science makes possible dimensional measurements of sound as many and as varied as are those of other means of artistic expression, employed, for example, in architecture. I would even say that since the young Russian scientist, [Leon] Theremin, has perfected his original instruments, and can now transform ethereal vibrations into tonal vibrations of any pitch, intensity, or quality that he may desire, the sound part of music would seem to have come quite within the reach of analysis. So it is not because of the elusiveness of sound vibrations that I consider it impossible to explain or judge a work of musical art; indeed, I have the same feeling about other works of art whether in painting, sculpture, or architecture. Would it be, then, that I do not accept the so-called classical laws of harmony, counterpoint, and so on? Whether I recognize their validity or not is of little importance to me in judging contemporary compositions, for these classical laws originated in works of the past; they have been formulated and adopted by teachers in their efforts to find a permanent basis, solid and suitable, for their courses of instruction; and this body of doctrine has undergone change after change in accommodating itself to new laws peculiar to new compositions appearing from time to time. No academic attempt to establish permanent laws, however, ever helped or hindered the advancement of work in art. The matter might be summed up by saying that in musical treatises there are no such laws as would be of any avail in judging a contemporary musical work of art. Apparently the uselessness of all such arguments must come from the fact that such would-be laws are dealing only with the obvious and superficial part of the work of art without ever reaching those infinitely minute roots of the artist's sensitiveness and personal reaction. The elusive roots, or sources, are often sensed as two in character: one might be called the national consciousness, its territory being rather extensive; while the other, the individual consciousness, seems to be the product of an egocentric process. Both defy classification and analysis as well, yet every sensitive artist perceives the value of their influence in the creation of a real work of art. The manifestation of these two types of consciousness in music may break or satisfy all the academic rules, but such circumstance is of insignificant importance compared with the real aim, namely, fullness and sincerity of expression. We have here to do, perhaps, with that inner motion which purposely sets our intelligence and perception to seek its own development in its own atmosphere and tradition—not its historical tradition, but the tradition which heredity makes one feel to be true to one's nature. Such search may be intensively selective, and then becomes a clearing process applied to our natural gifts and supervised by our individual consciousness. Here, again, I insist that no stated laws can be given whereby to judge the degree of perfection attained in this process on the part of the individual, inasmuch as what we are attempting to discover is only sensed and as yet unknown. So were I able to explain and demonstrate the value of my own works, it would then prove, at least from my personal point of view, that they are constructed altogether of obvious, superficial, tangible elements within easy reach of formal analysis, and, therefore, that these works of mine are not perfect works of art. The difficulty remains when one attempts either to classify or to state definitely relative estimates of one's contemporaries in music, not excepting those among one's own countrymen. Indeed from this point of view, any attempt to arrive at a definite judgment with respect to a work of art seems to me to be folly.

On the initial performance of a new musical composition, the first impression of the public is generally one of reaction to the more superficial elements of its music, that is to say, to its external manifestations rather than to its inner content. The listener is impressed by some unimportant peculiarity in the medium of expression, and yet the idiom of expression, even if considered in its completeness, is only the means and not the end in itself, and often it is not until years after, when the means of expression have finally surrendered all their secrets, that the real inner emotion of the music becomes apparent to the listener. Thus, for example, if we consider present-day reviews of the compositions of Arnold Schoenberg and Darius Milhaud, it often seems as though chromaticism and atonality on the one hand, and diatonicism versus polytonality on the other, were the only significant traits of these two artists; nevertheless, in either case, it often seems as though such a judgment would reveal but the garb concealing or adorning their emotional sensitiveness, and we should always remember that sensitiveness and emotion constitute the real content of a work of art. Furthermore, the acute and subtle perception guiding the artist in his creative work is itself in continuous evolution, for just as any of the ordinary senses may be trained and made to perceive better today than yesterday, so this perception within the individual and national heritage of atmosphere and tradition may become keener and keener year after year, leaving no place for standardized and permanent classification.

I may be able to express my thought more perfectly if we consider briefly these ideas of nationalism and individualism in their relations to music. And what I hazard to express in this connection is my individual understanding of the more striking characteristics of contemporary music as exhibited in the works of some of my friends. At all events, I hope in this way to illustrate my thought more adequately.

For example, in the works of Darius Milhaud, probably the most important of our younger French composers, one is frequently impressed by the vastness of the composer's conceptions. This quality of Milhaud's music is far more individual than his use, so frequently commented upon and often criticized, of polytonality (a conception of the simultaneous use of several tonalities, of which we may find embryonic examples as early as the chorals of J. S. Bach, in certain passages of Beethoven, and in the definite use thereof by Richard Strauss). If we consider broadly one of his larger works, the *Choéphores*, we soon discover that on attaining the climax of a series of utterances tragic in character, in the course of which the most sweeping use is made of all the resources of musical composition, including polytonal writing, Milhaud nevertheless reaches still profounder depths of his own artistic consciousness in a scene where a strong pathetic psalmody is accompanied only by percussion. Here it is no longer polytonality which expresses Milhaud, and yet this is one of the pages where Milhaud most profoundly reveals himself. Of similar significance is the fact that in one of his latest works, *Les malheurs d'Orphée*, in its recent American premiere at one of the New York concerts of Pro Musica, Milhaud's occasional use of polytonality is so intricately interwoven with lyric and poetic elements as to be scarcely distinguishable, while his acknowledged artistic personality reappears clothed with a certain clarity of melodic design altogether Gallic in character. Again, we might note the singularly dramatic qualities of [Marcel] Delannoy, the facile and popular musical content of works of [Francis] Poulenc, the accuracy of form and elegance of orchestration in Roland-Manuel, and the peculiar tendency on the part of G[eorges] Auric to etch his music sharply, often to the point of an acute and satiric vein. Such inherent and widely divergent traits appertain to different individuals rather than to a single school; and this could also be said of the genial music of Germaine Tailleferre. In Arthur Honegger, still another member of what a French critic has labeled the *Groupe de Six*, we find, not only individual traits, but hereditary and racial characteristics altogether different from those of the four composers just mentioned, and this racial consciousness of Honegger he expresses without reserve. From his musical education, received at the hands of French teachers on French soil, Honegger seems to have conserved a facility in writing which he uses for self-expression along the lines of German expansiveness, and his music remains true to his racial consciousness—that is to say, the German consciousness, for he was born of German-Swiss parentage. The later statement is meant neither in a derogatory sense, nor in one of praise; it simply says that, while we can reconcile the various tendencies expressed by Milhaud, Poulenc, and Auric, as being all equally rooted in French national consciousness, it is from the German national consciousness that the art of Honegger springs. If we should consider still other young French musicians, we should find this phase of racial consciousness again in evidence; for we should not find the German character in the curiously dramatic qualities of M. Delannoy's music, or in the refined and intimate music of Roland-Manuel.

This national consciousness of musicians distinctively German is expansive, while our French consciousness is one of reserve. In virtue of the indissoluble ties binding each to his respective national consciousness, it is, of course, inconceivable that either one should be able to express himself adequately in the language of the other. Nationalism does not deprive the composer either of his personal soul or of its individual expression, for each creative artist has within him laws peculiar to his own being. These laws, peculiar to the artist himself, are, perhaps, the most momentous elements at play in the whole process of musical creation; they seem to be determined through an interplay of national and individual consciousness; and they can be imparted to the artist by no teacher, for they spring from his own heritage, and are first perceived only by himself. Such laws in the course of years may become those of a school, of pupils, of imitators, or of followers, but whenever a real artist appears, he evolves from his own consciousness new laws peculiar to himself. Incidentally, I should like to remark that musicians who are true alike to their national consciousness and to their own individuality often appreciate compositions altogether different from their own, but a Germanized French musician or a Gallicized musician of Germany will have a tendency to fail in understanding the musical works of others— the hybrid failing to recognize other personalities because of the loss of its own individuality. If we should now consider our lawful portion of inheritance from other musicians, the evident value of such a heritage, and the eventual danger of plagiarism, I should place on the legitimate side exchanges in emotional expression, the influence of experimental or incomplete compositions, which may be absorbed or assimilated without loss either of individual or of national consciousness; while, on the opposite side, I would put all efforts, either through imitation or plagiarism, to conceal absence or weakness of personality. It may sometimes be extremely difficult to decide these questions with respect to a particular work, but here again, the keen perception of the artist is the only dependable guide. Perhaps one of the most curious cases of exchanges of influence is that of Hérold, Weber, and Rossini; these three composers were strongly influenced in turn by a common characteristic of their respective works—namely, their romanticism; but each of the three held these interchanges of influence subservient to his own respective national consciousness. It was French romantic music that Hérold wrote, Rossini's romanticism was obviously Italian, while Weber remained to the end a German romanticist. Such influences enlarge the horizon of the aspiring artist without contracting either his personality or his heritage. Relations of this sort in works of some of my predecessors or contemporaries I shall be pointing out later on in this lecture. It is very important to estimate these influences carefully, inasmuch as they may be of good or ill effect, depending upon the quality of the influence and even more upon the strength of the personality subjected to them. For example, the influence of Liszt on Wagner was altogether considerable, and yet the personality of the latter was in no way impaired, despite the generous way in which he used the artistic heritage of his father-in-law. The thematic influence of Liszt on Wagner is certainly more than obvious, but the aesthetic of Wagner, however extensive, is essentially individual. Another significant influence, somewhat unique, and deriving at least partially from [Emmanuel] Chabrier, is that of Eric Satie, which has had appreciable effect upon Debussy, myself, and indeed most of the modern French composers. Satie was possessed of an extremely keen intelligence. His was the inventor's mind par excellence. He was a great experimenter. His experiments may never have reached the degree of development or realization attained by Liszt; but, alike in multiplicity and importance, these experiments have been of inestimable value. Simply and ingeniously Satie pointed the way, but as soon as another musician took to the trail he had indicated, Satie would immediately change his own orientation and without hesitation open up still another path to new fields of experimentation. He thus became the inspiration of countless progressive tendencies, and while he himself may, perhaps, never have wrought out of his own discoveries a single complete work of art, nevertheless we have today many such works which might not have come into existence if Satie had never lived. This influence of his was not in the least dogmatic, and, for this reason, of all the greater value to other musicians. Debussy held him in the highest esteem. Influences such as his are as fertile soil, propitious to the growth of rare flowers, wherein the individual consciousness, the indispensable seed, nourished in better surroundings thus provided, may still unfold according to its own essential nature, national, racial, or individual.

As often as not, the national consciousness is the creative artist's original source of inspiration. For example, the objectivity and clarity of design exhibited by our earliest composers furnished a rich heritage to our incomparable C[laude] A[chille] Debussy, the most phenomenal genius in the history of French music. Does this mean to say that Debussy was only an imitator? Certainly not! Again, is the symbolism of Debussy, his so-called impressionism, at variance with the Gallic spirit? Quite the contrary, because beneath the fine and delicate lacework of atmospheric surface, one may easily discover a refined precision of design, characteristically French. His genius was obviously one of great individuality, creating its own laws, constantly in evolution, expressing itself freely, yet always faithful to French tradition. For Debussy, the musician and the man, I have had profound admiration, but by nature I am different from Debussy, and while I consider that Debussy may not have been altogether alien to my personal inheritance, I should identify also with the earlier phase of my evolution Gabriel Fauré, Emmanuel Chabrier, and Erik Satie. The aesthetic of Edgar Allan Poe, your great American, has been of singular importance to me, and also the immaterial poetry of Mallarmé—unbounded visions, yet precise in design, enclosed in a mystery of somber abstractions—an art where all the elements are so intimately bound up together that one cannot analyze, but only sense, its effect. Nevertheless I believe that I myself have always followed a direction opposite to that of Debussy's symbolism.

Let us now turn to another aspect of my own work which may be of more immediate interest to you. To my mind, the "blues" is one of your greatest musical assets, truly American despite earlier contributory influences from Africa and Spain. Musicians have asked me how I came to write "blues" as the second movement of my recently completed Sonata for Violin and Piano. Here again the same process, to which I have already alluded, is in evidence, for, while I adopted this popular form of your music, I venture to say that nevertheless it is French music, Ravel's music, that I have written. Indeed, these popular forms are but the materials of construction, and the work of art appears only on mature conception where no detail has been left to chance. Moreover, minute stylization in the manipulation of these materials is altogether essential. To understand more fully what I mean by the process to which I refer, it would be sufficient to have these same "blues" treated by some of your own musicians and by musicians of European countries other than France, when you would certainly find the resulting compositions to be widely divergent, most of them bearing the national characteristics of their respective composers, despite the unique nationality of their initial material, the American "blues." Think of the striking and essential differences to be noted in the "jazz" and "rags" of Milhaud, Stravinsky, Casella, Hindemith, and so on. The individualities of these composers are stronger than the materials appropriated. They mold popular forms to meet the requirements of their own individual art. Again—nothing left to chance; again—minute stylization of the materials employed, while the styles become as numerous as the composers themselves.

In my own work of composition I find a long period of conscious gestation, in general, necessary. During this interval, I come gradually to see, and with growing precision, the form and evolution which the subsequent work should have as a whole. I may thus be occupied for years without writing a single note of the work— after which the writing goes relatively rapidly; but there is still much time to be spent in eliminating everything that might be regarded as superfluous, in order to realize as completely as possible the longed-for final clarity. Then comes the time when new conceptions have to be formulated for further composition, but these cannot be forced artificially, for they come only of their own free will, and often originate in some very remote perception, without manifesting themselves until long years after.

For the last fifteen or twenty years musicians and critics alike have taken great interest in the two divergent tendencies I have already mentioned: atonality and polytonality. And in the impassioned discussions of partisans we have often heard or read that atonality is a blind alley leading nowhere, but I do not accept the validity of this opinion; because, while as a system it may be so, it certainly cannot be as an influence. In fact, the influence of Schoenberg may be overwhelming on his followers, but the significance of his art is to be identified with influences of a more subtle kind—not the system, but the aesthetic of his art. I am quite conscious of the fact that my *Chansons madécasses* are in no way Schoenbergian, but I do not know whether I ever should have been able to write them had Schoenberg never written. On the other hand, it has often been said that my music has influenced many of my contemporaries. In particular it has been claimed with some insistence that the earlier appearance of my *Jeux d'eau* possibly influenced Debussy in the writing of his "Jardins sous la pluie," while a coincidence, even more striking, has been suggested in the case of my *Habanera*; but comments of this sort I must leave to others. It could very well be, however, that conceptions, apparently similar in character, should mature in the consciousness of two different composers at almost the same time without implying direct influence of either one upon the other. In such cases, the compositions may have numerous external analogies, but we can feel the difference in individuality of the two composers, just as no two human beings are ever altogether identical—considering of course at the moment only those composers who have actually sought and discovered their own personality. Again, if under apparently similar outward expression we fail to find dissimilar inner manifestations, it is likely that one of the two composers is a plagiarist of the other.

But we have been wandering somewhat from the subject of our lecture, and, perhaps, for no better reason than that I am unable to say much more about my own compositions and the methods by which they have been brought into being. When the first stroke of a work has been written, and the process of elimination begun, the severe effort toward perfection proceeds by means almost intangible, seemingly directed by currents of inner forces, so intimate and intricate in character as to defy all analysis. Real art, I repeat, is not to be recognized by definitions, or revealed by analysis: we sense its manifestations and we feel its presence: it is apprehended in no other way.

Before closing this short address I wish to say again how very happy I am in visiting your country, and all the more so because my journey is enabling me to become still more conversant with those elements which are contributing to the gradual formation of a veritable school of American music. That this school will become notable in its final evolution I have not the slightest doubt, and I am also convinced that it will realize a national expression quite as different from the music of Europeans as you yourselves are different from them. Here again, for the nurture of the most sensitive and imaginative of our young composers we should consider national heritage in all its entirety. There are always self-appointed promoters of nationalism in plenty, who profess their creed with a vengeance, but rarely do they agree as to the means to be employed. Among these nationalists in music we can always distinguish two distinct clans constantly waging their warfare of criticism. Now criticism is easy, but art is difficult. Most of these nationalists are painstaking enough in criticism, but few of them are sufficiently so in self-examination One group believes that folklore is the only requisite to national music; the other predicts the birth of national music in the individual of today. Meanwhile, within the first clan itself dissension goes on: "Folklore? But what in particular is our folklore? Indian tunes? But are they American? . . . Negro spirituals? Blues? But are these American?" and so on, until nothing is left of national background. And the field is at last wide open for those musicians whose greatest fear is to find themselves confronted by mysterious urges to break academic rules rather than belie individual consciousness. Thereupon these musicians, good bourgeois as they are, compose their music according to the classical rules of the European epoch, while the folklorists, apostles of popular airs, shout in their purism: "Can this be American music if inspired by Europe?" We are thus caught up in a vicious and unproductive circle, unless we turn once more to the past and consider how certain works, held to be essentially national in character, were produced. Wagner is generally regarded as purely Germanic and yet, as we have already remarked, a great deal of his thematic material was derived from the highly imaginative Franz Liszt, a Hungarian whose own works often and indubitably exhibit a rich flavor of Hungarian folklore. It is quite certain that Wagner's remarkable achievement depended upon his success in formulating his own style of manifestation, yet one may doubt that he would ever have written as he did if the abundant wealth of material accumulated by Liszt had not been more or less at his disposal. For example, to the completion of such a work as *Tristan und Isolde*, Wagner's extraordinary skill in construction, Liszt's unusual thematic genius, and folklore as well—all made contribution. Folklore and individual consciousness are alike necessary; and, in nations that are still young from a musical point of view, persistent fidelity of search in these two directions seems to be the greatest lack on the part of composers. With respect to individual consciousness let us not deceive ourselves: its discovery and development is more often than not a lifelong process. Nor should individuality ever be confused with eccentricity. Now, as to collecting the popular songs of which the national folklore is made up, I could do no better than cite the remarkable record of two distinguished Hungarian musicians, Béla Bartók and Zoltán Kodály, in personality altogether unlike, but mutually interested in folklore. These gentlemen, from 1905 to 1918, collected more than twelve thousand such songs of Hungary and adjacent countries. Of this number at least six thousand are Hungarian, and Bartók says that he could easily collect an additional thousand every year. Moreover, while assembling in tangible form this incomparable national heritage of Hungarian musicians, Messrs. Bartók and Kodály have with equally painstaking care preserved the quality of its material in accurate documentary form by recording the songs on gramophone disks, which are capable of catching and holding permanently the most elusive of folklore characteristics, including small variations in pitch, intensity, and quality of sound, for which the cruder medium of our ordinary written musical notation is utterly inadequate.

In conclusion I would say that even if Negro music is not of purely American origin, nevertheless I believe it will prove to be an effective factor in the founding of an American school of music. At all events, may this national American music of yours embody a great deal of the rich and diverting rhythm of your jazz, a great deal of the emotional expression in your blues, and a great deal of the sentiment and spirit characteristic of your popular melodies and songs, worthily deriving from, and in turn contributing to, a noble national heritage in music.

Notes

[Text: Ravel, "Contemporary Music," *The Rice Institute Pamphlet* 15/2 (April 1928): 131–45. Reprinted by permission of the Rice University Press.]

10

ARNOLD SCHOENBERG

(1874–1951)

Arnold Schoenberg was a staunch opponent of the neoclassical movement of the 1920s. Its eclectic mixture of old and new seemed to him not only illogical but perverse, and he interpreted its simplicity, diatonicism, and foursquare rhythms as a denial of the far-reaching accomplishments of the late romantic period, with which he was always attuned. In his view, the tendency of neoclassical composers to return to traditional styles from the baroque and classical periods was supremely misguided, a denial of the very idea of historical evolution and progress.

Schoenberg's disdain for neoclassicism also had a personal dimension, marked by his feelings of rivalry with Igor Stravinsky—the most formidable representative of this movement. Prior to 1925 the two composers had cordial relations, but in that year Schoenberg read an interview in which Stravinsky declared, "I myself don't compose modern music at all nor do I write music for the future. I write for today."[1] Schoenberg interpreted these remarks as an attack upon his art and upon himself personally, and he responded sharply. At the 1925 festival of the International Society for Contemporary Music in Venice, both composers were present, Stravinsky to perform his recent Piano Sonata, Schoenberg to conduct his Serenade, Op. 24. When Schoenberg ran over his allotted time in rehearsing the Serenade, he declared that he was the only significant composer at the gathering, and tensions among supporters of both composers ran high.

Shortly thereafter Schoenberg fired a literary salvo at Stravinskian neoclassicism in the essay "Gesinnung oder Erkenntnis?" ("Opinion or Insight"), which was published in 1926 in the widely read yearbook of Universal Edition. Here he attacked the mixing of traditional musical features associated with tonality—triads, familiar cadences, ostinati and pedal points—with more modern elements associated with his own "emancipation of dissonance." This eclecticism is pure whim, Schoenberg contended, a juggling of styles carried out by composers who express only their own "opinion" about what music is. A composer would better exercise "insight" into the historical development of music, in which it is apparent that musical ideas can only be expressed through comprehensible forms that suggest a homogeneity of style.

Schoenberg's disaffection with neoclassicism was considerably augmented by the attitudes of German music critics of the later 1920s. Increasingly they declared neoclassicism to be synonymous with "new music," and several of them dismissed Schoenberg's brand of new music as something antiquated, out of touch with the spirit of the postwar period. This was the position taken in a review of the Venice festival by the Prague critic and music historian Erich Steinhard, published in 1925 under the title "Tonale, atonale und antiquierte Musik" ("Tonal, Atonal, and Antiquated Music") in the journal *Der Auftakt*, of which Steinhard was editor. The Serenade, Steinhard wrote, "sounded despairingly aged. This is really a music that 'goes on and on,' with enough mathematically calculated figures, rhythms, and chords to assail the eyes and brain. This Serenade is non-music of a sort that is entirely avoided by all musical young people, with the exception of a small Viennese circle. It is antiquated."[2]

In his lecture "New and Outmoded Music, or Style and Idea" Schoenberg not only continued his polemic against neoclassicism, which he now ironically and disdainfully identified with the term "New Music," but he also did battle with critic-historians like Steinhard. The text was first read as a lecture in Prague in October 1930, after which it was repeated, with relatively minor changes, at the Kulturbund in Vienna in February 1933. The text of the 1933 version is given here for the first time in an English translation.

After immigrating to America later in 1933, Schoenberg translated portions of the lecture into English, presumably for his own teaching and lecturing, and in November 1945 he returned to it, making a "new version, entirely reformulated, revised and translated" into English. This version was slightly retitled as "New Music, Outmoded Music, Style and Idea," and although it touches on many of the same themes as in the 1933 lecture, it is less trenchant in tone and shows Schoenberg's distance from the heat of battle with the neoclassicists of the 1920s. The 1945 version was published, with minor revisions, in the collection of his writings called *Style and Idea* (1950), an anthology that took its title from the title of the lecture, another indication that Schoenberg considered this text to be one of his major aesthetic statements.

In addition to a far-reaching discussion of the four terms contained it the title, Schoenberg presents in the lecture his own highly original theory of historical evolution, a theory that is closely connected with the aesthetics underlying twelve-tone composition. In Schoenberg's view, musical history evolved in recurrent cycles, each characterized by a distinctive way in which musical space was used. The classical period, for example, was characterized by an emphasis on melody, the horizontal dimension of space; the Renaissance and early baroque periods, by a polyphony that filled the vertical as well as the horizontal dimension. Just as Bach stood between these two periods, Schoenberg saw himself—especially through his "discovery" of the twelve-tone principle—as standing between the romantic period and a newly emerging modern era characterized by counterpoint.

Neoclassical works—"New Music," as Schoenberg cynically called them—ran contrary to the dictates of history. New Music can be easily recognized, Schoenberg says, by its style—diatonic, simple, and traditional. But since it collides with the requirements of historical evolution, it is devoid of "idea." This term caused Schoenberg more than a touch of difficulty; in fact, it is not clearly defined in his 1933 lecture other than by analogy. In the 1945 revision of the lecture he is more specific. An idea, he says there, may be viewed simply as a theme, better as the totality of a work, or better still as a principle by which tonal equilibrium is maintained throughout a composition. By this definition tonality embodies a musical idea, as does the twelve-tone principle, but any meaningful idea cannot be present in a work that mixes different and conflicting tonal principles.

Readers will also note in Schoenberg's lecture an attachment to the values of romanticism and an utter disdain for music critics (as he notes, most of the important German musical journalists of the 1920s were also music historians). The text is often heavy with irony and complex, although precise, in its manipulation of words, which are sometimes marshaled into the witty aphorisms and imaginative analogies for which the composer was well known.

Schoenberg's Writings: A Selective Bibliography (see also the Bibliography preceding essay no. 3)

Style and Idea. Edited by Leonard Stein, translated by Leo Black. London: Faber and Faber; New York: St. Martin's Press, 1975. Reprinted with minor revisions, Berkeley and Los Angeles: University of California Press, 1984. A collection of 105 essays, chosen by the editor. This is an expansion of a collection of fifteen essays, chosen by Schoenberg, and published with the assistance of Dika Newlin in 1950.

Stil und Gedanke: Aufsätze zur Musik. Edited by Ivan Vojtěch. Arnold Schönberg gesammelte Schriften, volume 1. N.p.: S. Fischer, 1976. Collection of seventy-four essays including the fifteen from the 1950 edition of *Style and Idea*. In German. The original German text of the 1930–33 version of the following lecture is found in this volume, pp.466–77.

—ɯ—

NEW AND OUTMODED MUSIC, OR STYLE AND IDEA

(*Neue und veraltete Musik, oder Stil und Gedanke*, 1930, revised 1933)

Here we have four terms in a plainly contrary relationship with one another. Their contrasts are so multifaceted, complex, and diverse that it would be difficult to follow through with all of their resulting combinations. It is, furthermore, as easy for me to do justice to the more difficult task—discussing the terms *style* and *idea*—as it is difficult for me even approximately to define the two easier terms—essentially easier because they were more easily thought up.

What is "New Music"? Clearly, a music that did not exist before. Music must always be new in the measure to which it aspires to be artistic. For only the new in art, only what has not been said before, is worthy of being said at all.

In fact, the art of any era is new. If we were to choose works by Josquin des Prez, Bach, Haydn, or those of any other great master, they would also be understood as new music. Because art means new art. But this is not what is intended by the inventors of this slogan [New Music]. Even calling them inventors is going too far, because there is no invention in attaching the label *new* to music that has originated in the last few years. They should instead be called *historians* of some sort, because this is the term for people who deal at most with important facts about music history but not with its meaning. Some of them have read that once, under the battle cry "New Art," the homophonic-melodic style of composition supplanted the contrapuntal one. Incidentally, this was a change that has often been repeated in the development of music. Because always when one of the two directions—one of the two basic dimensions of music—is dealt with exclusively, the other one is neglected, so that the next period looks to the development of the neglected dimension. If an era ignores the contrapuntal style and develops only the horizontal dimension, and succeeds in giving its melodies a roundedness and richness of content, then the next generation of competent musicians will try to acquire a similar skill in writing polyphony. Conversely, a superabundance of content and an excessive attention to the space occupied by the principal melody may lead this music, dominated by its upper voice, to great lengths, as it must, since everything is expressed ever more broadly and expansively in the top part of the texture, leaving the lower parts quite empty. This will begin to tire the keener minds, and it will naturally lead to a new generation who will once again turn to a more concise manner of composing, which will exploit musical space in all of its dimensions simultaneously.

The pseudo-historian has no awareness of this; he is satisfied with knowing facts and misunderstanding them. He confuses symptoms with causes. Musical evolution is not driven by whether or not listeners like some music or the other. Neither are the wishes of artists involved; they may toss out hundreds of battle cries, just as they always have done, without consequence! In the days of the contrapuntal style there were certainly just as many half-wits who yammered over beautiful melody as there were "academicians" during the period of a melodic emphasis who longed for the learned style. And just as certainly there were true artists who were unconcerned with the yammering of the one group or the longing of the other and instead quietly continued to compose. These are all just symptoms.

The cause is simply the force of music's evolution, which plainly consists in exploiting musical space in all of its dimensions so that the greatest and richest content will be brought into even the smallest space.

This evolution can only move slowly and gradually. Its goal can only be approached by small steps and roundabout ways; briefly stated, such works cannot be created overnight because the laws of comprehensibility will not allow it.

The new that can be conceived of, created, and passed on is tied to a state of mind that requires preliminary stages which can be passed through only under certain conditions. Certainly, we can entertain an idea that has no concrete shape. An inventor may well be capable of thinking independently of such shapes. But in art only things with form can be contemplated, and here the thinker is to a considerable extent tied to an existing representational apparatus. The newer his idea, the greater must be his effort to realize the demands of comprehensibility in its representation.

But the genuinely new, required of every art work, is not an issue for our bumbling historians. Instead, in their mistaken effort to see our own period as analogous to an earlier one, they issue their battle cry, which serves less to designate a new music than it does a music—still new even in their own false theories—which they label simply as *outdated* for the sake of convenience, thinking back to battles long since fought.

I am not prepared to say how things stand with outmoded music, because we know almost as little about New Music as we do about its partisans—if this is the right term for people from the musical provinces who lounged in the reserves, historically speaking, far from the real battlefront.

But we have also overlooked a very important observation. Before about 1750 Johann Sebastian Bach wrote piece after piece whose newness seems to me ever more unfathomable the older they become. He developed an art—"initiated" is a better term because he had no forerunners—whose true essence can be understood today only approximately. I cannot bring up something like this superficially, or I will be like one of these pseudo-historians. The newness in Bach's art can only be grasped if it is compared to the Netherlanders on one side and to Handel on the other. This will show that the secret contrapuntal art of the Netherlanders involved laws of contrapuntal relationship among *seven* notes. Bach was the first and only one to revive their secret laws and also to extend them to all *twelve* notes. The Netherlanders were so skilled at handling the relations among the seven notes of a scale that they were able to create shapes by unprecedented spatial transformations and displacements. But they used the remaining five tones outside of the scale only occasionally, dealing essentially with no more than seven. Bach clearly understood how to work with all twelve, despite the difficulty posed by inequality of temperament.

I cannot go further here with this issue, only to note that Handel made no similar accomplishment. Further, let me note that this is not the only aspect of the unprecedented newness of Bach's art, for such a godsend—something new, truly new—rarely arrives in isolation. It is plain that Bach wrote upper voices—without any degradation in the content of the subsidiary ones—whose formal characteristics leave far behind the art of Telemann, Keyser, or even his son Philipp Emanuel, who called Bach outmoded! So far as I know, it has not been observed that Bach was the first to use a principle that was not fully expounded upon until Mozart, specifically, the principle of *development through variation*.

This is the principle that allowed for the real origins of the classical style, and it is at the core of the newness of [Bach's] art. The reduction in importance of subsidiary lines was not the central issue—this was only one of the means by which the laws of comprehensibility were accommodated.

While in work after work Bach created a new art, his contemporaries could only ignore it and also its newness, as they attempted to make up another new art. We know that nearly a hundred years later, their new music led to the epoch of Haydn, Mozart, and Beethoven, when every great master carried around a secret wish for the contrapuntal art. But this had so completely disappeared from the horizon that all they could achieve in this manner of expression remained far behind their other creations.

But what remains of the works of those who first raised the battle cry of new music? What lives on in the music of a Telemann, a Keyser, a Philipp Emanuel Bach, or even a Handel, despite a renaissance which for a few years attempted to resuscitate him? Still, it cannot be denied that they initiated the beginning of a period of new music. This is proved by the existence of the Viennese classical school.

Two things more can be said: the first is that the new music of Bach's contemporaries was not *so* new in content, idea, or technique because Bach had already done this all. It was instead only a new cycle in the evolution of music, another battle over the appropriate use of the total musical space, as I have already observed and explained to you. It also involved—now I may use this term—a new or at least temporarily new *style*, that is, a different way of presenting musical ideas.

The second is that Bach's contemporaries were just as mistaken when they called his music outmoded as people are now when they use the same term. Now two hundred years later the situation is quite reversed—what was new is outmoded, and Bach is simply *timeless*.

But let's look more closely at the notion of outmoded music. We can find many examples of outmodedness in everyday life. If a man or woman has long hair, this is considered outmoded, although the next fashion may well return to it. Showing emotion is also outmoded, although plenty of emotion is expended in the battle against it. Since we have electric lights, candlelight is obviously outmoded, but wealthy Americans, even those who do not own castles in which electric wiring could not be installed without destroying important artworks on the walls and ceilings, even these wealthy Americans imitate the old aristocratic tradition of giving their parties by candlelight. And there are other modern people who imitate things simply because they have been imitated before.

So what does it mean to be outmoded? Long hair became so when women entered the professional world. Emotion, when the lack of time created by our busy schedules made it imperative to speak and listen to important matters in the most concise way, without any pathos or embellishment. Candlelight, when it became pointless and senseless to create extra work for oneself or for one's servants. What these phenomena have in common is a changed lifestyle—they make one's former activities counterproductive.

Can the same be said of music? What new lifestyle can make romantic music counterproductive? Have our lives lost all touch with romanticism? Are we more enthusiastic about being run over by our automobiles than the Romans were by their chariots? Do we no longer want to travel to the North Pole, which may have for us little more than an abstract, scientific interest? Do we no longer search for oil? Do we no longer fly over oceans, even though we ought to know that it will be worthwhile only when the trip by airship compared to modern air travel has come to be like the sail boat as compared to the modern ship? Even if there is no longer romanticism in any of these, then isn't it still found in our fascination with detective stories? The Indian stories of my youth were no more romantic—only the names are now changed!

But even if there is no more romanticism in modern life, art in all instances is still different from life. In life we need not be involved, but in art our involvement is everything. Art cannot exist without our help. It assumes that we will surrender ourselves to and accept its fiction, which is not life itself but only one of its symbols. *Symbol*—an image of the senses and their essence. Not this essence itself, only an image! Is this not romanticism? If I am not mistaken—it is difficult amid the rapid changes in modern philosophy to stay up-to-date—if I am not mistaken, this battle against romanticism has today long been recognized as irrelevant. But I can't guarantee this.

It is superfluous for someone to describe a house by saying that it has walls, windows, doors, roof, and the like. If one did something similar in an artwork, we could rightly say that it was outmoded. Well-known things that are cut and dried do not need to be repeated if they don't reveal new perspectives. No new or fanciful manner of presentation will change this. Only what has not yet been said is worth saying!

So we can't go further. Maybe a younger and more successful composer could help us. Here is one who has written that complex music is outmoded. Young people today no longer want to hear music "that they cannot understand."[3] I don't think that this is true, because young people still fly over oceans, travel to the North Pole, and give their lives for something as ephemeral as a speed record. Then again there are a number of young people who say, conversely, "Am I stupid when I understand the mindless drivel that is being played, even before it is finished?" Or, "This is complex music, and I *want* to learn to understand it!" I conclude from the existence of ocean pilots, North Pole explorers, and breakers of world records that young people are more readily inspired by the difficult, the dangerous, the mysterious, the deep, the recondite, the complex of thought than they are by things that they understand on first contact.

The great minds—those who pose such riddles to youth—never become outmoded. But let's not deceive ourselves—all of these purveyors of the new who write so stupidly that even the dumbest can understand them, even they do not become outmoded. They have always been among us and they always will. They are the eternal bystanders to the art of all ages, the makers of kitsch. In every era intelligent people are insulted when they are told things that any idiot can understand. I can find no characteristic of new music that can be judged outmoded other than its saying something that has already been said. I won't act as though I am unaware of the arguments directed at. . . . Yes, is it time for me to remove my mask? I won't act at all as though I am defending a third party when I polemicize against the aestheticians of the New Music.

I am well aware of most of the criticisms directed against my own outmoded music and that of others. For example, against its so-called chromaticism. People nowadays want to go back to composition with seven notes. I don't know that any particular achievement has come from this wish; I have already dealt with this question in my *Harmonielehre*. But why such a throwback should be seen as something new is just as unclear to me as why and for what purpose people want to "loosen" harmony; it's not clear to me, since I have pointed out new paths for the use of twelve tones, paths on which some day all will have to travel, even those who lie on their lazy hides and pour New Music into flimsy old wineskins. For *l'art pour l'art*, even if the art is outmoded!

New Music is said to be for everyone! It is music for "use" [*Gebrauchsmusik*]! But it is clear that it has no use. It is neither for the few or for the many—it is for no one. And, anyway, what use would it have? For some time now, such pieces have had success. This has created the impression with some people that such New Music gives pleasure. But, as I have said, it has long been clear that this "people's music" is the purest *l'art pour l'art*, even in the impure purpose for which it was composed, which no one recognized. Since no one really likes it, everyone can content himself with applauding it, but being careful not to express a desire to hear such a light piece a second time. In these circumstances many of the business-minded music-for-use proponents, for lack of use, became idealistic artists. Even more idealistic than the outmoded ones, who at least could hope for success after their deaths. These unwilling idealists can only expect a single use, just like wrapping paper. They compose without hope or desire for the future.

I depart only slightly from my subject when I turn from outmoded music to speak now about the practitioners of New Music. In the twelve years since their appearance [1918], they have written much music that now even they themselves consider outmoded. From the traits of their current works, not yet officially outmoded, a portrait can easily be drawn of their music which twelve years earlier was destined to be outmoded. Plainly, these traits are very distinctive, so much so that even the stupidest bloke—especially such a one—can immediately distinguish outmoded from New Music. This is because all of these traits make up what is called the *style* of a work. Anyone—regardless of how unartistic, how unconcerned about the work of creative people, regardless of what might occupy his thoughts or what desires fill his emotional life—will still aptly remark that a particular building is "Renaissance" in style, or that a room is "Biedermeier," or "modern." If it is a positive achievement that our elementary schools should inculcate such an ability, then they have done their job! At last a real accomplishment!

Since I have nothing to hide, I will tell you that I come from a time when there were still amateurs in music who were able to retain a melody—even one by Brahms—after only one hearing. This was a time when musicians could listen once to a canon and know how many voices it had, about its structure, plan, and other such facts; they could hear a variations piece, for example, and not have a moment's doubt about what was going on in it, and so forth. But I don't recall our talking much then about style, so this must be a more recent achievement.

Certainly there are some historians who are also good musicians. But in my youth they would not have been able to converse with us musicians if they had not been able—after hearing a work even once—to discuss, for example, why a six-four chord in a certain place was not pleasing. Maybe they were good at mimicry, a different type of mimicry from that of today. I dimly recall that some of their discussions, here and there, were embarrassingly suspicious. For them the main thing was that the six-four chord be present, whether or not it was used correctly, because otherwise they would have thought that history was at an end. Today mimicry has won out.

Earlier, a frog hid under a leaf; today, the leaf tries to change places with the frog. We musicians of yesterday recognized that a piece was classical when we heard the second violin play a filler part, something that the younger generation of German composers could no longer accept. These distinctions seemed to us then as large as they now are small. Woe to the frog who has never noticed this. Since frogs are such mimics, it is fitting that they now offer their protection to the leaves. To me it seems that they are asking the impossible of one another.

If the hand of every true expert has a single unmistakable characteristic, such that everything that it produces bears evidence of it, then it is probably unavoidable that this characteristic will attract more attention than the object to which it is attached. Still, we have a specific object, which a specific expert has produced in a specific way; the expert's hand, with all of its individuality, was set in motion only to produce this object. So a leaf is still a leaf and a frog is still a frog, even if they both try to act like the other.

And so it is with style. It is the sum of characteristics conferred by a creator upon an object. And what is created, the thing that comes under scrutiny, is the object. We could demand that a plum tree bear glass plums, pears, or felt hats, but I think that even the lower types of plum trees will refuse. A plum tree can only bear what corresponds to its nature, as idiosyncratic as this may be. Of all growing things it is only the Christmas tree that bears fruit different from its own; among animals only the Easter bunny, which not only lays eggs but painted ones at that. But we can't expect marvels like this from other functioning organisms. Whoever can do tricks like this can do nothing more, nothing that matters. Style is no particular costume, not a "fancy dress," not something to cover nakedness. Like nakedness itself, it can't be taken off. Whoever trades an object for a style gets nothing in return. Whoever imitates this nothing produces nothing. And whoever takes possession of this nothing gets what he deserves, for the style is worth no more than the object.

What we should really think about style is self-evident. Everything organic has style, that is, a number of internal and external characteristics that pertain only to it. These properties come both from the creator and the thing itself. Something inorganic may well also have these distinctive characteristics, but if they do not equal the mathematical product of the characteristics of a particular creator times the characteristics of the thing itself, then it is all senseless. It is just as senseless to choose the style that something created is to have in advance. If a person is a *true individual*, able to imagine an object in advance and in detail, knowledgeable of the powers of his own hand at the stage of purely imaginative contemplation, even before using it to shape his materials, then he can precisely indicate how the object will look upon completion. He is always tied to the object, and he knows that it has its own characteristics. But he would no more start by choosing a style than would the plum tree. They both leave this to human frogs, who inflate themselves to be as big as an ox or diminish themselves to the size of a leaf. It is not too sad when a frog quakes in fear for not being a leaf, but it is tragic when a leaf is afraid of being a leaf. The creative individual concerns himself little with the characteristic features, the trivialities, that will someday be used to describe his style. He is unconcerned that everything necessary must be done just right, that a certain outward form is observed. Instead, he is continually and exclusively occupied with his object, his idea.

So now I have arrived at that place where my enemies like to put me—with the *idea.* For I am indeed one who constructs—I admit it freely. I admit that I construct while others "shake themes out of their sleeves." I ponder and reconsider, while "true geniuses" don't have to do this or other such things. Before going further let me say that I am convinced that anyone who has a brain probably uses it. [Johann] Nestroy said, "Money alone doesn't bring happiness. You have to have it first!" But it is different with a brain. It is not entirely a disgrace to conceal one's brain, for it is modest not to flaunt it. But if others are not modest and mock those fortunate enough to have a brain, choosing to hide it, then forbearance can quickly come to an end. But those who have a brain and try to hide it will not be able do so. It will be plainly visible on them, like a decoration, or it will show up like a signature on their works or letters. Think of Beethoven, who received a letter from his brother Johann signed "landowner." He answered with a letter signed "brain owner." Was it an accident that Beethoven wrote "brain owner"? After all, he possessed many other distinctions—great pianism, inspiration, temperament, humor; he could write melodies and he had many other claims to fame, such as his character, his imagination, his iron will, etc. Why should he have called himself "brain owner"? Why not sleeve owner, since he certainly could write as many melodies as those who shook their sleeves. Here is what I think. A brain owner should not be discouraged. It doesn't matter whether one is a master sent straight from heaven, with all his wits; it doesn't matter whether one pretends to be stupid, whether he is or not. God can make anyone in his sleep into a master, but I think He will do this only when we have done our best, when we have used our brain and slaved away to the best of our abilities.

I am very happy if I have as much brain as I am accused of. I am not frightened that such accusations come even from people with whom I deal (I have after all no family tomb where I can find people with whom I would rather deal). I must directly endure many indirect blows to the head, and not at first suspecting their ill intent, I recognize their maliciousness only in retrospect. I was once so unsuspecting that I showed a writer too much brain, without expecting to be repaid in kind. But, quite the opposite, he pleasantly related the famous story by [Gustav] Meyrink, in which a toad asked a centipede how he knew which of his hundred feet to use first. The question caused the centipede to think about it so much that it lost its instinct for walking. I found the story amusing, because I could more consciously make a hundred feet move than this writer could two. An "instinctive" person like him can only use his legs for standing, because otherwise he would have to think how to get them started when they didn't move by themselves, which he would not be able to do. A person like this writes in just the same way; his writings leave just such an impression. If he climbs out of the bed of his instincts accidentally with his left foot first and unwittingly splashes in the stream of a conscious idea, then his right foot will splash in behind, and the fool won't even realize that he doesn't have another foot to prevent his going under, but only his arm or even his nose to sense which place he would have to get to. Or it would be left to his mouth to open wide and silently suppress a call for help. Because otherwise a soul might be in danger of being saved.

Ideas can only be respected by him who has his own, and respect can be paid only by him who deserves it. I once wrote, "An idea can wait because it is timeless."

I am surprised that readers of this sentence made just as little fuss about it as did its author. But I don't want to tiptoe around it, so an explanation must be given. I am always amazed at pliers. I find expressed in them a wonderful idea that I always contemplate with pleasure. If I press on the right handle, the top left piece will move inward. If I press on the left handle, then the top right will press against the left. They squeeze together because both arms cross and the hinge point is fixed. A small tool like this exerts a force that multiplies what I put into it, and it can do amazing things, even crushing metal. I don't know how old pliers are. But the significance of their realization of an idea could only be appreciated by a person who had gone back before their discovery. In any event the idea behind them remains highly admirable. Certainly there are machines today that can do what pliers do. Perhaps in the future we won't have to hammer nails in or pull them out, and pliers may become dispensable. But the idea behind them will live on, just as amazing as on the day the tool was invented.

This idea can wait because—like other ideas—it is timeless. An idea cannot die! I am surprised that all composers have not found such a simple way to protect their music from becoming outdated. Is there anything simpler? All it takes is one or two genuine ideas and it can't happen! But a few dangers are still lurking, which can indeed pose a threat. Perhaps no one will notice that you have strewn ideas before them. Or everyone will notice but no one will pay attention. Or it will be thrown in your teeth as a reproof. Or, finally, everyone will think that you are outmoded, without noting, understanding, or testing your ideas. You will have to stand there, not knowing whether this has happened because you are outmoded in your ability truly to think, or whether the grand gestures with which you are dismissed apply only to your *ideas* that are deemed outmoded. All the same, you know that they have not understood a single note that you have written.

Let me come now to my conclusion. New music is the music of new musical ideas. New ideas are revealed in new external guises. But music that is truly new can never become outmoded. On the other hand it is certainly possible that the listener can become dulled to certain effects that it produces, but I cannot pull out nails that haven't been driven in. It is possible that the listener's pattern of thought will change so that he will not be moved by a particular thought complex. There are certainly epochs in which mankind believes that it has evolved beyond what was earlier thought. But in no way can this harm ideas, for once they are conceived they continue to exist.

An idea cannot be assailed even if it is refuted. I have heard (I don't know if it's true and I don't really know much about it) that modern chess masters have already refuted many of the earlier chess strategies that were previously considered immortal. This does not diminish the value of these ideas; one can no more refute a valuable idea than one can say that America did not exist before its discovery. For the refutation itself to have value, there must have been something to refute, just as there must be something to discover for discovery to take place.

The presentation of an idea—like an immortal chess strategy—can shed light. Its refutation takes away only one instance of presentation and is itself validated by the failed insight that it once illuminated. But the presentation of a new style, prior to that of a new idea, is a comical misdeed that leads only to the sort of leapfrog that we see continually in today's music. To try to compose in the style of older composers is a venture best undertaken by composers who are the least familiar with the style. Their only hope for success is to make their listeners think that someone somewhere composed music like that.

Incidentally, it is just as senseless and futile to try to bring extramusical intentions into music. No chess master can use a strategy that is popular or generally understood, because his opponent will also understand it and it won't lead to a win. No mathematician can discover new mathematics understood by those who lack the necessary special training. I am glad that I understand Einstein just as poorly as I do Kant, for this leads me to believe that they are on to something. I can't be accused in this of a false modesty because I am very proud to know when I *don't* understand something. As it is I know enough about things that I understand. Accordingly, higher forms of art music cannot be understood by everyone (this does not refer to the vernacular art of a Johann Strauss, a Nestroy, or a Raimund). In mathematics there are things—lower levels—that everyone can indeed understand. So too there is music whose ideas and expression correspond to thoughts that are generally graspable and presentable, thoughts that everyone can understand. This is music with which others need not be involved. But it cannot be composed by those who presume to descend to the lower level without everyone knowing that they were once higher up.

Whoever thinks can only have one wish—to do his duty. Every other claim pressing in on him can only be irksome. Whoever thinks cannot influence its results by circumstances lying outside of the requirements of the thought itself. Two times two is four, regardless of whether we like it or not. One thinks for the sake of thought. Similarly, art can only be made for its own sake. An idea is born; it must be shaped, formed, and carried to its conclusion. For there is only *l'art pour l'art*, art for its own sake!

Notes

[Text: Schoenberg, "Neue und veraltete Musik, oder Stil und Gedanke," typescript from the Arnold Schoenberg Institute, Vienna. Translated by Bryan R. Simms. Used by permission of Lawrence Schoenberg.]

[1. Cited in Leonard Stein, "Schoenberg and 'Kleine Modernsky'," in *Confronting Stravinsky: Man, Musician, and Modernist*, ed. Jann Pasler (Berkeley: University of California Press, 1986): 324.]

[2. Erich Steinhard, "Tonale, atonale und antiquierte Musik: Notizen zum Musikfest in Venedig," *Der Auftakt* 5 (1925): 262.]

[3. Schoenberg may be referring to Kurt Weill. See essay no. 8.]

1 1

RALPH VAUGHAN WILLIAMS

(1872–1958)

The question that Ralph Vaughan Williams poses in the title of this essay, "Should Music Be National?" touched upon an explosive issue in European and American music between the world wars. To most observers nationalistic music represented a rebellion against both the German-led modernism of the late romantic period and the French-inspired International Neoclassical Style of the 1920s. The music coming from these two movements seemed to aspire to universality and timelessness and to suppress any overt sense of the place from which music stemmed. In the 1930s the terms nationalism and internationalism had also acquired a volatile political resonance in which the nationalists were often connected with antimodern artistic positions and right-wing and sometimes anti-Semitic political causes.

Despite these far-reaching implications and potential for misunderstanding, Vaughan Williams forcefully argues for the necessity of nationalism in music. All great music, he says, has grown from and speaks to the culture from which its composer arose. Only music that is nationalistic in this sense can hope for subsequent international esteem or permanence. All important music thus grows from the folk of a region or nation just as does the simplest folk song— one is different from the other only in proportion. Art exists to communicate broadly to people at the time that it is created; it cannot be futuristic or elitist, nor can it exist for its own sake in the spirit of *l'art pour l'art*.

Plainly, Vaughan Williams argues against the older romantic, Germanized viewpoint of such composers as Schoenberg or Busoni. He speaks instead for English folkloristic composers of his own period, including Gustav Holst, Percy Grainger, and Arnold Bax, and more broadly, for the regionalist-populist branch of interwar neoclassicism. The sentiments concerning American music expressed by Aaron Copland in *Music and Imagination* (see essay no. 23) will be found close to those of Vaughan Williams.

Ralph Vaughan Williams was one of the most prolific and skilled essayists on music of the twentieth century. His articles include technical and pedagogical writings, studies of folklore, reminiscences of other English musicians, and a large number of writings in which he reasserts his regionalist viewpoint about music. The essay "Should Music Be National?" originated in 1932 as the first of the Mary Flexner Lectures on the Humanities at Bryn Mawr College, and it contains an overview of themes to which he returned in more detail in subsequent lectures.

Vaughan Williams's Writings: A Selective Bibliography

National Music and Other Essays. Second edition. Oxford and New York: Oxford University Press, 1987. Contains the texts of the Bryn Mawr lectures from 1932, also "The Making of Music" (based on lectures at Cornell University in 1954), and other writings.

Heirs and Rebels: Letters Written to Each Other and Occasional Writings on Music by Ralph Vaughan Williams and Gustav Holst. Edited by Ursula Vaughan Williams and Imogen Holst. London: Oxford University Press, 1959.

—⟋ɯ⟍—

SHOULD MUSIC BE NATIONAL?
(1932)

Whistler used to say that it was as ridiculous to talk about national art as national chemistry. In saying this he failed to see the difference between art and science.

Science is the pure pursuit of knowledge and thus knows no boundaries. Art, and especially the art of music, uses knowledge as a means to the evocation of personal experience in terms which will be intelligible to and command the sympathy of others. These others must clearly be primarily those who by race, tradition, and cultural experience are the nearest to him; in fact those of his own nation, or other kind of homogeneous community. In the sister arts of painting and poetry this factor of nationality is more obvious, due in poetry to the Tower of Babel and in painting to the fact that the painter naturally tends to build his visual imagination on what he normally sees around him. But unfortunately for the art of music some misguided thinker, probably first cousin to the man who invented the unfortunate phrase "a good European," has described music as "the universal language." It is not even true that music has a universal vocabulary, but even if it were so it is the use of the vocabulary that counts and no one supposes that French and English are the same language because they happen to use twenty-five out of twenty-six of the letters of their alphabet in common. In the same way, in spite of the fact that they have a musical alphabet in common, nobody could mistake Wagner for Verdi or Debussy for Richard Strauss. And similarly, in spite of wide divergencies of personal style, there is a common factor in the music say of Schumann and Weber.

And this common factor is nationality. As Hubert Parry said in his inaugural address to the Folk-Song Society of England, "True Style comes not from the individual but from the products of crowds of fellow-workers who sift and try and try again till they have found the thing that suits their native taste. . . . Style is ultimately national."

I am speaking, for the moment, not of the appeal of a work of art, but of its origin. Some music may appeal only in its immediate surroundings; some may be national in its influence and some may transcend these bounds and be world-wide in its acceptance. But we may be quite sure that the composer who tries to be cosmopolitan from the outset will fail, not only with the world at large, but with his own people as well. Was anyone ever more local, or even parochial, than Shakespeare? Even when he follows the fashion and gives his characters Italian names they betray their origin at once by their language and their sentiments.

Possibly you may think this an unfair example, because a poet has not the common vocabulary of the musician, so let me take another example.

One of the three great composers of the world (personally I believe the greatest) was John Sebastian Bach. Here, you may say, is the universal musician if ever there was one; yet no one could be more local, in his origin, his life work, and his fame for nearly a hundred years after his death, than Bach. He was to outward appearance no more than one of a fraternity of town organists and "town pipers" whose business it was to provide the necessary music for the great occasions in church and city. He never left his native country, seldom even his own city of Leipzig. "World Movements" in art were then unheard of; moreover, it was the tradition of his own country which inspired him. True, he studied eagerly all the music of foreign composers that came his way in order to improve his craft. But is not the work of Bach built up on two great foundations, the organ music of his Teutonic predecessors and the popular hymn tunes of his own people? Who has heard nowadays of the cosmopolitan hero [Louis] Marchand, except as being the man who ran away from the court of Dresden to avoid comparison with the local organist Bach?

In what I have up to now said I shall perhaps not have been clear unless I dispose at once of two fallacies. The first of these is that the artist invents for himself alone. No man lives or moves or could do so, even if he wanted to, for himself alone. The actual process of artistic invention, whether it be by voice, verse, or brush, presupposes an audience; someone to hear, read, or see. Of course the sincere artist cannot deliberately compose what he dislikes. But artistic inspiration is like Dryden's angel which must be brought down from heaven to earth. A work of art is like a theophany which takes different forms to different beholders. In other words, a composer wishes to make himself intelligible. This surely is the prime motive of the act of artistic invention, and to be intelligible he must clothe his inspiration in such forms as the circumstances of time, place, and subject dictate.

This should come unselfconsciously to the artist, but if he consciously tries to express himself in a way which is contrary to his surroundings, and therefore to his own nature, he is evidently being, though perhaps he does not know it, insincere. It is surely as bad to be self-consciously cosmopolitan as self-consciously national.

The other fallacy is that the genius springs from nowhere, defies all rules, acknowledges no musical ancestry, and is beholden to no tradition. The first thing we have to realize is that the great men of music close periods; they do not inaugurate them. The pioneer work, the finding of new paths, is left to the smaller men. We can trace the musical genealogy of Beethoven, starting right back from Philipp Emanuel Bach, through Haydn and Mozart, with even such smaller fry as Cimarosa and Cherubini to lay the foundations of the edifice. Is not the mighty river of Wagner but a confluence of the smaller streams, Weber, Marschner, and Liszt?

I would define genius as the right man in the right place at the right time. We know, of course, too many instances of the time being ripe and the place being vacant and no man to fill it. But we shall never know of the numbers of "mute and inglorious Miltons" who failed because the place and time were not ready for them.

Was not Purcell a genius born before his time? Was not [Sir Arthur] Sullivan a jewel in the wrong setting?

I read the other day in a notice by a responsible music critic that "it only takes one man to write a symphony." Surely this is an entire misconception. A great work of art can only be born under the right surroundings and in the right atmosphere. Bach himself, if I may again quote him as an example, was only able to produce his fugues, his Passions, his cantatas, because there had preceded him generations of smaller composers, specimens of the despised class of "local musicians" who had no other ambition than to provide worthily and with dignity the music required of them: craftsmen perhaps rather than conscious artists. Thus there spread among the quiet and unambitious people of northern Germany a habit, so to speak, of music, the desire to make it part of their daily life, and it was into this atmosphere that John Sebastian Bach was born.

The ideal thing, of course, would be for the whole community to take to music as it takes to language from its youth up, naturally, without conscious thought or specialized training; so that, just as the necessity for expressing our material wants leads us when quite young to perfect our technique of speaking, so our spiritual wants should lead us to perfect our technique of emotional expression and above all that of music. But this is an age of specialization and delegation. We employ specialists to do more and more for us instead of doing it ourselves. We even get other people to play our games for us and look on shivering at a football match, instead of getting out of it for ourselves the healthy exercise and excitement which should surely be its only object.

Specialization may be all very well in purely material things. For example, we cannot make good cigars in England and it is quite right therefore that we should leave the production of that luxury to others and occupy ourselves in making something which our circumstances and climate permit of. The most rabid chauvinist has never suggested that Englishmen should be forced to smoke impossible cigars merely because they are made at home. We say quite rightly that those who want that luxury and can afford it must get it from abroad.

Now there are some people who apply this "cigar" theory to the arts and especially to music; to music especially, because music is not one of the "naturally protected" industries like the sister arts of painting and poetry. The "cigar" theory of music is then this—I am speaking of course of my own country England, but I believe it exists equally virulently in yours: that music is not an industry which flourishes naturally in our climate; that, therefore, those who want it and can afford it must hire it from abroad. This idea has been prevalent among us for generations. It began in England, I think, in the early eighteenth century when the political power got into the hands of the entirely uncultured landed gentry and the practice of art was considered unworthy of a gentleman, from which it followed that you had to hire a "damned foreigner" to do it for you if you wanted it, from which in its turn followed the corollary that the type of music which the foreigner brought with him was the only type worth having and that the very different type of music which was being made at home must necessarily be wrong. These ideas were fostered by the fact that we had a foreign court at St. James's who apparently did not share the English snobbery about homemade art and so brought the music made in their own homes to England with them. So, the official music, whether it took the form of Mr. Handel to compose an oratorio, or an oboe player in a regimental band, was imported from Germany. This snobbery is equally virulent to this day. The musician indeed is not despised, but it is equally felt that music cannot be something which is native to us and when imported from abroad it must of necessity be better.

Let me take an analogy from architecture. When a stranger arrives in New York he finds imitations of Florentine palaces, replicas of Gothic cathedrals, suggestions of Greek temples, buildings put up before America began to realize that she had an artistic consciousness of her own.

All these things the visitor dismisses without interest and turns to her railway stations, her offices and shops; buildings dictated by the necessity of the case, a truly national style of architecture evolved from national surroundings. Should it not be the same with music?

As long as a country is content to take its music passively there can be no really artistic vitality in the nation. I can only speak from the experience of my own country. In England we are too apt to think of music in terms of the cosmopolitan celebrities of the Queen's Hall and Covent Garden Opera. These are, so to speak, the crest of the wave, but behind that crest must be the driving force which makes the body of the wave. It is below the surface that we must look for the power which occasionally throws up a Schnabel, a Sibelius, or a Toscanini. What makes me hope for the musical future of any country is not the distinguished names which appear on the front page of the newspapers, but the music that is going on at home, in the schools, and in the local choral societies.

Can we expect garden flowers to grow in soil so barren that the wildflowers cannot exist there? Perhaps one day the supply of international artists will fail us and we shall turn in vain to our own country to supply their places. Will there be any source to supply it from? You remember the story of the *nouveau riche* who bought a plot of land and built a stately home on it, but he found that no amount of money could provide him straightaway with the spreading cedars and immemorial elms and velvet lawns which should be the accompaniment of such a home. Such things can only grow in a soil prepared by years of humble toil.

Hubert Parry in his book, *The Evolution of the Art of Music*, has shown how music like everything else in the world is subject to the laws of evolution, that there is no difference in kind but only in degree between Beethoven and the humblest singer of a folk song. The principles of artistic beauty, of the relationships of design and expression, are neither trade secrets nor esoteric mysteries revealed to the few; indeed if these principles are to have any meaning to us they must be founded on what is natural to the human being. Perfection of form is equally possible in the most primitive music and in the most elaborate.

The principles which govern the composition of music are, we find, not arbitrary rules, nor as some people apparently think, barriers put up by mediocre practitioners to prevent the young genius from entering the academic grove; they are not the tricks of the trade or even the mysteries of the craft, they are founded on the very nature of human beings. Take, for example, the principle of repetition as a factor of design: either the cumulative effect of mere reiteration, such as we get in the Trio of the Scherzo of Beethoven's Ninth Symphony, or in a cruder form in Ravel's *Bolero*; or the constant repetition of a ground bass as in Bach's Organ Passacaglia or the Finale of Brahms's Fourth Symphony. Travelers tell us that the primitive savage as soon as he gets as far as inventing some little rhythmical or melodic pattern will repeat it endlessly. In all these cases we have illustrations of the fundamental principle of emphasis by repetition.

After a time the savage will get tired of his little musical phrase and will invent another and often this new phrase will be at a new pitch so as to bring into play as many new notes as possible. Why? Because his throat muscles and his perceptive faculties are wearied by the constant repetition.

Is not this exactly the principle of the second subject of the classical sonata, which is in a key which brings into play as many new sounds as possible? Then we have the principle of symmetry also found in primitive music when the singer, having got tired in turn with his new phrase, harks back to the old one.

And so I could go on showing you how Beethoven is but a later stage in the development of those principles which actuated the primitive Teuton when he desired to make himself artistically intelligible.

The greatest artist belongs inevitably to his country as much as the humblest singer in a remote village—they and all those who come between them are links in the same chain, manifestations on their different levels of the same desire for artistic expression, and, moreover, the same nature of artistic expression.

I am quite prepared for the objection that nationalism limits the scope of art, that what we want is the best, from wherever it comes. My objectors will probably quote Tennyson and tell me that "We needs must love the highest when we see it" and that we should educate the young to appreciate this mysterious "highest" from the beginning. Or perhaps they will tell me with Rossini that they know only two kinds of music, good and bad. So perhaps we had better digress here for a few moments and try to find out what good music is, and whether there is such a thing as absolute good music; or even if there is such an absolute good, whether it must not take different forms for different hearers. Myself, I doubt if there is this absolute standard of goodness. I think it will vary with the occasion on which it is performed, with the period at which it was composed and with the nationality of those that listen to it. Let us take examples of each of these—firstly, with regard to the occasion. The Venusberg music from *Tannhäuser* is good music when it comes at the right dramatic moment in the opera, but it is bad music when it is played on an organ in church. I am sorry to have to tell you that this is not an imaginary experience. A waltz of Johann Strauss is good music in its proper place as an accompaniment to dancing and festivity, but it would be bad music if it were interpolated in the middle of the St. *Matthew Passion*. And may we not even say that Bach's B Minor Mass would be bad music if it were played in a restaurant as an accompaniment to eating and drinking?

Secondly, does not the standard of goodness vary with time? What was good for the fifteenth century is not necessarily good for the twentieth. Surely each new generation requires something different to satisfy its different ideals. Of course there is some music that seems to defy the ravages of time and to speak a new message to each successive generation. But even the greatest music is not eternal. We can still appreciate Bach and Handel or even Palestrina, but Dufay and Dunstable have little more than a historical interest for us now. But they were great men in their day and perhaps the time will come when Bach, Handel, Beethoven, and Wagner will drop out and have no message left for us. Sometimes of course the clock goes round full circle and the twentieth century comprehends what had ceased to have any meaning for the nineteenth. This is the case with the modern revival of Bach after nearly one hundred and fifty years of neglect, or the modern appreciation of Elizabethan madrigals. There may be many composers who have something genuine to say to us for a short time and for that short time their music may surely be classed as good. We all know that when an idiom is new we cannot detect the difference between the really original mind and the mere imitator. But when the idiom passes into the realm of everyday commonplace then and then only we can tell the true from the false. For example, any student at a music school can now reproduce the tricks of Debussy's style, and therefore it is now, and only now, that we can discover whether Debussy had something genuine to say or whether when the secret of his style becomes common property the message of which that style was the vehicle will disappear.

Then there is the question of place. Is music that is good music for one country or one community necessarily good music for another? It is true that the great monuments of music, the *Missa Papae Marcelli*, or the *St. Matthew Passion*, or the Ninth Symphony, or *Die Meistersinger*, have a worldwide appeal, but first they must appeal to the people, and in the circumstances where they were created. It is because Palestrina and Verdi are essentially Italian and because Bach, Beethoven, and Wagner are essentially German that their message transcends their frontiers. And even so, the *St. Matthew Passion*, much as it is loved and admired in other countries, must mean much more to the German, who recognizes in it the consummation of all that he learnt from childhood in the great traditional chorales which are his special inheritance. Beethoven has a universal meaning, but to the German, who finds in it that same spirit exemplified in its more homely form in those *Volkslieder* which he learnt in his childhood, he must also have a specialized meaning.

Every composer cannot expect to have a worldwide message, but he may reasonably expect to have a special message for his own people and many young composers make the mistake of imagining they can be universal without at first having been local. Is it not reasonable to suppose that those who share our life, our history, our customs, our climate, even our food, should have some secret to impart to us which the foreign composer, though he be perhaps more imaginative, more powerful, more technically equipped, is not able to give us? This is the secret of the national composer, the secret to which he only has the key, which no foreigner can share with him and which he alone is able to tell to his fellow countrymen. But is he prepared with his secret? Must he not limit himself to a certain extent so as to give his message its full force? For after all it is the millstream forcing its way through narrow channels which gathers strength to turn the water wheel. As long as composers persist in serving up at second-hand the externals of the music of other nations, they must not be surprised if audiences prefer the real Brahms, the real Wagner, the real Debussy, or the real Stravinsky to their pale reflections.

What a composer has to do is to find out the real message he has to convey to the community and say it directly and without equivocation. I know there is a temptation each time a new star appears on the musical horizon to say, "What a fine fellow this is, let us try and do something like this at home," quite forgetting that the result will not sound at all the same when transplanted from its natural soil. It is all very well to catch at the prophet's robe, but the mantle of Elijah is apt, like all second-hand clothing, to prove the worst of misfits. How is the composer to find himself? How is he to stimulate his imagination in a way that will lead him to voicing himself and his fellows? I think that composers are much too fond of going to concerts—I am speaking now, of course, of the technically equipped composer. At the concert we hear the finished product. What the artist should be concerned with is the raw material. Have we not all about us forms of musical expression which we can take and purify and raise to the level of great art? Have we not all around us occasions crying out for music? Do not all our great pageants of human beings require music for their full expression? We must cultivate a sense of musical citizenship. Why should not the musician be the servant of the state and build national monuments like the painter, the writer, or the architect?

Come muse, migrate from Greece and Ionia,

Cross out please those immensely overpaid accounts,

That matter of Troy and Achilles' wrath, and Aeneas', Odysseus' wanderings,

Placard "removed" and "to let" on the rocks of your snowy Parnassus,

Repeat at Jerusalem, place the notice high on Jaffa's gate and on Mount Moriah,

The same on the walls of your German, French and Spanish castles, and Italian collections,

For know a better, fresher, busier sphere,

A wide untried domain awaits, demands you.

Art for art's sake has never flourished among the English-speaking nations. We are often called inartistic because our art is unconscious. Our drama and poetry have evolved by accident while we thought we were doing something else, and so it will be with our music. The composer must not shut himself up and think about art; he must live with his fellows and make his art an expression of the whole life of the community. If we seek for art we shall not find it. There are very few great composers, but there can be many sincere composers. There is nothing in the world worse than sham good music. There is no form of insincerity more subtle than that which is coupled with great earnestness of purpose and determination to do only the best and the highest, the unconscious insincerity which leads us to build up great designs which we cannot fill and to simulate emotions which we can only experience vicariously. But, you may say, are we to learn nothing from the great masters? Where are our models to come from? Of course we can learn everything from the great masters and one of the great things we can learn from them is their sureness of purpose. When we are sure of our purpose we can safely follow the advice of St. Paul "to prove all things and to hold to that which is good." But it is dangerous to go about "proving all things" until you have made up your mind what is good for you.

First, then, see your direction clear and then by all means go to Paris, or Berlin, or Peking if you like and study and learn everything that will help you to carry out that purpose.

We have in England today a certain number of composers who have achieved fame. In the older generation Elgar and Parry, among those of middle age Holst and Bax, and of the quite young Walton and Lambert. All these served their apprentice-ship at home. There are several others who thought that their own country was not good enough for them and went off in the early stages to become little Germans or Frenchmen. Their names I will not give to you because they are unknown even to their fellow countrymen.

I am told that when grape vines were first cultivated in California the vineyard masters used to try the experiment of importing plants from France or Italy and set-ting them in their own soil. The result was that the grapes acquired a peculiar indi-vidual flavor, so strong was the influence of the soil in which they were planted. I think I need hardly draw the moral of this, namely, that if the roots of your art are firmly planted in your own soil and that soil has anything individual to give you, you may still gain the whole world and not lose your own souls.

Notes

[Text: Vaughan Williams, "Should Music Be National?," in *National Music and Other Essays*, second edition (Oxford: Oxford University Press, 1987). Reprinted by permission of Oxford University Press.]

IGOR STRAVINSKY (1882–1971)

ROLAND-MANUEL (1891–1966)

Igor Stravinsky's *Poetics of Music* consists of the texts of six Charles Eliot Norton lectures given in French at Harvard University in 1939 and 1940. In the third lecture, "The Composition of Music," the composer addressed the issue of the creative process in music, which he explained squarely in the spirit of neoclassicism, the movement of which Stravinsky was the leader. The romantic notions of inspiration, high art, freedom, and pure imagination are played down in his explanation of creativity and replaced by Apollonian ideas of calculation, equilibrium, willpower, discovery, craftsmanship, and self-limitation. As if to underscore that his conception of the creative process was antiromantic, the composer makes a lengthy digression to criticize the music dramas of Wagner, which are, he says, the products of a debased culture, a "religion for those who have no religion." He also places a high value on tradition in new music, "a living force that animates and informs the present," he concludes. Thus in 1939 Stravinsky appears to have accepted the longstanding critics' interpretation of neoclassicism as essentially a "back to. . ." movement, although in his earlier writings he had expressed skepticism about this notion, finding the essence of his music much more in its objectivity and avoidance of emotiveness—a product, that is, of its own day.[1]

Poetics of Music was once thought to be an authoritative statement concerning neoclassicism, spoken by its leading figure. It is now known that these texts were ghostwritten by the musicologist and composer Roland-Manuel (the pen name of Roland-Alexis Manuel Lévy), a revelation that has considerably diminished their importance. Stravinsky provided Roland-Manuel with an outline of the content that he wished to cover in the lectures, and Roland-Manuel visited the composer in April 1939 at a clinic near Geneva, where Stravinsky was being treated for tuberculosis, to discuss them further. Roland-Manuel worked on the texts closely with Stravinsky's fellow Russian émigré Pierre Suvchintsky, who was the primary author of the fifth lecture—a scathing critique of music in the Soviet Union.

In addition to guidelines from and discussions with the composer, Roland-Manuel also availed himself of statements earlier attributed to Stravinsky. The opening of the third lecture, for example, is taken almost word for word from Stravinsky's remarks made during an interview on the French radio conducted by the Parisian critic Serge Moreux in 1938.[2] Roland-Manuel also drew from Stravinsky's *Chronicles of My Life*, perhaps unaware that this autobiography was itself ghostwritten by Stravinsky's friend Walter Nuvel. He also drew significantly on the recently published *Introduction à la poétique* by Paul Valéry, a work that he much admired, finding in it an aesthetic of artistic creativity that seemed appropriate to Stravinsky's music.

The issue of authenticity plagues all of Stravinsky's writings on music. His longer essays—*Chronicles of My Life* (1935–36), *Poetics of Music* (1939), and six volumes of conversations with his assistant Robert Craft (1958–69)—were ghostwritten, although they reflect his ideas to an extent. His shorter writings, even his interviews, are also suspect. After reading the text of an interview given by Stravinsky in New York in 1925, Arnold Schoenberg immediately saw the problems created by Stravinsky's failure to speak his own mind. Schoenberg wrote in the margin: "What is given here as utterances by Stravinsky one does not have to take too seriously because one can't. He himself is not so serious about it, otherwise he would put more weight on being quoted exactly as to what he meant to say. Most of it is nonsense which I did not expect of him, and it is difficult to distinguish what I do expect from him."[3]

Stravinsky's Writings: A Selective Bibiliography

Stravinsky, Igor. *An Autobiography*. New York: W. W. Norton, 1962. Translation of *Chroniques de ma vie* (1935–36).

———. *Poetics of Music in the Form of Six Lessons*. Translated by Arthur Knodel and Ingolf Dahl. Cambridge: Harvard University Press, 1947.

———. *Selected Correspondence*. Edited by Robert Craft. Three volumes. New York: Alfred A. Knopf, 1982–85.

Stravinsky, Igor, and Robert Craft. *Conversations with Igor Stravinsky*. Garden City: Doubleday, 1959. Reprinted, Berkeley: University of California Press, 1980.

———. *Dialogues and a Diary*. Garden City: Doubleday, 1968. Reprinted without Craft's diary as *Dialogues*, Berkeley: University of California Press, 1982.

———. *Expositions and Developments*. Garden City: Doubleday, 1962. Reprinted, Berkeley: University of California Press, 1981.

———. *Memories and Commentaries*. Garden City: Doubleday, 1960. Reprinted, Berkeley: University of California Press, 1981.

———. *Retrospectives and Conclusions*. New York: Alfred A. Knopf, 1969. Reprinted in *Themes and Conclusions*, Berkeley: University of California Press, 1982.

———. *Themes and Episodes*. New York: Alfred A. Knopf, 1966. Reprinted in *Themes and Conclusions*, Berkeley: University of California Press, 1982.

White, Eric Walter. *Stravinsky: The Composer and His Works*. Second edition. Berkeley and Los Angeles: University of California Press, 1979. Contains nine essays by Stravinsky in an appendix. Among these see especially "Some Ideas About My Octuor" (1924), "Avertissement" (1927), and "Interview avec Serge Moreux de *L'intransigeant* pour la Radiodiffusion, Paris" (1938, in French only).

—❦—

"THE COMPOSITION OF MUSIC" FROM *POETICS OF MUSIC*

("De la composition musicale" from *Poétique musicale*, 1939)

We are living at a time when the status of man is undergoing profound upheavals. Modern man is progressively losing his understanding of values and his sense of proportions. This failure to understand essential realities is extremely serious. It leads us infallibly to the violation of the fundamental laws of human equilibrium. In the domain of music, the consequences of this misunderstanding are these: on one hand there is a tendency to turn the mind away from what I shall call the higher mathematics of music in order to degrade music to servile employment and to vulgarize it by adapting it to the requirements of an elementary utilitarianism—as we shall soon see on examining Soviet music. On the other hand, because the mind itself is ailing, the music of our time, and particularly the music that calls itself and believes itself *pure*, carries within it the symptoms of a pathologic blemish and spreads the germs of a new original sin. The old original sin was chiefly a sin of knowledge; the new original sin, if I may speak in these terms, is first and foremost a sin of non-acknowledgment—a refusal to acknowledge the truth and the laws that proceed therefrom, laws that we have called fundamental. What then is this truth in the domain of music? And what are its repercussions on creative activity?

Let us not forget that it is written: "*Spiritus ubi vult spirat*" (St. John, 3:8). What we must retain in this proposition is above all the word *will*. The Spirit is thus endowed with the capacity of willing. The principle of speculative volition is a fact.

Now it is just this fact that is too often disputed. People question the direction that the wind of the spirit is taking, not the rightness of the artisan's work. In so doing, whatever may be your feelings about ontology or whatever your own philosophy and beliefs may be, you must admit that you are making an attack on the very freedom of the spirit—whether you begin this large word with a capital or not. If a believer in Christian philosophy, you would then also have to refuse to accept the idea of the Holy Spirit. If an agnostic or atheist, you would have to do nothing less than refuse to be a *free-thinker*. . .

It should be noted that there is never any dispute when the listener takes pleasure in the work he hears. The least informed of music-lovers readily clings to the periphery of a work; it pleases him for reasons that are most often entirely foreign to the essence of music. This pleasure is enough for him and calls for no justification. But if it happens that the music displeases him, our music-lover will ask you for an explanation of his discomfiture. He will demand that we explain something that is in its essence ineffable.

By its fruit we judge the tree. Judge the tree by its fruit then, and do not meddle with the roots. Function justifies an organ, no matter how strange the organ may appear in the eyes of those who are not accustomed to see it functioning. Snobbish circles are cluttered with persons who, like one of Montesquieu's characters, wonder how one can possibly be a Persian. They make me think unfailingly of the story of the peasant who, on seeing a dromedary in the zoo for the first time, examines it at length, shakes his head and, turning to leave, says, to the great delight of those present: "It isn't true."

It is through the unhampered play of its functions, then, that a work is revealed and justified. We are free to accept or reject this play, but no one has the right to question the fact of its existence. To judge, dispute, and criticize the principle of speculative volition which is at the origin of all creation is thus manifestly useless. In the pure state, music is free speculation. Artists of all epochs have unceasingly testified to this concept. For myself, I see no reason for not trying to do as they did. I myself having been created, I cannot help having the desire to create. What sets this desire in motion, and what can I do to make it productive?

The study of the creative process is an extremely delicate one. In truth, it is impossible to observe the inner workings of this process from the outside. It is futile to try to follow its successive phases in someone else's work. It is likewise very difficult to observe oneself. Yet it is only by enlisting the aid of introspection that I may have any chance at all of guiding you in this essentially fluctuating matter.

Most music-lovers believe that what sets the composer's creative imagination in motion is a certain emotive disturbance generally designated by the name of "inspiration."

I have no thought of denying to inspiration the outstanding role that has devolved upon it in the generative process we are studying; I simply maintain that inspiration is in no way a prescribed condition of the creative act, but rather a chronologically secondary manifestation.

Inspiration, art, artist—so many words, hazy at least, that keep us from seeing clearly in a field where everything is balance and calculation through which the breath of the speculative spirit blows. It is afterwards, and only afterwards, that the emotive disturbance which is at the root of inspiration may arise—an emotive disturbance about which people talk so indelicately by conferring upon it a meaning that is shocking to us and that compromises the term itself. Is it not clear that this emotion is merely a reaction on the part of the creator grappling with that unknown entity which is still only the object of his creating and which is to become a work of art? Step by step, link by link, it will be granted him to discover the work. It is this chain of discoveries, as well as each individual discovery, that gives rise to the emotion—an almost physiological reflex, like that of the appetite causing a flow of saliva—this emotion which invariably follows closely the phases of the creative process.

All creation presupposes at its origin a sort of appetite that is brought on by the foretaste of discovery. This foretaste of the creative act accompanies the intuitive grasp of an unknown entity already possessed but not yet intelligible, an entity that will not take definite shape except by the action of a constantly vigilant technique.

This appetite that is aroused in me at the mere thought of putting in order musical elements that have attracted my attention is not at all a fortuitous thing like inspiration, but as habitual and periodic, if not as constant, as a natural need.

This premonition of an obligation, this foretaste of a pleasure, this conditioned reflex, as a modern physiologist would say, shows clearly that the idea of discovery and hard work is what attracts me.

The very act of putting my work on paper, of, as we say, kneading the dough, is for me inseparable from the pleasure of creation. So far as I am concerned, I cannot separate the spiritual effort from the psychological and physical effort; they confront me on the same level and do not present a hierarchy.

The word *artist* which, as it is most generally understood today, bestows on its bearer the highest intellectual prestige, the privilege of being accepted as a pure mind—this pretentious term is in my view entirely incompatible with the role of the *homo faber*.

At this point it should be remembered that, whatever field of endeavor has fallen to our lot, if it is true that we are *intellectuals*, we are called upon not to cogitate, but to perform.

The philosopher Jacques Maritain reminds us that in the mighty structure of medieval civilization, the artist held only the rank of an artisan. "And his individualism was forbidden any sort of anarchic development, because a natural social discipline imposed certain limitative conditions upon him from without." It was the Renaissance that invented the artist, distinguished him from the artisan and began to exalt the former at the expense of the latter.

At the outset the name artist was given only to the Masters of Arts: philosophers, alchemists, magicians; but painters, sculptors, musicians, and poets had the right to be qualified only as artisans.

> Plying divers implements,
>
> The subtile artizan implants
>
> Life in marble, copper, bronze,

says the poet [Joachim] Du Bellay. And Montaigne enumerates in his *Essays* the "painters, poets and other artizans." And even in the seventeenth century, La Fontaine hails a painter with the name of *artisan* and draws a sharp rebuke from an ill-tempered critic who might have been the ancestor of most of our present-day critics.

The idea of work to be done is for me so closely bound up with the idea of the arranging of materials and of the pleasure that the actual doing of the work affords us that, should the impossible happen and my work suddenly be given to me in a perfectly completed form, I should be embarrassed and nonplused by it, as by a hoax.

We have a duty toward music, namely, to invent it. I recall once during the war when I was crossing the French border a gendarme asked me what my profession was. I told him quite naturally that I was an inventor of music. The gendarme, then verifying my passport, asked me why I was listed as a composer. I told him that the expression "inventor of music" seemed to me to fit my profession more exactly than the term applied to me in the documents authorizing me to cross borders.

Invention presupposes imagination but should not be confused with it. For the act of invention implies the necessity of a lucky find and of achieving full realization of this find. What we imagine does not necessarily take on a concrete form and may remain in a state of virtuality, whereas invention is not conceivable apart from actual working out.

Thus, what concerns us here is not imagination in itself, but rather creative imagination: the faculty that helps us to pass from the level of conception to the level of realization.

In the course of my labors I suddenly stumble upon something unexpected. This unexpected element strikes me. I make a note of it. At the proper time I put it to profitable use. This gift of chance must not be confused with that capriciousness of imagination commonly called fancy. Fancy implies a predetermined will to abandon oneself to caprice. The aforementioned assistance of the unexpected is something quite different. It is a collaboration immanently bound up with the inertia of the creative process and is heavy with possibilities which are unsolicited and come most appositely to temper the inevitable over-rigorousness of the naked will. And it is good that this is so.

"In everything that yields gracefully," G. K. Chesterton says somewhere, "there must be resistance. Bows are beautiful when they bend only because they seek to remain rigid. Rigidity that slightly yields, like Justice swayed by Pity, is all the beauty of earth. Everything seeks to grow straight, and happily, nothing succeeds in so growing. Try to grow straight and life will bend you."

The faculty of creating is never given to us all by itself. It always goes hand in hand with the gift of observation. And the true creator may be recognized by his ability always to find about him, in the commonest and humblest thing, items worthy of note. He does not have to concern himself with a beautiful landscape; he does not need to surround himself with rare and precious objects. He does not have to put forth in search of discoveries: they are always within his reach. He will have only to cast a glance about him. Familiar things, things that are everywhere, attract his attention. The least accident holds his interest and guides his operations. If his finger slips, he will notice it; on occasion, he may draw profit from something unforeseen that a momentary lapse reveals to him.

One does not contrive an accident: One observes it to draw inspiration therefrom. An accident is perhaps the only thing that really inspires us. A composer improvises aimlessly the way an animal grubs about. Both of them go grubbing about because they yield to a compulsion to seek things out. What urge of the composer is satisfied by this investigation? The rules with which, like a penitent, he is burdened? No: he is in quest of his pleasure. He seeks a satisfaction that he fully knows he will not find without first striving for it. One cannot force oneself to love; but love presupposes understanding, and in order to understand, one must exert oneself.

The same problem was posed in the Middle Ages by the theologians of pure love. To understand in order to love; to love in order to understand: We are here not going around in a vicious circle; we are rising spirally, providing that we have made an initial effort, have even just gone through a routine exercise.

Pascal has specifically this in mind when he writes that custom "controls the automaton, which in its turn unthinkingly controls the mind. For there must be no mistake," continues Pascal, "we are automatons just as much as we are minds . . . ."

So we grub about in expectation of our pleasure, guided by our scent, and suddenly we stumble against an unknown obstacle. It gives us a jolt, a shock, and this shock fecundates our creative power.

The faculty of observation and of making something out of what is observed belongs only to the person who at least possesses, in his particular field of endeavor, an acquired culture and an innate taste. A dealer, an art-lover who is the first to buy the canvases of an unknown painter who will be famous twenty-five years later under the name of Cézanne—doesn't such a person give us a clear example of this innate taste? What else guides him in his choice? A flair, an instinct from which this taste proceeds, a completely spontaneous faculty anterior to reflection.

As for culture, it is a sort of upbringing which, in the social sphere, confers polish upon education, sustains and rounds out academic instruction. This upbringing is just as important in the sphere of taste, and is essential to the creator who must ceaselessly refine his taste or run the risk of losing his perspicacity. Our mind, as well as our body, requires continual exercise. It atrophies if we do not cultivate it.

It is culture that brings out the full value of taste and gives it a chance to prove its worth simply by. its application. The artist imposes a culture upon himself and ends by imposing it upon others. That is how tradition becomes established.

Tradition is entirely different from habit, even from an excellent habit, for habit is by definition an unconscious acquisition and tends to become mechanical, whereas tradition results from a conscious and deliberate acceptance. A real tradition is not the relic of a past irretrievably gone; it is a living force that animates and informs the present. In this sense the paradox which banteringly maintains that everything which is not tradition is plagiarism, is true. . .

Far from implying the repetition of what has been, tradition presupposes the reality of what endures. It appears as an heirloom, a heritage that one receives on condition of making it bear fruit before passing it on to one's descendants.

Brahms was born sixty years after Beethoven. From the one to the other, and from every aspect, the distance is great; they do not dress the same way, but Brahms follows the tradition of Beethoven without borrowing one of his habiliments. For the borrowing of a method has nothing to do with observing a tradition. "A method is replaced: a tradition is carried forward in order to produce something new." Tradition thus assures the continuity of creation. The example that I have just cited does not constitute an exception, but is one proof out of a hundred of a constant law. This sense of tradition which is a natural need must not be confused with the desire which the composer feels to affirm the kinship he finds across the centuries with some master of the past.

My opera *Mavra* was born of a natural sympathy for the body of melodic tendencies, for the vocal style and conventional language which I came to admire more and more in the old Russo-Italian opera. This sympathy guided me quite naturally along the path of a tradition that seemed to be lost at the moment when the attention of musical circles was turned entirely toward the music drama, which represented no tradition at all from the historical point of view and which fulfilled no necessity at all from the musical point of view. The vogue of the music drama had a pathological origin. Alas, even the admirable music of *Pelléas et Mélisande,* so fresh in its modesty, was unable to get us into the open, in spite of so many characteristics with which it shook off the tyranny of the Wagnerian system.

The music of *Mavra* stays within the tradition of Glinka and Dargomyzhsky. I had not the slightest intention of reestablishing this tradition. I simply wanted in my turn to try my hand at the living form of the *opéra-bouffe* which was so well suited to the Pushkin tale which gave me my subject. *Mavra* is dedicated to the memory of composers, not one of whom, I am sure, would have recognized as valid such a manifestation of the tradition they created, because of the novelty of the language my music speaks one hundred years after its models flourished. But I wanted to renew the style of these dialogues-in-music whose voices had been reviled and drowned out by the clang and clatter of the music drama. So a hundred years had to pass before the freshness of the Russo-Italian tradition could again be appreciated, a tradition that continued to live apart from the main stream of the present, and in which circulated a salubrious air, well adapted to delivering us from the miasmic vapors of the music drama, the inflated arrogance of which could not conceal its vacuity.

I am not without motive in provoking a quarrel with the notorious "synthesis of the arts." I do not merely condemn it for its lack of tradition, its *nouveau riche* smugness. What makes its case much worse is the fact that the application of its theories has inflicted a terrible blow upon music itself. In every period of spiritual anarchy wherein man, having lost his feeling and taste for ontology, takes fright at himself and at his destiny, there always appears one of these gnosticisms which serve as a religion for those who no longer have a religion, just as in periods of international crises an army of soothsayers, fakirs, and clairvoyants monopolizes journalistic publicity. We can speak of these things all the more freely in view of the fact that the halcyon days of Wagnerism are past and that the distance which separates us from them permits us to set matters straight again. Sound minds, moreover, never believed in the paradise of the synthesis of the arts and have always recognized its enchantments at their true worth.

I have said that I never saw any necessity for music to adopt such a dramatic system. I shall add something more: I hold that this system, far from having raised the level of musical culture, has never ceased to undermine it and finally to debase it in the most paradoxical fashion. In the past one went to the opera for the diversion offered by facile musical works. Later on one returned to it in order to yawn at dramas in which music, arbitrarily paralyzed by constraints foreign to its own laws, could not help tiring out the most attentive audience in spite of the great talent displayed by Wagner.

So, from music shamelessly considered as a purely sensual delight, we passed without transition to the murky inanities of the "art-religion," with its heroic hardware, its arsenal of warrior-mysticism, and its vocabulary seasoned with an adulterated religiosity. So that as soon as music ceased to be scorned, it was only to find itself smothered under literary flowers. It succeeded in getting a hearing from the cultured public thanks only to a misunderstanding which tended to turn drama into a hodge-podge of symbols, music itself into an object of philosophical speculation. That is how the speculative spirit came to lose its course and how it came to betray music while ostensibly trying to serve it the better.

Music based upon the opposite principles has, unfortunately, not yet given proofs of its worth in our own period. It is curious to note that it was a musician who proclaimed himself a Wagnerian, the Frenchman Chabrier, who was able to maintain the sound tradition of dramatic art in those difficult times and who excelled in the French *opéra-comique* along with a few of his compatriots, at the very height of the Wagnerian vogue. Is not this the tradition that is continued in the sparkling group of masterpieces that are called *Le médecin malgré lui, La colombe, Philémon et Baucis* of Gounod; *Lakmé, Coppélia, Sylvia* of Léo Delibes; *Carmen* by Bizet; *Le roi malgré lui, L'étoile* of Chabrier; *La béarnaise, Véronique* of Messager—to which has just recently been added *La chartreuse de Parme* by young Henri Sauguet?

Think how subtle and clinging the poison of the music drama was to have insinuated itself even into the veins of the colossus Verdi.

How can we help regretting that this master of the traditional opera, at the end of a long life studded with so many authentic masterpieces, climaxed his career with *Falstaff,* which, if it is not Wagner's best work, is not Verdi's best opera either?

I know that I am going counter to the general opinion that sees Verdi's best work in the deterioration of the genius that gave us *Rigoletto, Il trovatore, Aida,* and *La traviata.* I know I am defending precisely what the elite of the recent past belittled in the works of this great composer. I regret having to say so; but I maintain that there is more substance and true invention in the aria "La donna è mobile," for example, in which this elite saw nothing but deplorable facility, than in the rhetoric and vociferations of the *Ring.*

Whether we admit it or not, the Wagnerian drama reveals continual bombast. Its brilliant improvisations inflate the symphony beyond all proportion and give it less real substance than the invention, at once modest and aristocratic, that blossoms forth on every page of Verdi.

At the beginning of my course I gave notice that I would continually come back to the necessity for order and discipline; and here I must weary you again by returning to the same theme.

Richard Wagner's music is more improvised than constructed, in the specific musical sense. Arias, ensembles, and their reciprocal relationships in the structure of an opera confer upon the whole work a coherence that is merely the external and visible manifestation of an internal and profound order.

The antagonism of Wagner and Verdi very neatly illustrates my thoughts on this subject.

While Verdi was being relegated to the organ-grinder's repertory, it was fashionable to hail in Wagner the typical revolutionary. Nothing is more significant than this relegation of order to the muse of the street corners at the moment when one found sublimity in the cult of disorder.

Wagner's work corresponds to a tendency that is not, properly speaking, a disorder, but one which tries to compensate for a lack of order. The principle of the end-less melody perfectly illustrates this tendency. It is the perpetual becoming of a music that never had any reason for starting, any more than it has any reason for ending. Endless melody thus appears as an insult to the dignity and to the very function of melody which, as we have said, is the musical intonation of a cadenced phrase. Under the influence of Wagner the laws that secure the life of song found themselves violated, and music lost its melodic smile. Perhaps his method of doing things answered a need; but this need was not compatible with the possibilities of musical art, for musical art is limited in its expression in a measure corresponding exactly to the limitations of the organ that perceives it. A mode of composition that does not assign itself limits becomes pure fantasy. The effects it produces may accidentally amuse, but are not capable of being repeated. I cannot conceive of a fantasy that is repeated, for it can be repeated only to its detriment.

Let us understand each other in regard to this word fantasy. We are not using the word in the sense in which it is connected with a definite musical form, but in the acceptation which presupposes an abandonment of oneself to the caprices of imagination. And this presupposes that the composer's will is voluntarily paralyzed. For imagination is not only the mother of caprice, but the servant and handmaiden of the creative will as well.

The creator's function is to sift the elements he receives from her, for human activity must impose limits upon itself. The more art is controlled, limited, worked over, the more it is free.

As for myself, I experience a sort of terror when, at the moment of setting to work and finding myself before the infinitude of possibilities that present themselves, I have the feeling that everything is permissible to me. If everything is permissible to me, the best and the worst; if nothing offers me any resistance, then any effort is inconceivable, and I cannot use anything as a basis, and consequently every under-taking becomes futile.

Will I then have to lose myself in this abyss of freedom? To what shall I cling in order to escape the dizziness that seizes me before the virtuality of this infinitude? However, I shall not succumb. I shall overcome my terror and shall be reassured by the thought that I have the seven notes of the scale and its chromatic intervals at my disposal, that strong and weak accents are within my reach, and that in all of these I possess solid and concrete elements which offer me a field of experience just as vast as the upsetting and dizzy infinitude that has just frightened me. It is into this field that I shall sink my roots, fully convinced that combinations which have at their disposal twelve sounds in each octave and all possible rhythmic varieties promise me riches that all the activity of human genius will never exhaust.

What delivers me from the anguish into which an unrestricted freedom plunges me is the fact that I am always able to turn immediately to the concrete things that are here in question. I have no use for a theoretic freedom. Let me have something finite, definite—matter that can lend itself to my operation only insofar as it is com-mensurate with my possibilities. And such matter presents itself to me together with its limitations. I must in turn impose mine upon it. So here we are, whether we like it or not, in the realm of necessity. And yet which of us has ever heard talk of art as other than a realm of freedom? This sort of heresy is uniformly widespread because it is imagined that art is outside the bounds of ordinary activity. Well, in art as in everything else, one can build only upon a resisting foundation: Whatever constantly gives way to pressure constantly renders movement impossible.

My freedom thus consists in my moving about within the narrow frame that I have assigned myself for each one of my undertakings.

I shall go even farther: my freedom will be so much the greater and more meaningful the more narrowly I limit my field of action and the more I surround myself with obstacles. Whatever diminishes constraint diminishes strength. The more constraints one imposes, the more one frees oneself of the chains that shackle the spirit.

To the voice that commands me to create I first respond with fright; then I reassure myself by taking up as weapons those things participating in creation but as yet outside of it; and the arbitrariness of the constraint serves only to obtain precision of execution.

From all this we shall conclude the necessity of dogmatizing on pain of missing our goal. If these words annoy us and seem harsh, we can abstain from pronouncing them. For all that, they nonetheless contain the secret of salvation: "It is evident," writes Baudelaire, "that rhetorics and prosodies are not arbitrarily invented tyrannies, but a collection of rules demanded by the very organization of the spiritual being, and never have prosodies and rhetorics kept originality from fully manifesting itself. The contrary, that is to say, that they have aided the flowering of originality, would be infinitely more true."

Notes

[Text: Stravinsky, "The Composition of Music," Chapter 3 in *Poetics of Music in the Form of Six Lessons*, translated by Arthur Knodel and Ingolf Dahl (Cambridge: Harvard University Press, 1947). Used by permission of the Harvard University Press.]

[1. See Stravinsky's essays "Some Ideas About My Octuor" and "Avertissement" in Eric Walter White, *Stravinsky: The Composer and His Works*, 2nd edition (Berkeley and Los Angeles: University of California Press, 1979): Appendix A.]

[2. Its text is given in White's *Stravinsky* (see note no. 1). Robert Craft has remarked about this interview: "Stravinsky had written his replies beforehand and he read them from a typescript." See Igor and Vera Stravinsky, *A Photograph Album, 1921 to 1971.* (New York: Thames and Hudson, 1982): 28.]

[3. Leonard Stein, "Schoenberg and 'Kleine Modernsky'," in *Confronting Stravinsky: Man, Musician, and Modernist*, edited by Jann Pasler (Berkeley: University of California Press, 1986): 324.]

13

PAUL HINDEMITH

(1 8 9 5 – 1 9 6 3)

Paul Hindemith's essay on musical inspiration was based on texts from his Charles Eliot Norton lectures at Harvard University in 1949 and 1950. He was the second musician to deliver these prestigious lectures, preceded a decade earlier by Igor Stravinsky (see essay no. 12). The book that stemmed from the talks at Harvard, *A Composer's World*, proved to be his most detailed statement of his musical aesthetic, indeed a synthesis of ideas and interests that came to him during the different stages of his career. In the book the composer enunciates an ideal conception of music that is, in general, consistent with a neoclassic or objectivist viewpoint inherited from the interwar period, but with a greater emphasis on the spiritual and ethical dimension of music. His book is also filled with a bitter dissatisfaction with the intellectual and artistic climate of his own time and with the many false directions that he found in music from earlier in the century.

Hindemith's ideas about music resurrect the rebellion against late romantic musical values, returning to arguments that were more characteristic of 1920 than 1950. He forcefully rejects the possibility of a steady progress or evolution in musical language, he dismisses *l'art pour l'art* aestheticism of the early twentieth century, and he has nothing good to say about the notion that difficult music could be validated by any prospect for future understanding. He was ambiguous about the audience for serious music, at once insisting that composers communicate to a large group of listeners but at the same time unable to hide his contempt for the taste of the masses. He saves his most bitter critique for the direction in music represented by Schoenberg. Although he does not mention Schoenberg by name, Hindemith's diatribe against the musical and ethical failures of atonality and twelve-tone composition makes plain the object of his dissatisfaction.

These feelings are evident in his discussion of "Musical Inspiration," which is the title of the pivotal chapter in *A Composer's World*. A composer's ideas, says Hindemith, come to him suddenly, as though unbidden, whereupon his musical vision captures them in their entirety in a chrysalis that is preserved until it can be shaped by his technique into a comprehensible form. Inspiration is always limited, Hindemith says, by musical materials, which create timeless boundaries and unalterable constraints upon the artist's imagination. These materials, he says, are inevitably earth-bound. If a composition is to have value, if it is to communicate and stimulate an emotional response in its listeners, then its tones must maintain an analogy with physical reality. The twelve tones cannot be treated as equal, as in atonal composition, but must instead be differentiated in their relative weights. Tonality must be maintained, otherwise the listener will be cast into a disagreeable feeling of weightlessness.

In addition to writing and lecturing on aesthetic issues, Hindemith was an important music theorist. His most significant theoretical treatise, the first volume of *Unterweisung im Tonsatz* (The Craft of Musical Composition), had the purpose of stating "basic principles of composition, derived from the natural characteristics of tones, and consequently valid for all periods." His theories, like his music, reject both the enshrinement of traditional tonality and the unstructured freedom of atonality.

Hindemith Writings: A Selective Bibliography

Aufsätze, Vorträge, Reden. Zurich: Atlantis, 1994. Relatively few of these essays and lectures are available in English translations.

A Composer's World. Cambridge: Harvard University Press, 1952.

The Craft of Musical Composition. Three volumes, 1937–70. Hindemith's most important theoretical work. Volumes 2 and 3 deal with composition in two and three parts, respectively, and volume 1 states Hindemith's theory of tonal coherence.

Johann Sebastian Bach: Heritage and Obligation. New Haven: Yale University Press, 1952.

—ɯ—

"MUSICAL INSPIRATION"
FROM A COMPOSER'S WORLD
(1952)

If music influences the intellectual and emotional realms of our mental activities, there must exist for each effect achieved in these realms a corresponding cause. The material of musical construction—successions of differently shaped sounds in their infinite number of combinations—provides these causes. It is the composer who is supposed to know about the intimate relation of musical causes and intellectual-emotional effects, and to steer the successions of sound consciously and skillfully to the point where they exert their expected influence. There is no doubt that in weighing and comparing causes and effects he must have, beyond all craftsmanship, an innate gift of measuring the relationship in manner and intensity of these two components of musical impressions. A certain divination is necessary to lift such an evaluating process beyond the primitive level of materialistic calculation or simple empiricism. Recognizing such loftiness in a composer's endeavors, we are readily inclined to attribute to him what seems to be the most characteristic quality of the composing mind which differentiates him from the sober, noncomposing crowd: the possession of creative ideas, of musical inspiration.

Although we must admit that musical inspiration is, in its ultimate profundity, as unexplainable as our capacity of thinking in general, we must not think of it as an irrational, entirely uncontrollable mental manifestation. After all, musical inspiration, like any other kind of artistic or scientific inspiration is not without bounds. It operates within the limitations drawn by both the material qualities of the artistic medium that causes the aforesaid effects and the state of mental erudition and preparedness in the mind of the individual who experiences them.

Recognizing these limitations will help us to understand more clearly the possibilities of an artist's imagination. Thus, if we know the specific limitations a poet encounters in using a certain language with its characteristic features, we shall not expect him to force his material into realms of expression that are alien to its qualities; we shall not confuse the poet's inspiration with the composer's, which in turn is limited materially by the entirely different properties of his working stuff, the succession of sounds. And what is true with the poet's and the musician's constructive materials is likewise true with respect to those of the painter, the architect, the sculptor, and other artists.

Beyond the specific limitations prescribed by each single art's material of construction, the composer seems to be limited in a way peculiar to his craft and unknown to the other creative artists. This craft, although through the immateriality and meaninglessness of its building stuff it is forced to dwell technically on a very high level of sublimation and abstraction, seems, with respect to its immediate impression on the recipient, of a lower value than all the other arts. Since music relies so much on our emotions, which come and go as they choose, unchecked and undirected by our reason, it occupies a place at the borderline between the arts and mere sensual impressions. Its effects seem to be similar to those exerted upon the uncontrollable senses of smell and taste. In all other arts it is our power of reasoning that has to be satisfied first, before an aesthetic enjoyment of an artist's creation can be had: The words of a poem must be understood in their verbal meaning before its structural beauty or spiritual loftiness can be appreciated; the subject of a painting or its abstract lineations must enter our consciousness before any emotional reaction can take place. With music it is different. It touches our emotions first and we are the helpless victims of its attacks. Only after the emotional reaction has been released by the sounds of music can our power of reasoning take possession of the artistic impression and transform it into aesthetic satisfaction—by way of mental construction, as we know. This reverse mode of action in the impressional stimulation of a musical composition is the reason for the comparatively low level on which music makes its initial appeal, as has just been mentioned.

Of course we know that music compensates its recipients in a manner not accessible to other arts. The range of emotions it can touch is infinitely larger, the variety within this range is unlimited, the tempo of consecutive emotions is unbelievably fast. We know the reason for this: The emotions released by music are no real emotions, they are mere images of emotions that have been experienced before, and we know about our unconscious technique of uncovering them in their mental hiding places. Paintings, poems, sculptures, works of architecture, after having impressed us consciously in the manner mentioned, do not—contrary to music—release images of feelings; instead they speak to the real, untransformed, and unmodified feelings. (Of course, additional memories of previous feelings may always participate in enhancing the artistic effect.) Gaiety released by examples of these arts is real gaiety, not a stored-away recollection of a formerly experienced gaiety; sadness is real sadness. This is proved by the fact that these real feelings lack entirely the range, variety, and speed of the images of feelings evoked by music, with their delirious, almost insane manner of appearance. Unlike these images of feelings, they are relatively uncomplicated, need time to develop and to fade out, and cannot appear in rapid succession.

2

One kind of limitation is common to all the arts: They are subject to the boundaries circumscribed by our common human and terrestrial sensual experiences of time and space. No artist, no craftsman was ever able to transgress these limitations, notwithstanding the commonplace usage of metaphorical, vague, and exaggerating terms in artistic discussions which to the uninitiated could easily suggest that such results have been attained or at least attempted. Neither could he suggest immeasurable largeness, as seen in the scientific field of astronomy, nor could he create an image of infinite smallness, as known in physics. The arts in this respect are, in spite of their great suggestive power, truly and immovably earth-bound.

The effects of an art on our receptive capacity may employ the element of space only, as do architecture, sculpture, and painting; or the element of time only, as does poetry; or it may operate in both, as do the drama and the moving pictures. It is again the art of music that cannot be caught in a net of temporal and spatial relations as easily as the other arts. We cannot deny that musical progressions evoke in our mind sensations of both a temporal and a spatial nature, but the following investigation will show that the sensations of musical time and musical space are not identical with time and space as felt in our everyday life or in the aesthetic effects of nonmusical works of art.

Musical time in its effect on our feelings is easily comprehensible as long as it uses temporal arrangements that are not essentially different from normal time. This is the case when it is totally or predominantly expressed in a metrical succession of temporal units, whose principal property is regular recurrence. Here as in actual time a row of one hundred beats is nothing but a row of one hundred beats, and its sum total is counted and felt as such. Doubts may arise only with respect to the beginning of the row, and the abatement of our attention may result in some other irregularities of judgment. If our place of observation is at the end of this row—meaning that we have heard it in its entirety up to its last beat—and we are looking back at its course, we feel that this series of one hundred beats, in spite of some more or less important subdivisions, could have ended earlier or have been continued to any temporal point further on without suffering an essential change in its structure and our evaluation of it.

But there is another form of musical time whose effects are quite different from those of normal time or of musical time as expressed in metrical successions. Here, in contrast to meter, irregularity in duration is the essential condition, irregularity which possibly is heightened to incommensurability. This is musical time expressed in forms of rhythm. The term "rhythm" is here used in its widest sense and includes everything irregular from the smallest nonmetrical motif to what is usually covered by the term "musical form." Music theory generally is not inclined to recognize in metrical and rhythmical forms two essentially different temporal orders of musical material. In fact, in our music in which melody and harmony are linked together mainly with the aid of meter, it is not wholly easy to separate meter from rhythm. But experimentally, in the music theorist's laboratory, so to speak, the basic dissimilarity of meter and rhythm can be proved. We can understand this dissimilarity by comparing our everyday actions as a series of temporally irrational successions of time intervals with the metrically organized time intervals as measured by watches, clocks, and other time-dividing devices. In musical time, as expressed in rhythmical forms, the time interval, covered by our row of one hundred beats, contains many rhythmical motifs which, although usually they can be measured by these beats, have just as little in common with them as have our temporally irrational actions with the clock's ticking. To understand such a succession as a rhythmic structure and not merely as a metrically organized row, we have to wait until it reaches its end. Then the complete form will appear to our analyzing mind as a new unit and not, as it appeared in meter, as an accumulation of single units. All the nonmetrical constituent parts of this new unit, although in their own rhythmic form clearly circumscribed, have now lost their individual meaning and are nothing but subordinate parts of this new entity. Now our place of observation has changed. We are no longer looking back on the past course of the row; we are above it, so to speak, and are looking down and can take in with one single glance the temporal form in its totality—indivisible, unrepeatable, unchangeable. We may say that musical time in this moment produced an effect which in normal time is nonexistent. This effect of comprehending as a new superunit what in the course of its development was built up by smaller units is borrowed from our spatial experiences, where this comprehensive judgment is a most commonplace fact—and yet it was the result of a strictly temporal operation.

3

Musical space is at least as far removed from our normal spatial concepts as was musical time in its rhythmic form of appearance from our temporal experiences. This seems strange, for even laymen without any musical training use the expression "ascending" for tone successions in which the second component has a higher number of vibrations per second, and conversely name "descending" any succession moving in the opposite direction. Actually there are in music no such spatial distinctions as high and low, near and far, right and left that correspond with the same definitions in real nonmusical space. Yet it is undeniable that successions of tones bring about effects of spatial feelings which in their obviousness are convincing even to the entirely untrained mind. Since neither the loudness nor the color of tones can produce or influence this effect, it must be the pitch relation among tones that is the reason for it.

To understand the connection between the movement from tone to tone in music on the one hand and the feeling of spatial movement on the other, we must again, as we did in our discussion of the emotional effects of music, find the common denominator of both factors. This time the equation is: The physical effort which we know is necessary to change from one tone position to another equals the physical effort we imagine when we think of a change of position in our common physical experience. Going from one given tone up to a tone with a higher vibration frequency is accomplished, in human voices and in string and wind instruments, with an increase in the energy of tone production. The amount of energy involved in such movement may be almost undiscernible (as in a violinist's progressing from the tone A of the open string to the next C), or it may be a tremendous physical effort, as when a tenor sings the same progression with full voice. But the absolute amount of energy involved counts only so far as our nonmusical interest in the performer himself or our sentimental reactions derived from his performance are concerned. It is the relative amount of energy that counts for our evaluation of musical space. Going to a tone of a higher frequency number means some effort, no matter how great or how small this effort in single cases may be. The recognition of this effort leads us to the comparison: Lifting some physical object from its place to a higher place means some effort; going from a tone of lower frequency to a tone of higher frequency means some effort; consequently one effort reminds me of the other, and since the lifting of the physical object took place in real space, the musical effect also reminds me of space. Going from a given tone to a tone of lower vibration frequency again reminds me of a change in position of a physical object, this time from a higher to a lower place, and again a spatial feeling connected with music is established by comparison.

This all is true without limitation in respect to singers' voices; it holds with wind instruments and, to a high degree, with string instruments too, since the close relationship of all these instruments to the singing voice is always recognizable. But in keyboards this natural equalization of spatial height with musical height has dwindled to almost nothing, and the mere horizontal change of the hand's position does not distinguish between ascending and descending. That even with these highly artificial arrangements we still feel the correspondences strain-up and relax-down, is explainable only through our previous experiences with singing voices and string and wind instruments.

When we talked about the emotional effects of music, we found that no image of a feeling could be evoked in our mind, unless a real feeling, suffered earlier, could be recalled. With the recognition of musical space we again see that only in reference to our experiences in real space can we have an analogous image of space in our mind, evoked by music. If this is true we can go one step further.

Musical space is felt—again by analogy with our experiences in real space—as three-dimensional. If we describe movements proceeding in a three-dimensional space as going up and down, right and left, forth and back, we can easily see their equivalents in musical space. A spatial up and down corresponds with the musical straining and releasing of vibrational tensions (as mentioned); right and left has its correspondence in the harmonic and melodic relations that exist between the successive components of each musical progression; and the feeling of spatial depth, as expressed by the motion forth and back, is symbolized musically similar to the construction which produces the effect of perspective in painting. In painting the impression of visual depth is created by so drawing all receding lines of the picture's objects that their prolongations meet in one single point—the vanishing point; and in musical perspective, all harmonies, whether resulting from the vertical (up and down) distance between tones, or by the summing-up effect of consecutive tones in melodies, will by our analytic capacity be understood as in close relationship to tones which, by frequent recurrence, or by favorable position in the structure, or finally by support received from other tones, will be felt as tones superior to the others; tones that occupy the place of fundamentals, of tonics.

4

Is it necessary to operate with the concept of musical space? Can we not conceive music that exists without reference to any real or imagined space? It seems that it is not possible to think of music as of something completely removed from any spatial conception, so long as we believe that music is supposed to touch our emotional life and to prompt us into the activity of simultaneous reconstruction. Since music revives in our minds the images of feelings which are inevitably connected with memories of spaces in which the originals of these images occurred to us, imaginary spaces will always show up simultaneously with the images of feelings.

If it is not possible to conceive music without any reference to images of spatial feelings, must we necessarily project all our three-dimensional experiences into our musical space? Could we not restrict ourselves to an image of a two-dimensional space by omitting the reference of harmonies to fundamental tones, to tonics, to the effect similar to perspective in painting? Do not many works of the pictorial arts renounce this effect? There was in musical history a time when these effects of perspective—or of tonality, as the technical term goes—were unknown to musicians. This was at a time before harmonies were used consciously and when music consisted only of melodic lines. Even nowadays in many countries and cultures that are not under the domination of Western musical techniques and habits, harmony is either unknown or flatly rejected as an unwelcome addition to the native material of music, and people with this exclusively melodic conception of music cannot have any effect of sounding perspective—or of tonality, as expressed by harmonic reference to tonal fundamentals (although of course other means of tonal organization are applied). With harmony it seems to go as with the tree of the knowledge of good and evil: once you have tasted its fruits, you have lost your innocent approach to the facts of life. For us, after our musical development has gone through about a thousand years of musical knowledge that consisted exclusively of harmonized musical structures, it is quite impossible to understand melodic lines without harmonic and tonal implications. The intervals produced by the successive tones of melodies have, in addition to their melodic function, harmonic significance, and we cannot fail to perceive it. These harmonies, again without our active interpretational participation, assemble around fundamental tones, as did the vertical harmonies, and thus again produce the effect of tonal perspective. In painting it is up to the painter to decide whether he wants to have perspective as a part of the pictorial effect or not. In music we cannot escape the analogous effect of tonal unification, of tonality. The intervals which constitute the building material of melodies and harmonies fall into tonal groupments, necessitated by their own physical structure and without our consent.

Have we not heard many times of tendencies in modern music to avoid these tonal effects? It seems to me that attempts at avoiding them are as promising as attempts at avoiding the effects of gravitation. Of course, we can use airplanes to fly away from the center of gravitation, but is not an airplane the best evidence for our incapacity to escape gravitation? Tonality doubtless is a very subtle form of gravitation and in order to feel it in action we do not even need to take our usual musical detour from actual experience via the image of it, released by music. It suffices to sing in a chorus or a madrigal group to experience the strength of tonal gravitation: to sense how a synoptic tonal order has a healthy, refreshing effect on our moods and how structures that in their obscurity reach the point of impracticability lead to real physical pain.

Certainly, there is a way to escape the effects of earthly gravitation, by using a powerful rocket that overshoots the critical point of terrestrial attraction, but I cannot see how music's less harmful projectiles could ever reach this point or its imaginary equivalent. And yet, some composers who have the ambition to eliminate tonality, succeed to a certain degree in depriving the listener of the benefits of gravitation. To be sure they do not, contrary to their conviction, eliminate tonality: they rather avail themselves of the same trick as those sickeningly wonderful merry-go-rounds on fair grounds and in amusement parks, in which the pleasure-seeking visitor is tossed around simultaneously in circles, and up and down, and sideways, in such fashion that even the innocent onlooker feels his inside turned into a pretzel-shaped distortion. The idea is, of course, to disturb the customer's feeling of gravitational attraction by combining at any given moment so many different forms of attraction that his sense of location cannot adjust itself fast enough. So-called atonal music, music which pretends to work without acknowledging the relationships of harmonies to tonics, acts just the same as those devilish gadgets; harmonies both in vertical and in horizontal form are arranged so that the tonics to which they refer change too rapidly. Thus we cannot adjust ourselves, cannot satisfy our desire for gravitational orientation. Again spatial dizziness is the result, this time in the sublimated realm of spatial images in our mind.

I personally do not see why we should use music to produce the effect of seasickness, which can be provided more convincingly by our amusement industry. Future ages will probably never understand why music ever went into competition with so powerful an adversary.

There is one strange fact about the feeling of musical space that has no equivalent in our ordinary spatial experiences: one of its imaginary, but nevertheless strongly felt dimensions coincides with the effects of musical time. What we feel as the spatial effect of moving sidewards, is accomplished musically by moving horizontally from one sounding unit to another, and this is exactly what produces the effect of musical time. The two different functions of one and the same factor do not have any disturbing effect on our interpretation of musical facts; musical time and musical space are felt as two clearly distinctive facts in musical progressions, and yet we know and feel that at some points they are interlocked, in a way that is unknown to normal time and normal space. We have already seen how musical time usurped a typical spatial effect with the fact that the cumulative single temporal units of a musical form produce a new entity, in which the total effect is not equal to the sum total of the single effects. Now we see that musical space in turn penetrates the realm of musical time.

I said before that no artist or craftsman could in his work suggest immeasurable largeness nor infinite smallness. Even less can he give in a work of art an idea of the relativity of normal time and normal space by means that are perceptible to our senses. Although this concept can be expressed in numbers and words, we can never experience it actually, as it is too far removed from our terrestrial sphere of knowledge. Yet music seems to be the only earthly form of expression which in the properties of its constructive material permits us to have sensations that are a very faint allusion to the feeling of beings to whom the universal concept of the relativity and interchangeability of time and space is an ordinary experience.

5

Within the framework of musical time and musical space the musical action takes place, in which the composer's ideas are the actors who by harmonic, melodic, and rhythmic circumstances are turned into tragic or comic characters, their tragedies and comedies being of the kind that lives in the stored-away world of the listener's images of emotions.

The word "idea" is a very vague term for what we really mean when we talk of the composer's creative imagination. The German word *Einfall* is the perfect expression needed in our situation. *Einfall*, from the verb *einfallen*, to drop in, describes beautifully the strange spontaneity that we associate with artistic ideas in general and with musical creation in particular. Something—you know not what—drops into your mind—you know not whence—and there it grows—you know not how—into some form—you know not why. This seems to be the general opinion, and we cannot blame the layman if he is unable to find rational explanations for so strange an occurrence.

Even many composers, although the rather prosaic labor of writing musical symbols on paper absorbs about ninety-nine per cent of their work, look at the apparently unprompted appearance of their own ideas with amazement. They are in a permanent state of artistic narcissism, compared with which the harmless self-admiration of the original Narcissus is but child's play. They will tell you about their creations as they would about natural phenomena or heavenly revelations. You have the impression, not that they themselves did their composing, but that "it" composed within them almost in spite of their own existence. It is admirable how people can throughout a lifetime maintain this naive self-confidence. We can merely envy them, that in spite of all professed temporary doubts in their craftsmanship they constantly think of themselves as exceptional examples of mankind, as incarnations of some supernatural being.

Let us look with a somewhat more temperate attitude at the ideas, the *Einfälle* that populate our stage set up by musical space and musical time. When we talk about *Einfälle* we usually mean little motifs, consisting of a few tones—tones often not even felt as tones but felt merely as a vague curve of sound. They are common to all people, professionals and laymen alike; but while in the layman's mind they die away unused in their earliest infancy, as said before, the creative musician knows how to catch them and subject them to further treatment. I know a scientist who said: "Everybody can have—and has—scientific ideas, but it takes a scientist to know what to do with them." I am very much inclined to include musical ideas in this statement. Who can be sure that the inner singing and ringing that any Mr. or Mrs. X feels bubbling up in a musically uncultivated mind—we talked about it in the first chapter—is not, in its unshaped authenticity, at least as beautiful and satisfactory as—and perhaps even better than—the greatest composer's unshaped inner singing and ringing? It is exciting to know how primitive, commonplace, colorless, and insignificant the first ideas, the primordial *Einfälle*, of even extraordinary musical masters are. But it seems almost more exciting to recognize the specific talent with which those masters keep their ideas fresh and, despite all mutations, basically intact, during the sometimes considerably long interval of time required for the treatment of these ideas. In this they are led by tradition, by the presumptive conditions of performance of the future piece, by its purpose and style, and, to a minor degree, by personal whims and fancies that may add certain flavors to the final form. Sometimes a composer may drive his musical material, on its way from the *Einfall* to its completion in a piece, through a tremendous barrier of frustrations which may suppress most of the aforesaid considerations and lead, even with the very first attempts at treating the basic material, to formulations of utter strangeness.

Although it is not possible to watch the source of the singing and ringing in other people's minds—it is not wholly easy even to analyze one's own mind far back into those remote regions of origin and creation—we can in some cases get glimpses of the early fate of musical ideas. To be sure, in order to be observable they must already have crossed the limitations of their first specterlike appearance and have gained some primordial form, either mentally by addition of the results of constructive conclusions, or even visibly in some jotted-down notes on paper. For the most part, only the mental form will exist, until a more extensive treatment brings the rudimentary material into some musically organized, yet still very primitive shape. Jotted-down notes can be regarded as the first steps away from the source, only if a composer's experience of many years has taught him to reduce the normally very long route from his brain to his writing hand. It is in the rare cases, when composers of this kind have left us some of these first-step sketches, that we can imaginatively trace these embryonic structures back to their still more elemental form, the original inner singing and ringing. Fortunately for our argument, one great composer left us a good many of these first-step sketches. I am referring to the sketch books of Beethoven.

In them we find many of the well-known themes which we are accustomed to think of as the most nearly perfect, the most convincing, the most suitable thematic creations: themes so homogeneous, so integrated, that they must have sprung up like the fully armed Minerva out of Jupiter's head. And yet we see them go through a process of transformation and conversion which sometimes gives us five or more intermediate steps from the first structural treatment to the final version. Some of the first versions are in quality so far below the final form, that we would be inclined any time to attribute their invention to Mr. X. And to watch the plodding through those many stages of development is oftentimes rather depressing: if that is the way a genius works, chiseling and molding desperately in order to produce a convincing form, what then is the fate of the smaller fellows? Perhaps it is always true that in working from the tiniest and almost imperceptible spark of structural invention up to an intelligible musical form, a petty composer is very much like Beethoven. If only the work involved in reaching this goal really counted, there would be many a genius. The petty composer could do the same, technically, as the real genius did, and he would almost be justified in feeling godlike—as so many authors did and do—because he was able to turn his bubbling inner singing and ringing into music, which Mr. and Mrs. X could never do.

Does all this mean that the genius and the average producer of music are of the same stuff; that in reality there are no such things as musical imagination, ideas, *Einfälle*; and that by mere accident one individual happens to develop into a Beethoven while the other just as accidentally remains an unknown sixth-rate musician? No. It merely means that if we want to understand the power that animates the ideational personages on our scene of musical time and space, we must not ramble through the mental regions that are common to Mr. X, the untalented composer, and the genius. It means that the regions of genuine musical creation are so far beyond our everyday experiences, that Mr. X will never know what they are and the untalented composer will never enter their inner secrets. Mr. X may always have all the wonderful ideas necessary for an excellent work of art; the little fellow may possess the acutest technique, which permits him to develop the most rudimentary ideas into forms of sound. But what the genius has—and what is far beyond their reach—is vision.

6

What is musical vision? We all know the impression of a very heavy flash of lightning in the night. Within a second's time we see a broad landscape, not only in its general outlines but with every detail. Although we could never describe each single component of the picture, we feel that not even the smallest leaf of grass escapes our attention. We experience a view, immensely comprehensive and at the same time immensely detailed, that we never could have under normal daylight conditions, and perhaps not during the night either, if our senses and nerves were not strained by the extraordinary suddenness of the event.

Compositions must be conceived the same way. If we cannot, in the flash of a single moment, see a composition in its absolute entirety, with every pertinent detail in its proper place, we are not genuine creators. The musical creator, like any other creative individual, is permitted to share with the demiurge the possession of vitalizing visions; but it is the privilege of the demiurge to transform them into concrete existence without any interfering technical obstacle, whereas the creative musician, by reason of his earthly heritage, has to overcome many hurdles between them and their realization. If he is a genuine creator he will not feel disturbed or discouraged by this fact. Not only will he have the gift of seeing—illuminated in his mind's eye as if by a flash of lightning—a complete musical form (though its subsequent realization in a performance may take three hours or more); he will have the energy, persistence, and skill to bring this envisioned form into existence, so that even after months of work not one of its details will be lost or fail to fit into his photomental picture. This does not mean that any F-sharp in the 612th measure of the final piece would have been determined in the very first flash of cognition. If the seer should in this first flash concentrate his attention on any particular detail of the whole, he would never conceive the totality; but if the conception of this totality strikes his mind like lightning, this F-sharp and all the other thousands of notes and other means of expression will fall into line almost without his knowing it. In working out his material he will always have before his mental eye the entire picture. In writing melodies or harmonic progressions he does not have to select them arbitrarily, he merely has to fulfill what the conceived totality demands. This is the true reason for Beethoven's apparently more than philistine bickering with his material: a desire not to improve or to change any *Einfall* but to accommodate it to the unalterable necessities of an envisioned totality, even if with all his technical skill and experience he has to press it through five or more versions that distort it past recognition.

The man of average talent may have visions too; but instead of seeing them in the clarity of lightning, he perceives dark contours which he has not the divination to fill out appropriately. He may have lots of exciting and wonderful single ideas which he patches together in order to get a musical form that corresponds with his shadowy idea, after the formula: the greater the number of beautiful details, the more beautiful the overall picture must be. For those gifted with flashlike visions, this hunting for beautiful details seems to be useless, since in fulfilling the demands of the vision they have no choice as to the kind and shape of building material; they can only try to obey these demands and find the sole suitable solution. If they should disregard them completely and consider a search for beautiful details justifiable, they would not be creative artists, any more than a philatelist is—or any other assembler of valuables, who with all his efforts succeeds merely in getting together a collection, never in creating an organism.

It is obvious that a composer, during the long period the notation of his work requires, is always in danger of losing the original vision of it. The flashlike picture may fade out, the outlines may dissolve, many details may disappear in darkness. One of the characteristics of the talent of a creative genius seems to be the ability to retain the keenness of the first vision until its embodiment in the finished piece is achieved. There is no doubt that this embodiment, if it is to appear as a true realization of the vision, can come to life only with the assistance of a great amount of technical skill. Skill can never make up for lack of vision, but on the other hand a vision will never receive its true materialization if a composer's technique does not provide every means towards this end. Yet, compositional technique can be acquired even by noncomposers, while clear visions are the privilege of real creative talent.

To acquire a decent technique in composition seems not to be too difficult. After all, there are a restricted number of rules of thumb concerning voice leading, harmonic progressions, tonal arrangements, and so forth, which are basically valid in all kinds of musical settings, regardless of style and purpose. The fact that after four or five years of study many so-called composers are leaving our schools with sufficient practical knowledge in the craft of putting tones together seems to prove this point. But the technique of composition, like the technique of any other art, is a deceptive thing. You may manage the few basic rules of construction with all their combinative possibilities pretty well, and yet the highest degree of subtlety, in which each technical item is in congruence with the respective part of the vision, again may be attained by no one but the genius. There are relatively few masterworks in which this ultimate congruence can be felt. Even in our stockpile of classical music which by common agreement consists of works written by superior composers not many pieces fulfill those highest requirements. True, there are many other great and excellent works, which in their artistic value are by no means less important. They may in their ability to speak as human creations to human beings be closest to our hearts, but it is in those few uncontested masterpieces that we feel the breath of universality and eternity, because their particular kind of perfection, the absolute coincidence of intention and realization, is almost superhuman.

The fact that very few masterworks display this congruence of vision and materialization shows us that even the individual possessing the greatest gift and the highest technical skill is not always able to reach this goal. A tremendous effort is necessary in order to work towards it; not merely a technical effort, but a moral effort, too—the effort to subject all considerations of technique, style, and purpose to this one ideal: congruence. Again, it is the aspiration towards the ideal unity of the Augustinian and the Boethian attitudes towards music which must ennoble our endeavors and which on the other hand pushes, as we know, the final goal into an utter remoteness close to inaccessibility.

7

Many composers will never feel an urge to exert efforts of this kind, others may not want to have their pleasant musical microcosm disturbed by such artistic obligations, and those who have the intuitive knowledge will not always summon the moral energy to force themselves very far forward on this thorny path. As for the listeners, the consumers, their feeling that in a composition the moral effort has been made at all, will be a sign that this composition has the hallmark of a work of art, and the perceptible amount of this effort will be considered the measurement for its artistic value. The more the composer feels impelled by his moral determination to drive the technical part of his work as close as possible to the goal of congruence, the higher seems to us the work's convincing quality. Other works, in which the composer's moral effort cannot be perceived, need not be bad music. They may have a pleasant, entertaining, touching effect. As mere technical mechanisms they may be without flaw. They may evoke wonderful emotional images in our mind, they may readily lead us to mentally reconstruct their forms; yet they may not impress us as works of art.

In addition to those composers who in their indolence or ignorance do not want to be bothered with the kind of problems discussed in this book, there are others who flatly deny the ethic power of music, nor do they admit any moral obligation on the part of those writing music. For them music is essentially a play with tones, and although they spend a considerable amount of intelligence and craftsmanship to make it look important, their composition can be of no greater value, as a sociological factor, than bowling or skating, and its intellectual or philosophical importance must necessarily be counted in the same class with the doings of snake worshipers and similar fetishistic isolationists. Nevertheless, there must in the minds of these creators exist some driving power that makes up for the lack of moral compulsion, at least dynamically, and keeps their writing apparatus well greased.

For some of them musical composition is identical with the problem of finding extramusical rules of tone distribution. The lack of any reasonable physical or psychological basis does not prevent their establishing such systems of organization; nor are they discouraged by the general impracticability of their creations and by the unresponsiveness of their audiences. It must be a peculiar satisfaction to follow laws of one's own invention, possibly laws that have no validity—or almost none—for other composers.

Others see in composition a safety valve for the mental overpressure from which they suffer. Like people who have the irresistible urge to talk, they need some mental activity that gives them relief. Writing music is just the thing. It is preferable to incessant talking, since even the lowest grade of chatter must make some sense, whereas writing music is not subject to so rigid a requirement. Besides this amenity it gives its producer an air of sophistication and fortifies his ego.

Still another group, in an attempt to replace with an apparent rationality what is lacking morally, develops an oversublimated technique which produces images of emotions that are far removed from any emotional experiences a relatively normal human being ever has. In doing so they advocate an esoteric *art pour l'art*, the followers of which can only be emotional imps, monsters, or snobs.

All these composers forget one important fact: music, as we practice it, is in spite of its trend towards abstraction, a form of communication between the author and the consumer of his music. If with the method just described we try to push the listener into the background, the picture will be filled with something that is less pleasant than the dullest ignorance of a dumb group of listeners: our own selfishness. William H. Vanderbilt's maxim "the public be damned" would seem to be one of those composers' working rules; or else they claim that audiences have to rubber-stamp whatever they deem necessary to dump upon them; or, finally, they may say: "The present world does not understand my music, but in two hundred years people will be mature enough to follow me." Even if in exceptional cases it may happen that composers are discovered who were never heard in their lifetime two hundred years previous, this attitude is utterly unartistic, since it neglects one of the main reasons for artistic communication: the altruistic desire to present something of one's own to one's fellow men. An artist would be justified in retiring into this unproductive res-ignation only if he were convinced that he had done everything in his power to make himself understood by his contemporaries. If he cannot succeed in doing so, in one form or another, there will be very slight chance that posterity will recognize him as a great genius. It is more likely, however, that his composing is, except for himself, of no value to anyone living either now or two hundred years hence.

There are also many other producers of music who turn their backs on our ideals: those to whom music is nothing but a business proposition; those whose com-posing is a pleasant pastime without any reason or aim; those who compose just because they cannot stop; and those who are merely public entertainers. We need not discuss their activities, since we know that they add nothing to the great trea-sury of useful music and that many of them do not have the least ambition to be counted among those contributing to this noble objective. Nor need we tarry with the man who has all the necessary ambition but no talent whatsoever.

Notes

[Text: Hindemith, "Musical Inspiration," Chapter 4 in A Composer's World (Cambridge: Har-vard University Press, 1952). Reprinted by permission of the Harvard University Press.]

PART III

MUSIC IN THE
AGE OF ANXIETY, 1950–1975

MUSICAL CULTURE IN EUROPE AND AMERICA FOLLOWING World War II was shaped by the same spirit that troubled all of society. A great anxiety was felt everywhere in the world, imparted by the Cold War, the horrific revelations of the Holocaust, and by the continued threat of warfare, then all the more menacing in light of nuclear weaponry. The war itself had left Europe in chaos, its inhabitants having suffered a nearly total loss of control over their lives. It had revealed an overwhelming power inherent in science and technology, which soon began to invade every corner of daily life. In America there followed a new era of wealth and materialism, and by the 1960s popular culture had risen to such towering influence in society as to make many observers question the very future of classical music.

In an environment such as this, neoclassicism and traditionalism, the dominant styles in music before the war, were soon swept from the center of attention in the international culture for modern music. After 1950 a youthful generation of musicians that included Milton Babbitt in America, Karlheinz Stockhausen in Germany, and Pierre Boulez in France began to create a new style of music that more closely mirrored the society around it. The new music of the 1950s emphasized, first of all, an enormous degree of control, as though musicians hoped to compensate in art for what had long seemed lacking in daily life. The reestablishment of control expressed itself in an imperious demand for conformity to a new way of thinking about music. Boulez spoke in this dogmatic tone when he declared (see essay no. 14) that all nonserialist composers were "useless." Control within the music itself was often reasserted by the application of systems that partially automated the process of composition. The most important of these was "total serialism," by which the order of appearance of pitches, durations, registers, types of attack, and other features of a work was governed by intricate precompositional arrangements. Total serialism amounted to a radical reinterpretation of Schoenberg's twelve-tone method, as it supplanted a composer's once-intuitive choices by the dictates of preplanned systems.

A depersonalization entered music by the use of such automated and seemingly rational procedures. Indeed, the overt expression of emotion in the new music was now suppressed, as though the war had drained mankind of all of its emotional reserves. Music was often abstract and as complex as scientific discourse. If music was unemotional, what then was its content? This is the question most frequently addressed in the group of essays that follows. Perhaps surprisingly, it was American composers who took the most unorthodox positions on this issue. John Cage proposed a music in which there was no content at all, in the normal sense of the term. A piece of music for Cage was to be purely an occasion in which the listener could experience sounds and silences, completely devoid of artistic communication from the composer. Milton Babbitt suggested that the intricate systems that governed the structure of a composition could be equivalent to its content.

Neither of these alternatives was wholeheartedly embraced by the Europeans, who wanted music to have meaning, although they quarreled about what that meaning was to be or how it was to be achieved. Luciano Berio held that music had to reflect the freedom of a nontotalitarian society, and he saw in serialism nothing less than a return to fascism. Luigi Nono demanded that a new piece of music must have meaning in the sense that it would document social realities at a particular point in history. None of these authors mentions traditional expressivity or emotion as a concept that was still appropriate to music.

But a more traditional approach to composition continued to exist during the 1950s and 1960s, as an extension of the neoclassical and populist styles of the prewar period. This more conservative language had many adherents, especially in the United States, among them Aaron Copland, Samuel Barber, Leonard Bernstein, William Schuman, and David Diamond. Their music, while accorded respect and support, was in many modern music circles demoted to a secondary status. The neoclassical composers who had established their careers in the 1930s now had different reactions to the collision between their individual artistic temperaments and the new and seemingly foreign musical culture. Igor Stravinsky and Elliott Carter completely dispensed with neoclassicism and adopted the reigning modernist idiom. Others were more cautious, making only moderate concessions to the new taste. Copland, Roger Sessions, Dmitri Shostakovich, and Benjamin Britten, for example, began to use their own adaptations of the twelve-tone method, but their music remained far more traditional than that of their successful younger colleagues. Others, including Arthur Honegger and Paul Hindemith, spoke out and bitterly condemned the postwar musical culture.

One aspect of the thinking of established neoclassical composers in this unsympathetic age is shown in a lecture given in 1964 by Benjamin Britten (essay no. 18). Britten simply ignores the new style and speaks entirely from the standpoint of a regionalist-populist English composer of 1930. Still, the writings of most of these older figures make it clear that they felt great dissatisfaction with the new musical culture and often bitterness toward the society that had produced it. In many cases the music that they wrote in the 1950s and 1960s received relatively little attention until the 1990s, when the doctrinaire aspects of the postwar period had largely faded from memory.

14

PIERRE BOULEZ
(B .   1 9 2 5)

The incendiary essay "Schoenberg Is Dead" was written by Pierre Boulez for the English modern music journal *Score*, where it appeared in 1952, shortly after the death of Arnold Schoenberg on July 13 of the previous year. It was far from the laudatory eulogy that everyone must have anticipated, appropriate to the passing of one of the century's leading composers. Schoenberg's twelve-tone music was instead dismissed by Boulez as a "catastrophe," as "a direction as wrong as any in the history of music." The title of the article was thus doubly provocative, as Schoenberg was declared dead both physically and in his relevance for future musical developments. In a letter to John Cage of December 1951, Boulez confessed that the polemic tone of the article came from his wish to separate himself from "dodecaphonic academicians"—no doubt a jab at his former teacher René Leibowitz, whom he had come to find pedantic in his attachment to the Viennese twelve-tone idiom. The article was slightly expanded in 1966 and returned to French for inclusion in Boulez's collection of essays called *Relevés d'apprenti (Stocktakings from an Apprenticeship)*, and it is this later version that is given here in translation.

Boulez's condemnation of Schoenberg's twelve-tone music came from his belief that it contained an excessive residue of traditionalism. Boulez found this in three primary areas: texture, form, and the lack of serialization outside of pitch. His generalizations deserve further scrutiny, as they are only partially accurate descriptions of Schoenberg's twelve-tone music. Regarding form, it is true, as Boulez says, that Schoenberg used patterns derived from earlier tonal music. The first movement of the String Quartet No. 4, Op. 37, or the Woodwind Quintet, Op. 26, for example, relate to traditional sonata form, as the composer himself indicated. But Schoenberg's application of these forms is intentionally superficial, virtually a parody of the classical procedures. Boulez's generalization otherwise does not hold true, since Schoenberg derives the essential elements of form precisely from the workings of his dodecaphonic method.[1]

Boulez comes to the central issue of his dissatisfaction with Schoenberg in the matter of texture. Schoenberg's twelve-tone works are, in fact, based on traditional homophonic and polyphonic textures, the outcome of an intricate theory of cyclic historical development in music that he developed as the twelve-tone method crystallized in his thinking. Schoenberg outlines his ideas on the relationship of texture to historical evolution in his lecture-essay "New and Outmoded Music, or Style and Idea," essay no. 10 in this anthology. But by the 1950s and 1960s traditional uses of theme, line, and chord were out of favor among the leading modernist composers, who experimented with numerous alternatives. Boulez himself profited from the pointillistic textures that he found in Webern's music and, differently expressed, in works of the late 1940s by his teacher Olivier Messiaen. The experience with electronic music of the 1950s led composers toward even newer ideas concerning texture—Iannis Xenakis, for example, used the resources of musique concrète to develop textures from slowly evolving masses of sound, which in turn inspired new avenues in works of the 1960s by Krzysztof Penderecki and György Ligeti.

But Boulez is wide of the mark when he states that Schoenberg only applied tone rows to create musical themes. Schoenberg used row forms thematically mainly at the beginning of a work or at a structural juncture. Elsewhere their notes are normally spread throughout a texture, and there the important themes do not directly duplicate the pitch content of the original row or any of its forms.

In his later writings and lectures, Boulez continued to express his disappointment with Schoenberg's twelve-tone music, but without the sharply dogmatic tone that led him to declare, as in this essay, all nonserial composers "useless." In a lecture given in 1976 at the opening of the Arnold Schoenberg Institute in Los Angeles, he remarked:[2]

> I was severely criticized some years ago for having written an essay entitled "Schoenberg est mort." I thought then, and I still think, that all that criticism came from stumbling over the title and not reading further into the essay itself. And I am sure that what I meant then, and what I still mean today (and very precisely), is just this: that mannerism after Schoenberg is absolutely dead in its very beginning; and that invention through Schoenberg is the only vital solution. And in many ways, a composer of this importance has to die through his real successors.

Boulez's Writings: A Selective Bibliography

Boulez on Music Today. Translated by Susan Bradshaw and Richard Rodney Bennett. Cambridge: Harvard University Press, 1971. Translation of *Penser la musique aujourd'hui* (Paris, 1964).

Conversations with Célestin Deliège. London: Eulenburg Books, 1976. Translation of *Par volonté et par hasard: Entretiens avec Célestin Deliège* (Paris, 1975).

Orientations: Collected Writings by Pierre Boulez. Edited by Jean-Jacques Nattiez. Translated by Martin Cooper. Cambridge: Harvard University Press, 1986. A translation of *Points de repère* (Paris, 1981, revised 1985).

Stocktakings from an Apprenticeship. Edited by Paule Thévenin. Translated by Stephen Walsh. Oxford: Clarendon Press, 1991. Translation of *Relevés d'apprenti* (Paris, 1966); earlier translated by Herbert Weinstock as *Notes of an Apprenticeship* (New York, 1968).

—ɯ—

SCHOENBERG IS DEAD

(*Schönberg est mort*, 1952, revised 1966)

Where do we stand with regard to Schoenberg?

This is certainly one of the most urgent questions that confronts us; and yet it is elusive and baffling, and perhaps cannot be satisfactorily answered.

There is no point in denying that the "case" of Schoenberg is primarily annoying for its flagrant incompatibilities.

Paradoxically, the central experiment of his work is premature precisely in so far as it lacks ambition. Or we can happily reverse the proposition and say that its ambition is at its greatest precisely where its code is most outworn. It is arguable that this ambiguity is the source of that disturbing misunderstanding which in turn prompts those more or less conscious, more or less violent reservations one feels toward a body of work which, in spite of everything, one knows to be absolutely necessary.

For with Schoenberg we witness one of the most important upheavals that the language of music has ever been called on to undergo. Admittedly the actual material does not change: the twelve semitones; it is the way the material is organized that is called in question: from tonal organization we move to serial organization. How did this idea of the series come about? At what point in Schoenberg's work? And as a result of what deductions? In tracing this genealogy, we may come nearer to explaining certain intractable inconsistencies.

We may start by saying that Schoenberg's discoveries are essentially morphological. The development starts with the post-Wagnerian vocabulary and ends up with the "suspension" of tonality. Although there are already signs of a clear tendency in *Verklärte Nacht*, in the First Quartet, Op. 7, in the Chamber Symphony, it is only in certain pages of the Scherzo and Finale of the Second Quartet, Op. 10, that we find a real break for freedom. All the works I have just mentioned are therefore in some sense preparatory; we may reasonably allow ourselves to regard them now as above all documentary.

Tonality is effectively suspended in the Three Piano Pieces of Op. 11. Thereafter the experiments become increasingly intense until they culminate in the resounding triumph of *Pierrot lunaire*. We may observe in the technique of these scores three remarkable features: the principle of perpetual variation, or non-repetition; the preponderance of "anarchic" intervals—those which yield the greatest tension in terms of tonality—and the gradual elimination of that tonal interval par excellence, the octave; and a clear preoccupation with counterpoint.

There is already inconsistency—if not contradiction—in these three characteristics. The variations principle in fact does not go well with a strict, even academic, contrapuntal technique. In strict canon, especially, where the consequent is an exact copy of the antecedent—in rhythm as well as pitch—we get a major internal contradiction. If, on the other hand, the canon is at the octave, it is easy to imagine the extreme antagonism between a series of horizontal events governed by a principle of tonal abstention and a vertical control that emphasizes the strongest of all tonal intervals.

Nevertheless one can detect here a discipline which will have fruitful consequences; we should particularly note the possibility, as yet embryonic, of a series of intervals passing from the horizontal to the vertical and vice versa: the separation of the notes of a given thematic cell from the rhythmic figure which produced it, so that the cell becomes a series of absolute intervals (to use the term in its mathematical sense).

To return to the use of what I have called "anarchic" intervals. In the works of this period we very often find fourths followed by diminished fifths, major thirds followed by major sixths, with all the inversions and dovetailings to which these two figures can be subjected. We notice here a preponderance of those intervals (where the texture is linear) or chords (where there is a vertical build-up) which are least reducible to the classical harmonic norm of superimposed thirds. On the other hand, we may observe the abundance of disjunct intervals, which give the range a feeling of distension, and hence the importance attached to the absolute pitch of each note, something which had scarcely ever been hinted at before.

This approach to musical material has prompted a good deal of defensive "aestheticizing" and special pleading, but with no attempt to generalize the problem. Schoenberg himself wrote on this subject in a way which seems to authorize the use of the term *expressionism*: "In my first works in the new style I was particularly guided, in both the details and the whole of the formal construction, by very powerful expressive forces, not to mention a sense of form and logic acquired from tradition and well developed through hard work and conscientiousness."[3]

No further comment is called for, and one can but applaud this initial phase, in which the musical thought is perfectly balanced by the purely formal aspects of the experimentation. In short, aesthetics, poetics, and technique are all in phase—if I may again use a mathematical term—whatever flaws one may be able to find in these areas individually. (I deliberately avoid discussion of the intrinsic value of post-Wagnerian expressionism.)

In the series of works beginning with the Serenade, Op. 24, Schoenberg seems to have been overtaken by his own innovation, with the no-man's-land of strictness locatable to the Five Piano Pieces, Op. 23.

This Op. 23 is the extreme point of equilibrium and the first manifesto of serial technique, to which we are introduced by the fifth piece, a waltz: it is worth pondering on this essentially "expressionist" coincidence of the first dodecaphonic composition with a German romantic formal stereotype. ("Prepare yourself with serious immobilities," as Satie might have said.) We are here in the presence of a new way of organizing sound, rudimentary as yet, but which will be codified above all in the Suite for Piano, Op. 25, and the Wind Quintet, Op. 26, before reaching a conscious schematization in the Variations for Orchestra, Op. 31.

Schoenberg is open to bitter reproach for this exploration of dodecaphony, pursued so determinedly in a direction as wrong as any in the history of music.

I do not say this lightly. Why then?

We may recall that the series arose, in Schoenberg, from an ultrathematicization in which, as we have seen, the intervals of the theme can be regarded as absolute, free of any rhythmic or expressive obligation. (The third piece of Op. 23, which is based on a five-note series, is particularly significant in this respect.)

It has to be admitted that this ultrathematicization is the underlying principle of the *series*, which is no more than its logical outcome. Moreover, the confusion between theme and series in Schoenberg's serial works is sufficiently expressive of his inability to envisage the world of sound brought into being by serialism. For him dodecaphony is nothing more than a rigorous means for controlling chromaticism; beyond its role as regulator, the serial phenomenon passed virtually unnoticed by Schoenberg.

What then was his main ambition once a chromatic synthesis—or safety net—had been established by serialism? To create works of the same nature as those of the old sound-world which he had only just abandoned, works in which the new technique would "prove itself." But how could the new technique be properly tested if one took no trouble to find specifically serial structures? And by structure I mean everything from the generating of the component materials right up to the global architecture of the work. In a word, Schoenberg never concerned himself with the logical connection between serial forms as such and derived structure.

This seems to be the reason for the futility of most of his serial output. Since the preclassical and classical forms which predominate are historically unconnected with dodecaphony, a yawning chasm opens up between the infrastructures of tonality and a language whose organizational principles are as yet but dimly perceived. Not only does the actual intention fail, since the language is not supported by the architecture, but the very opposite happens: The architecture annuls any possibility of organization that the new language may possess. The two worlds are incompatible: and yet he has tried to justify the one by the other.

This could hardly be called a valid way of working, and it yields results which can simply be discounted: the worst kind of misconception, a sort of lopsided "romantico-classicism" whose well-intentionedness is not its least repellent feature. It certainly does not show much faith in serial organization to deprive it of its own modes of development in favor of others that seem safer, a reactionary attitude which left the door open for every kind of more or less shameful survival, as we can now proceed to demonstrate.

The persistence, for example, of accompanied melody; of counterpoint based on the idea of a leading voice and secondary voice (*Hauptstimme* and *Nebenstimme*). I do not hesitate to call this one of the most unfortunate inheritances from the sclerosis of hybrid romanticism. Echoes of a dead world can be heard not only in these outworn concepts but equally in the actual technique. From Schoenberg's pen flows a stream of infuriating clichés and formidable stereotypes redolent of the most wearily ostentatious romanticism: all those endless anticipations with expressive accent on the harmony note, those fake appoggiaturas, those arpeggios, tremolandos, and note-repetitions, which sound so terribly empty and which so utterly deserve the label "secondary voices"; finally, the depressing poverty, even ugliness, of rhythms in which a few tricks of variation on classical formulae leave a disheartening impression of bonhomous futility.

How can one associate oneself unreservedly with an output that displays such contradictions, such illogic? If only it displayed them within a strict technique—the one saving grace! But what are we to think of Schoenberg's American period, which shows utter disarray and the most wretched disorientation? How are we to judge this reinstatement of polarized and even tonal functions, if not as one further (and unnecessary) proof of his lack of grasp and cohesion? From now on technical rigor is abandoned. The interval of an octave, the false cadence, the strict canon at the octave, all reappear. Such an approach achieves a lack of coherence which can only be described as a *reductio ad absurdum* of Schoenbergian incompatibility. Have we arrived at a new musical methodology merely so as to reconstruct the old one? So monstrous a trick of incomprehension leaves me speechless: the "case" of Schoenberg embodies a "catastrophe" which will doubtless remain exemplary.

Could it have been otherwise? It would be naively arrogant today to answer "no." Nevertheless it is possible to see why Schoenberg's serial music was doomed to stalemate. First, the investigation of serialism was one-sided: it neglected rhythm, and even, strictly speaking, sound, in the sense of dynamics and mode of attack. Who would dare to blame him for that? One may, on the other hand, point to a remarkable preoccupation with timbre, in the sense of *Klangfarbenmelodie*, which could be generalized into a timbre series. But the real reason for the stalemate lies in a profound misunderstanding of serial FUNCTIONS as such, as engendered, that is, by the actual serial principle—there are traces of them, but in an embryonic rather than effective form. By this I mean that Schoenberg saw the series as a lowest common denominator which would guarantee the semantic unity of the work, but that the linguistic components generated by this means are organized according to a preexistent, nonserial, rhetoric. This, to my mind, is the central provoking, UNEVIDENCE of a body of work without intrinsic unity.

The unevidence of Schoenberg's in the field of serialism has prompted enough defections or prudent disappearances to call for some response.

It is not leering demonism but the merest common sense which makes me say that, since the discoveries of the Viennese School, all nonserial composers are USELESS (which is not to say that all serial composers are useful). It will hardly do to answer in the name of so-called liberty, for this liberty has a strong flavor of ancient servitude. If the Schoenbergian stalemate is a fact, we shall not find a valid solution to the problem posed by the epiphany of a contemporary language by simply spiriting it away.

Perhaps we should start by dissociating serialism as such from the work of Schoenberg. People have confused the two with patent delight and ill-concealed dishonesty. It is easy to forget that a certain Webern ploughed the same furrow; admittedly (so thick are the smokescreens of mediocrity) hardly anyone has heard of him. Perhaps we might tell ourselves that serialism is a logical consequence of history—or historically logical, if you prefer. Perhaps we might, like this Webern, investigate the musical EVIDENCE arising from the attempt at generating structure from material. Perhaps we might enlarge the serial domain with intervals other than the semitone: micro-intervals, irregular intervals, complex sounds. Perhaps we might generalize the serial principle to the four constituents of sound: pitch, duration, dynamics/attack, and timbre. Perhaps . . . Perhaps . . . we might expect of a composer some imagination, a certain measure of asceticism, a bit of intelligence, and finally a sensibility which will not blow away in the first breeze.

We should anyway guard against seeing Schoenberg as a sort of Moses dying within sight of the Promised Land, having brought the sacred tablets of the law from a Sinai which many insist on confusing with Valhalla. (Meanwhile, the "Dance Round the Golden Calf" is in full swing.) We are certainly indebted to him for *Pierrot lunaire* . . . and a few other more-than admirable works—*pace* the mediocrities all around us, who would like to limit the damage to "Central Europe."

But it is now essential to dispose of the ambiguity and contradiction: it is time to resolve the stalemate. There is no room in this conclusion for any gratuitous bravado, still less any bland fatuity, but only a rigor impervious to weakness of compromise. So let us not hesitate to say, without any silly desire for scandal, but equally without shamefaced hypocrisy or pointless melancholy:
SCHOENBERG IS DEAD.

Notes

[Text: Boulez, "Schönberg est mort," from *Relevés d'apprenti*, translated by Stephen Walsh in *Stocktakings from an Apprenticeship* (Oxford: Oxford University Press, 1991). Used by permission of David Higham Associates.]

[1. This issue is addressed further in Martha MacLean Hyde, "The Roots of Form in Schoenberg's Sketches," *Journal of Music Theory* 24 (1980): 1–136.]

[2. Pierre Boulez, "Through Schoenberg to the Future," *Journal of the Arnold Schoenberg Institute* 1 (1977): 123–24.]

[3. Here Boulez cites Schoenberg's essay "Opinion or Insight," found in *Style and Idea* (Berkeley and Los Angeles: University of California Press, 1984): 262.]

15

MILTON BABBITT

(B. 1916)

Babbitt's famous and often-reprinted article "Who Cares If You Listen?" is based on the radical premise that the content of a musical composition can be identical to its form. What a contemporary work communicates to its listener is not emotion, dramatic conflict, social awareness, or any other such traditional idea, but instead the abstract form and architecture that guided the composer in creating the work. Since these have evolved far beyond the understanding of most people, it follows that there is no longer a reason for a composer to present his music to the public at large.

Many of Babbitt's contemporaries found this premise extreme, even in a period known for music of great complexity and abstraction, music that in general made few concessions to its audiences. It was contradicted, for example, by the influential critical theory of writers such as Theodor Adorno, for whom modern music had to communicate the conflicts of society. It was also far removed from the aesthetic of such earlier modernists as Arnold Schoenberg, who believed that structures guiding the composer had virtually no relevance to the listener, who should instead receive an idea from a musical work that ultimately reflected the "spirit of mankind." Babbitt's point of view was most stridently opposed by European composers, who were often seeking new ways in which music could be relevant to postwar society. The writings by Luciano Berio and Luigi Nono found later in this anthology contain responses aimed at least partly at Babbitt.

To understand Babbitt's provocative article, the reader must first identify the music about which he speaks, which he designates only as "contemporary," "advanced," and "serious." He gives four characteristics of the form inherent in this music, which allow it to be defined more precisely. First, it is music that uses an "efficient" tonal vocabulary. All pitch classes in such a work have an equally high level of importance in the total structure—none can be added or omitted without changing the work in a basic way. Second, each musical event has a large number of "functions," suggesting that each appears as the result of its occurrence in an integrated serialized system that coordinates and interconnects the choice of pitch classes, registers, durations, dynamic levels, and timbres. Third, each work is formally independent from preexisting constructive patterns. Each composition, that is, establishes its own form rather than relying on the standardized formal types of a common practice. Fourth, the compositional system is an extension of procedures developed in earlier serialized music (e.g., Schoenberg's twelve-tone method), which were uncovered by a systematic formal analysis.

These four ideas neatly characterize Babbitt's own "totally serialized" works composed beginning in the late 1940s, and they have partial relevance to music of the early 1950s by Europeans, such as Pierre Boulez and Karlheinz Stockhausen. Straightforward examples of Babbitt's idea of total organization can be found in his Three Compositions for Piano (1947). In each of these pieces the order of occurrence of pitch classes, registers, and points of attack in a measure is governed by a single precompositional plan for serialization. A highly unified and relatively automated system thus creates the form of the work, which is also, Babbitt says, its content.

Babbitt's writings consist primarily of analytic essays that explore the twelve-tone system using a mathematical model derived from set theory. This model was of the utmost importance to American composers and music theorists of the 1960s and 1970s. Theorists, in particular, soon began to imitate Babbitt's terminology and his mathematical apparatus. Babbitt's original title for this essay was "The Composer as Specialist," which was changed by his editor to a more inflammatory alternative—a change of which Babbitt has never approved.

Babbitt's Writings: A Selective Bibliography

"Set Structure as a Compositional Determinant," *Journal of Music Theory* 5 (1961): 72–94. Technical discussion of the phenomenon of "combinatoriality" in twelve-tone music.

"Some Aspects of Twelve-Tone Composition." *Score* 12 (1955): 53–61. Babbitt's first important essay, in which he outlines his conclusions concerning the twelve-tone systems of Schoenberg and Webern and their implications for composers in the future.

"Twelve-Tone Invariants as Compositional Determinants," *Musical Quarterly* 46 (1960): 246–59. Technical discussion of the phenomenon of "invariance" as it occurs in the twelve-tone works of Schoenberg and Webern.

"Twelve-Tone Rhythmic Structure and the Electronic Medium," *Perspectives of New Music* 1 (1962): 49–79. Puts forward a system for transferring the manipulations of pitch in twelve-tone music to its durational aspect.

Words about Music. Edited by Stephen Dembski and Joseph N. Straus. Madison: University of Wisconsin Press, 1987. The text of lectures given by Babbitt at the University of Wisconsin in 1983.

—⟁—

WHO CARES IF YOU LISTEN?
(THE COMPOSER AS SPECIALIST)
(1958)

This article might have been entitled "The Composer as Specialist" or, alternatively, and perhaps less contentiously, "The Composer as Anachronism." For I am concerned with stating an attitude toward the indisputable facts of the status and condition of the composer of what we will, for the moment, designate as "serious," "advanced," contemporary music. This composer expends an enormous amount of time and energy—and, usually, considerable money—on the creation of a commodity which has little, no, or negative commodity value. He is, in essence, a "vanity" composer. The general public is largely unaware of and uninterested in his music. The majority of performers shun it and resent it. Consequently, the music is little performed, and then primarily at poorly attended concerts before an audience consisting in the main of fellow professionals. At best, the music would appear to be for, of, and by specialists.

Towards this condition of musical and societal "isolation," a variety of attitudes has been expressed, usually with the purpose of assigning blame, often to the music itself, occasionally to critics or performers, and very occasionally to the public. But to assign blame is to imply that this isolation is unnecessary and undesirable. It is my contention that, on the contrary, this condition is not only inevitable, but potentially advantageous for the composer and his music. From my point of view, the composer would do well to consider means of realizing, consolidating, and extending the advantages.

The unprecedented divergence between contemporary serious music and its listeners, on the one hand, and traditional music and its following, on the other, is not accidental and—most probably—not transitory. Rather, it is a result of a half-century of revolution in musical thought, a revolution whose nature and consequences can be compared only with, and in many respects are closely analogous to, those of the mid-nineteenth-century revolution in mathematics and the twentieth-century revolution in theoretical physics. The immediate and profound effect has been the necessity for the informed musician to reexamine and probe the very foundations of his art. He has been obliged to recognize the possibility, and actuality, of alternatives to what were once regarded as musical absolutes. He lives no longer in a unitary musical universe of "common practice," but in a variety of universes of diverse practice.

This fall from musical innocence is, understandably, as disquieting to some as it is challenging to others, but in any event the process is irreversible, and the music that reflects the full impact of this revolution is, in many significant respects, a truly "new" music. Apart from the often highly sophisticated and complex constructive methods of any one composition, or group of compositions, the very minimal properties characterizing this body of music are the sources of its "difficulty," "unintelligibility," and—isolation. In indicating the most general of these properties, I shall make reference to no specific works, since I wish to avoid the independent issue of evaluation. The reader is at liberty to supply his own instances; if he cannot (and, granted the condition under discussion, this is a very real possibility), let him be assured that such music does exist.

First. This music employs a tonal vocabulary which is more "efficient" than that of the music of the past, or its derivatives. This is not necessarily a virtue in itself, but it does make possible a greatly increased number of pitch simultaneities, successions, and relationships. This increase in efficiency necessarily reduces the "redundancy" of the language, and as a result the intelligible communication of the work demands increased accuracy from the transmitter (the performer) and activity from the receiver (the listener). Incidentally, it is this circumstance, among many others, that has created the need for purely electronic media of "performance." More importantly for us, it makes ever heavier demands upon the training of the listener's perceptual capacities.

Second. Along with this increase of meaningful pitch materials, the number of functions associated with each component of the musical event also has been multiplied. In the simplest possible terms, each such "atomic" event is located in a five-dimensional musical space determined by pitch-class, register, dynamic, duration, and timbre. These five components not only together define the single event, but, in the course of a work, the successive values of each component create an individually coherent structure, frequently in parallel with the corresponding structures created by each of the other components. Inability to perceive and remember precisely the values of any of these components results in a dislocation of the event in the work's musical space, an alteration of its relation to all other events in the work, and—thus—a falsification of the composition's total structure. For example, an incorrectly performed or perceived dynamic value results in destruction of the work's dynamic pattern, but also in false identification of other components of the event (of which this dynamic value is a part) with corresponding components of other events, so creating incorrect pitch, registral, timbral, and durational associations. It is this high degree of "determinacy" that most strikingly differentiates such music from, for example, a popular song. A popular song is only very partially determined, since it would appear to retain its germane characteristics under considerable alteration of register, rhythmic texture, dynamics, harmonic structure, timbre, and other qualities.

The preliminary differentiation of musical categories by means of this reasonable and usable criterion of "degree of determinacy" offends those who take it to be a definition of qualitative categories, which—of course—it need not always be. Curiously, their demurrers usually take the familiar form of some such "democratic" counterderfinition as: "There is no such thing as 'serious' and 'popular' music. There is only 'good' and 'bad' music." As a public service, let me offer those who still patiently await the revelation of the criteria of Absolute Good an alternative criterion which possesses, at least, the virtue of immediate and irrefutable applicability: "There is no such thing as 'serious' and 'popular' music. There is only music whose title begins with the letter 'X,' and music whose title does not."

Third. Musical compositions of the kind under discussion possess a high degree of contextuality and autonomy. That is, the structural characteristics of a given work are less representative of a general class of characteristics than they are unique to the individual work itself. Particularly, principles of relatedness, upon which depends immediate coherence of continuity, are more likely to evolve in the course of the work than to be derived from generalized assumptions. Here again greater and new demands are made upon the perceptual and conceptual abilities of the listener.

Fourth, and finally. Although in many fundamental respects this music is "new," it often also represents a vast extension of the methods of other musics, derived from a considered and extensive knowledge of their dynamic principles. For, concomitant with the "revolution in music," perhaps even an integral aspect thereof, has been the development of analytical theory, concerned with the systematic formulation of such principles to the end of greater efficiency, economy, and understanding. Compositions so rooted necessarily ask comparable knowledge and experience from the listener. Like all communication, this music presupposes a suitably equipped receptor. I am aware that "tradition" has it that the lay listener, by virtue of some undefined, transcendental faculty, always is able to arrive at a musical judgment absolute in its wisdom if not always permanent in its validity. I regret my inability to accord this declaration of faith the respect due its advanced age.

Deviation from this tradition is bound to dismiss the contemporary music of which I have been talking into "isolation." Nor do I see how or why the situation should be otherwise. Why should the layman be other than bored and puzzled by what he is unable to understand, music or anything else? It is only the translation of this boredom and puzzlement into resentment and denunciation that seems to me indefensible. After all, the public does have its own music, its ubiquitous music: music to eat by, to read by, to dance by, and to be impressed by. Why refuse to recognize the possibility that contemporary music has reached a stage long since attained by other forms of activity? The time has passed when the normally well-educated man without special preparation could understand the most advanced work in, for example, mathematics, philosophy, and physics. Advanced music, to the extent that it reflects the knowledge and originality of the informed composer, scarcely can be expected to appear more intelligible than these arts and sciences to the person whose musical education usually has been even less extensive than his background in other fields. But to this, a double standard is invoked, with the words "music is music," implying also that "music is just music." Why not, then, equate the activities of the radio repairman with those of the theoretical physicist, on the basis of the dictum that "physics is physics"? It is not difficult to find statements like the following, from the *New York Times* of September 8, 1957: "The scientific level of the conference is so high . . . that there are in the world only 120 mathematicians specializing in the field who could contribute." Specialized music, on the other hand, far from signifying "height" of musical level, has been charged with "decadence," even as evidence of an insidious "conspiracy."

It often has been remarked that only in politics and the "arts" does the layman regard himself as an expert, with the right to have his opinion heard. In the realm of politics, he knows that this right, in the form of a vote, is guaranteed by fiat. Comparably, in the realm of public music, the concertgoer is secure in the knowledge that the amenities of concert going protect his firmly stated "I didn't like it" from further scrutiny. Imagine, if you can, a layman chancing upon a lecture on "Pointwise Periodic Homeomorphisms." At the conclusion, he announces: "I didn't like it." Societal conventions being what they are in such circles, someone might dare inquire: "Why not?" Under duress, our layman discloses precise reasons for his failure to enjoy himself; he found the hall chilly, the lecturer's voice unpleasant, and he was suffering the digestive aftermath of a poor dinner. His interlocutor understandably disqualifies these reasons as irrelevant to the content and value of the lecture, and the development of mathematics is left undisturbed. If the concertgoer is at all versed in the ways of musical lifesmanship, he also will offer reasons for his "I didn't like it"—in the form of assertions that the work in question is "inexpressive," "undramatic," "lacking in poetry," etc., etc., tapping that store of vacuous equivalents hallowed by time for: "I don't like it, and I cannot or will not state why." The concertgoer's critical authority is established beyond the possibility of further inquiry. Certainly he is not responsible for the circumstance that musical discourse is a never-never land of semantic confusion, the last resting place of all those verbal and formal fallacies, those hoary dualisms that have been banished from rational discourse. Perhaps he has read, in a widely consulted and respected book on the history of music, the following: "to call him [Tchaikovsky] the 'modern Russian Beethoven' is footless, Beethoven being patently neither modern nor Russian. . . ." Or, the following, by an eminent "nonanalytic" philosopher: "The music of Lourié is an ontological music. . . . It is born in the singular roots of being, the nearest possible juncture of the soul and the spirit. . . ." How unexceptionable the verbal peccadilloes of the average concertgoer appear beside these masterful models. Or, perhaps, in search of "real" authority, he has acquired his critical vocabulary from the pronouncements of officially "eminent" composers, whose eminence, in turn, is founded largely upon just such assertions as the concertgoer has learned to regurgitate. This cycle is of slight moment in a world where circularity is one of the norms of criticism. Composers (and performers), wittingly or unwittingly assuming the character of "talented children" and "inspired idiots" generally ascribed to them, are singularly adept at the conversion of personal tastes into general principles. Music they do not like is "not music," composers whose music they do not like are "not composers."

In search of what to think and how to say it, the layman may turn to newspapers and magazines. Here he finds conclusive evidence for the proposition that "music is music." The science editor of such publications contents himself with straightforward reporting, usually news of the "factual" sciences; books and articles not intended for popular consumption are not reviewed. Whatever the reason, such matters are left to professional journals. The music critic admits no comparable differentiation. He may feel, with some justice, that music which presents itself in the marketplace of the concert hall automatically offers itself to public approval or disapproval. He may feel, again with some justice, that to omit the expected criticism of the "advanced" work would be to do the composer an injustice in his assumed quest for, if nothing else, public notice and "professional recognition." The critic, at least to this extent, is himself a victim of the leveling of categories.

Here, then, are some of the factors determining the climate of the public world of music. Perhaps we should not have overlooked those pockets of "power" where prizes, awards, and commissions are dispensed, where music is adjudged guilty, not only without the right to be confronted by its accuser, but without the right to be confronted by the accusations. Or those well-meaning souls who exhort the public "just to listen to more contemporary music," apparently on the theory that familiarity breeds passive acceptance. Or those, often the same well-meaning souls, who remind the composer of his "obligation to the public," while the public's obligation to the composer is fulfilled, manifestly, by mere physical presence in the concert hall or before a loudspeaker or—more authoritatively—by committing to memory the numbers of phonograph records and amplifier models. Or the intricate social world within this musical world, where the salon becomes bazaar, and music itself becomes an ingredient of verbal canapés for cocktail conversation.

I say all this is not to present a picture of a virtuous music in a sinful world, but to point up the problems of a special music in an alien and inapposite world. And so, I dare suggest that the composer would do himself and his music an immediate and eventual service by total, resolute, and voluntary withdrawal from this public world to one of private performance and electronic media, with its very real possibility of complete elimination of the public and social aspects of musical composition. By so doing the separation between the domains would be defined beyond any possibility of confusion of categories, and the composer would be free to pursue a private life of professional achievement, as opposed to a public life of unprofessional compromise and exhibitionism.

But how, it may be asked, will this serve to secure the means of survival for the composer and his music? One answer is that, after all, such a private life is what the university provides the scholar and the scientist. It is only proper that the university, which—significantly—has provided so many contemporary composers with their professional training and general education, should provide a home for the "complex," "difficult," and "problematical" in music. Indeed, the process has begun; and if it appears to proceed too slowly, I take consolation in the knowledge that in this respect, too, music seems to be in historically retarded parallel with now sacrosanct fields of endeavor. In E. T. Bell's *Men of Mathematics*, we read: "In the eighteenth century the universities were not the principal centers of research in Europe. They might have become such sooner than they did but for the classical tradition and its understandable hostility to science. Mathematics was close enough to antiquity to be respectable, but physics, being more recent, was suspect. Further, a mathematician in a university of the time would have been expected to put much of his effort on elementary teaching; his research , if any, would have been an unprofitable luxury. . . ." A simple substitution of "musical composition" for "research," of "academic" for "classical," of "music" for "physics," and of "composer" for "mathematician," provides a strikingly accurate picture of the current situation. And as long as the confusion I have described continues to exist, how can the university and its community assume other than that the composer welcomes and courts public competition with the historically certified products of the past, and the commercially certified products of the present?

Perhaps for the same reason, the various institutes of advanced research and the large majority of foundations have disregarded this music's need for means of survival. I do not wish to appear to obscure the obvious differences between musical composition and scholarly research, although it can be contended that these differences are no more fundamental than the differences among the various fields of study. I do question whether thes differences, by their nature, justify the denial to music's development of assistance granted these other fields. Immediate "practical" applicability (which may be said to have its musical analogue in "immediate extensibility of a compositional technique") is certainly not a necessary condition for the support of scientific research. And if it be contended that such research is so supported because in the past it has yielded eventual applications, one can counter with, for example, the music of Anton Webern, which during the composer's lifetime was regarded (to the very limited extent that it was regarded at all) as the ultimate in hermetic, specialized, and idiosyncratic composition; today, some dozen years after the composer's death, his complete works have been recorded by a major record company, primarily—I suspect—as a result of the enormous influence this music has had on the postwar, nonpopular, musical world. I doubt that scientific research is any more secure against predictions of ultimate significance than is musical composition. Finally, if it be contended that research, even in its least "practical" phases, contributes to the sum of knowledge in the particular realm, what possibly can contribute more to our knowledge of music than a genuinely original composition?

Granting to music the position accorded other arts and sciences promises the sole substantial means of survival for the music I have been describing. Admittedly, if this music is not supported, the whistling repertory of the man in the street will be little affected, the concert-going activity of the conspicuous consumer of musical culture will be little disturbed. But music will cease to evolve, and, in that important sense, will cease to live.

Notes

[Text: Babbitt, "Who Cares If You Listen?," *High Fidelity* 8 (February 1958): 38–40, 126. Used by permission of Milton Babbitt.]

16

JOHN CAGE

(1 9 1 2 – 9 2)

In his essay "History of Experimental Music in the United States," John Cage defines the notion of "experimental" music in a precise though narrow way, limiting it to an "action the outcome of which is not foreseen." By this definition experimental music is restricted to indeterminate works—primarily the music composed by Cage himself and others in his circle after about 1950. Cage explored two types of indeterminacy, one of the composition, the other of performance. In the first, as in his piano piece *Music of Changes* (1951), the composer chooses the musical materials to write down guided by chance operations; in the second type, the musical materials are not fully notated, sometimes not notated at all. An example is Cage's Concert for Piano and Orchestra (1958), which consists of a collection of graphic notations upon which the performers improvise. Clearly, the resulting sounds are unforeseen by the composer, and the work is hence "experimental."

In his article, Cage also touches on twentieth-century American composers with new musical ideas, even if not "experimental," but it is his own indeterminate music that is his principal concern. Such music, he says, is not an object that communicates ideas or feelings but is instead a process "providing experience not burdened by psychological intentions on the part of the composer." It avoids gestures of continuity, it is not involved with any objective, and it is close to nature. The composer's basic material is space and emptiness, which Cage designates ironically as "silence"; within this space, sounds of any type may occur. He contends that such music is urgently necessary in modern society.

The article resulted from Cage's appearance in 1958 at the Internationale Ferienkurse für Neue Musik in Darmstadt, an occasion that considerably increased his international influence and ultimately led to new directions in European music. The article was first published in a German translation in the *Darmstädter Beiträge zur neuen Musik*, the journal associated with the Darmstadt Summer Courses. In the early 1950s Darmstadt was nearly synonymous with abstract and partially automated composition, often in the vein of "total serialization." By 1958, however, a distinct dissatisfaction with this idiom was widely felt, as composers sought alternatives that could bring meaning back into their music while allowing it to remain in the modernist postwar style that was still thought necessary. Numerous stylistic alternatives were devised by European figures— Bernd Alois Zimmermann's collages, Berio's "live processes," Xenakis's "stochastic" soundscapes, Pousseur's absurdist theater among them. The freely improvisatory element of Cage's indeterminacy now emerged as another alternative, although its underlying philosophy, in which the personality of the composer and the capacity of the music to communicate were intentionally eliminated, was unsettling to many; indeed, it seemed to be a return to the depersonalization of totally organized music of the earlier 1950s. It is not surprising that several leading European composers greeted Cage with skepticism, even vigorous rejection. An example of the latter is found in Luigi Nono's lecture-essay "Historical Presence in Music Today," essay no. 17 in this anthology.

John Cage was an eloquent spokesman for his philosophy; indeed he is perhaps the most skillful writer of any major composer of the twentieth century. His many essays and lectures show his precise and easy use of language, which combines sophisticated ideas with lightness, wit, and irony.

Cage's Writings: A Selective Bibliography

Empty Words. Middletown, CT: Wesleyan University Press, 1979.

Silence. Middletown, CT: Wesleyan University Press, 1961. A collection of lectures and writings by Cage to 1961. *Silence* is by far the most important collection of Cage's writings.

A Year From Monday. Middletown, CT: Wesleyan University Press, 1967.

I-VI. Cambridge: Harvard University Press, 1990. Cage's Charles Eliot Norton lectures from 1988–89.

John Cage Writer: Previously Uncollected Pieces. Edited by Richard Kostelanetz. New York: Limelight Editions, 1993.

—⚭—

HISTORY OF EXPERIMENTAL MUSIC IN THE UNITED STATES
(1959)

Once when Daisetz Teitaro Suzuki was giving a talk at Columbia University he mentioned the name of a Chinese monk who had figured in the history of Chinese Buddhism. Suzuki said, "He lived in the ninth or the tenth century." He added, after a pause, "Or the eleventh century, or the twelfth or thirteenth century or the fourteenth."

About the same time, Willem de Kooning, the New York painter, gave a talk at the Art Alliance in Philadelphia. Afterwards there was a discussion: questions and answers. Someone asked De Kooning who the painters of the past were who had influenced him the most. De Kooning said, "The past does not influence me; I influence it."

A little over ten years ago I acted as music editor for a magazine called *Possibilities*. Only one issue of this magazine appeared. However: in it, four American composers (Virgil Thomson, Edgard Varèse, Ben Weber, and Alexei Haieff) answered questions put to them by twenty other composers. My question to Varèse concerned his views of the future of music. His answer was that neither the past nor the future interested him; that his concern was with the present.

Sri Ramakrishna was once asked, "Why, if God is good, is there evil in the world?" He said, "In order to thicken the plot." Nowadays in the field of music, we often hear that everything is possible; (for instance) that with electronic means one may employ any sound (any frequency, any amplitude, any timbre, any duration); that there are no limits to possibility. This is technically, nowadays, theoretically possible and in practical terms is often felt to be impossible only because of the absence of mechanical aids which, nevertheless, could be provided if the society felt the urgency of musical advance. Debussy said quite some time ago, "Any sounds in any combination and in any succession are henceforth free to be used in a musical continuity." Paraphrasing the question put to Sri Ramakrishna and the answer he gave, I would ask this: "Why, if everything is possible, do we concern ourselves with history (in other words with a sense of what is necessary to be done at a particular time)?" And I would answer, "In order to thicken the plot." In this view, then, all those interpenetrations which seem at first glance to be hellish—history, for instance, if we are speaking of experimental music—are to be espoused. One does not then make just any experiment but does what must be done. By this I mean one does not seek by his actions to arrive at money but does what must be done; one does not seek by his actions to arrive at fame (success) but does what must be done; one does not seek by his actions to provide pleasure to the senses (beauty) but does what must be done; one does not seek by his actions to arrive at the establishing of a school (truth) but does what must be done. One does something else. What else?

In an article called "New and Electronic Music," Christian Wolff says: "What is, or seems to be, new in this music?. . . One finds a concern for a kind of objectivity, almost anonymity—sound come into its own. The 'music' is a resultant existing simply in the sounds we hear, given no impulse by expressions of self or personality. It is indifferent in motive, originating in no psychology nor in dramatic intentions, nor in literary or pictorial purposes. For at least some of these composers, then, the final intention is to be free of artistry and taste. But this need not make their work 'abstract,' for nothing, in the end, is denied. It is simply that personal expression, drama, psychology, and the like are not part of the composer's initial calculation: they are at best gratuitous.

"The procedure of composing tends to be radical, going directly to the sounds and their characteristics, to the way in which they are produced and how they are notated."

"Sound come into its own." What does that mean? For one thing: it means that noises are as useful to new music as so-called musical tones, for the simple reason that they are sounds. This decision alters the view of history, so that one is no longer concerned with tonality or atonality, Schoenberg or Stravinsky (the twelve tones or the twelve expressed as seven plus five), nor with consonance and dissonance, but rather with Edgard Varèse who fathered forth noise into twentieth-century music. But it is clear that ways must be discovered that allow noises and tones to be just noises and tones, not exponents subservient to Varèse's imagination.

What else did Varèse do that is relevant to present necessity? He was the first to write directly for instruments, giving up the practice of making a piano sketch and later orchestrating it. What is unnecessary in Varèse (from a present point of view of necessity) are all his mannerisms, of which two stand out as signatures (the repeated note resembling a telegraphic transmission and the cadence of a tone held through a crescendo to maximum amplitude). These mannerisms do not establish sounds in their own right. They make it quite difficult to hear the sounds just as they are, for they draw attention to Varèse and his imagination.

What is the nature of an experimental action? It is simply an action the outcome of which is not foreseen. It is therefore very useful if one has decided that sounds are to come into their own, rather than being exploited to express sentiments or ideas of order. Among those actions the outcomes of which are not foreseen, actions resulting from chance operations are useful. However, more essential than composing by means of chance operations, it seems to me now, is composing in such a way that what one does is indeterminate of its performance. In such a case one can just work directly, for nothing one does gives rise to anything that is preconceived. This necessitates, of course, a rather great change in habits of notation. I take a sheet of paper and place points on it. Next I make parallel lines on a transparency, say five parallel lines. I establish five categories of sound for the five lines, but I do not say which line is which category. The transparency may be placed on the sheet with points in any position and readings of the points may be taken with regard to all the characteristics one wishes to distinguish. Another transparency may be used for further measurements, even altering the succession of sounds in time. In this situation no chance operations are necessary (for instance, no tossing of coins) for nothing is foreseen, though everything may be later minutely measured or simply taken as a vague suggestion.

Implicit here, it seems to me, are principles familiar from modern painting and architecture: collage and space. What makes this action like dada are the underlying philosophical views and the collagelike actions. But what makes this action unlike dada is the space in it. For it is the space and emptiness that is finally urgently necessary at this point in history (not the sounds that happen in it—or their relationships) (not the stones—thinking of a Japanese stone garden—or their relationships but the emptiness of the sand which needs the stones anywhere in the space in order to be empty). When I said recently in Darmstadt that one could write music by observing the imperfections in the paper upon which one was writing, a student who did not understand because he was full of musical ideas asked, "Would one piece of paper be better than another: one for instance that had more imperfections?" He was attached to sounds and because of his attachment could not let sounds be just sounds. He needed to attach himself to the emptiness, to the silence. Then things—sounds, that is—would come into being of themselves. Why is this so necessary that sounds should be just sounds? There are many ways of saying why. One is this: In order that each sound may become the Buddha. If that is too Oriental an expression, take the Christian Gnostic statement: "Split the stick and there is Jesus."

We know now that sounds and noises are not just frequencies (pitches): that is why so much of European musical studies and even so much of modern music is no longer urgently necessary. It is pleasant if you happen to hear Beethoven or Chopin or whatever, but it isn't urgent to do so anymore. Nor is harmony or counterpoint or counting in meters of two, three, or four or any other number. So that much of Ives (Charles Ives) is no longer experimental or necessary for us (though people are so used to knowing that he was the first to do such and such). He did do things in space and in collage, and he did say, Do this or this (whichever you choose), and so indeterminacy which is so essential now did enter into his music. But his meters and rhythms are no longer any more important for us than curiosities of the past like the patterns one finds in Stravinsky. Counting is no longer necessary for magnetic tape music (where so many inches or centimeters equal so many seconds): magnetic tape music makes it clear that we are in time itself, not in measures of two, three, or four or any other number. And so instead of counting we use watches if we want to know where in time we are, or rather where in time a sound is to be. All this can be summed up by saying each aspect of sound (frequency, amplitude, timbre, duration) is to be seen as a continuum, not as a series of discrete steps favored by conventions (Occidental or Oriental). (Clearly all the Americana aspects of Ives are in the way of sound coming into its own, since sounds by their nature are no more American than they are Egyptian.)

Carl Ruggles? He works and reworks a handful of compositions so that they better and better express his intentions, which perhaps ever so slightly are changing. His work is therefore not experimental at all but in a most sophisticated way attached to the past and to art.

Henry Cowell was for many years the open sesame for new music in America. Most selflessly he published the New Music Edition and encouraged the young to discover new directions. From him, as from an efficient information booth, you could always get not only the address and telephone number of anyone working in a lively way in music, but you could also get an unbiased introduction from him as to what that anyone was doing. He was not attached (as Varèse also was not attached) to what seemed to so many to be the important question: Whether to follow Schoenberg or Stravinsky. His early works for piano, long before Varèse's *Ionization* (which, by the way, was published by Cowell), by their tone clusters and use of the piano strings, pointed towards noise and a continuum of timbre. Other works of his are indeterminate in ways analogous to those currently in use by Boulez and Stockhausen. For example: Cowell's *Mosaic Quartet*, where the performers, in any way they choose, produce a continuity from composed blocks provided by him. Or his *Elastic Musics*, the time lengths of which can be short or long through the use or omission of measures provided by him. These actions by Cowell are very close to current experimental compositions which have parts but no scores, and which are therefore not objects but processes providing experience not burdened by psychological intentions on the part of the composer.

And in connection with musical continuity, Cowell remarked at the New School before a concert of works by Christian Wolff, Earle Brown, Morton Feldman, and myself, that here were four composers who were getting rid of glue. That is: Where people had felt the necessity to stick sounds together to make a continuity, we four felt the opposite necessity to get rid of the glue so that sounds would be themselves.

Christian Wolff was the first to do this. He wrote some pieces vertically on the page but recommended their being played horizontally left to right, as is conventional. Later he discovered other geometrical means for freeing his music of intentional continuity. Morton Feldman divided pitches into three areas, high, middle, and low, and established a time unit. Writing on graph paper, he simply inscribed numbers of tones to be played at any time within specified periods of time.

There are people who say, "If music's that easy to write, I could do it." Of course they could, but they don't. I find Feldman's own statement more affirmative. We were driving back from some place in New England where a concert had been given. He is a large man and falls asleep easily. Out of a sound sleep, he awoke to say, "Now that things are so simple, there's so much to do." And then he went back to sleep.

Giving up control so that sounds can be sounds (they are not men: they are sounds) means for instance: the conductor of an orchestra is no longer a policeman. Simply an indicator of time—not in beats—like a chronometer. He has his own part. Actually he is not necessary if all the players have some other way of knowing what time it is and how that time is changing.

What else is there to say about the history of experimental music in America? Probably a lot. But we don't need to talk about neoclassicism (I agree with Varèse when he says neoclassicism is indicative of intellectual poverty), nor about the twelve-tone system. In Europe, the number twelve has already been dropped and in a recent lecture Stockhausen questions the current necessity for the concept of a series. Elliott Carter's ideas about rhythmic modulation are not experimental. They just extend sophistication out from tonality ideas towards ideas about modulation from one tempo to another. They put a new wing on the academy and open no doors to the world outside the school. Cowell's present interests in the various traditions, Oriental and early American, are not experimental but eclectic. Jazz per se derives from serious music. And when serious music derives from it, the situation becomes rather silly.

One must make an exception in the case of William Russell [1905–1992]. Though still living, he no longer composes. His works, though stemming from jazz—hot jazz—New Orleans and Chicago styles—were short, epigrammatic, original, and entirely interesting. It may be suspected that he lacked the academic skills which would have enabled him to extend and develop his ideas. The fact is, his pieces were all expositions without development and therefore, even today, twenty years after their composition, interesting to hear. He used string drums made from kerosene cans, washboards, out-of-tune upright pianos; he cut a board such a length that it could be used to play all the eighty-eight piano keys at once.

If one uses the word "experimental" (somewhat differently than I have been using it) to mean simply the introduction of novel elements into one's music, we find that America has a rich history: the clusters of Leo Ornstein, the resonances of Dane Rudhyar, the Near-Eastern aspects of Alan Hovhaness, the tack piano of Lou Harrison, my own prepared piano, the distribution in space of instrumental ensembles in works by Henry Brant, the sliding tones of Ruth Crawford and, more recently, Gunther Schuller, the microtones and novel instruments of Harry Partch, the athematic continuity of clichés of Virgil Thomson. These are not experimental composers in my terminology, but neither are they part of the stream of European music which though formerly divided into neoclassicism and dodecaphony has become one in America under Arthur Berger's term, *consolidation*: consolidation of the acquisitions of Schoenberg and Stravinsky.

Actually America has an intellectual climate suitable for radical experimentation. We are, as Gertrude Stein said, the oldest country of the twentieth century. And I like to add: in our air way of knowing nowness. Buckminster Fuller, the dymaxion architect, in his three-hour lecture on the history of civilization, explains that men leaving Asia to go to Europe went against the wind and developed machines, ideas, and Occidental philosophies in accord with a struggle against nature; that, on the other hand, men leaving Asia to go to America went with the wind, put up a sail, and developed ideas and Oriental philosophies in accord with the acceptance of nature. These two tendencies met in America, producing a movement into the air, not bound to the past, traditions, or whatever. Once in Amsterdam, a Dutch musician said to me, "It must be very difficult for you in America to write music, for you are so far away from the centers of tradition." I had to say, "It must be very difficult for you in Europe to write music, for you are so close to the centers of tradition." Why, since the climate for experimentation in America is so good, why is American experimental music so lacking in strength politically (I mean unsupported by those with money [individuals and foundations], unpublished, undiscussed, ignored), and why is there so little of it that is truly uncompromising? I think the answer is this: Until 1950 about all the energy for furthering music in America was concentrated either in the League of Composers or in the ISCM (another way of saying Boulanger and Stravinsky on the one hand and Schoenberg on the other). The New Music Society of Henry Cowell was independent and therefore not politically strong. Anything that was vividly experimental was discouraged by the League and the ISCM. So that a long period of contemporary music history in America was devoid of performances of works by Ives and Varèse. Now the scene changes, but the last few years have been quiet. The League and the ISCM fused and, so doing, gave no concerts at all. We may trust that new life will spring up, since society like nature abhors a vacuum.

What about music for magnetic tape in America? Otto Luening and Vladimir Ussachevsky call themselves experimental because of their use of this new medium. However, they just continue conventional musical practices, at most extending the ranges of instruments electronically and so forth. The Barrons, Louis and Bebe, are also cautious, doing nothing that does not have an immediate popular acceptance. The Canadian Norman McLaren, working with film, is more adventurous than these—also the Whitney brothers in California. Henry Jacobs and those who surround him in the San Francisco area are as conventional as Luening, Ussachevsky, and the Barrons. These do not move in directions that are as experimental as those taken by the Europeans: Pousseur, Berio, Maderna, Boulez, Stockhausen, and so forth. For this reason one can complain that the society of musicians in America has neither recognized nor furthered its native musical resource (by "native" I mean that resource which distinguishes it from Europe and Asia—its capacity to easily break with tradition, to move easily into the air, its capacity for the unforeseen, its capacity for experimentation). The figures in the ISCM and the League, however, were not powerful aesthetically, but powerful only politically. The names of Stravinsky, Schoenberg, Webern are more golden than any of their American derivatives. These latter have therefore little musical influence, and now that they are becoming quiescent politically, one may expect a change in the musical society.

The vitality that characterizes the current European musical scene follows from the activities of Boulez, Stockhausen, Nono, Maderna, Pousseur, Berio, etc. There is in all of this activity an element of tradition, continuity with the past, which is expressed in each work as an interest in continuity whether in terms of discourse or organization. By critics this activity is termed post-Webernian. However, this term apparently means only music written *after* that of Webern, not music written *because of* that of Webern: there is no sign of *Klangfarbenmelodie*, no concern for discontinuity—rather a surprising acceptance of even the most banal of continuity devices: ascending or descending linear passages, crescendi and diminuendi, passages from tape to orchestra that are made imperceptible. The skills that are required to bring such events about are taught in the academies. However, this scene will change. The silences of American experimental music and even its technical involvements with chance operations are being introduced into new European music. It will not be easy, however, for Europe to give up being Europe. It will, nevertheless, and must: for the world is one world now.

History is the story of original actions. Once when Virgil Thomson was giving a talk at Town Hall in New York City, he spoke of the necessity of originality. The audience immediately hissed. Why are people opposed to originality? Some fear the loss of the status quo. Others realize, I suppose, the fact that they will not make it. Make what? Make history. There are kinds of originality: several that are involved with success, beauty, and ideas (of order, of expression: i.e., Bach, Beethoven); a single that is not involved, neuter, so to say. All of the several involved kinds are generally existent and only bring one sooner or later to a disgust with art. Such original artists appear, as Antonin Artaud said, as pigs: concerned with self-advertisement. What is advertised? Finally, and at best, only something that is connected not with making history but with the past: Bach, Beethoven. If it's a new idea of order, it's Bach; if it's a heartfelt expression, it's Beethoven. That is not the single necessary originality that is not involved and that makes history. That one sees that the human race is one person (all of its members parts of the same body, brothers—not in competition any more than hand is in competition with eye) enables him to see that originality is necessary, for there is no need for eye to do what hand so well does. In this way, the past and the present are to be observed and each person makes what he alone must make, bringing for the whole of human society into existence a historical fact, and then, on and on, in continuum and discontinuum.

Notes

[Text: Cage, "History of Experimental Music in the United States," 67–75 in *Silence* (Middletown, Connecticut: Wesleyan University Press, 1961). © 1973 by John Cage, Wesleyan University Press, reprinted by permission of University Press of New England.]

17

LUIGI NONO

(1924–1990)

Nono's "Historical Presence in Music Today" originated as a lecture at the Darmstadt Summer Courses for New Music in 1959. It was published shortly afterward in the journal *Melos,* in a German version edited by Nono's student Helmut Lachenmann, whereupon it was given the new title "Gitterstäbe am Himmel der Freiheit" ("Prison Bars in the Heaven of Freedom"). Shortly thereafter, it appeared in shortened versions in several different languages. The complete lecture appears here for the first time in English. It remains Nono's most controversial and often cited statement on music. In it he enunciates his belief that contemporary composers have a duty to embody in their music distinctive aspects of the social and artistic situation of their own time. In this context he attacks the music and artistic outlook of John Cage, in which he finds a pernicious renunciation of a composer's responsibility to history.

Cage and his music had attracted considerable attention at Darmstadt the previous summer (1958). The American visitor had read three lectures concerning indeterminacy and its philosophical basis, and, joined by the pianist David Tudor, he played several of his own chance pieces, in addition to new music by Earle Brown, Morton Feldman, and Christian Wolff. This represented a very different approach to music from what was customary at Darmstadt, where rationality and strict organization were the order of the day. The music of Luigi Nono—long a mainstay of the Darmstadt School—was squarely in the doctrinaire manner of postwar European serialism. True to his belief that music must address issues of the present day, Nono chose texts concerning society and politics, often reflecting his own strict Marxist philosophy.

Before dealing with Cage, however, Nono turns his attention to another "product of American culture," Joseph Schillinger, who like Cage is guilty of avoiding his duty to history. The choice of Schillinger is certainly odd. Before his death in 1943 he was known primarily as a teacher of popular music (George Gershwin was one of his students). His book *The Mathematical Basis of the Arts,* published posthumously and cited by Nono, is a dense exploration of numerical phenomena and art, having little relevance to postwar music. Plainly enough, Nono was referring not to Schillinger per se but to the automated, mathematized compositions of the early 1950s by figures such as Babbitt and Boulez. These were abstract works that for Nono had no connection to the social issues of their time. Later in his lecture Nono is more specific in his condemnation of such music, in which composers, he says, willingly remove their own intellectual control and allow the musical elements to unfold according to some dehumanized system.

Finally Nono arrives at John Cage, whom he attacks vigorously. He accuses Cage of intellectual apathy, rampant egotism and ambition, and making false promises of freedom. The sound elements of his works are pure decoration, and worst of all, the withdrawal of the composer's intentions—a premise of indeterminate composition—negates the relevance of Cage's music to its time, neutralizing its role as an artifact that could speak to and about a specific point in history. Instead of chance or collage, Nono proposes a synthesis of rational composition intertwined with interesting and expressive elements. Nono experimented with this amalgamation in his own music of the 1960s, at which time he turned to electronic composition.

Nono's Writings: A Selective Bibliography

"The Historical Reality of Music Today." *Score* 27 (1960): 41–45. A translation of a shortened version of "Presenza storica nella musica d'oggi."

Texte: Studien zu seiner Musik. Edited by Jürg Stenzl. N.p.: Atlantis, 1974. Contains Nono's complete literary oeuvre to 1974. Very few of his writings have been translated into English.

—ɯ—

HISTORICAL PRESENCE IN MUSIC TODAY

(*Presenza storica nella musica d'oggi*, 1959)

There flourishes today—in creative matters as in those of criticism and analysis—a widespread tendency to place an artistic or cultural phenomenon not in its historical context, to view it not in light of its origins or the elements that shaped it, not in relation to its pertinence to and effect upon the present day, not in relation to its inherent possibilities for illuminating the future, but, instead, to view it exclusively for its own sake, in and of itself, only in relation to that fixed moment when it appeared.

Not only does this reject the organization of history, but even history itself, together with its evolutionary and constructive process.

moi, Antonin Artaud, je suis mon fils,	me, Antonin Artaud, I am my son
mon père, ma mère,	my father, my mother,
et moi;	and myself;
niveleur du périple imbécile où s'enferre	leveller of the idiotic trip that's tangled up in
l'engendrement,	breeding,
le périple papa-maman	the trip papa-mama
et l'enfant.[1]	and baby.

This is the manifesto of those who imagine that they can inaugurate, *ex abrupto,* a new era in which everything on the agenda must be "new," those who are seeking an easy way to establish themselves as beginning and end, as gospel.

That's the agenda. It reminds us of the anarchist's gesture of dropping a bomb as the sole and final way to create the illusion of a clean slate, a desperate reaction to a situation that one cannot control, either historically or personally. It is an agenda that entirely lacks the constructive impetus characteristic of the true revolutionary, who—clearly conscious of where things stand—brings about the collapse of existing structures to create room for new and emerging ones.

They reject not only history and its shaping forces, they go so far as to see in them fetters constraining the so-called "spontaneous freedom" of man's creative spirit. Two theoretical positions—different in concept but similar in consequence—have been advanced to support this ideology. They come from two men who are products of American culture: Joseph Schillinger (actually of Russian birth) and John Cage. In recent years their ideas have exerted, both directly and indirectly, a confusing influence in Europe. At the beginning of the first chapter ("Art and Nature") of his book *The Mathematical Basis of the Arts,* which was published in New York in 1948, Joseph Schillinger presents a theory of creative freedom and its absence:

> If art implies selectivity, skill and organization, ascertainable principles must underlie it. Once such principles are discovered and formulated, works of art may be produced by scientific synthesis. There is a common misunderstanding about the freedom of an artist as it relates to self-expression. No artist is really free. He is subjected to the influences of his immediate surroundings in the manner of execution and confined to the material media at his hand. If an artist were truly free, he would speak his own individual language. In reality, he speaks only the language of his immediate geographical and historical boundaries. There is no artist known who, being born in Paris, can express himself spontaneously in the medium of Chinese 4th century A.D., nor is there any composer, born and reared in Vienna, who possesses an inborn mastery of the Javanese gamelan.
>
> The key to real freedom and emancipation from local dependence is through scientific method.[2]

Schillinger affirms the binding of a person to his historical and geographical location, but he condemns this relation as an impediment to spontaneous expression. If his assertion, "No artist is really free," were actually true, then nowhere in the course of history would there have been art. For art and freedom are synonymous whenever a person expresses his awareness, insight, and choice at a definite moment within the constructive historical process, whenever he consciously and decisively engages in the process of liberation that history is destined to fulfill. Schillinger's demand for a scientific synthesis as the only way of making art *free* leads us to think of mass production, whose fundamental principle is indeed scientific but which completely erases all characteristic features from a work, that is, its vital power to contribute to the time in which it originated and to become a testament to its time.

Taking shelter in a scientific principle or mathematical relation without concern for the whys and wherefores, the function of this principle, removes the raison d'être from all otherwise valid phenomena by effacing their historical identity as distinctive artifacts of their period, sending us back to the "dark ages" of dogmatic principles. The observance of a schematic principle (of a scientific or mathematical sort) never gives life to an artwork; instead, this comes invariably from synthesis—the outcome of dialectic—between a principle and its realization in history; that is, its individuation at a particular point in time—not earlier or later.

John Cage, the other of the two, uses a different method to support his long-held philosophy of timelessness (doing so apparently without having to sacrifice his indifference to the present historical moment). He bases his aesthetic on sayings of the sages of Imperial China. These are wonderfully apt so long as one ignores the fact that, in the epoch when they were made, they belonged to the political and religious program of the ruling dynasties and were used to attack the concept of historical development. They were intended to counteract a lessening of the power of the gods of that period wrought by the passing of time. But Imperial China is dead, its intellectual organization is dead, and the process of history has given the lie to all of its programmatic documents, unmasking them for their vain exaltation of the ego. The remark of Daisetz Teitaro Suzuki, "He lived in the ninth or the tenth century. Or the eleventh century, or the twelfth or thirteenth century or the fourteenth," recounted by John Cage in his article in the 1959 *Darmstädter Beiträge*, is irrelevant to the indispensable historical thought of today.[3] A similarly static idea of time arose in the Holy Roman Empire, which, as a reflection of the Kingdom of God on earth, intended to maintain its fixed hierarchic order for all time. But the church, which had to reconcile its active religious mission with this secular power structure, could never preserve a fixed structure. It was upset by events such as the founding of the Jesuit order in the sixteenth century or the institution of the worker priesthood in France today, developments forced by the incorruptible and unavoidable progress of history.

With a smug naïveté we offer a new alternative to the apparently collapsing European state of mind, dispelling its depression by replacing the young European's apathetic "It doesn't matter" with the morally rejuvenative "*I* am time—*I* am space!" We thereby spare him a responsibility to his place in time, a responsibility that has now taken on considerable proportions—apparently too large and too burdensome for many. *This* is a capitulation in the face of time, a cynical flight from responsibility, explainable only as the flight of one whose ambition (more or less hidden) for the aggrandisement of his ego has flagged on account of the defeats dealt him by history. Inwardly he has become small and poor, outwardly all the more reliant on an absolute "spirit of the age," which, so he hopes, will not threaten the prerogatives of his ego and deliver him from disgrace at the hands of time. It is a yearning for a naive and everlasting innocence by those who feel guilty but will not consciously own up to it. They are only too willing to buy their way out of such necessities, ready to pay even with their own vitality of mind, even though they don't have much of this currency left to spend.

It takes courage and power to recognize one's time and to decide in its favor. It is much easier to stick one's head in the sand: "We're free since we have no choice;

we're free since we are dead; free as a rock; just as the slave who has castrated himself is free from his instincts. Seriously now, we're free because we have put blinders in front of our faces."

This is the mentality written on their calling card, which is new although the mentality is very old in both a historical and clinical sense. It brings us face to face with a fully moribund and reactionary consequence of the individual's vain and centuries old assertion of his own ego. Just when the frail European spirit staggers toward it, grasping it as a quick and easy means of "deliverance," it is exposed for what it is.

The halt in intellectual activity leads on one hand to apathy by the individual and on the other to an ever larger role for materials. A mere contemplation of these will apparently have to satisfy us in our future experience with music.

Precisely here, in a mentality that sees no alternative to a depressing dichotomy between intellect and material, we find the greatest failure of intellectual power. The intellect, seeking only to be the faithful mirror of material, becomes its slave, without asking whether or to what degree it is meaningful; the material, on the other hand, is entrusted quite by itself with a capacity to communicate, and the apathetic intellect can only stand by in reverential silence as it takes on automatized shapes. From these two equally impoverished alternatives we usually choose the second, since the intellect has already showed itself to be creatively ineffective.

But it is really not a question of two alternatives, but only a single one. This is the conscious, responsible recognition of materials by the intellect, a discovery achieved mutually as the one acts upon the other. This one true and necessary approach is clearly foreign to John Cage, who asks: "Are notes notes or are they Webern?"[4] One could answer by the question, "Are people people or are they heads, feet, hands, stomachs?" Without this mutual interpenetration of conception and technique—unthinkable without a clear underlying intellectual conception—any communication inherent in materials is lost as they become mere decoration and ornament, at best a vain diversion for an ego of regal proportions or one that is in for some deadly serious listening.

Anything can be made into a decoration. A very easy way is to take elements from one culture and place them in an unrelated culture, stripping them of their original meaning. This is *collage*, which is quite old. An example in architecture is the cathedral at Aachen, which was built around 800 A.D. in imitation of the cathedral of S. Vitale in Ravenna, built 200 years earlier. This represented the transplanting of a culture, a transplanting that has significance in intellectual history. The cathedral was a symbol of the idea of conquest which then prevailed with a ruler whose ideological aspirations for imposing his culture on a foreign one made its construction recommendable. Collage was also valued by the Venetians in their golden period, when trophies plundered from other cultures were used to deck out their own city. These collages had a moral virtue only for never having to dissemble as to what they really were. A block in S. Marco that plainly came from another culture had the unmistakable effect of documenting a historical period characterized by the plundering of foreign trophies.

The methods of collage descend from imperialist thought. There is no real difference between the use of a hollow Indian drum as a trash can in a modern European house and the use of orientalisms as attractive ornaments in the arts and crafts of Western culture. Rather than a fruitful study of the intellectual products of foreign cultures—which is highly necessary and recommendable—we pillage these creations with brutal indifference and aesthetic titillation, to profit from the fascination for exotic items. And then we try to justify this by muttering philosophical thoughts from bygone cultures.

These justifications, as they are commonly phrased nowadays at Darmstadt, acquire an added pungency when adjectives such as "free" and "spontaneous" are sprinkled on. The technical concept used to support these terms is the old idea of "improvisation." Improvisation in old Chinese music was based on notated sources in which only the parameter of pitch was fixed while the others were freely improvised. The performers of such improvisations were always restricted to certain castes, among which the rules were passed on from generation to generation. It should never be forgotten that such improvisations were cultic events, always referring to a higher being, to a god.

In the *commedia dell'arte* we encounter a technically related type of improvisation. Their plots were reduced to a few general formulas. These defined the space within which actors were free to improvise dialogue and action and which, as regards staging, outlined the fundamental situations in which the characters came into contact. This type of freedom did not last long. Influenced by a few dominant actors who had come to excel in all areas of their craft, ensuing generations limited themselves to imitating and profiting from their high achievements. The earlier multifaceted art declined into purely virtuosic acting and rigid ceremony, lacking in creative power.

And today? Today they would have us believe that improvisation is liberating, a guarantee of freedom of the ego. So too its opposite—order is dismissed as compulsion, an incarceration of the ego. This opposition, as John Cage and his circle represented it at Darmstadt, is not only a muddled juggling of terms but also an attempt to mislead naive beginners by mixing up composition with speculation.

To draw an analogy between so-called "totally organized" composition and political systems is to engage in a pitifully gross example of mind control, which seeks to replace freedom as an exercise of free will with something quite different. The plainly rhetorical application of the terms freedom and bondage in an artistic or creative context is merely another attempt to inflame—and a very simple one at that. It instills a distrust of important concepts—including intellectual order, artistic discipline, clarity, and purity—a distrust explained by the hatred that fills those who cannot distinguish between the concept of order and miltary or political subjugation. These people tangle concepts together, showing that they are unable to extricate themselves—inwardly or outwardly—from the past. For them "freedom" arises when they allow instinct to supersede their capacity for analytic thought. Their idea of freedom is intellectual suicide, analogous to the medieval Inquisition, which contended that a person who was trapped in the bondage of the devil could be freed by being burned at the stake. These "freedom aesthetes" have no understanding of the genuine idea of creative freedom—a consciously acquired capacity for identifying and facing up to the necessary demands of one's own time.

Chance, their universal panacea, has been on the minds of composers of every period, provided that this term is understood as a means for expanding the empirical horizon, as a path leading to a broader knowledge. But to use the term chance and its acoustic by-products in the sense of discovery that can replace genuine decision-making can only be a method for those who fear decisions and the freedom that they entail.

There is no need for history to discredit these individuals, because their coin has long been exposed as counterfeit. They think that they are free, but their euphoria prevents them even from noticing the prison bars that stand across their heavenly freedom. Music as a historical presence will always be the legacy of those who consciously yield to the process of history and who, at every moment in this process, make decisions with the full clarity of their intuition and logical perception. As they sense vital needs they will open new possibilities for new fundamental structures. Art lives and will continue to fulfill its role in history. And there is still much wonderful work to be done.

Notes

[Text: "Gitterstäbe am Himmel der Freiheit" ("Prison Bars in the Heaven of Freedom"), *Melos* 27 (1960): 69–75. Translated by Bryan R. Simms. Reprinted by the permission of Nuria Schoenberg Nono and the Archivio Luigi Nono, Venice. The title from the first edition in *Melos* is replaced here by "Presenza storica nella musica d'oggi," the title used by Nono when the text was first presented as a lecture.]

1. Quoted in Georges Charbonnier, *Antonin Artaud* (Paris: Pierre Seghers, 1959): 16. [The poem is extracted from Artaud's *Ci-gît* (1947). Nono's reference here to Artaud may be a jab at Boulez, who often alluded approvingly to Artaud's surrealistic writing. "I can observe in his writings," wrote Boulez in the 1958 essay 'Sound and Word,' "the basic pre-occupations of music today."]

[2. Joseph Schillinger, *The Mathematical Basis of the Arts* (New York: Philosophical Library, 1948), 3.]

[3. "History of Experimental Music in the United States," in Cage, *Silence* (Middletown, CT: Wesleyan University Press, 1961), 67–75. This article, which is also reprinted in this anthology, first appeared in a German translation in the *Darmstädter Beiträge zur neuen Musik*, 3 (1959).]

[4. Nono probably refers to Cage's lecture entitled "Communication," given at Darmstadt in September 1958. In its version printed in *Silence* (p. 41), Cage writes, "Are sounds just sounds or are they Beethoven?"]

BENJAMIN BRITTEN

(1 9 1 3 – 1 9 7 6)

When it was published in 1964, Benjamin Britten's short address "On Winning the First Aspen Award" went directly against the spirit of its time. Here Britten reformulates the regionalist-populist musical aesthetic that was widespread before World War II, and he implicitly rejects the orthodoxy of the postwar avant-garde. For Britten, music should be tailored to a specific use, intentionally accommodating a certain audience and circumstance of performance. Its purpose is to bring pleasure, which should be immediately and broadly felt, to the community in which the music is heard. This viewpoint about music is familiar from the writings of composers in the 1920s and 1930s; virtually identical sentiments had been expressed in 1932, for example, by Ralph Vaughan Williams in his lecture "Should Music Be National?" (essay no. 11). Although it was not Britten's way to criticize his younger contemporaries, his description of music of the avant-garde as "pretentious nonsense" made it clear that he had little sympathy for the new directions in music since the 1950s.

Britten rarely wrote about music. When he came to America in 1939 he began to contribute essays to several periodicals, music criticism then being a popular sideline for American composers. But with his return to England and growing success as a composer in the mid-1940s, his writings became infrequent.

Britten's Writings: A Selective Bibliography

"Au Revoir to the U. S. A." *Modern Music* 19 (1941–42): 100–101.

"Conversation with Benjamin Britten." *Tempo* 6 (1944): 4–5.

"England and the Folk-Art Problem." *Modern Music* 18 (1941): 71–75.

—〰—

ON WINNING THE FIRST ASPEN AWARD

(1964)

When last May President Alvin C. Eurich and Chairman Robert O. Anderson told me they wished to travel the five thousand miles from Aspen to Aldeburgh to have a talk with me, they hinted that it had something to do with an Aspen Award for Services to the Humanities—an award of very considerable importance and size. I imagined that they felt I might advise them on a suitable recipient, and I began to consider what I should say. Who would be suitable for such an honor? What kind of person? Doctor, priest, social worker, politician? An artist? Yes, possibly (that, I imagined, could be the reason that Mr. Anderson and Professor Eurich thought I might be the person to help them). So I ran through the names of the great figures working in the arts among us today. It was a fascinating problem, rather like one's schooltime game of ideal cricket elevens or, slightly more recently, ideal casts for operas—but I certainly won't tell which of our great poets, painters, or composers came to the top of my list.

Mr. Anderson and Professor Eurich paid their visit to my home in Aldeburgh. It was a charming and courteous visit, but it was also a knockout. It had not occurred to me, frankly, that it was I who was to be the recipient of this magnificent award, and I was stunned. I am afraid my friends must have felt I was a tongue-tied host. But I simply could not imagine why I had been chosen for this very great honor. I read again the simple and moving citation. The key word seemed to be *humanities*. I went to the dictionary to look up its meaning. I found *humanity*: "the quality of being human" (well, that applied to me all right). But I found that the plural had a special meaning: "Learning or literature concerned with human culture, as grammar, rhetoric, poetry, and especially the ancient Latin and Greek classics." (Here I really had no claims since I cannot properly spell even in my own language, and when I set Latin I have terrible trouble over the quantities.) *Humanitarian* was an entry close beside these, and I supposed I might have some claim here, but I was daunted by the definition: "One who goes to excess in his human principles (in 1855 often contemptuous or hostile)." I read on, quickly, *Humanist*: "One versed in humanities," and I was back where I started. But perhaps, after all, the clue was in the word *human*, and I began to feel that I might have a small claim.

I certainly write music for human beings—directly and deliberately. I consider their voices, the range, the power, the subtlety, and the color potentialties of them. I consider the instruments they play—their most expressive and suitable individual sonorities, and where I may be said to have invented an instrument (such as the slung mugs of *Noye's Fludde*) I have borne in mind the pleasure the young performers will have in playing it. I also take note of the *human* circumstances of music, of its environment and conventions; for instance, I try to write dramatically effective music for the theater—I certainly don't think opera is better for not being effective on the stage. I fear some people think that effectiveness must be superficial. And the best music to listen to in a great Gothic church is the polyphony that was written for it and took account of the great resonance: this was my approach in *War Requiem*— I calculated it for a big reverberant acoustic, and that is where it sounds best. I believe therefore in *occasional* music, although I admit there are some occasions that can intimidate one—I do not envy Purcell writing his "Ode to Celebrate King James's Return to London from Newmarket." On the other hand, almost every piece I have ever written has been composed with a certain occasion in mind, and usually for definite performers, and certainly always *human* ones.

You may ask perhaps: how far can a composer go in thus considering the demands of people, of humanity? At many times in history the artist has made a conscious effort to speak with the voice of the people. Beethoven certainly tried, in works as different as the *Battle of Vittoria* and the Ninth Symphony, to utter the sentiments of a whole community. From the beginning of Christianity there have been musicians who have wanted and tried to be the servants of the church to express the devotion and convictions of Christians as such. Recently we have had the example of Shostakovich, who set out in his *Leningrad* Symphony to present a monument to his fellow citizens, an explicit expression for them of their own endurance and heroism. At a very different level, one finds composers such as Johann Strauss and George Gershwin aiming at providing the people with the best dance music and songs that they were capable of making. And I can find nothing wrong with the objectives—declared or implicit—of these men, nothing wrong with offering to my fellowmen music that may inspire them or comfort them, touch them or entertain them, even educate them, directly and with intention. On the contrary, it is the composer's duty, as a member of society, to speak to or for his fellow human beings.

When I am asked to compose a work for an occasion, great or small, I want to know in some detail the conditions of the place where it will be performed, the size and acoustics, what instruments or singers will be available and suitable, the kind of people who will hear it, and what language they will understand—and even sometimes the age of the listeners and performers. For it is futile to offer children music by which they are bored, or which makes them feel inadequate or frustrated, which may set them against music forever; and it is insulting to address anyone in a language that he does not understand. The text of my *War Requiem* was perfectly in place in Coventry Cathedral—the Owen poems in the vernacular, and the words of the Requiem Mass familiar to everyone—but it would have been pointless in Cairo or Peking.

During the act of composition one is continually referring back to the conditions of performance—as I have said, the acoustics and the forces available, the techniques of the instruments and the voices—such questions occupy one's attention continuously and certainly affect the stuff of the music. In my experience they are not only a restriction but a challenge, an inspiration. Music does not exist in a vacuum. It does not exist until it is performed, and performance imposes conditions. It is the easiest thing in the world to write a piece virtually or totally impossible to perform—but oddly enough that is not what I prefer to do; I prefer to study the conditions of performance and shape my music to them.

Where does one stop, then? In answering people's demands? It seems that there is no clearly defined "Halt" sign on this road. The only brake that one can apply is that of one's own private and personal conscience; when that speaks clearly, one must halt; and it can speak for musical or nonmusical reasons.

In the last six months I have been several times asked to write a work as a memorial to the late President Kennedy. On each occasion I have refused—not because in any way I was out of sympathy with such an idea; on the contrary, I was horrified and deeply moved by the tragic death of a very remarkable man. But for me I do not feel the time is ripe; I cannot yet stand back and see it clearly. I should have to wait very much longer to do anything like justice to this great theme. But had I, in fact, agreed to undertake a limited commission, my artistic conscience would certainly have told me in what direction I could go, and when I should have to stop.

There are many dangers that hedge round the unfortunate composer; pressure groups that demand true proletarian music, snobs who demand the latest avant-garde tricks; critics who are already trying to document today for tomorrow, to be the first to find the correct pigeonhole definition. These people are dangerous—not because they are necessarily of any importance in themselves, but because they may make the composer, above all the young composer, self-conscious, and instead of writing his own music, music that springs naturally from his gift and personality, he may be frightened into writing pretentious nonsense, or deliberate obscurity. He may find himself writing more and more for machines, in conditions dictated by machines, and not by humanity; or, of course, he may end by creating grandiose claptrap when the real talent is for dance tunes or children's piano pieces. Finding one's place in society as a composer is not a straightforward job. It is not helped by the attitude toward the composer of some societies.

My own, for instance, semi-socialist Britain, and conservative Britain before it, has for years treated the musician as a curiosity to be barely tolerated. At a tennis party in my youth I was asked what I was going to do when I grew up—what job I was aiming at. "I am going to be a composer," I said. "Yes, but what else?" was the answer. The average Briton thought, and still thinks, of the arts as suspect and expensive luxuries. The Manchester counselor who boasted he had never been to a concert and didn't intend to go is no very rare bird in England. By Act of Parliament, each local authority in England is empowered to spend a 6d.[six pence] rate on the arts. In fact, it seems that few of them spend more than one twentieth of this—a sign of no very great enthusiasm! Until such a condition is changed, musicians will continue to feel out of step in our semi-welfare state.

But if we in England have to face a considerable indifference, in other countries conditions can have other, equally awkward effects. In totalitarian regimes, we know that great official pressure is brought to bring the artist into line and make him conform to the state's ideology. In the richer capitalist countries, money and snobbishness combine to demand the latest, newest manifestations, which I am told go by the name in this country of "foundation music."

The *ideal* conditions for an artist or musician will never be found outside the *ideal* society, and when shall we see that? But I think I can tell you some of the things that any artist demands from any society. He demands that his art shall be accepted as an essential part of human activity and human expression; and that he shall be accepted as a genuine practitioner of that art and consequently of value to the community; reasonably, he demands a secure living from society, and a pension when he has worked long enough; this is a basis for society to offer a musician, a modest basis. In actual fact there are very few musicians in my country who will get a pension after forty years' work in an orchestra or in an opera house. This must be changed; we must at least be treated as civil servants. Once we have a material status, we can accept the responsibility of answering society's demands on us. And society should and will demand from us the utmost of our skill and gift in the full range of music-making. (Here we come back to occasional music.) There should be special music made and played for all sorts of occasions: football matches, receptions, elections (why not?), and even presentations of awards. I would have been delighted to have been greeted with a special piece composed for today. It might have turned out to be another piece as good as the cantata Bach wrote for the municipal election at Mühlhausen, or the galliard that Dowland wrote as a compliment to the Earl of Essex. Some of the greatest pieces of music in our possession were written for special occasions, grave or gay. But we shouldn't worry too much about the so-called permanent value of our occasional music. A lot of it cannot make much sense after its first performance, and it is quite a good thing to please people even if only for today.

That is what we should aim at—pleasing people today as seriously as we can, and letting the future look after itself. Bach wrote his *St. Matthew Passion* for performance on one day of the year only—the day which in the Christian church was the culmination of the year, to which the year's worship was leading. It is one of the unhappiest results of the march of science and commerce that this unique work, at the turn of a switch, is at the mercy of any loud roomful of cocktail drinkers—to be listened to or switched off at will, without ceremony or occasion.

The wording of your institute's constitution implies an effort to present the arts as a counterbalance to science in today's life. And though I am sure you do not imagine that there is not a lot of science, knowledge, and skill in the art of making music (in the calculation of sound qualities and colors, the knowledge of the technique of instruments and voices, the balance of forms, the creation of moods, and the development of ideas), I would like to think you are suggesting that what is important in the arts is not the scientific part, the analyzable part of music, but the something that emerges from it but transcends it, which cannot be analyzed because it is not in it, but of it. It is the quality which cannot be acquired by simply the exercise of a technique or a system: It is something to do with personality, with gift, with spirit. I simply call it magic—quality which would appear to be by no means unacknowledged by scientists, and which I value more than any other part of music.

It is arguable that the richest and most productive eighteen months in our music history is the time when Beethoven had just died, when the other nineteenth-century giants, Wagner, Verdi, and Brahms, had not begun; I mean the period in which Franz Schubert wrote the *Winterreise*, the C Major Symphony, his last three piano sonatas, the C Major String Quintet, as well as a dozen other glorious pieces. The very creation of these works in that space of time seems hardly credible; but the standard of inspiration, of magic, is miraculous and past all explanation. Though I have worked very hard at the *Winterreise* the last five years, every time I come back to it I am amazed not only by the extraordinary mastery of it—for Schubert knew exactly what he was doing (make no mistake about that) and he had thought profoundly about it. But each time the magic is renewed, and the mystery remains. This magic comes only with the sounding of the music, with the turning of the written note into sound—and it only comes (or comes most intensely) when the listener is one with the composer, either as performer himself or as a listener in active sympathy. Simply to read a score in one's armchair is not enough for evoking this quality.

Indeed, this magic can be said to consist of just the music that is not in the score. Sometimes one can be quite daunted when one opens the *Winterreise*—there seems to be nothing on the page. One must not exaggerate; the shape of the music and its substance is perfectly clear—sometimes, as in his last great B-flat Sonata, elaborately so. What cannot be indicated on the printed page are the innumerable small variants of rhythm and phrasing which make up the performer's contribution. In the *Winterreise*, it was not possible for Schubert to indicate exactly the length of rests and pauses, or the color of the singer's voice or the clarity or smoothness of consonants. This is the responsibility of each individual performer, and at each performance he will make modifications. The composer expects him to; he would be foolish if he did not. For a musical experience needs three human beings at least. It requires a composer, a performer, and a listener; and unless these three take part together there is no musical experience.

The experience will be that much more intense and rewarding if the circumstances correspond to what the composer intended: if the *St. Matthew Passion* is performed on Good Friday in a church, to a congregation of Christians; if the *Winterreise* is performed in a room, or in a small hall of truly intimate character to a circle of friends; if *Don Giovanni* is played to an audience which understands the text and appreciates the musical allusions. The further one departs from these circumstances, the less true and more diluted is the experience likely to be. One must face the fact today that the vast majority of musical performances take place as far away from the original as it is possible to imagine. I do not mean simply *Falstaff* being given in Tokyo, or the Mozart Requiem in Madras. I mean, of course, that such works can be audible in any corner of the globe, at any moment of the day or night—through a loudspeaker, without question of suitability or comprehensibility. Anyone, anywhere, at any time, can listen to the B Minor Mass upon one condition only: that they possess a machine. No qualification is required of any sort—faith, virtue, education, experience, age. Music is now free for all. If I say the loudspeaker is principal enemy of music, I don't mean that I am not grateful to it as a means of education or study, or as an evoker of memories. But it is not part of true musical experience. Regarded as such, it is simply a substitute, and dangerous because deluding. Music demands more from a listener than simply the possession of a tape machine or a transistor radio. It demands some preparation, some effort—a journey to a special place, saving up for a ticket, some homework on the program perhaps, some clarification of the ears and sharpening of the instincts. It demands as much effort on the listener's part as the other two corners of the triangle, this holy triangle of composer, performer, and listener.

This award is the latest of the kindnesses for which I am indebted to your country. I first came to the United States twenty-five years ago, at the time when I was a discouraged young composer—muddled, fed up and looking for work, looking to be used. I was most generously treated here, by old and new friends, and to all of these I can never be sufficiently grateful. Their kindness was past description; I shall never forget it. But the thing I am most grateful to your country for is this: It was in California, in the unhappy summer of 1941, that, coming across a copy of the poetical works of George Crabbe in a Los Angeles bookshop, I first read his poem of *Peter Grimes*; and, at this same time reading a most perceptive and revealing article about it by E. M. Forster. I suddenly realized where I belonged and what I lacked. I had become without roots, and when I got back to England six months later I was ready to put them down. I have lived since then in the same small corner of East Anglia, near where I was born. And I find as I get older that working becomes more and more difficult away from that home. I plot and plan my music when I am away on tour, and I get great stimulus and excitement from visiting other countries. With a congenial partner, I like giving concerts, and in the last years we have traveled as far as Vancouver and Tokyo, Moscow and Java. I like making new friends, meeting new audiences, hearing new music. But I belong at home—there—in Aldeburgh. I have tried to bring music to it in the shape of our local festival; and all the music I write comes from it. I believe in roots, in associations, in backgrounds, in personal relationships. I want my music to be of use to people, to please them, to "enhance their lives" (to use Berenson's phrase). I do not write for posterity: in any case, the outlook for that is somewhat uncertain. I write music, now, in Aldeburgh, for people living there, and further afield, indeed for anyone who cares to play it or listen to it. But my music now has its roots in where I live and work. And I only came to realize that in California in 1941.

People have already asked me what I am going to do with your money. I have even been told in the post and press exactly how I ought to dispose of it. I shall of course pay no attention to these suggestions, however well- or ill-intentioned.

The last prize I was given went straight away to the Aldeburgh Festival, the musical project I have most at heart. It would not surprise me if a considerable part of the Aspen award went in that direction; I have not really decided. But one thing I know I want to do; I should like to give an annual Aspen prize for a British composition. The conditions would change each year. One year it might be for a work for young voices and a school orchestra, another year for the celebration of a national event or centenary, another time a work for an instrument whose repertory is small— but in any case for specific or general usefulness. And the jury would be instructed to choose only that work which was a pleasure to perform and inspiriting to listen to. In this way I would try to express my interpretation of the intention behind the Aspen Institute, and to express my warmest thanks, my most humble thanks, for the unbelievable honor which you have awarded me today.

Notes

[Text: Britten, "On Winning the First Aspen Award," *Saturday Review* 47/3 (August 22, 1964): 37–39, 51. Reprinted by permission of the Aspen Institute for Humanistic Studies.]

1 9

L U C I A N O   B E R I O

(B .   1 9 2 5)

Berio's "Meditation on a Twelve-Tone Horse" is a polemical assault upon strict-ly organized and serialized composition of the 1950s and 1960s. By 1968, when Berio's essay was published, most of the leading European composers had already turned away from strict serialism, but in America total organization in music still had many adherents. One such was Milton Babbitt. In his essay "Who Cares If You Listen?" (essay no. 15), Babbitt had postulated that intricate systems of total serialization were indispensable to modern music, if it was "to continue to live." He contended that the contemporary serial composer need-ed to analyze earlier twelve-tone works, by implication those of Schoenberg and Webern, to derive strategies that could then be extended in a far more sys-tematic and integrated manner in new compositions.

This is the viewpoint attacked by Berio. It is futile, he writes, to analyze historically bygone works—the works of Schoenberg, for example—with the intention of redirecting their form (or content) into modern compositions. The meaning of any artwork is inseparable from the time and culture in which it is written and cannot be historically transplanted. To try to do so, he says, is com-parable to the misguided attempt by earlier linguists to get at the underlying meaning of a language by analyzing its external sounds and symbols. Language, like composition, rests instead upon an underlying idea or meaning—a deep structure—which is transformed until it achieves its outward shape. A twelve-tone apparatus is solely "theory," which, like grammar in language, can only assist the listener in understanding a work. It cannot produce a meaningful utter-ance. The authoritarian insistence on serialism, Berio concludes, is nothing less than fascism.

In this complex argument Berio is indebted not only to structuralist writ-ers such as Claude Lévi-Strauss and Noam Chomsky, but also to the critical the-ory of Theodor Adorno. In 1938 Adorno wrote a widely read article, "On the Fetish Character in Music and the Regression of Listening," in which he argued that both classical and popular music had become commercialized to the extent of becoming a capitalistic festish. Now Berio revives the analogy by declaring that serialized music has also become a fetish—an object adored by contem-porary musicians far beyond its inherent value. Also reminiscent of Adorno's writings is the pseudo-Marxist discussion of a composer's responsibility to soci-ety. Although music cannot directly improve society, Berio admits, it must still be composed in a manner that will not imitate antisocial phenomena such as racism and fascism, both of which he finds alarmingly analogous to twelve-tone systems.

For Berio the alternative to the fascistic implications of totally serialized music was an approach in which "process," rather than form, was front and center. The presence especially of "live processes" could imbue music with a content that was distinguishable from form but still abstract and original, attuned, that is, to the spirit of the postwar decades. In practical terms these objectives were realized by composers including Berio, Pierre Boulez, and George Crumb by turning to the human voice. In Berio's works of the 1960s, including *Circles*, *Sequenza III*, *Visage*, and "O King" from *Sinfonia*, the vocal idiom suggests new ways in which music can embody meaning, different from traditional emotional communication as well as from Babbitt's dogmatic formalism.

Especially in the 1950s and 1960s, Berio was an active and important essayist on modern music. He was the editor of a modern music journal, *Incontri musicali*, and his writings appeared also in other Italian and international journals. Few of them are available in English. He has been less active as a writer since the 1970s, although his published interviews are good sources of his ideas on contemporary issues. A bibliography of his writings to 1976 is given by Claudio Annibaldi in the article on Berio in *The New Grove Dictionary of Music and Musicians*.

Berio's Writings: A Selective Bibliography

Berio, Luciano. *Two Interviews*. Translated and edited by David Osmond-Smith. New York: Marion Boyars, 1985.

Muller, Theo. "'Music Is Not a Solitary Act': Conversation with Luciano Berio." *Tempo* 199 (1997): 16–20.

—⟨𝔪⟩—

MEDITATION ON A
TWELVE-TONE HORSE
(1968)

Thanks to Italy's political situation, it was not until 1945 that I first had the opportunity to see and hear the works of Schoenberg, Stravinsky, Webern, Hindemith, Bartók, and Milhaud. I was already nineteen years old. Of that crucial period let me simply say that among the many thoughts and emotions aroused in me by these encounters, one is still intact and alive within me today: anger—anger at the realization that fascism had until that moment deprived me of knowledge of the most essential musical achievements of my own culture; further, that it was capable of actually falsifying spiritual reality.

Today, so many years afterward, talk of "cultural development," "the art explosion," "free expression," may make my recollected anger seem out of place. Yet, beneath the glossy surface of contemporary artistic liberality, a more subtle form of fascism is taking shape: a disguised fascism which, while it is not at the moment depriving us of any current "information," is threatening all the same to change our conscience and our recognition of our responsibilities in regard to music as a social act.

I refer to what H. M. Enzensberger calls the industrialization of conscience, which praises maturity and at the same time stifles maturity, which builds monuments to "culture" which bear no relation to cultural reality, which praises peace and makes war, which buys and sells all: work, the worker's conscience, happiness, symphonies, life and death, mail-order guns, and a label for every truth.

This is why I choose to vent my remembered anger here in commenting on the responsibility of the composer at a historical moment so grave and so crucial that to limit myself to anecdotes about my life in music would almost seem a shirking of that very responsibility. Furthermore, ideas in music (like any other ideas) are cumulative, and I am not so falsely modest as to claim I can capsulize into ten minutes what took me twenty years to experience and achieve.

We all know that music can't lower the cost of bread, is incapable of stopping (or starting, for that matter) wars, cannot eradicate slums and injustice. Never before, however, have responsible composers felt so compelled to challenge the meaning of and reasons for their works in relation to the world of events. Yet we are constantly faced with the ludicrous image of the Great Society composer, occupied with the assembly-line production and collection of well-made, cleverly-imitated musical objects. Never has *the composer* come so dangerously close to becoming an extraneous, or merely decorative, figure in his own society.

Composition deals with the invention and elaboration of patterns of expectation; that is, creating modes of conditioning the perception of a willing listener. This is true even of the composer who loudly declares his disregard for the audience's reaction; unless he is deaf, the composer himself plays the role of a mini-audience.

Between the various modes of "systems" (I'm really speaking of poetics) and the ideological configuration of the society there is always a strong relationship. This relationship is not a simple, deterministic one, as certain kinds of pseudo-Marxian thinking would suggest (a "decadent society produces decadent music"), but rather a dialectic one. Historical evolution modifies not only social structure but codes of esthetic perception as well. The modes that allow us to abstract and to interpret the discreet moments of that evolution must themselves undergo constant adjustment. For this reason every meaningful work can be considered an expression of a doubt, an experimental step in a poetic process, an acknowledgement of the need continuously to modify, to reinterpret, to verify, to renounce forever the comfortable utopia of a super-code that would guarantee absolutely faultless communication.

The ideology of the culture industry tends to freeze experience into schemes and manners: formation becomes "form"; an instrument, "gadget"; a social ideal, "party." Schoenberg's and Webern's poetics, "the twelve-tone system." To me, instead, it is essential that the composer be able to prove the relative nature of musical processes: their structural models, based on past experience, generate not only rules but also the transformation and the destruction of those very rules.

A composer's awareness of the plurality of functions of his own tools forms the basis for his responsibility just as, in everyday life, every man's responsibility begins with recognition of the multiplicity of human races, conditions, needs, and ideals. I would go as far as to say (as my anger comes back) that any attempt to codify musical reality into a kind of imitation grammar (I refer mainly to the efforts associated with the twelve-tone system) is a brand of fetishism which shares with fascism and racism the tendency to reduce live processes to immobile, labeled objects, the tendency to deal with formalities rather than substance. Claude Lévi-Strauss describes (though to illustrate a different point) a captain at sea, his ship reduced to a frail raft without sails, who, by enforcing a meticulous protocol on his crew, is able to distract them from the nostalgia for a safe harbor and from the desire for a destination.

A more specific comment on musical theory (a subject which is bound to remain abstract unless its functions are specified in advance) may clarify my beliefs. I find a discussion on musical theory meaningful only in relation to analysis and to specific problems of musical education, and then only to the extent that it allows different methods of analysis of the same poetic development; that is, musical theory is concerned mainly with finding constants in the history of musical development and with examining the interaction between them.

The methods and concepts used in the description of these constants and their interaction have something to do with the way we actually perceive them in a culturally defined time and space. This is simply to say that a theory of music is based principally on those factors that condition our perception in prominent ways: in tonal music, for instance, harmonic and metric aspects; in more recent music, the integration of any sound phenomenon—from speech to instrument, from "noise" to "sound"—into a generalized harmonic continuum.

In science, theory involves treatment of underlying regularities in phenomena and often the planning and prediction of the future on the basis of these regularities. In music, however, we create to a certain extent the material for analysis. Musical theory, then, is a tool for historical analysis, which becomes effective on the condition of accepting a piece of music not as an item, an isolated artifact, but as partaking of a complex environment in process.

This is why I am very much against the formalistic and escapist attitude of twelve-tone composition. In losing himself in the manipulation of a dozen notes, a composer runs the risk of forgetting that these notes are simply symbols of reality; he may, in addition, end up ignoring what sound really is.

A composer can give a descriptive analysis of his own work and can bring to bear the analytical tools from past musical experience. A structural description of a piece of music cannot, however, account for the meaning of that piece unless it is placed in a historical continuity. By the same token a "theory" derived from analysis can never legitimately be used as a tool for producing music. Attempts to do this betray an idea of musical language based solely on procedures for combining elements, which is, to say the least, irrelevant to any serious discussion of music.

Such a concept of music gives rise to the well-known query which opens many "theoretical" discussions these days: "How did he get the notes?" Shuffling notes with the illusion that one is dealing with the formation of music is like using words like "peace" and "freedom" in speaking about Vietnam without touching the underlying relationships that constitute the real and horrifying meaning of that rotten war.

But rather than pursue that unhappy metaphor, let me turn to another, this time from linguistics. The choice is logical, with all one hears about "language of music," "musical grammar," and such, and discussions of music always seem to demand an eventual resort to metaphor anyway.

Recently a major breakthrough was witnessed in the field of linguistics. At its head was Noam Chomsky, who pointed out the need to abandon the dead end of taxonomic linguistics, which is based on segmentation and classification of elements. These elements are found by "discovery procedures" which are considered supremely scientific by some because they are applied only to given sequences of sounds without regard to the underlying structure of the language. This is a consequence of the notion that the sequence of sounds represents the structure of the sentence in some direct way.

Chomsky's insight was that one must begin, not with discreet units (in a loose sense, sounds) but with a semantically meaningful deep structure, from which is derived, by a series of operations, the surface structure, which is then assigned a phonetic form. The grammar, then, which describes these steps, shows how the sense of a sentence is related to its words. Chomsky repeatedly asserts that a grammar is a theory of language in that it describes what a person must know in order to speak and understand, but that it is not a model for the speaker or the hearer; that is, it does not explain the language user's ability, nor can it be used *to produce* language.

The parallels to music here are not accidental. The composer's steps always imply theoretical experience. But he is, so to speak, condemned by the very nature of his responsibilities never to succeed fully in reconciling theory and practice. To use Adorno's terms, "the problem facing the composer is not so much how to organize a musical meaning but rather how to give a meaning to organization."

There is the story of the man who stopped his watch, which had been running slow, so that it would at least give the exact time twice a day. The composer's watch is always too slow or too fast. Still, he falsifies the nature of his work and abdicates his responsibilities if he stops the mechanism to assure himself a narrow range of absolute accuracy and security. He is bound, instead, to resist surrendering to the prejudice of *the theory* and be prepared to face the multiple character of experience. He must find conceptual schemes open enough to allow him to select, to process, to combine the many aspects of reality, always bearing in mind that any signficant musical idea is not the result of a neo-positivistic procedure, but a system of interrelationships in progress.

A theory cannot substitute for meaning and idea; a discrete analytical tool can never be turned to creation by dint of polishing and perfecting it. It is poetics which guide discovery and not procedural attitudes; it is idea and not style.

This basic fact has been missed those who insist on trying to create a twelve-tone utopia of "twelve-tone coherence" by forcing on us the dubious gift of twelve-tone melodies in which, as someone has written, "the twelve-tone rhythmic structuralization is totally identical [sic] with the structuralization of the twelve tones." Alas, this industrialized twelve-tone horse, dull on the outside and empty inside, [is] constantly being perfected and dragged to a new Troy in the shadow of an ideological war long since fought and won by responsible minds like Schoenberg, with neither systems nor scholarship for armor!

Notes

[Text: Berio, "Meditation on a Twelve-Tone Horse," *Christian Science Monitor*, 15 July 1968. (1968 The Christian Science Publishing Society. All rights reserved. Reprinted with permission.]

PART IV

RETURNING TO
THE KNOWN, 1970–

AS THE ANXIETIES THAT MARKED POSTWAR SOCIETY BEGAN
to wane in the 1970s, the music that mirrored that society also changed. An earlier
dogmatic insistence on conformity relaxed into a live-and-let-live mood, in which
composers were more willing to coexist than to criticize. Automated systems of composition, including total serialism, almost entirely disappeared as composers again
came to rely on traditional methods of composing and on their artistic intuition. The
tendency toward depersonalization, which once unified such apparent opposites as
serialism and chance, was gradually dispelled by a return to expressivity, even to outright displays of emotion. Most significantly, the desire to forget the past in music—
so important in the 1950s among composers such as Boulez—yielded to an opposite
tendency by which musicians consciously referred in their new works to one or more
preexisting and well-established styles.

This reestablishing of contact with the musical past is, in fact, the principal
theme that underlies the two essays that follow. George Rochberg uses the term
renewal to describe a return to tradition, which can, he says, once again allow music
to sing and dance. John Harbison speaks of "rebuilding and reconnecting" as the
essential task facing the contemporary composer. Neither writer specifies any particular style or form that should be revived, but for both, the profile of music must be
made to reveal known values for it to be in tune with the culture of the present day.

Harbison, like many younger American composers of the present day, urges a
rapprochement with popular music, something little in evidence in the 1950s and
1960s. He makes the safe assumption that the most significant musical past in the
lives of young composers will now be popular music—not the works of Boulez, Babbitt, Schoenberg, or the earlier masters. As serious musicians they should aim to relo-
cate the vitality of popular music in the more durable classical forms.

20

GEORGE ROCHBERG

(B. 1918)

The criticisms that George Rochberg levels at modernist composers in his essay "Reflections on the Renewal of Music" are evidence of a new spirit in European and American music that emerged clearly in the 1970s and still exists now at the end of the twentieth century. Like other major aesthetic changes in the twentieth century, the new outlook of the 1970s was based on a rejection of what went immediately before. Rochberg dismisses music whose content can be located only in its form and works that are so innovative as to have no apparent association with the past. The music of Boulez and his followers was a special object of Rochberg's displeasure. Boulez had long spoken out against music that attempted to renew the past. In his essay "Bach's Moment" (1951), for example, Boulez had referred to composers of such works as "scavengers" and "grave robbers." "How can one respect these prophets of 'back to' or a 'reactivation,'" he concluded, "when their most blatant aim is security, and their chief motive a lack of courage."[1]

In this essay Rochberg vigorously attacks Boulez's viewpoint. The attempt to forget the past is narcissistic, he says, a "curse" prefigured by a philosophy of progress carried over from the early twentieth century. It is a discredited outlook that has only served to block the fertile stylistic renewals that have so often occurred in music history. The music that has come from such a philosophy is mere "anarchic hash," only an "aberration" in history, he concludes.

Rochberg also signals a new philosophy for the 1970s in his demand that music should have emotional content. A unifying thread in the music and aesthetic theory of avant-garde composers of the 1950s was the avoidance of emotion. For Milton Babbitt the content of music could be simply its form, for Luciano Berio it was "live processes," for Luigi Nono it was historical responsibility, for John Cage there was no such content at all. Unlike Rochberg, none of these composers called for a return to the human heart as a proper subject for new music. Rochberg's conclusion is that a return to emotional expressivity can only be achieved by a return to traditional elements: music, he says, must once again sing and dance.

In his many essays George Rochberg has been a relentless critic of postwar modernism, not at all content with the new live-and-let-live attitude that has prevailed among his contemporaries. Both his writings and his musical compositions show an almost continual search for and experimentation with alternatives to the orthodoxies of the 1950s. In his music these have included twelve-tone composition, textural and spatial composition, collage, neoromanticism, and polystylism.

Rochberg's Writings: A Selective Bibliography

The Aesthetics of Survival: A Composer's View of Twentieth-Century Music. Edited by William Bolcolm. Ann Arbor: University of Michigan Press, 1984. A collection of Rochberg's essays.

"Fiddlers and Fribbles, or, Is Art a Separate Reality?" *New Literary History* 18 (1987): 257–79.

The Hexachord and Its Relation to the TwelveTone Row. Bryn Mawr: Theodore Presser, 1955. An early theoretical speculation relating to Rochberg's music and to the general analytic spirit of the 1950s.

"Can the Arts Survive Modernism? (A Discussion of the Characteristics, History and Legacy of Modernism)." *Critical Inquiry* 11 (1984): 317–40. A diatribe against the values of modernist composers of the 1950s and later.

———ɯɯ———

REFLECTIONS ON THE RENEWAL
OF MUSIC
(1972)

When Mahler called Bruckner "half-baked" and Brahms "overdone," he was exercising his very strong sense of skepticism regarding the value of their achievements. Obviously, judgments produced by the skeptical temper are not necessarily true for all people. Yet, for an artist, they are basic to decisions he must make for himself. They affect his views not only of the work of others but of his own as well and determine to a great extent what he will willfully take, i.e., borrow or "steal," from another, how he will allow himself to be influenced, and what he will accept into his personal canon.

The capacity for self-indulgence is the measure of the lack of self-critical faculties, rationalizations notwithstanding, whether offered in the guise of aesthetics or not. Skepticism, therefore, is one of the primary requisites of mental awareness, the sharpness of a natural or developed acumen which tests everything in order to discover what is good or authentic. The development of critical powers leads to the capacity to make discriminating judgments without which there is no taste; and without taste there is no art. For what we call "art" is ultimately—however else it may be defined—the habitual exercise of projecting fine judgments of subtle and specific perceptions. That is why the gross, generalized, and nonspecific perceptions of today's avant-gardists fall outside the range of art and have been dubbed "anti-art." The self-declared avant-gardist lacks, among other things, precisely that skeptical temper of mind which develops the critical powers leading finally to taste, subtlety, grace, proportion—in a word, art.

Borges's[2] notion that history may be the record of the infinitely varying individual inflections of a universal mind contains more than one refutation of commonly-held beliefs. Among them is the belief in the necessity or desirability of originality,[3] the motive force which seems to supply the energy for change itself and offers the justification for asserting the aggressive tendencies of the ego, whether in art, politics, business, etc. From Borges's notion one can proceed directly and easily to the consideration of how influence—which produces resemblance, replication, reminiscence through emulation of manner or substance, or both—operates from one man to another, from one epoch to another, even to the inclusion of outright borrowing, i.e., exact repetition. But, then, in the case of direct borrowing, from whom is one taking if not from one's larger self, providing, of course, one accepts Borges's idea that each of us is, indeed, a single individual filament of a vast, interconnected cosmic nervous system, one cell of a complex far-flung organism. Narcissistic individualism, which thrives chiefly on the belief in originality and rationalizes the excesses of self-indulgence, is a kind of metaphysical cop-out.

By an act of pure fantasy the Florentine Camerata reached across centuries to the drama of ancient Greece and came up with monody and opera. If ancient Greek drama had persisted without change into the time of the late Renaissance, baroque and subsequent opera might never have occurred. How different is modern opera from Greek drama as it was actually performed? We shall never know. But in the mental space carved out by the historical loss of the actual practice of Greek drama there grew a myth of how it was; and out of the myth and the urge to resuscitate Greek tragedy, music renewed itself. We are still living off the energies of that act of renewal.

Another of the many refutations of commonly held beliefs implicit in Borges's idea of history is the long-cherished notion of the linear causal progression of human events buttressed in our time by the dizzying speed of the changes by which science and technology have "advanced" our civilization. To be a victim of the idea of change as endemic to the course of man's motion through time is nothing short of a curse on the artist. For it deprives him on every side of the reality and value of the past experience of human beings whose earlier contributions must be considered as valid as his own, but for different reasons, if his own are to be considered valid by others who will come later: If one wipes the slate clean of others, in order to satisfy some misguided notion of being "contemporary," one's own fate is, by the same token, equally guaranteed null and void. There is no virtue in starting all over again. The past refuses to be erased. Unlike Boulez, I will not praise amnesia.

The history of music leapfrogs its way across the centuries. The "perfect art" of the Netherlanders, overridden by monody, lives in renewed form in Schoenberg and Webern; the fugal art of Bach, overridden by the sonata, comes to life again, albeit imbued with a new psychology and purpose, in Beethoven, the master of the sonata; the ground-bass variation technique, overridden by the harmonic variation, is reborn in Brahms's Fourth Symphony; Stravinsky resurrects Pergolesi in *Pulcinella*; Webern, in his *Klangfarben* version of Bach's Ricercare from *The Musical Offering*, virtually writes a new work; Ives's *Concord Sonata* treats the motto of Beethoven's Fifth Symphony as an underlying presence; and so on. All acts of renewal through uses of the past renew both that past drawn upon and that present in which the act occurs. Far from being acts of weakness or signs of the depletion of creative energy, they reveal a profound wisdom about the paradox of time, which does not consume itself and its products as if it were fire, but gathers up into itself everything which has occurred in it, preserving everything as the individual mind preserves its individual memories. The myth is more important than the fact.

It is not at all true that this is the "Age of McLuhan" any more than it is the "Age of Schoenberg," or "of Stravinsky," or of anyone else. This is the cliché language of the media and of simple-minded critics and historians who need to pin tags on phenomena. Nor is it at all true that there is a single tradition which operates along the track of a main line with station stops at Bach, Beethoven, Brahms, etc. If one can accept in whole or in part the idea of a universal mind, endlessly producing a repertoire of recurring images and forms, one immediately appreciates the rule of human conduct and culture: an emergent procession of varieties of parallel, simultaneous patterns of living and believing, frequent juxtapositions of opposites in these patterns, frequent and violent overt conflicts between such patterns, subtle conflicts and tension between related but different patterns, and so forth.

Like every other time, ours is a vast mix which refuses to be reduced to neatly packaged verbal categories. If Brahms does not belie the "Age of Wagner" concept, then Debussy does; if not Debussy, then Verdi; and so on. Verbal consistencies are not more fruitful than aesthetic ones. (Music, like existence itself, is susceptible to description but not to analysis.) To insist on either verbal or aesthetic consistencies is to limit the world at any given moment of individual perception only to what that individual eye can see, ear hear, mind perceive; it is to refuse, especially, the contradictory evidence of other observers and other consciousnesses which are equally limited. Like the nineteenth century, the twentieth presents us with nothing but contradictions, and only the partisan thinks he sees clearly.

Schoenberg probably suffered more from a sense of ongoing linear change and the pressure of historical consciousness than any other major composer of the twentieth century. He was overly concerned with his ultimate position in history and as a result became too self-conscious about how he worked, how his work affected others, etc. History has nothing to do with creation and is not a sufficient motive force for a man's actions. When it enters the stream of consciousness and becomes a criterion for the evaluation of oneself and others, it tends to corrode and destroy. Taken as an abstraction, history is a constant danger to human thought and life.

In his story "The Aleph,"[4] Borges describes a poet and his work, in a way the very model of a certain variety of contemporary composer, in these words: "He read me many another stanza, each of which obtained his approbation and profuse commentary, too. There was nothing memorable in any of them. I realized that the poet's labor lay not with the poetry, but with the invention of reasons to make the poetry admirable; naturally, this ulterior and subsequent labor modified the work for him, but not for others." Like a stain on the tissue of time, the self-indulgent verbiage of proclamation and justification will remain as sometime documents of our collective confusions; but the work which it attempted to make "admirable" will have long since faded from the field of memory.

The desperate search in the second half of the twentieth century for a way out of cultural replication, i.e., being influenced by others, borrowing, leapfrogging, etc., has let loose a veritable Pandora's box of aberrations which have little or nothing to do with art, but everything to do with being "successful" historically or commercially. Even the critics, no longer willing to be left out or behind, have joined in the hue and cry for "the new"; they celebrate and rationalize it. Self-indulgence is now the rule. By a series of typical paradoxes only powerful creative spirits like Brahms, Mahler, Bartók, and Stravinsky remain skeptical of everything but authentic values and, therefore, continue the process of cultural replication by refracting all previous music through their individual, particular natures; the avant-gardists, wanting to start all over again, make anarchic hash of music, partially by invoking the philosophies of the East and doctrines of noncausality and indeterminacy, among others.

What was advertised as the "exhaustion of tonality" at the end of the nineteenth century, descriptions by historians beginning typically with *Tristan* and tracing the demise through the new Viennese School, may simply have been an incapacity on the part of composers to continue to produce a viable tonal music which could stand comparison with the best work of the eighteenth and nineteenth centuries. Even if we grant the emergence of new perceptions and sensibilities, it does not follow that authentic values must be cast aside every time a new device or procedure is discovered. Culture, like time, its guardian, proceeds by slow accretion and eventually absorbs everything of value. By the same token nothing of value is ever lost. This is the only faith that a serious artist can live by, provided that he has made something worth preserving, even though he will never really know the fate of his work.

We live with two distinct yet interrelated realities: the world of nature which includes man as a biogenetic reflection of nature's urge toward consciousness, and the world of man which includes art as a spiritual reflection of that self-awareness nature has given him. Art is neither a mirror nor a substitute for the world. It is an addition to that universal reality which contains natural man and shows the infinite varieties of ways that man can be. William Faulkner put it much more simply when he said that art was a way of declaring that "Kilroy was here." However we phrase it, art preserves the reality of man's presence on earth. It is part of his urge toward the physical survival of the race and the spiritual immortality of the individual. Its fantastic nature does not change this striving one iota. On the contrary, it intensifies, confirms, and purifies it; for man, though he may be a failure in the realms of social and political order, is primarily and essentially a craftsman and maker of symbols and metaphors. This is his true gift, his real nature.

What cannot be remembered cannot be preserved. The true intent of art is to preserve human consciousness. The Homeric epics and the Old Testament—to cite just two examples—existed, we are told, in centuries-old oral traditions before being written down more than two thousand years ago. If the dislocation of tradition which afflicts us had befallen the ancient Greeks and Hebrews, we would not know the poetic glories of the *Odyssey* and the *Iliad* or the vast sweep of human experience recorded in *Genesis* through *Deuteronomy*. We would be bereft of two of the richest sources and deposits of human metaphor and symbol. Why, then, do composers today think that music which they admit cannot be remembered earns them, merely because they wrote it, the right to preservation and transmission? They produce for obsolescence while secretly hoping for immortality.

It is curious that *Le sacre du printemps* is the subject of rhythmic analysis, *Wozzeck* of structural analysis, and more recently *Lulu* of harmonic and intervallic analysis, not to speak of rhythmic and metric analysis. They are treated as though the balletic and theatrical impulses which brought them to life are as nothing compared with the formal designs and patterns which articulate their audible surfaces. The primal energy and sensuality of *Le sacre*, the heartbreak of human noncomprehension and the cruelty of the human condition which are basic to *Wozzeck*, the heartlessness of lust, the poison of soullessness depicted in *Lulu*—all this is disregarded as though it were of no account. The passions of man, which are the very heart of theater and theater music, seem to escape or to embarrass those who write about music today. The gestures which embody dramatic functions and form the real and audible stuff of music remain, analysis notwithstanding, the only reasons why these works have entered their respective repertoires and will undoubtedly remain there. As obvious as all this is, or ought to be, it is completely overlooked by legions of composer-theorists who are lost in the labyrinth of academic abstractions.

There can be no justification for music, ultimately, if it does not convey eloquently and elegantly the passions of the human heart. Who would care to remember the quartets of Beethoven or Bartók if they were merely demonstrations of empty formalisms? What claim would Chopin have on us if he had merely given us the abstractions of shape, gesture, and motion through time? Debussy was being celebrated only a few years ago as one of the patron saints of pure instrumental timbre as a compositional virtue. How he would have writhed to be reduced to the size of his idolators! More recently, interest has been shown in Varèse's penchant for symmetry. All well and good; but one could hardly claim that this describes or explains in any meaningful way the passion, bite, and force of his rhetoric, the real reasons we value him. The insistence by all on ignoring the dramatic, gestural character of music, while harping on the mystique of the minutiae of abstract design for its own sake, says worlds about the failure of much new music. Like mushrooms in the night, there has sprung up a profusion of false, half-baked theories of perception, of intellection, of composition itself. The mind grows sterile, and the heart small and pathetic.

The enlargement of mental perspective teaches us that consciousness, whose core is the central nervous system, is radial, not linear. Earth-time embraces man through his entire slow, tortuous advance up the ladder of evolution. No matter how far up that ladder he may climb, no matter how far away from his beginnings he may find himself as the decades, centuries, and eons elapse, he will bear within him all that he ever was. What profit is there, then, for man to shorten his perspective to man-time, that tiny scale of measurement by which men count their days and actions? Man-time is a distorting mirror in which, by ever so slight a shift of position, men can create false images, reduce the significant to smallness, inflate the insignificant to largeness. Music without a cosmology will not move the soul; nor will it illumine the heart.

The cosmogony of the ancients and primitives, expressed in magic, rites, and rituals, which invested the world around them with signs and symbols of the unknown, paradoxically ensured the survival of these peoples; for through their seemingly unsophisticated notions they preserved the sense of awe and mystery in the face of a cosmos into which man had seemingly stumbled. And we? Because we have lost that precious sense of the magic and mystery of existence, we have no cosmogony. (Physics and astronomy are poor substitutes.) Because we have no cosmogony, we are finally, but surely not suddenly, faced with the problem of whether man can survive his own thoughtlessness and arrogance, his collective *hubris*. Mahler was the last composer to intuit that music belongs to cosmogony and is supported by it. What was it Beethoven was supposed to have said? "Music is the one corporeal entrance into an incorporeal realm which comprehends us but which we cannot comprehend." Even if we suppose that Beethoven did not say it, would the statement be less true?

The renewal of music depends on the renewal of the art of composition itself. If we value Wagner and Brahms for the power of their harmony, why, then, have we given up harmony? If we value Mozart and Chopin for the elegance of their melodies, why, then, have we given up the melodic line? If in the combination of many voices a radiant polyphony emerges, why have we given up counterpoint? Ballet cannot exist without rhythmic pulsation and periodicities any more than opera can exist without the accompanied aria. Both are rooted in myth, fairy-tale, real or imagined history, the embodiments and extensions of man's passionate nature. Nontheatrical music is not necessarily less dramatic. It must still move and touch us. The enlargement of the timbral palette is made at the sacrifice of the melodic phrase, the rhythmic period. If there is value in this enlargement it will come only with its direct and concrete association with discernible, memorable melodies and rhythms, polyphonic combinations, and textural composites which articulate that longing for a reality which is man's best and perhaps only true claim to existence. History will not help us; but the past, which is ever-present, can.

The renewal of music is linked to the survival of man. In his prophetic introduction to *Magister Ludi*, published in 1946, Hermann Hesse refers to the treatise of an ancient Chinese philosopher who describes "the music of decline" as a reflection of the chaos and disorderly state of men's affairs. It is painful, to say the least, to consider that ours may be or, in fact, is such a "music of decline." Man the human being must learn to reconcile himself to a universe in which he is or is not a welcome guest (how can one tell?) simply in order to survive physically—which means acknowledging the limits of his biogenetic nature, as well as the delicate balance of nature itself and his relation to that balance. In the same way, man the musician must learn to reconcile himself to the limits of music which inhere in his central nervous system and to stop torturing sound into shapes and gestures whose meanings, if they have any, suggest that man has lost the power of musical speech and has reduced himself to inarticulateness. To sing is to project the subtle inflections of the human psyche; to dance is to project the subtle inflections of the human body and its musculature. The renewal of music lies in the direction of reasserting both, simply and directly.

The gestures of twentieth-century music do not invalidate those of the eighteenth or nineteenth centuries, any more than Western music invalidates Indian music, or vice versa. When authentic, they are extensions of the psychology of musical expression. In no way can it be claimed that they supersede the vast continuities, the grander and more serene gestures of tonal music. They are primarily investigations of previously unexposed and unexplored areas of the human psyche and have value insofar as they articulate those areas of sensation, feeling, and emotion with clarity of means and eloquence of utterance. These narrow-chested gestures of our time often tend to be peripheral to the major, earlier gestures of music and describe, as it were, a series of vague and tenuous probes and lines of movement, extending from the ghostly shadowlands of the surreal to the gravity-free, time-frozen sensations of cosmic space-longing, from the randomness of causality-free projections to the overdetermined, tightly woven structures of total organizations. There is no contradiction in suggesting that the renewal of music depends on the fullest possible use of the human imagination, the only recognizable limit being the central nervous system, which potentially includes, therefore, all the gestures, old and new, of which music is capable. Translated into practice, this would mean the use of every device and every technique appropriate to its specific gestural repertory in combination with every other device and technique until theoretically all that we are and all that we know is bodied forth in the richest, most diverse music ever known to man, *ars combinatoria.*

Notes

[Text: Rochberg, "Reflections on the Renewal of Music," *Current Musicology* 13 (1972): 75–82. Used by permission of *Current Musicology.*]

[1. Pierre Boulez, "Bach's Moment," translated by Stephen Walsh in Boulez, *Stocktakings from an Apprenticeship* (Oxford: Clarendon Press 1991): 13.]

2. Jorge Luis Borges (b. 1899), Argentine poet and philosophical essayist. In "Pascal's Sphere," which appears in *Other Inquisitions, 1937–1952* (New York, 1966), 5–8, Borges remarks: "Perhaps universal history is the history of the diverse intonation of a few metaphors" (p. 8).

3. A unique discussion of the belief in the necessity of artistic originality can be found in Leonard B. Meyer, *Music, the Arts, and Ideas* (Chicago, 1967), especially pp. 54–67, 188.

4. *A Personal Anthology* (New York, 1967), 138–54.

21

JOHN HARBISON

(B. 1938)

John Harbison's "Uses of Popular Music" and "Accessibility" were two of six talks given to the composition seminar at the Berkshire Music Center in 1984. His audience was a group of young composers, and the presentations outlined both practical and idealistic concerns faced by contemporary composers. Harbison's texts were imbued with the new spirit of classical music in America of the 1970s and 1980s, a nondogmatic attitude that supported a composer's freedom to bring into new music elements from anywhere in its history and from any existing style.

The presentation titled "Accessibility" addresses simplicity versus complexity in new music, referring to the collision between forbidding modernist works of the 1950s and 1960s and the more direct and accessible idiom that had been ever more prominent since the 1970s. From Harbison's eclectic and nondoctrinaire viewpoint, the distinction is illusory, since simple works are often complex beneath their surface, and difficult works are sometimes based on predictable archetypes. Composers should ignore such distinctions and seek to formulate their own valid language, based on connections with all of musical culture.

In an earlier talk entitled "History," Harbison had argued that composers should construct their own past, their own network of associations and influences, rather than conform to a doctrinaire style. "The compositional task becomes one of rebuilding and reconnecting," he said, "rather than following a dialectic line." This observation is quite the opposite of the demand for conformity expressed by leading composers of the 1950s, including Babbitt, Nono, and Boulez, and it echoes the more recent thinking of a composer such as George Rochberg (see essay no. 20) in its call for renewal and contact with known values and musical styles.

Harbison's network of connections to the past also admits popular music, as he explains in the talk titled "Uses of Popular Music." Here he praises the musical richness of popular songs composed primarily in the 1930s and 1940s. These have a value that is nourishing to the classical composer, he says, going far beyond the vapid emblems of adolescence found in rock.

Harbison's Writings: A Selective Bibliography

"Six Tanglewood Talks," *Perspectives of New Music* 23/2 (1984–85): 12–22 and 24/1 (1985-86): 46–60.

Review of *Copland: 1900 Through 1942,* by Aaron Copland and Vivian Perlis (New York, 1984). In *Musical Quarterly* 71 (1985): 95–98.

Review of *Contemplating Music: Challenges to Musicology,* by Joseph Kerman (Cambridge, MA, 1985). In *Musical Quarterly* 72 (1986): 416–18.

—⁓—

TWO TANGLEWOOD TALKS

(1984)

Uses of Popular Music

Concert music makes up only a tiny percentage of the music played and heard today, and accounts for an even smaller percentage of the revenues earned by music. To most of the people in the world, *music* is TV music, movie music, and above all pop music (the latter recently having also taken on a visual form). These musics are elective— someone has caused them to begin by buying a ticket or turning on a set or record player. There is also a great deal of nonelective music, played in supermarkets, airports, hotel lobbies, and even outdoor public spaces. It is clear now that most people regard music as an accompaniment to something: at best an enhancer, like a wine at a meal, at worst an environmental accident which can create habits and dependencies of a passive kind.

Although ambient music is an important sociological subject, I want to address here that "vernacular" music which is *experienced* and retained, and which becomes an important part of people's lives. Such music is major competition for concert music. It is also a potential nourishment for concert music.

All the most vital forms of pop music stemmed from jazz originally, but pure jazz has now become relatively limited in public appeal. The jazz public resembles, even overlaps with the concert music public; it is even much like the new music public, gradually emerging from years in the ghetto underground.

Early in the century jazz was *not* esoteric: it gave birth to the first unimported American popular music. This popular music was created by two symbiotic forces, the musical comedy and tin pan alley writers, and the nightclub, radio, and phonograph record performers. The unit of currency was the "tune," the best of which originated as theater songs. A tune became a "hit" when many interpreters played and sang it, each in their own way, and many copies of the sheet music were sold. (The sheet music represented the original, authoritative version of the tune, rendered in the exact detail the composer wanted, and requiring an advanced performer to play it at home.) A tune became a "standard" when this process continued over many years, through generations, until the tune literally entered the popular subconscious. Each era was proud to contribute a few standards, hardy emblems of the vitality of their times.

It is these standards that I began playing, solo and in groups, around 1950, an inheritance I took for granted, though I was very aware of the quality of some of these perennials. They were often as demanding as any "art" music. I remember working hard to make sure that all the harmonies were right in the bridge of *Body and Soul*, that the common tones which brought about the fabulous transitions back to the A sections of *The Song Is You* and *All the Things You Are* were given enough weight, that the second chord of *Foggy Day* was *not* a diminished chord but a minor sixth (I was shocked and grateful to be corrected on that by a fastidious trumpet player). It was a hard exhilarating school, harder and more exhilarating than the learning and performance of baroque continuo parts ten years later, because it was a living language. What my colleagues and I were fortunate to be sharing was a late flowering of a disciplined, linguistically demanding improviser's art, based on the melodic and harmonic inventions of some of America's greatest musicians—Kern, Gershwin, Rodgers, Berlin, Warren, Van Heusen, and many others. To this day I'm told, by composers who experienced the same kind of background, that we are still "composing out those changes."

The late fifties was the last time this was a culturally central activity. Those who later became composers of concert music—Kraft, Schuman, Previn, Schuller, Martirano, and countless others—were still close to the public pulse when they went out to play those standards on their jazz jobs.

I remember sensing the presence of a powerful interloper around 1956, when the first rockers began moving us out of our club! About the same time the musical comedy, the fountainhead of the best songs, began to founder. As a teenager I was already aware that "the standards" I carried in my head were becoming less a shared common "melos," more the property of buffs. I listened among the hit parade tunes for something I thought had that quality. I found *Too Late Now!*

But it *was* too late, that song was by Burton Lane, survivor from a different age.

The tunes were gradually being replaced by the groups, or the hero performers, who were bigger than their tunes. It isn't *Heartbreak Hotel* or *Hound Dog* that survives as a cultural artifact, it is *Elvis Presley* or his posthumous doubles singing them. Sheet music disappeared or became hopelessly primitive. The *song* became the *record*: few tunes circulated among performers; they were instead identified definitely with a single recorded performance, which that performer tried to duplicate exactly in live performance or "lip-synched" to the record. The beat, the harmonies, and the forms emphasized clear reiterated shapes ("hooks"), root position chords, and hypnotic, crushing pulsations, physicality and presence above all.

Partly through this drastic grammatical simplification, partly through new marketing techniques, pop music found a wider public than ever before. In spite of the anachronistic presence of some actual tunewriters, like the Beatles, I became aware of a steadily narrowing vocabulary as I taught, through many years, a course called Practical Harmony for nonclassical musicians. I will never forget the response to one of my assignments, the writing out of a lead-sheet for *Nice Work If You Can Get It*, giving the melody only. I was glad none of the class had ever heard Gershwin's version. I thought they would be thrilled by his evasive, dapper strategies. Their versions were unanimous, firmly in the mid-seventies root position cut. I then played Gershwin for them; they were deeply unimpressed, found him "complicated," "weird," and "wrong." I knew I was in alien country.

Soon after, I was asked by a very gifted composition student and "crossover" pianist to show him what I heard in "all that grey music" I like—Bach cantatas, thirties Stravinsky, etc. He was himself already an accomplished handler of "gesture," "areas," and "colors," and was asking out of genuine curiosity and good humor that will eventually carry him over all obstacles. I chose Cantata 23, one of the greatest, and greyest, and we went virtually bar by bar. Then the Stravinsky *Symphony of Psalms*—I think it stayed grey for him, while it glowed for me.

Am I making too much of these and other encounters if I begin asking wild questions?

1. Does the root position, static harmony, the modal triadic droning in Duran Duran songs mean I should worry about an atrophy of purposeful harmonic progression among young concert composers?

2. Does the young pianist who rides roughshod over the deceptive cadence at the end of the Mozart G Minor Piano Quartet do so because Kiss has a repertoire of four chords and that isn't one of them?

3. Is the young cellist whose choreography is better than her timing, who does not *feel* the drop to E♭ early in the Schubert Quintet, mesmerized by the gestural, exaggerated monotone of David Bowie?

4. Does the distance from *For All We Know* to *Beat It* signify the approaching end of structural hearing?

Each generation believes deep down that the other generation's music is somehow wrong—maybe good but unnatural, unfaithful to experience. This perception finds double force with popular music. Pop music is above all the music of adolescence, sometimes prolonged adolescence. Every generation feels their pop music was the last good pop music, because they feel their early years were the last good early years. Adults nurse their generation's hits in their memories to their dying day because their most irreversible moments danced to that pulse. But then on their dying day it all dies, all except the standards and the few things that have achieved an artistic life, because for the most part they are associations with events and emotions, not durable freestanding musical objects. This is the poignancy of pop to each generation: its mortality and frailty. This is why pop music dates so comically and touchingly, so even the *beat* of the last decade seems so quaint and unhip.

This is why I will always believe *Teach Me Tonight* is a wonderful song (I hope it is); it is a blonde in forty crinolines and extra makeup who refused to be taught. This is why the only popular music we can honestly and viably incorporate into our compositional style is that of our own adolescence. It is the perishable icon we seek to enshrine in something more durable, to find its essence, to strip it of its nostalgia and trap only its vitality.

It is up to you to find out what to do with yours, and me with mine; it could take us the rest of our lives.

Accessibility

Commentators and audience members speak of the accessibility or difficulty of a piece as if composers really have a choice in these matters. I suppose it is good public relations for composers to perpetrate the myth that we are always in total control. I believe that in our less high-pressure tasks we can be. In writing music for a specific public occasion, or for a television program, or for a dance by circus elephants, we have to be able to shoot for an exact mark. But in our highest-striving work, when we seek out the livest, high-yeast material, we can't be fully in the driver's seat: the ideas, if they are really alive, have their own life, and sometimes all our planning, expectation and habits must be prepared for adjustment, or abandonment. It is not a lack of technique that causes this lack of willful control. In fact it takes a lot of ready technique to deal with the unforeseen situations that can arise when the material has strong legs.

Most of us composers, after we have had the experience of having a piece veer off to a different place than we expected or planned, begin to realize that our freedom of choice is an illusion. We cannot choose the kind of music we write—accessible, difficult, complex, simple—any more definitively than we choose our shoe size or our hair color.

We can and must do things to maximize our abilities—if we write too many notes and confuse our intentions we can try to be more economical; if we are too monochromatic and over-refined we must strive for the clearest contrasts. But we can't change our basic nature, only discover it, so that audiences and critics who take credit for our accessibility or bristle at our difficulty are assuming more control of our fates than we have. "He sold out," we often hear, as a comment about an accessible piece the hearer didn't like. But no one ever sold out! Instead, their character, their genes, their fatal pull emerges. The result may be great, it may be weak and venal, but it is beyond planning and design. Its realization can be hastened, but never *determined* by the pull of the marketplace. (Besides, the yield from a "sellout," at least in concert music, is so paltry it is hardly worth the trouble.)

One of the most futile recurrent musical discussions, one which takes place in public and private, is the pitched battle between champions of simplicity and complexity. The unjustly neglected serial composer from Rhode Island argues that only complex music really lasts, that the greatest music is always unappreciated in its time, and cites Bach as a typical example of a composer of challenge and intricacy who waited a century for vindication. The successful opera composer from North Dakota counters that great music is always acclaimed in its time, citing Verdi's immense popularity, his function as a great Dickensian novelist in tones, remembering the crowd carrying him home on their shoulders after the first performance of *Falstaff*.

Then the combatants may even attempt to co-opt each others' composers. The apostle of complexity explains that the appreciation of Verdi's music was based on aberrant sociological factors, that if it is good music, and he admits it probably is, the real essence of the music was and is structurally complex, that in fact the structure of the briefest Verdi aria is of great linguistic density, but imperfectly analyzed and heard even by those who purport to like it. The challenger for simplicity points out that Bach's music, beneath its surface elaboration, is based on primitive universal archetypes, rooted in dance forms, based on folk tunes and chorales, and his obscurity in 1720 was a historical accident due to his unfortunate location in a provincial backwater.

There is truth in all of these self-serving tortuous arguments. It is true that music of simple surface can be structurally complex. The reverse is also true. It is true that at every historical point we have had good composers with advanced perspectives, and good ones with conservative tendencies. Compounding the confusion, sometimes the simple surface is at one with the progressive tendencies, as with Telemann and C. P. E. Bach, sometimes the complex style seeks to put the brake on history, as with Brahms and J. S. Bach.

We often hear that all great music, however strange, quirky, and intricate, will become clear with time. It won't. The *Grosse Fuge* has not, the Schoenberg Fourth Quartet has not, any more than Yeats's "Sailing to Byzantium" unlocks like a nursery rhyme to its grandchildren. Difficult minds like Schoenberg and Beethoven continue to hurl their challenge, and their achievements may even *grow* in mystery. This can happen to "first-hearing" pieces as well, like some of the transparent jewels in Schütz's *Geistliche Chormusik*, or Monostatos' slaves in the *Magic Flute*, or the end of *Les noces*.

Let's try some formulas, according to journalistic canons of today:

1. difficult = advanced

2. accessible = conservative

3. advanced = Steve Reich

4. conservative = Roger Sessions

5. difficult = advanced = Steve Reich!

6. accessible = conservative = Roger Sessions!

We need to step back from all of this and observe that we have only the most tenuous grip on what simple and complex, accessible and difficult mean in music. Recent work in analysis confirms our experience that a Schumann song can be structurally more intricate than one by Dallapiccola, though many listeners will find the Dallapiccola less accessible. But before we conclude from this that idiom and dissonance are the determining factors we must deal with my introduction-to-music class which rabidly preferred the "gutsy" music of Varèse's *Octandre* to the "boring, hokey" love duet from *La bohème*.

It turns out that legitimate concepts like *accessible* and *difficult* are mainly servants of fads and swings of taste. One hearer says, "the music is accessible," he means he likes it. Another says the same thing: he doesn't like it, he implies that it may be superficial or complacent. Categories and labels usually are little more than hidden protestations of affection or aversion, inchoate appetites that crave support, even from worn-out adjectives.

When I arrived in Pittsburgh to take up my position as Resident Composer, I was asked if my programming there would be representative of the "American spectrum." The answer was no, I was not objective. I would try to do things I believed were good. "Does that mean, then, that we will hear music only of the ultraconservative, romantic, accessible type you espouse?" The answer was no, if I understood the question. "I advocate among other things the music of Sessions, Carter, Davies, Lerdahl, and Wuorinen, not quite the sort of category you describe." Under the circumstances, I don't really understand why I write that ultraconservative, romantic, accessible music, but if I could find something exactly like my own music I probably would do two things: 1) program it, and 2) stop composing because it would no longer be necessary.

We are all quickly imprisoned by our labels, if we don't make immediate creative and polemical efforts to struggle free. Whatever our supposed allegiances, we need to give leadership on the principles of open listening, listening based on real points of contact rather than surfaces.

One of our most strenuous and generous tasks as musicians is to hear value, when it is present, in a work of a distant aesthetic persuasion. We probably can't love such pieces, we may not wish to promote them, but we can enlarge our spirits by receiving them openly. It is not an act of crucial artistic necessity—only the things we really love will influence our own course—but it is an act of musical citizenship, of community.

It is fortunate that such acts of musical citizenship are more frequent now than they were twenty years ago. And they mean most when they come from people with strongly etched aesthetic positions. There is nothing duller or blander than the true pluralist, the person who says, "I like it all, let the flowers bloom, let the games begin." This kind of democracy is already far too celebrated among our art funders. A healthy community is one with many passionately held, diverse viewpoints, which will fight vigorously, but which admit, in moments of painful stretching, that there might also be something else.

The challenge to composers is to discover their own nature. I was aided in this by a couple of chance remarks made by Michael Steinberg in the mid-sixties.

1) "Rachmaninoff might be a better composer than Stefan Wolpe."

2) "Why should we assume that all composers of conservative tendencies are second-rate, and why should we musicians be content to turn over this direction to the second rate?"

In the early seventies it took more nerve, it was more out of step to explore a nonchromatic language than now. The chromatic revolution had been certified by the universities, was socially and academically acceptable.

Nowadays we may be reaching the point were "far-out" might start to mean something again. Younger composers are fortunate that they confront in their early years an unpressured multiplicity of options; the rewards will be clear. They will get earlier confidence, they will emerge younger, and they will take music somewhere that will surprise the generation that preceded them.

We must demand of ourselves and of our colleagues works of structural power, of urgency, of necessity. If we can understand them at once, fine; we must not ostracize or jealously regard those of our number who possess a genuine unforced popular touch. But if we don't get the new piece immediately, but only that crucial sense of wanting to go back, we must lead our fellow listeners and critics in the determination to go back, to give the difficult language a chance to ripen in our minds, or just go on being difficult.

Twenty years hence, some of us will remember, but few will care under what banner all these pieces marched into the world.

Notes

[Text: "Accessibility" and "Uses of Popular Music" from "Six Tanglewood Talks," *Perspectives of New Music* 23/2 (1984–85): 12–22 and 24/1 (1985–86): 46–60. Reprinted by permission of John Harbison and *Perspectives of New Music*.]

PART V

THE SEARCH FOR
AN AMERICAN
MUSICAL LANGUAGE

THE HISTORY OF CLASSICAL COMPOSITION IN AMERICA IN the twentieth century in large part duplicates that in Europe, although in some areas American musicians have traveled on separate routes. Before World War I most classical composers in America—Horatio Parker, Edward MacDowell, and Charles Griffes are examples— received their training in Germany, and they imitated modern German or French models of composition. American musical culture had a distinctly German accent at this time. But this alignment changed dramatically at the end of World War I, when France began to provide the primary artistic models for American composers, as it did for their compatriot writers and painters. The artistic alliance that was formed at this time between the two countries is discussed authoritatively by Elliott Carter in his essay "France-America Ltd." (essay no. 24).

The International Neoclassical Style, whose most eminent practitioner was Stravinsky, was eagerly adopted by American figures, especially those who had obtained their training in Europe in the 1920s and 1930s. The music of Roger Sessions, Walter Piston, and some of the compositions of Aaron Copland from the 1930s are examples of this internationalist and modernistic musical idiom. At the same period in America there flourished a regionalist-populist style—simpler, less dissonant, often folkloric, and more distinctively American than was possible with neoclassicism per se. Music composed by Copland, Virgil Thomson, and Roy Harris includes examples of this more homespun idiom. Copland's lecture "The Composer in Industrial America" (essay no. 23) speaks from the perspective of a composer who aspired to master both the modernist and the populist approaches of the interwar period.

Following World War II American composers such as Milton Babbitt and John Cage rose to a position of greater international prominence than had American musicians heretofore. Despite many disputes that erupted between the Americans and their European colleagues, the music of both groups was in general similar in its common tendencies toward control, use of system, depersonalization, and technology.

Since the 1960s and 1970s America has been increasingly the source of important new musical ideas. The style of minimalism, born in the 1960s in New York in the works of the American composers Philip Glass, Steve Reich, Terry Riley, and La Monte Young, has been and continues to be imitated by musicians around the world. In the last twenty years the Americans have been rather more eager than the Europeans to depart from doctrinaire aspects of postwar modernism and to adopt a variety of simpler styles that often incorporate elements from pop and rock—all blended together with a happy tolerance for all of music.

There has also existed in America, mainly in the first half of the century, a distinctively naive approach to composition, which was intentionally independent of European traditions and movements. One of the best known figures in this development is Harry Partch (1901–74), and aspects of the music of Charles Ives and John Cage draw upon this untutored and homemade conception of what music can be. Ives's vernacular aesthetic is outlined in the Notes to his *114 Songs* (essay no. 22).

2 2

CHARLES IVES

(1 8 7 4 – 1 9 5 4)

After suffering a heart attack in October, 1918, Charles Ives, perhaps sensing his own mortality, decided to publish some of his music to make it better known. For this, he selected pieces composed considerably earlier, his *Concord* Piano Sonata and a selection of earlier songs, which he then published at his own expense. To help explain the ideas behind the Sonata, he also wrote an accompanying pamphlet, titled *Essays Before a Sonata*, and for the song collection, which he called *114 Songs*, he appended the Notes that are reproduced here. These appeared untitled in minuscule type, at the conclusion of the song book, although they are now often called a "Postface," the term given to them in an edition by Howard Boatwright. The *Essays* and these Notes are Ives's most detailed statement of his own highly distinctive musical aesthetic.

The Notes recapitulate and extend ideas first presented in the *Essays*. In the Epilogue of this earlier treatise, the composer draws a distinction in music between what he calls "manner" and "substance." Manner—a quality marked by a polished form, conventional beauty and unity, and commercial appeal—is of no value. Only substance is important in music. It resides in a spiritual and ethical content that is also to be found in everyday life. In the Notes to the *114 Songs*, the composer elaborates upon this duality. Art, he says, cannot flourish if it is practiced as a "whole," that is, as a closed system sealed off from life or as something engaged in for its own sake in the manner of *l'art pour l'art*. Instead, to have substance, or something important to say, it must be integrated into the everyday and practiced naturally and instinctively by common people. Everyone, he says, has an artistic, even creative, insight which comes as naturally as admiring the beauty of a sunset. The future of music will lie in the hands of the common man who "while digging his potatoes will breathe his own Epics, his own Symphonies."

Ives was guided in his thinking by the idealism of American transcendentalist writers such as Thoreau and Emerson and by the antielitist sentiments of Walt Whitman. Although he was apparently uninfluenced by the writings of European composers of his day, he still addresses many of the same issues that concerned European musicians of the 1920s and 1930s. His distinction between manner and substance echoes Schoenberg's discourse on style and idea in music (see essay no. 10), and his antielitist viewpoint concerning art has a close parallel in the thinking of Ralph Vaughan Williams (essay no. 11) among other populist composers. Like many of his European counterparts he rebelled against the implications of high art of the late romantic period. Indeed, he found in the works of Wagner, Debussy, Tchaikovsky, and Richard Strauss only the emptiness of manner. His own search for substance in music led him to his distinctively regionalist and sometimes naive style, which paralleled the European neoclassicist reaction to romanticism while remaining entirely isolated from it.

Ives's *Essays Before a Sonata* and Notes to *114 Songs* reveal a conversational style of writing, which was sometimes turgid and always rambling. His remarks in the Notes about his own songs are awkward and self-deprecating, as though anticipating the lack of understanding for them that he fully anticipated.

Ives's Writings: A Selective Bibliogaphy

Memos. Edited by John Kirkpatrick. New York: W. W. Norton, 1972. An autobiograpical sketch made by Ives in 1931 and 1932.

Essays Before A Sonata, The Majority and Other Writings. Edited by Howard Boatwright. New York: W. W. Norton, 1962. A selection of Ives's writings, including a version of the Notes to *114 Songs* (called a "Postface" by the editor).

—ɯ—

NOTES TO 114 SONGS
(1922)

Greek philosophers, ward-politicians, unmasked laymen, and others, have a saying that bad-habits and bad-gardens grow to the "unintendedables"; whether these are a kind of "daucus carota," "men," "jails" or "mechanistic theories of life" is not known,—but the statement is probably or probably not true. The printing of this collection was undertaken primarily, in order to have a few clear copies that could be sent to friends who, from time to time, have been interested enough to ask for copies of some of the songs; but the job has grown into something different,—it contains plenty of songs which have not been and will not be asked for. It stands now, if it stands for anything, as a kind of "buffer state,"—an opportunity for evading a question, somewhat embarrassing to answer,—"Why do you write so much—,which no one ever sees?" There are several good reasons, none of which are worth recording.

Another, but unconvincing, reason for not asking publishers to risk their capital or singers their reputation, may be charted to a theory,—(perhaps it is little more than a notion, for many do not agree with it,—to be more exact, a man did agree with it once; he had something to sell,—a book, as I remember, called, "The Truth about Something," or "How to write Music while Shaving!") Be that as it may,—our theory has a name—it is, "The balance of values," or "The circle of sources"; (in these days, of chameleon efficiency, every whim must be classified under a scientific sounding name, to save it from investigation). It stands something like this: That an interest in any art-activity, from poetry to baseball is better, broadly speaking, if held as a part of life, or of a life, than if it sets itself up as a whole,—a condition verging, perhaps, towards a monopoly or possibly a kind of atrophy of the other important values, and hence reacting unfavorably upon itself. In the former condition, this inter-est, this instinctive impulse, this desire to pass from "minor to major," this artistic-intuition, or whatever you call it, may have a better chance to be more natural, more comprehensive, perhaps, freer and so more tolerant,—it may develop more muscle in the hind legs and so find a broader vantage ground for jumping to the top of a fence, and more interest in looking around,—if it happens to get there.

Now all this may not be so; the writer certainly cannot and does not try to prove it so by his own experience, but he likes to think the theory works out somewhat in this way. To illustrate further (and to become more involved): if this interest, and everyone has it, is a component of the ordinary life,—if it is free primarily to play the part of the, or a, reflex, subconscious-expression, or something of that sort, in rela-tion to some fundamental share in the common work of the world, as things go, is it nearer to what nature intended it should be, than if, as suggested above, it sets itself up as a whole,—not a dominant value only, but a complete one? If a fiddler or poet does nothing all day long but enjoy the luxury and drudgery of fiddling or dreaming, with or without meals, does he or does he not, for this reason, have anything valu-able to express?—or is whatever he thinks he has to express less valuable than he thinks?

This is a question which each man must answer for himself. It depends to a great extent, on what a man nails up on his dashboard as "valuable." Does not the sinking back into the soft state of mind (or possibly a non-state of mind) that may accept "art for art's sake," tend to shrink rather than toughen up the hitting mus-cles,—and incidentally those of the umpire or the grand stand, if there be one? To quote from a book that is not read: "Is not beauty in music too often confused with something which lets the ears lie back in an easy-chair? Many sounds that we are used to, do not bother us, and for that reason are we not too easily inclined to call them beautiful? . . . . Possibly the fondness for personal expression,—the kind in which self-indulgence dresses up and miscalls freedom,—may throw out a skin-deep arrangement, which is readily accepted at first as beautiful—formulae that weaken rather than toughen the musical-muscles. If a composer's conception of his art, its functions and ideals, even if sincere, coincide to such an extent with these groove-colored permutations of tried out progressions in expedience, so that he can arrange them over and over again to his delight—has he or has he not been drugged with an overdose of habit-forming sounds? And as a result do not the muscles of his clientele become flabbier and flabbier until they give way altogether and find refuge only in exciting platitudes,—even the sensual outbursts of an emasculated rubber stamp,—a "Zaza," a "Salome" or some other money-getting costume of effeminate manhood? In many cases probably not,—but there is this tendency."[1]

If the interest, under discussion, is the whole and the owner is willing to let it rest as the whole, will it not produce something less vital than the ideal which under-lies, or which did underlie it? And is the resultant work from this interest as free as it should be from a certain influence of reaction which is brought on or, at least, is closely related to the artist's over-anxiety about its effect upon others?

And to this, also, no general answer must be given,—each man will answer it for himself,—if he feels like answering questions. The whole matter is but one of the personal conviction. For as Mr. Sedgwick says in his helpful and inspiring little book about Dante, "in judging human conduct,"—and the manner in which an interest in art is used has to do with human conduct,—"we are dealing with subtle mysteries of motives, impulses, feelings, thoughts that shift, meet, combine and separate like clouds."[2]

Every normal man,—that is, every uncivilized or civilized human being not of defective mentality, moral sense, etc., has, in some degree, creative insight (an unpopular statement) and an interest, desire and ability to express it (another unpopular statement). There are many, too many, who think they have none of it, and stop with the thought or before the thought. There are a few who think (and encourage others to think) that they and they only have this insight, interest, etc. . . . and that (as a kind of collateral security) they and they only know how to give true expression to it, etc. But in every human soul there is a ray of celestial beauty (Plotinus admits that), and a spark of genius (nobody admits that).

If this is so, and if one of the greatest sources of strength,—one of the greatest joys, and deepest pleasures of men, is giving rein to it in some way, why should not every one instead of a few, be encouraged, and feel justified in encouraging everyone including himself to make this a part of every one's life and his life,—a value that will supplement the other values and help round out the substance of the soul?

Condorcet, in his attitude toward history,—Dryden, perhaps when he sings [in "A Song for St. Cecilia's Day"] "—from heavenly harmony, This universal frame began . . . . . The diapason closing full in man,"—more certainly Emerson in the "Over-soul" and "common-heart" seem to lend strength to the thought that this germ-plasm of creative-art, interest and work is universal, and that its selection-theory is based on any condition that has to do with universal encouragement. Encouragement here is taken in the broad sense of something akin to unprejudiced and intelligent examination, to sympathy and unconscious influence,—a thing felt rather than seen. The problem of direct encouragement is more complex and exciting but not as fundamental or important. It seems to the writer that the attempts to stimulate interest by elaborate systems of contents, prizes, etc., are a little overdone nowadays. Something of real benefit to art may be accomplished in this way—but perhaps the prizes may do the donors more good than the donatees. Possibly the pleasure and satisfaction of the former in having done what they consider a good deed, may be far greater than the improvement in the quality of the latter's work. In fact, the process may have an enervating effect upon the latter,—it may produce more Roderick Hudsons [the title character of a novel by Henry James] than Beethovens. Perhaps something of greater value could be caught without this kind of bait. Perhaps the chief value of the plan to establish a "course at Rome" to raise the standard of American music (or the standard of American composers—which is it?) may be in finding a man strong enough to survive it. To see the sunrise a man has but to get up early, and he can always have Bach in his pocket. For the amount of a month's wages, a grocery-clerk can receive "personal instruction" from Beethoven, and other *living* "conservatories." Possibly, the more our composer accepts from his patrons, "et al.," the less he will accept from himself. It may be possible that a month in a "Kansas wheat field" will do more for him than three years in Rome. It may be, that many men—perhaps some of genius—(if you won't admit that all are geniuses) have been started on the downward path of subsidy by trying to write a thousand dollar prize poem or a ten thousand dollar prize opera. How many masterpieces have been prevented from blossoming in this way? A cocktail will make a man eat more, but will not give him a healthy, normal appetite (if he had not that already). If a bishop should offer a "prize living" to the curate who will love God the hardest for fifteen days, whoever gets the prize would love God the least,—probably. Such stimulants, it strikes us, tend to industrialize art, rather than develop a spiritual sturdiness—a sturdiness which Mr. Sedgwick says shows itself in a close union between spiritual life and the ordinary business of life, against spiritual feebleness which shows itself in the separation of the two. And for the most of us, we believe, this sturdiness would be encouraged by anything that will keep or help us keep a normal balance between the spiritual life and the ordinary life. If for every thousand dollar prize a potato field be substituted, so that these candidates of "Clio" can dig a little in real life, perchance dig up a natural inspiration, art's-air might be a little clearer—a little freer from certain traditional delusions,—for instance, that free thought and free love always go to the same café—that atmosphere and diligence are synonymous. To quote Thoreau incorrectly: "When half-Gods talk, the Gods walk!" Everyone should have the opportunity of not being over-influenced. But these unpopular convictions should stop,—"On ne donne rien si libéralement que ses conseils" [nothing is given so freely as advice].

A necessary *part* of this *part* of progressive evolution (for they tell us now that evolution is not always progressive) is that everyone should be as free as possible to encourage everyone, including himself, to work, and to be willing to work where this interest directs,—"to stand and be willing to stand, unprotected, from all the showers of the absolute which may beat upon him,—to use or learn to use or, at least, to be unafraid of trying to use, whatever he can, of any and all lessons of the infinite which humanity has received and thrown to him—that nature has exposed and sacrificed for him,—that life and death have translated for him," *until* the products of his labor shall beat around and through his ordinary work,—shall strengthen, widen and deepen all his senses, aspirations, or whatever the innate power and impulses may be called, which God has given man.

Everything from a mule to an oak, which nature has given life has a right to that life, and a right to throw into that life all the values it can. Whether they be approved by a human mind or seen with a human eye, is no concern of that right. The right of a tree, wherever it stands, is to grow as strong and as beautiful as it can whether seen or unseen,—whether made immortal by a Turner,—translated into a part of Seraphic architecture or a kitchen table. The instinctive and progressive interest of every man in art, we are willing to affirm with no qualification, will go on and on, ever fulfilling hopes, ever building new ones, ever opening new horizons, until the day will come when every man while digging his potatoes will breathe his own Epics, his own Symphonies (operas if he likes it): and as he sits of an evening in his back-yard and shirt sleeves smoking his pipe and watching his brave children in *their* fun of building *their* themes, for *their* sonatas of *their* reality,—will hear the transcendental strains of the day's symphony, resounding in their many choirs, and in all their perfection, through the west wind and the tree tops!

It was not Mark Twain but the "Danbury News Man" who became convinced that a man never knows his vices and virtues until that great and solemn event, that first sunny day in spring when he wants to go fishing, but stays home and *helps* his wife clean house. As he lies on his back under the bed,—under all the beds,—with nothing beneath him but tacks and his past life,—with his soul (to say nothing of his vision), full of that glorious dust of mortals and carpets,—with his finger-tips rosey with the caresses of his mother-in-law's hammer (her annual argument),—as he lies there taking orders from the hired girl, a sudden and tremendous vocabulary comes to him. Its power is omnipotent, it consumes everything,—but the rubbish heap. Before it his virtues quail, hesitate and crawl carefully out of the cellar window; his vices,—even they go back on him,—even they can't stand this,—he sees them march with stately grace (and others) out of the front door. At this moment there comes a whisper,—the still small voice of a "parent on his father's side"—"Vices and Virtues! Vices and Virtues! they ain't no sech things,—but ther'e a tarnal lot of 'em." Wedged in between the sewing machine and the future he examines himself, as every man in his position should do,—"What has brought me to this?—Where am I? Why do I do this?"—"these are natural inquiries. They have assailed thousands before our day; they will afflict thousands in years to come and probably there is no form of interrogation so loaded with subtle torture,—unless it is to be asked for a light in a strange depot by a man you've just selected out of seventeen thousand as the one man the most likely to have a match. Various authors have various reasons for bringing out a book, and this reason may or may not be the reason they give to the world; I know not and care not. It is not for me to judge the world unless I am elected. It is a matter which lies between the composer and his own conscience, and I know of no place where it is less likely to be crowded. . . . . . Some have written a book for money: I have not. Some for fame: I have not. I have not written a book for any of these reasons or for all of them together. In fact, gentle borrower, I have not written a book at all"—I have merely cleaned house. All that is left is out on the clothes line,—but it's good for a man's vanity to have the neighbors see him—on the clothes line.

For some such or different reason; through some such or different process this volume,—this package of paper, uncollectible notes, marks of respect and expression, is now thrown, so to speak, at the music fraternity, who for this reason will feel free to dodge it on its way—perhaps to the waste basket. It is submitted as much or more in the chance that some points for the better education of the composer may be thrown back at him, than that any of the points the music may contain may be valuable to the recipient.

Some of the songs in this book, particularly among the later ones, cannot be sung,—and if they could perhaps might prefer, if they had a say, to remain as they are,—that is, "in the leaf,"—and that they will remain in this peaceful state is more than presumable. An excuse (if none of the above are good enough) for their existence, which suggests itself at this point, is that a song has a *few* rights the same as other ordinary citizens. If it feels like walking along the left hand side of the street—passing the door of physiology or sitting on the curb, why not let it? If it feels like kicking over an ash can, a poet's castle, or the prosodic law, will you stop it? Must it always be a polite triad, a "breve gaudium," a ribbon to match the voice? Should it not be free at times from the dominion of the thorax, the diaphragm, the ear and other points of interest? If it wants to beat around in the valley, to throw stones up the pyramids, or to sleep in the park, should it not have some immunity from a Nemesis, a Rameses, or a policeman? Should it not have a chance to sing to itself, if it can sing?—to enjoy itself, without making a bow, if it can't make a bow?—to swim around in any ocean, if it can swim, without having to swallow "hook and bait" or being sunk by an operatic greyhound? If it happens to feel like trying to fly where humans cannot fly,—to sing what cannot be sung—to walk in a cave, on all fours,—or to tighten up its girth in blind hope and faith, and try to scale mountains that are not—Who shall stop it!

—*In short, must a song*

always be a song!

C. E. I [CHARLES EDWARD IVES]

Notes

[Text: Charles Ives. Notes at the conclusion of *114 Songs* (self-published, 1922): unpaginated.]

[1. The quotation is freely drawn from the *Essays Before a Sonata*.]

[2. Henry Sedgwick, *Dante: An Elementary Book for Those Who Seek in the Great Poet the Teacher of Spiritual Life* (New Haven: Yale University Press, 1918).]

23

AARON COPLAND

(1900-1990)

In "The Composer in Industrial America," Aaron Copland discusses the proper role for American musicians of the 1950s from the populist standpoint that had emerged in musical aesthetics of the 1920s and 1930s. There must be a serious music in America, he says, that will reflect upon and be relevant to its overwhelmingly "industrial" society—Copland's polite term for a materialistic culture in his homeland that he more pointedly describes as "crude" and "crass." It would be futile for composers in general to turn their backs on their own society by writing relatively complex music, he says. Ironically, this is precisely the direction that American music took just after Copland issued this admonishment. He also reflects on the two dominant styles of interwar music—one relatively severe and modernistic, the other populist, traditional, and relatively simple. Both styles can and should coexist, he recommends, just as they have in his own oeuvre and as they did in general in circles of modern music in Europe and America between the world wars. Artistic music can relate even to an industrial society, he concludes, by an affirmative emotionality that focuses attention on and depicts the human condition within that society.

Copland's "The Composer in Industrial America" originated as the fifth of his Charles Eliot Norton lectures delivered in 1951 and 1952 at Harvard University. Their texts were then published under the title *Music and Imagination*. Copland later speculated that the lectures had taken on a musical shape:

> *The value of these lectures depended partly on the overall shaping of the material. I thought of them as similar to a musical composition with two large movements (the two sets of lectures), each including three separate but related sections. In the first three lectures, which were delivered in the fall of 1951, I attempted to develop in a logical way the subject of the imagination in connection with musical experience; in the second set, delivered in the spring of 1952, I was concerned with the public rather than the musical imagination.*[1]

Copland's comparison of his writings to his music is apposite, as both have great ease, clarity, and conciseness. He characteristically tended to understate his importance as an essayist: "I am not a professional writer," he said. "Although I tended to think that music was either too hard to write about or not worth writing about at all, I periodically published articles and books, sometimes developed from lectures."[2] In fact Copland was one of the most insightful chroniclers and critics of American modern music of the twentieth century. An example in this essay is his estimation of the music of Charles Ives, an authoritative critique that will repay careful study.

Copland's Writings: A Selective Bibliography

Copland on Music (Garden City, NY: Doubleday, 1960). A collection of essays.

Music and Imagination. Cambridge: Harvard University Press, 1952. The six Charles Eliot Norton lectures given at Harvard University, 1951–52.

The New Music: 1900–1960. New York: Mentor, 1968. Originally published in 1941 as *Our New Music*, updated to account for developments following World War II.

What To Listen For In Music. Second edition. New York: Mentor, 1957. Based on a course in music appreciation given in 1936 and 1937 at the New School for Social Research in New York.

—ɯ—

"THE COMPOSER IN INDUSTRIAL AMERICA" FROM MUSIC AND IMAGINATION

(1952)

Is it sheer chance, I sometimes wonder, that no one has ever published an adequate critical summary of the whole field of American serious composition? There are, of course, several compendiums containing mostly biographical data and lists of works, but no one has yet attempted to summarize what our composers have accomplished, nor to say what it feels like to be a composer in industrial America. What sort of creative life the composer leads, what his relation to the community is or should be—these and many other interesting facets of the composer's life have hardly been explored.

My colleague, the American composer Elliott Carter, once said to me that in his opinion only an imaginative mind could possibly conceive itself a composer of serious music in an industrial community like the United States. Actually it seems to me that we Americans who compose alternate between states of mind that make composition appear to be the most natural and ordinary pursuit and other moods when it seems completely extraneous to the primary interests of an industrial environment. By temperament I lean to the side that considers composing in our community as a natural force—something to be taken for granted—rather than the freakish occupation of a very small minority of our citizens.

And yet, judging the situation dispassionately, I can see that we ought not to take it for granted. We must examine the place of the artist and composer in our kind of society, partly to take account of its effect on the artist and also as a commentary on our society itself. The fact is that an industrial society must prove itself capable of producing creative artists of stature, for its inability to do so would be a serious indictment of the fundamental tenets of that society.

From the moment that one doesn't take composing for granted in our country, a dozen questions come to mind. What *is* the composer's life in America? Does it differ so very much from that of the European or even the Latin American composer of today? Or from the life of United States composers in other periods? Are our objectives and purposes the same as they always have been? These questions and many related ones are continually being written about by the literary critic, but they are infrequently dealt with in the musical world. I can best consider them by relating them to my own experience as a creative artist in America. Generalizing from that experience it may be possible to arrive at certain conclusions. This engenders an autobiographical mood, but it is impossible to avoid it if I am to use myself as guinea pig.

My own experience I think of as typical because I grew up in an urban community (in my case, New York City) and lived in an environment that had little or no connection with serious music. My discovery of music was rather like coming upon an unsuspected city—like discovering Paris or Rome if you had never before heard of their existence. The excitement of discovery was enhanced because I came upon only a few streets at a time, but before long I began to suspect the full extent of this city. The instinctual drive toward the world of sound must have been very strong in my case, since it triumphed over a commercially minded environment that, so far as I could tell, had never given a thought to art or to art expression as a way of life.

Scenes come back to me from my early high school years. I see myself digging out scores from the dusty upstairs shelves of the old Brooklyn Public Library on Montague Street; here were riches of which my immediate neighbors were completely unaware. Those were the impressionable years of exploration. I recall nights at home alone singing to myself the songs of Hugo Wolf—living on a plane which had no parallel in the rest of my daily life. Or explaining to a school friend, after hearing one of my first orchestral concerts in the Brooklyn Academy of Music, in the days before radio and recorded symphonies, what a large orchestra sounded like. I've forgotten my exact description except for the punch line: "And then, and then," I said, after outlining how the instrumental forces were gradually marshaled little by little, "and then—the whole orchestra came in." This was musical glory manifesting itself. Most of all I remember the first time I openly admitted to another human being that I intended to become a composer of music. To set oneself up as a rival of the masters: what a daring and unheard-of project for a Brooklyn youth! It was summertime and I was fifteen years old—and the friend who heard this startling confession might have laughed at me. Fortunately, he didn't.

The curious thing, in retrospect, is the extent to which I was undisturbed by the ordinariness of the workaday world about me. It didn't occur to me to revolt against its crassness, for in the last analysis it was the only world I knew, and I simply accepted it for what it was. Music for me was not a refuge or a consolation; it merely gave meaning to my own existence, where the world outside had little or none. I couldn't help feeling a little sorry for those to whom music and art in general meant nothing, but that was their own concern. As for myself, I could not imagine my own life without it.

It seems to me now, some thirty-five years later, that music and the life about me did not touch. Music was like the inside of a great building that shut out the street noises. They were the noises natural to a street; but it was good to have the quiet of the great building available, not as a haven or a hiding place, but as a different and more meaningful place.

Here at the start, I imagine, is a first difference from the European musician, whose contacts with serious music, even when delayed must seem entirely natural, since "classical music" is German, English, French, Italian, and so forth—has roots, in other words, in the young composer's own background. In my America, "classical" music was a foreign importation. But the foreignness of serious music did not trouble me at all in those days: my early preoccupations were with technique and expressivity. I found that I derived profound satisfaction from exteriorizing inner feelings—at times, surprisingly concrete ones—and giving them shape. The scale on which I worked at first was small—two-or three-page piano pieces or songs—but the intensity of feeling was real. It must have been the reality of this inner intensity I speak of which produced the conviction that I was capable of some day writing a longer, and perhaps, significant work. There is no other way of explaining a young artist's self-assurance. It is not founded on faith alone (and of course there can be no certainty about it), but some real kernel there must be, from which the later work will grow.

My years in Europe from the age of twenty to twenty-three made me acutely conscious of the origins of the music I loved. Most of the time I spent in France, where the characteristics of French culture are evident at every turn. The relation of French music to the life around me became increasingly manifest. Gradually, the idea that my personal expression in music ought somehow to be related to my own back-home environment took hold of me. The conviction grew inside me that the two things that seemed always to have been so separate in America—music and the life about me—must be made to touch. This desire to make the music I wanted to write come out of the life I had lived in America became a preoccupation of mine in the twenties. It was not so very different from the experience of other young American artists in other fields, who had gone abroad to study in that period; in greater or lesser degree, all of us discovered America in Europe.

In music our problem was a special one: it really began when we started to search for what Van Wyck Brooks calls a usable past. In those days the example of our American elders in music was not readily at hand. Their music was not often played except perhaps locally. Their scores were seldom published, and even when published, were expensive and not easily available to the inquiring student. We knew, of course, that they too had been to Europe as students, absorbing musical culture, principally in Teutonic centers of learning. Like us, they came home full of admiration for the treasures of European musical art, with the self-appointed mission of expounding these glories to their countrymen.

But when I think of these older men, and especially of the most important among them—John Knowles Paine, George Chadwick, Arthur Foote, Horatio Parker—who made up the Boston school of composers at the turn of the century, I am aware of a fundamental difference between their attitude and our own. Their attitude was founded upon an admiration for the European art work and an identification with it that made the seeking out of any other art formula a kind of sacrilege. The challenge of the Continental art work was not: can we do better or can we also do something truly our own, but merely, can we do as well. But of course one never does "as well." Meeting Brahms or Wagner on his own terms one is certain to come off second best. They loved the masterworks of Europe's mature culture not like creative personalities but like the schoolmasters that many of them became. They accepted an artistic authority that came from abroad, and seemed intent on conforming to that authority.

I do not mean to underestimate what they accomplished for the beginnings of serious American musical composition. Quite the contrary. Within the framework of the German musical tradition in which most of them had been trained, they composed industriously, they set up professional standards of workmanship, and encouraged a seriousness of purpose in their students that long outlasted their own activities. But judged purely on their merits as composers, estimable though their symphonies and operas and chamber works are, they were essentially practitioners in the conventional idiom of their own day, and therefore had little to offer us of a younger generation. No doubt it is trite to say so, but it is none the less true, I think, that a genteel aura hangs about them. There were no Dostoyevskys, no Rimbauds among them; no one expired in the gutter like Edgar Allan Poe. It may not be gracious to say so, but I fear that the New England group of composers of that time were in all their instincts overgentlemanly, too well-mannered, and their culture reflected a certain museumlike propriety and bourgeois solidity.

In some strange way Edward MacDowell, a contemporary of theirs, managed to escape some of the pitfalls of the New Englanders. Perhaps the fact that he had been trained from an early age in the shadow of the Conservatoire at Paris and had spent many subsequent years abroad gave him a familiarity in the presence of Europe's great works that the others never acquired. This is pure surmise on my part; but it is fairly obvious that, speaking generally, his music shows more independence of spirit, and certainly more personality than was true of his colleagues around 1900. It was the music of MacDowell, among Americans, that we knew best, even in 1925. I cannot honestly say that we dealt kindly with his work at that period; his central position as "foremost composer of his generation" made him especially apt as a target for our impatience with the weaknesses and orthodoxies of an older generation. Nowadays, although his music is played less often than it once was, one can appreciate more justly what MacDowell had: a sensitive and individual poetic gift, and a special turn of harmony of his own. He is most successful when he is least pretentious. It seems likely that for a long time MacDowell's name will be secure in the annals of American music, even though his direct influence as a composer can hardly be found in present-day American music.

The search for a usable past, for musical ancestors, led us to examine most closely, as was natural, the music of the men who immediately preceded our own time—the generation that was active after the death of MacDowell in 1908. It was not until about that period that some of our composers were able to shake off the all-pervasive German influence in American music. With Debussy and Ravel, France had reappeared as a world figure on the international musical scene, and French impressionism became the new influence. Composers like Charles Martin Loeffler and Charles T. Griffes were the radicals of their day. But we see now that if the earlier Boston composers were prone to take refuge in the sure values of the academic world, these newer men were in danger of escaping to a kind of artistic ivory tower.

As composers, they seemed quite content to avoid contact with the world they lived in. Unlike the poetry of Sandburg or the novels of Dreiser or Frank Norris, so conscious of the crude realities of industrial America, you will find no picture of the times in the music of Loeffler or Griffes. The danger was that their music would become a mere adjunct to the grim realities of everyday life, a mere exercise in polite living. They loved the picturesque, the poetic, the exotic—medievalisms, Hinduisms, Gregorian chants, *chinoiseries*. Even their early critics stressed the "decadent" note in their music.

Despite this *fin-de-siècle* tendency, Charles Griffes is a name that deserves to be remembered. He represents a new type of composer as contrasted with the men of Boston. Griffes was just an ordinary small-town boy from Elmira, New York. He never knew the important musical people of his time and he never managed to get a better job than that of music teacher in a private school for boys, outside Tarrytown, New York. And yet there are pages in his music where we recognize the presence of the truly inspired moment. His was the work of a sentient human being, forward-looking, for its period, with a definite relationship to the impressionists and to Scriabin. No one can say how far Griffes might have developed if his career had not been cut short by death in his thirty-sixth year in 1920. What he gave those of us who came after him was a sense of the adventurous in composition, of being thoroughly alive to the newest trends in world music and to the stimulus that might be derived from such contact.

Looking backward for first signs of the native composer with an interest in the American scene one comes upon the sympathetic figure of Henry F. Gilbert. His special concern was the use of Negro material as a basis for serious composition. This idea had been given great impetus by the arrival in America in 1892 of the Bohemian composer, Anton Dvořák. His writing of the *New World* Symphony *in* the new world, using melodic material strongly suggestive of Negro spirituals, awakened a desire on the part of several of the younger Americans of that era to write music of local color, characteristic of one part, at least, of the American scene. Henry Gilbert was a Boston musician, but he had little in common with his fellow New Englanders, for it was his firm conviction that it was better to write a music in one's own way, no matter how modest and restricted its style might be, than to compose large works after a foreign model. Gilbert thought he had solved the problem of an indigenous expression by quoting Negro or Creole themes in his overtures and ballets. What he did was suggestive on a primitive and pioneering level, but the fact is that be lacked the technique and musicianship for expressing his ideals in a significant way.

What, after all, does it mean to make use of a hymn tune or a cowboy tune in a serious musical composition? There is nothing inherently pure in a melody of folk source that cannot be effectively spoiled by a poor setting. The use of such materials ought never to be a mechanical process. They can be successfully handled only by a composer who is able to identify himself with, and re-express in his own terms, the underlying emotional connotation of the material. A hymn tune represents a certain order of feeling: simplicity, plainness, sincerity, directness. It is the reflection of those qualities in a stylistically appropriate setting, imaginative and unconventional and not mere quotation, that gives the use of folk tunes reality and importance. In the same way, to transcribe the cowboy tune so that its essential quality is preserved is a task for the imaginative composer with a professional grasp of the problem.

In any event, we in the twenties were little influenced by the efforts of Henry Gilbert, for the truth is that we were after bigger game. Our concern was not with the quotable hymn or spiritual: we wanted to find a music that would speak of universal things in a vernacular of American speech rhythms. We wanted to write music on a level that left popular music far behind—music with a largeness of utterance wholly representative of the country that Whitman had envisaged.

Through a curious quirk of musical history the man who was writing such a music—a music that came close to approximating our needs—was entirely unknown to us. I sometimes wonder whether the story of American music might have been different if Charles Ives and his work had been played at the time he was composing most of it—roughly the twenty years from 1900 to 1920. Perhaps not; perhaps he was too far in advance of his own generation. As it turned out, it was not until the thirties that he was discovered by the younger composers. As time goes on, Ives takes on a more and more legendary character, for his career as composer is surely unique not only in America but in musical history anywhere.

In the preceding chapter I mentioned the abundance of imagination in the music of Ives, its largeness of vision, its experimental side, and the composer's inability to be self-critical. Here I want to be more specific and stress not so much the mystical and transcendental side of his nature—the side that makes him most nearly akin to men like Thoreau and Emerson—but rather the element in his musical speech that accounts for his acceptance of the vernacular as an integral part of that speech. That acceptance, it seems to me, was a highly significant moment in our musical development.

Ives had an abiding interest in the American scene as lived in the region with which he was familiar. He grew up in Danbury, Connecticut, but completed his schooling at Yale University, where he graduated in 1898. Later he moved on to New York, where he spent many years as a successful man of business. Throughout his life one gets the impression that he was deeply immersed in his American roots. He was fascinated by typical features of New England small-town life: the village church choir, the Fourth of July celebration, the firemen's band, a barn dance, a village election, George Washington's Birthday. References to all these things and many similar ones can be found in his sonatas and symphonies. Ives treated this subject matter imaginatively rather than literally. Don't think for an instant that he was a mere provincial with a happy knack for incorporating indigenous material into his many scores. No, Ives was an intellectual, and what is most impressive is not his evocation of a local landscape but the overall range and comprehensiveness of his musical mind.

Nevertheless Ives had a major problem in attempting to achieve formal coherence in the midst of so varied a musical material. He did not by any means entirely succeed in this difficult assignment. At its worst his music is amorphous, disheveled, haphazard—like the music of a man who is incapable of organizing his many different thoughts. Simultaneity of impression was an idea that intrigued Ives all his life.

As a boy he never got over the excitement of hearing three village bands play on different street corners at the same time. Ives tried a partial solution for reproducing this simultaneity of effect, which was subsequently dubbed "musical perspective" by one music critic. He composed a work which is a good example of this device. It is called *Central Park in the Dark,* dates from 1907, and, like many of Ives's works, is based on a poetic transcription of a realistic scene. The composer thought up a simple but ingenious method for picturing this scene, thereby enhancing what was in reality a purely musical intention. Behind a velvet curtain he placed a muted string orchestra to represent the sounds of the night, and before the curtain he placed a woodwind ensemble which made city noises. Together they evoke Central Park in the dark. The effect is almost that of musical cubism, since the music seems to exist independently on different planes. This so-called musical perspective makes use of music realism in order to create an impressionistic effect.

The full stature of Ives as composer will not be known until we have an opportunity to judge his output as a whole. Up to now, only a part of his work has been deciphered and published. But whatever the total impression may turn out to be, his example in the twenties helped us not at all, for our knowledge of his work was sketchy—so little of it had been played.

Gradually by the late twenties, our search for musical ancestors had been abandoned or forgotten, partly, I suppose, because we became convinced that there were none—that we had none. We were on our own, and something of the exhilaration that goes with being on one's own accompanied our very action. This self-reliant attitude was intensified by the open resistance to new music that was typical in the period after the First World War. Some of the opposition came from our elders—conservative composers who undoubtedly thought of us as noisy upstarts, carriers of dangerous ideas. The fun of the fight against the musical philistines, the sorties and strategies, the converts won, and the hot arguments with dull-witted critics partly explain the particular excitements of that period. Concerts of new music were a gamble: who could say whether Acario Catapos of Chile, or Josef Hauer of Vienna, or Kaikhosru Sorabji of England was the coming man of the future? It was an adventuresome time—a time when fresh resources had come to music and were being tested by a host of new composers with energy and ebullient spirits.

Sometimes it seems to me that it was the composers who were the very last to take cognizance of a marked change that came over the musical scene after the stimulating decade of the twenties. The change was brought about, of course, by the introduction for the first time of the mass media of distribution in the field of music. First came the phonograph, then the radio, then the sound film, then the tape recorder, and now television. Composers were slow to realize that they were being faced with revolutionary changes: they were no longer merely writing their music within an industrial framework of what had previously been our comparatively restricted musical life. One of the crucial questions of our times was injected: How are we to make contact with this enormously enlarged potential audience without sacrificing in any way the highest musical standards?

Jacques Barzun recently called this question the problem of numbers. "A huge increase in the number of people, in the number of activities, and possibilities, of desires and satisfactions, is the great new fact." Composers are free to ignore this "great new fact" if they choose; no one is forcing them to take the large new public into account. But it would be foolish to sidestep what is essentially a new situation in music: foolish because musical history teaches that when the audience changes, music changes. Our present condition is very analogous to that in the field of books. Readers are generally quick to distinguish between the book that is a best-seller by type and the book that is meant for the restricted audience of intellectuals. In between there is a considerable body of literature that appeals to the intelligent reader with broad interests. Isn't a similar situation likely to develop in music? Aren't you able even now to name a few best-seller compositions of recent vintage? Certainly the complex piece—the piece that is "born difficult"—is an entirely familiar musical manifestation. But it is the intelligent listener with broad interests who has tastes at the present time which are difficult to define. Composers may have to relinquish old thinking habits and become more consciously aware of the new audience for whom they are writing.

In the past, when I have proffered similar gratuitous advice on this subject, I have often been misinterpreted. Composers of abstruse music thought they were under attack, and claimed that complexities were natural to them—"born that way," a contention that I never meant to dispute. I was simply pointing out that certain modes of expression may not need the full gamut of post-tonal implications, and that certain expressive purposes can be appropriately carried out only by a simple texture in a basically tonal scheme. As I see it, music that is born complex is not inherently better or worse than music that is born simple.

Others took my meaning to be a justification for the watering down of their ideas for the purposes of making their works acceptable for mass consumption. Still others have used my own compositions to prove that I make a sharp distinction between those written in a "severe" and those in a "simple" style. The inference is sometimes drawn that I have consciously abandoned my earlier dissonant manner in order to popularize my style—and this notion is applauded enthusiastically; while those of a different persuasion are convinced that only my so-called "severe" style is really serious.

In my own mind there never was so sharp a dichotomy between the various works I have written. Different purposes produce different kinds of work, that is all. The new mechanization of music's media has emphasized functional requirements, very often in terms of a large audience. That need would naturally induce works in a simpler, more direct style than was customary for concert works of absolute music. But it did not by any means lessen my interest in composing works in an idiom that might be accessible only to cultivated listeners. As I look back, it seems to me that what I was trying for in the simpler works was only partly the writing of compositions that might speak to a broader audience. More than that they gave me an opportunity to try for a more homespun musical idiom, not so different in intention from what attracted me in more hectic fashion in my jazz-influenced works of the twenties. In other words, it was not only musical functionalism that was in question, but also musical language.

This desire of mine to find a musical vernacular, which, as language, would cause no difficulties to my listeners, was perhaps nothing more than a recrudescence of my old interest in making a connection between music and the life about me. Our serious composers have not been signally successful at making that kind of connection. Oblivious to their surroundings, they live in constant communion with great works, which in turn seems to make it *de rigueur* for them to attempt to emulate the great works by writing one of their own on an equivalent plane. Do not misunderstand me. I entirely approve of the big gesture for those who can carry it off. What seems to me a waste of time is the self-deceiving "major" effort on the part of many composers who might better serve the community by the writing of a good piece for high school band. Young composers are especially prone to overreaching themselves—to making the grand gesture by the writing of ambitious works, often in a crabbed style, that have no future whatever. It is unrealistic and a useless aping, generally of foreign models. I have no illusion, of course, that this good advice will be heeded by anyone. But I like to think that in my own work I have, by example, encouraged the notion that a composer writes for different purposes and from different viewpoints. It is a satisfaction to know that in the composing of a ballet like *Billy the Kid* or in a film score like *Our Town*, and perhaps in the *Lincoln Portrait*, I have touched off for myself and others a kind of musical naturalness that we have badly needed along with "great" works.

An honest appraisal of the position of the American composer in our society today would find much to be proud of, and also much to complain about. The worst feature of the composer's life is the fact that he does not feel himself an integral part of the musical community. There is no deep need for his activities as composer, no passionate concern in each separate work as it is written. (I speak now not of my own personal experience, but of my observation of the general scene.) When a composer is played he is usually surrounded by an air of mild approval; when he is not played no one demands to hear him. Performances in any case are rare events, with the result that very few composers can hope to earn a livelihood from the music they write. The music-teaching profession has therefore been their principal resource, and the composing of music an activity reserved for their spare time. These are familiar complaints, I know, perhaps immemorial ones; but they show little sign of abatement, and in the aggregate they make composers as a group an unhappy lot, with the outward signs of unhappiness ranging from open resentment to inner frustration.

On the brighter side of the ledger there is the cheering fact that numerically there are many more active composers than there once were. There is private encouragement on the part of certain foundations and individuals, and prizes and commissions are much more frequently given. An occasional radio station or recording company will indicate a spurt of interest. The publishers have shown signs of gratifying awakening, by a willingness to invest in the future of unknowns. The music critics are, generally speaking, more open-minded in their attitude, more ready to applaud than they were a quarter of a century ago. And best of all, there appears to be a continual welling up of new talents from all parts of America that augurs well for our composing future.

In the final analysis the composer must look for keenest satisfaction in the work that he does—in the creative art itself. In many important respects creation in an industrial community is little different from what it has always been in any community. What, after all, do I put down when I put down notes? I put down a reflection of emotional states: feelings, perceptions, imaginings, intuitions. An emotional state, as I use the term is compounded of everything we are: our background, our environment, our convictions. Art particularizes and makes actual these fluent emotional states. Because it particularizes and because it makes actual, it gives meaning to *la condition humaine*. If it gives meaning it necessarily has purpose. I would even add that it has moral purpose.

One of the primary problems for the composer in an industrial society like that of America is to achieve integration, to find justification for the life of art in the life about him. I must believe in the ultimate good of the world and of life as I live it in order to create a work of art. Negative emotions cannot produce art; positive emotions bespeak an emotion about something. I cannot imagine an artwork without implied convictions; and that is true also for music, the most abstract of the arts.

It is this need for a positive philosophy which is a little frightening in the world as we know it. You cannot make art out of fear and suspicion; you can make it only out of affirmative beliefs. This sense of affirmation can be had only in part from one's inner being; for the rest it must be continually reactivated by a creative and yea-saying atmosphere in the life about one. The artist should feel himself affirmed and buoyed up by his community. In other words, art and the life of art must mean something, in the deepest sense, to the everyday citizen. When that happens, America will have achieved a maturity to which every sincere artist will have contributed.

Notes

[Text: Copland, "The Composer in Industrial America," Chapter 6 in *Music and Imagination* (Cambridge: Harvard University Press, 1952). Reprinted by permission of the Harvard University Press.]

[1. Aaron Copland and Vivian Perlis, *Copland Since 1943* (New York: St. Martin's Press, 1989), 177.]

[2. Ibid., 175.]

2 4

ELLIOTT CARTER

(B. 1908)

Elliott Carter is ideally suited to trace the cultural connections in modern music between France and the United States. He grew up in New York in a Francophile family and is said to have learned to speak French even before English. He studied at Harvard University at a time when the nearby Boston Symphony Orchestra, under the leadership of Serge Koussevitsky, was performing an unprecedented number of new works of French and American provenance. He went abroad in 1932 to attend the École Normale de Musique in Paris, and, following the example of such predecessors as Walter Piston and Aaron Copland, he also studied privately with Nadia Boulanger. In Paris he saw firsthand the close cultural ties between the modern arts in France and America that had existed since the end of World War I, and he witnessed the power exerted by Igor Stravinsky in the solidification of a new order in music—the International Neoclassical Style—that found ever more devoted adherents among younger American musicians.

The influence of French culture upon the development of musical modernism in America is Carter's topic in this essay, which is presented here for the first time in an English translation. The author points to several aspects of direct French influence in America—the teaching of Boulanger, the presence in Boston of Koussevitsky, and the French orientation of American modern musical societies, including the Society Pro-Musica, International Composers' Guild, and League of Composers. At the same time, he explores the circumstances that have made musical culture in America different from that of France. Among the most important, he says, are the different cultural aspirations of those occupying the upper classes in the two countries. The lack of a long cultural tradition in America and the presence of a pervasively bourgeois society have produced here, Carter says, a distinctive musical culture that is diverse to the point of incoherence.

The time frame of Carter's study of intercultural exchange begins essentially in 1920. Before then there was relatively little connection in music between France and the United States, except for what stemmed from isolated areas of French immigration, such as New Orleans. Before World War I, America's European model for music was Germany. Virtually all of the leading American composers near the turn of the century received their advanced musical education in Germany, and their own music was shaped primarily by new ideas coming from Germany. So strong was the German grip on American music at this time that a native musician such as Charles Ruggles changed his name to Carl, hoping that its German sound would create opportunities for him. The German influence quickly evaporated during World War I, after which

France became the source of new ideas in modern music, leading to a cultural affinity between the two countries that still exists in the present day.

Elliott Carter began to publish reviews and essays on music in 1937, shortly after his return from France. These first appeared in the journal *Modern Music*, and he has since written over one hundred articles for many of the leading musical and literary periodicals. His article "France-America Ltd." was written for the catalogue of an exhibition "Paris-New York" at the Musée National d'Art Moderne in Paris in 1977, commemorating the opening there of the Pompidou Center.

Carter's Writings: A Selective Bibliography

Collected Essays and Lectures, 1937–1995. Edited by Jonathan W. Bernard. Rochester, NY: University of Rochester Press, 1997.

Flawed Words and Stubborn Sounds: A Conversation with Elliott Carter, by Allen Edwards. New York: W. W. Norton, 1971.

The Writings of Elliott Carter: An American Composer Looks at Modern Music. Edited by Else Stone and Kurt Stone. Bloomington and London: Indiana University Press, 1977. Sixty-nine articles and reviews are reprinted.

—⁂—

FRANCE-AMERICA LTD.

(France Amérique Ltd., 1977)

Concert music, imported from Europe during the eighteenth and nineteenth centuries, found itself faced with a rather special problem in adapting to the social conditions of America. Constantly threatened with extinction by the spectacular success of popular music and by the ever-increasing costs of concerts, it has never benefited from the assiduous efforts of a discriminating, music-loving upper class, with clearly defined cultural goals, capable of imposing its tastes. The cultural habits that have favored the elaborate development of repertoires and performance methods that constitute the world of music could never have come into existence in Europe without such an upper class. It is indeed surprising that America was able to attain such a high degree of musical development without a comparable tradition.

Composers in America found themselves faced with a dilemma, especially at the beginning, before they had the support of predecessors who had already struggled with this problem. Being citizens of a country whose history and society were different from those of Europe, and aspiring to master an art highly developed by European musicians to express their own preoccupations, they often judged their own efforts inept or mediocre, and the public quite agreed with them. Now, however, that they have attained a professional level equal to that of their European colleagues, the situation remains difficult because, in the concert and opera repertory, the public always finds of most value the European "masterpieces," which define the tastes and expectations of performers, public, and even many composers.

For the typical concertgoer, the question of American music has usually come down to comparing it in quality to European music. Yet European audiences look to American music for an American character distinct from that of Europe, while many Americans are searching for an authentic and personal music that attains an elevated musical level without preoccupation with "being American." Despite enormous difficulties, our composers had to try to find their own way—a way that would be a reflection of their personal experiences. Of course, it was the European musical aesthetic itself that impelled all composers, particularly in the nineteenth century, to find a national style, to demonstrate originality within the framework of the rules of musical decorum and therefore to find in their environment a musical material that would make them distinctive. In America, this material was above all the music of the Blacks and the Indians.

Of the three great musical cultures of the nineteenth century, the German and the Italian were introduced into our cities by the crowds of immigrants coming from every social class of these countries. These immigrants did all they could to maintain continuity with their former way of life. They formed choral societies, symphony orchestras, and opera companies. The French, by comparison, have not exerted the same influence, for despite their active role at the periphery, in Louisiana and in Québec, there were few of them in the big cities. This situation does not seem likely to change despite the predictions of the British historian Arnold Toynbee, who wrote in the 1930s that French culture was bound to spread in the United States as the result of two new waves of immigration, flowing down from Canada and up from Louisiana, that would meet in Washington. What we know and what we have always known about French culture (if rather superficially) are the ideas of Rousseau, Montesquieu, and de Tocqueville, which have become an integral part of our political structure.

Apart, then, from the situation in Louisiana, other aspects of French culture have had only a weak effect on the general population; it was of interest to the rich and cultivated classes who saw in bourgeois and aristocratic France the ideal of a luxurious and elegant life. Concert music, like all artistic objects, evoked and probably still evokes in the eyes of Americans the same image of refinement and distinction, and for that reason has always had great works of French music in its repertoire. By the same token, the larger public greeted with pleasure French performers and conductors who, having accepted posts here, often drew highly qualified instrumentalists from the Conservatoire. It is hardly surprising to find that many an American seriously aspiring to a musical career, impressed by the talent and authority of French musicians and by the respect they inspired, wished to study in Paris.

During the postwar periods of the twentieth century, such musical studies were encouraged by the French and American governments by means of generous stipends. The American Conservatory was founded in 1921 at Fontainebleau for such students. And after the First World War, thanks to the devaluation of the franc, many Francophile American artists and writers were able to live in Paris—Ezra Pound, Gertrude Stein, Ernest Hemingway, Man Ray, Virgil Thomson, George Antheil—and their presence there attracted many others. These "expatriates" were drawn by the contemporary art then flourishing in Paris, and by the respect paid by the French to the artist, which contrasted with the disdain accorded by Americans at the time. It was during these years that the influence of French and Russian music gave a new and important direction to American music.

Throughout the nineteenth century, and even earlier, French composers of symphonic and operatic music were preoccupied with incorporating folk and popular music into their works. For instance, the treatment of Spanish music by Bizet, Lalo, and Chabrier—not to mention Debussy and Ravel—implied the inclusion of a dramatic element, of animation, of local color and nostalgia, and also of an enlarged musical continuity when these folkloric materials were assimilated by the "great music" of the concert hall. The reconciliation of these two styles, that of folklore and that of symphonic music, owing to French musicians of the romantic period, inevitably gave birth to national schools, in particular the Spanish school, which followed the French example while adapting it to its needs, and also to a certain extent the Russian school, where the flair exhibited by Berlioz and others for the brilliant and the picturesque suggested interesting innovations. This model even reached as far as New Orleans, where Louis Moreau Gottschalk, a former pupil of Berlioz, composed pieces of Creole charm, like "Le bananier" and "La bamboula."

The relationships between concert music and popular music cut across several different phases connected to the development of romanticism and of European politics. At the beginning of the twentieth century, the "Wild Men" of Russia undertook to accentuate the basic and primitive aspects of their music and finally, in reaction against the romantic style, they distorted popular music (very often the music of the carnival or circus), in the manner of Satie or *Les Six*, in order to accentuate its roughness, it repetitive aspect, and its almost pathetic banality. In *Renard* (1916) and *L'histoire du soldat* (1918), Stravinsky succeeded in combining these two styles in a new and convincing way, in part inherited from the French musicians he had had contact with and in part completely original. This synthesis inevitably had repercussions everywhere.

Among the young American composers, such music aroused a great deal of interest, notably because it often took their own popular music as a point of departure: the cakewalk (as in Debussy), ragtime, and jazz. They soon saw there a path which could lead to a new American style, the vitality of which would be much stronger than that of any preceding efforts at a romantic style—efforts which had never been convincing except for those of Charles Ives.

To encourage this tendency, Serge Koussevitsky, conductor of the Boston Symphony during the 1920s and 1930s and one of the defenders of contemporary music from France and Russia, urged American composers to form a national school comparable to the Russian Five: he commissioned and performed American works that conformed to this tendency. His advisor for contemporary repertoire was reportedly Nadia Boulanger, who already at this time was attracting a good number of American students to Paris.

Indeed, just after the First World War, a great deal of contemporary music was being played in the United States, thanks principally to the efforts of French musicians who had become established here. The French pianist Robert Schmitz, with the help of the Alliance Française, inaugurated a series of concerts of modern music, given by what was called at first the Franco-American Society, later the Society Pro-Musica (whose board comprised Charles Ives, Edgard Varèse, and the harpist and French composer Carlos Salzedo). Besides giving concerts that included a great deal of new French music, this group organized touring programs devoted to Bartók, Prokofiev, Stravinsky, Milhaud, and Honegger, which were heard all over the American continent. In 1927, in New York, this Society premiered several movements of Ives's Fourth Symphony, and on the same program was heard Milhaud's *Les malheurs d'Orphée*, conducted by the composer. At the same time, Edgard Varèse and Carlos Salzedo organized the more innovative International Composers' Guild, under the auspices of which they had their own works performed. These two avant-garde organizations came into existence thanks to the initiative of French musicians, and shortly thereafter the Americans created the League of Composers to promote the music of their own country. For, at that moment, numerous American musicians had already begun to wax indignant at the importance constantly accorded to European music, to the detriment of their own. They felt the same way as Debussy did in regard to the Germans, when he wrote:

> It is obvious that we have been more than welcoming toward German musicians. In fifty years, we will see what remains of our present-day infatuation. We love everything that comes from outside. Like children, we clap our hands before a work that comes from afar . . . without understanding the real value or solidity of that work, without asking ourselves whether we can feel a sincere emotion, thrill to spirits that are foreign to ours.

Because of the American Conservatory in Fontainebleau and its teachers, numerous young American students of composition were drawn to Paris during the 1920s, recognizing the possibilities of "modern music" and finding no teacher in the United States who took this music seriously. They knew of only two such teachers in Europe—Arnold Schoenberg and Nadia Boulanger—and, given the anti-German feeling after the First World War, most Americans interested in new music went to Paris. In this way began Nadia Boulanger's career as teacher and as inspiration, whose influence is felt even today. It is thanks to her above all that French culture has exerted an influence on American music since the 1920s right up to the present day.

This remarkable teacher, whose first students were those at Fontainebleau at the beginning of the 1920s, and who later taught at the École Normale and at the Paris Conservatoire, could be considered the message-bearer of the Stravinskian aesthetic. For not only did she always present his works as exemplary models of contemporary music (and this in each new period of Stravinsky's work), but her own musical tastes also evolved parallel to those of Stravinsky himself—who, during his neoclassic period (1919–53), occupied an ever higher position in the history of music, in the estimation of contemporary musicologists. When Stravinsky came to be interested in the quartets of Beethoven, the cantatas of Bach, the music of the Renaissance or the Middle Ages, or later in Webern and other twelve-tone music, Mlle. Boulanger lost little time in drawing her students' attention to these same works and analyzing them in detail. In this way, the anti-Wagnerian and anti-Straussian tastes of the Russian composer found an echo in the tastes of Nadia Boulanger. Often one had the impression that it was she, before Stravinsky himself, who was making these happy discoveries from the distant past which enchanted so many of us. Following the artistic production of Stravinsky year after year, she often presented her students with unexpected opinions about the music of the past. They followed this with enormous gratitude, because Mlle. Boulanger was giving them an opportunity to observe at close quarters the creative activity of Stravinsky. In any case, her teaching demonstrated an intuitive grasp of numerous aspects of musical composition (she could cite at the piano, from memory, an impressive number of examples) and an ability to show the student, with supporting examples, how he could have solved a problem. Her remarkably sustained attention, her musical perspicacity, and the personal interest she bore toward her students were things for which all of them remain deeply grateful.

Her teaching, over the course of a half-century, revealed a constant evolution: she changed over the years as did most musicians, including Stravinsky. The group of students in the 1920s, which included Aaron Copland, Walter Piston, and Roy Harris, founders of the new Americanism, always found her open-minded about all new music. She read the entire score of *Wozzeck* or *Le sacre du printemps* at the piano while her pupils added whatever her hands could not reach, all the while discussing the musical writing, so marvelously inventive in those works, on the same level as if it were Beethoven. Her perspicacity and her acuity of judgment were such that quite a few other composers, like Roger Sessions and Virgil Thomson, who never really studied with her, sent her their scores for her to look at and criticize. It seems that even Honegger and Stravinsky did this too.

During the 1930s, she became much less open to the Viennese School and to Bartók, for like many other young musicians of the time—Hindemith, Milhaud, Copland—she had turned away, little by little, from what had indeed already begun to seem like "old-fashioned modernism." Some, who had just come to devote themselves to the music of the preceding generation, felt betrayed, especially when she held up to them Stravinsky's *Perséphone* as a model.

At the time, Nadia Boulanger showed moderate enthusiasm for some new French music, especially Poulenc, but the composers of an older generation, such as Fauré, Debussy, and Ravel, whose works she adored and spoke of out of a profound knowledge, were an entirely different matter. And all during those years, without letup, she read through scores of old music that had been brought to light by musicologists. During her classes she would draw her students' attention to a ballade of Machaut, or some French composer of madrigals, or to Monteverdi; her recordings of their music left us with vivid proof of her intelligence and musical sensibility. Even though Mlle. Boulanger was always presenting new things to her students, nonetheless she remained fundamentally attached to a traditional curriculum, owing to her belief that students should develop a perfect mastery of harmony, counterpoint, solfège, and orchestration. The verve that she brought to teaching even the simplest little harmony exercise succeeded in transforming this sort of routine into a vivid clarification of fundamental musical matters, no matter what the style.

More recently, the interest which she brought to late Stravinsky and to Webern impelled her to deepen her acquaintance with the work of Boulez—and when her students today attempt to compose in this style, her criticisms are of great help to them.

For some time, the particular tastes of the 1930s prevailed with her students and gave rise to the light and charming style of the "Boulangerie," as it was then christened. Nadia Boulanger favored this manner in those of her students whose talent lent itself to it. But this was true of only a few, while many others partook of the great expansion of the spirit that permitted her to help young composers from all points on the globe to find their own way. Echoing the fervor of so many of her students, Saint-John Perse wrote, on the occasion of her eightieth birthday:

> Nadia, the passing centuries may bring changes of aspect, changes of language, but Music, your Century [in the sense of "world"], has no masks to shed; it is consciousness of existence, more than any art and more than any science of language.
>
> To you, Nadia, both freeman and vassal in the great musical family, but bound only to that divination which submits to no servitude, no school and no ritual.
>
> To her of whom Paul Valéry spoke to me one day during the years between the two world wars, in these simple words: "She is Music personified" (and music to him was always to be equated with "intelligence").
>
> To her whom I saw, in America during the darkest hours of the Western drama [World War II], living among us as apostle and sibyl: animator, instigator, educator, and liberator, her ear open to all music and her soul to all breaths, a leaf herself trembling in an immense foliage.
>
> Honor and thanks be rendered to her in the name of music itself.[1]

In conclusion, the uncertainty in assessing the influence of French culture, and indeed the influence of any culture on another, is that only certain aspects are transferable, and it is hard to tell which ones. In the first place, as I have said, since America did not have an upper class capable of forming the public taste, particularly in music where such influence could have no material interest, the structure of the musical profession was erected on a foundation completely different from that of Europe. That amounts to saying that the public, so numerous and fervent in our concert halls, is in large part conservative, not out of hostility towards contemporary music but rather because they feel baffled by it. Moreover, in a culture where there exists no official, institutionalized system of instruction like that of the Conservatoire, through which almost everyone who wants to be part of the musical profession must pass, musical instruction is of extremely variable quality, sometimes excellent, sometimes very mediocre. Of course this does not encourage the development of a public well disposed to respect American artists and, all too often, the public prefers European artists whose credentials inspire more confidence. In consequence, the terms "conservative" and "avant-garde" signify something that is radically different from what they mean in the more homogeneous European artistic milieux. In fact, such designations really cannot be applied to American music in their European sense, even though many critiques try to impose them without seeing what the real situation is. For if there is one thing that can be said of American composers, it is that, despite their efforts, they do not constitute a school and their art remains, as a whole, anarchic by European standards. In fact, the greater part of our cultural life greatly lacks such coherence as would provide a stable social basis and despite a recent surge of public opinion in favor of more extensive government support for the arts—the sort of support that Europe has had for generations—it is highly unlikely that an agreement to plan and build an institution comparable to the Centre Pompidou or the Cité de la Musique would ever be approved by the American government. All our museums, all our cultural institutions are private foundations financed by individuals, and if they are supported by the government it is only on the condition that half the subvention has already been provided by individuals. Therein lies the basic difference between French and American culture.

Notes

[Text: Carter, "France Amérique Ltd.," in Paris—New York (Paris: Centre d'Art et de Culture Georges Pompidou / Musée National d'Art Moderne, 1977): 7–11. Translated by Jonathan W. Bernard and reviewed by the author, who has also made a few small changes for this publication. Carter's French text is probably a translation from an English-language original that is now apparently lost.]

[1. This translation makes no pretense of being adequate to the text of St.-John Perse in any literary sense. For this reason, Perse's original words, which are poetic and at times highly elliptical, are given below. The translator wishes to thank Joël-François Durand, his colleague at the University of Washington School of Music, for assistance in rendering some points in this translation. The original French reads as follows:

"Nadia, les siècles changent de visage et changent de langage, mais la Musique, votre Siècle, n'a point de masques à dépouiller, étant plus qu'aucun art et plus qu'aucune science du langage, connaissance de l'être.

A vous, Nadia, libre et vassale dans la grande famille musicale, mais à cette seule divination soumise, qui n'est d'aucun servage, d'aucune école et d'aucun rite.

A Celle qu'entre deux guerres Paul Valéry m'adressait un jour avec ces simples mots: 'Elle est la Musique en personne' (et la musique pour lui, toujours, se couronnait d' 'intelligence').

A Celle qu'en Amérique, aux heures les plus sombres du drame occidental, j'ai vue vivre parmi nous sa vie d'apôtre et de sibylle: animatrice, instigatrice, éducatrice et libératrice, l'oreille à toutes sources et l'âme à tous le souffles, feuille elle-même frémissante dans l'immense feuillage.

Honneur et grâces soient rendus au nom de la musique même."]

PART VI

JAZZ FROM
THE COMPOSER'S
POINT OF VIEW

Jazz has been one of America's greatest contributions to twentieth-century culture. Essentially a mix of folk and popular music, it has exhibited such richness, vitality of spirit and expressivity, and so persistent a capacity for fusing with a variety of musical styles that it has proved to be a shaping force in classical music throughout the century.

The relationship of jazz to the art of composition is complex, in large part because the spirit of jazz is so often encountered in a merger with different and sometimes even unrelated forms of musical expression. In the present day, most musicians assume that jazz is essentially an improvised type of music in which composition, strictly speaking, plays a subsidiary or negligible role. But earlier, especially in the 1920s when jazz first burst upon the attention of the American and European publics, improvisation was not thought to be a crucial element, instead, it was only one style among many in which the spirit of jazz could manifest itself. The possibility that jazz can be essentially a product of strict musical composition has always been argued, as the articles by Duke Ellington and Gunther Schuller (essays no. 29 and 30) show. The conflicts inherent in any attempt to define jazz rigidly or to confine it either to the improvisational or compositional dimensions are vividly portrayed in the essays that follow.

In these six articles the reader will find six different descriptions of jazz. Duke Ellington and Gunther Schuller emphasize a compositional viewpoint through which jazz can be shaped into an integrated structure comparable to classical music. Aaron Copland and Virgil Thomson define jazz as a rhythmic style, based on the ragtime prototype of a rhythmically irregular melody superimposed on a regular accompaniment. The music that they call jazz was all written down in the form of popular songs, character pieces for piano, and dance music. For Jelly Roll Morton, jazz was an alternative to ragtime, essentially a style of playing that used swinging rhythms with improvisational liberties in the written or preexisting music. Darius Milhaud perceptively notes that two very different types of music were called jazz—one essentially improvised and purely expressive, the other composed and used functionally for dancing. Both seemed to him to stem from a common African origin.

2 5

DARIUS MILHAUD

(1 8 9 2 – 1 9 7 4)

Darius Milhaud's first contact with jazz came just after World War I, when he returned to Paris from a wartime sojourn in Brazil with the French diplomatic corps. The jazz that he heard at this time was mainly dance music played by the orchestras of Paul Whiteman and Billy Arnold—music that Milhaud later termed "Broadway" jazz. Its idiom was even then being imitated in modern works by Satie, Auric, and Stravinsky, all of whom found it entirely compatible with the emerging neoclassical style. Milhaud's *Caramel mou* (1920), a "shimmy" for jazz band, was his own artistic reflection on this type of music.

A visit to New York City in 1922 introduced him to a very different type of jazz, which proved to be much more stimulating to his imagination as a composer. In his autobiography *My Happy Life* he describes a visit to a Harlem club:

> *Harlem had not yet been discovered by the snobs and aesthetes: we were the only white folk there. The music I heard was absolutely different from anything I had ever heard before, and was a revelation to me. Against the beat of the drums, the melodic lines criss-crossed in a breathless pattern of broken and twisted rhythms. A Negress whose grating voice seemed to come from the depths of the centuries, sang in front of the various tables. With despairing pathos and dramatic feeling, she sang over and over again to the point of exhaustion, the same refrain to which the constantly changing melodic pattern of the orchestra wove a kaleidoscopic background.* [1]

Back in Paris during the following year Milhaud recorded his ideas about Harlem and Broadway jazz in the article "L'Évolution du jazz-band et la musique des nègres d'Amérique du Nord," which was published in May of that year in *Le courrier musical*, for which Milhaud was then a regular contributor. The essay was soon republished in German and English, and it long remained one of the most perceptive early studies of the complex subject of jazz.

After his trip to Harlem, Milhaud realized that there were two types of music then called jazz. One was played primarily by white musicians in dance bands throughout the world. The performers relied mainly on written compositions and arrangements, their playing was polished and crisp in rhythm, and the instrumentalists used outré techniques such as exaggerated vibrato, mute effects, and sliding between tones. The dance music itself was characterized by syncopated melody accompanied in a regular rhythm.

The other type of jazz was performed by African-American musicians, such as those whom he had heard in Harlem in 1922. This was a supremely

expressive and personal music, relying far more on improvisation, and less polished than its Broadway cousin. In 1923 it was still virtually unknown to Europeans, indeed very little known even to most Americans. Milhaud was the first
European composer to imitate this idiom in a classical composition, in his ballet
La création du monde (1923), which he composed at the same time that he
wrote this article.

Milhaud was virtually alone among important classical composers of the
early 1920s in his high artistic appraisal of jazz. Other composers at this time—
even those who used jazz idioms in their music—were inclined to view it as
primitive or ephemeral, often a symbol of American brashness and high spirits,
but not a source of deep or enduring expression. For Milhaud, on the contrary,
it was the equal of even the greatest classical music in its power to express
human spirituality.

A year after Milhaud's article appeared in *Le courrier musical*, it was published in an English translation in the American magazine *Living Age* under the
title "The Jazz Band and Negro Music." This was a faulty translation that was
made from a German version rather than from Milhaud's original. The article is
given here in a new translation made from Milhaud's 1923 original text.

Milhaud's Writings: A Selective Bibliography

My Happy Life. Translated by Donald Evans, George Hall, and Christopher Palmer. London and New
York: Marion Boyars, 1995. This is an expanded version of Milhaud's earlier autobiography, *Notes without
Music*.

Notes sur la musique: Essais et chroniques. Edited by Jeremy Drake. Paris: Flammarion, 1982. A collection
of Milhaud's many essays, interviews, and reviews and a complete bibliography of his writings. In French.

—⟊—

THE EVOLUTION OF THE JAZZ BAND
AND MUSIC OF THE NEGROES
OF NORTH AMERICA
(*L'Évolution du jazz-band et la musique des nègres d'Amérique du nord*, 1923)

In 1918 the jazz band arrived from New York at the Casino de Paris, brought to us by
Gaby Deslys and Mr. Pilcer. Here I won't dwell on the shock, the sudden awakening
that this rhythmic style produced on us, with sounds that until then had never been
brought together and now all at once were put before us. In it we heard the importance of syncopation in its rhythms and melodies, situated on a bedrock of dull regu-
larity that was as basic as circulating blood, as a heartbeat or its pulsations; we heard
an emphasis on percussion in which all the percussion instruments—their names
known from our orchestration manuals—were simplified and made into a single com-

plex instrument. When Mr. Buddy, the "drummer" of the Syncopated Orchestra, played a percussion solo, we heard a structured piece, rhythmically balanced, with an unbelievable variety of expression coming from the many different sounds of the percussion family, all members of which he played at once. We heard a new instrumental technique: the piano played with the dryness and precision of a drum or banjo; the saxophone was brought back; the trombone, using glissandos to give it the most contemporary means of expression, plays the sweetest melodies, as does the trumpet. Both instruments often use mute, portamento, vibrato from the slide or valves, and flutter tonguing. We heard the clarinet in the high register with attacks so aggressive, a tone so powerful, such slides and shaking of notes as to baffle our best players. The banjo appeared, with a dry and nervous sound, more resonant than the harp or the pizzicati of a string quartet. We heard the very unusual playing of the violin, harsh and shrill, using the widest vibrato and the slowest glissandos.

The power of jazz comes from a novelty of technique that extends to all of its elements. In rhythm there is an exploration of resources resulting from the constant use of syncopation, opening up in this music a realm of expression with the simplest means that does not need a rich or varied orchestration. In 1920–21 you just had to hear Jean Wiéner on piano and Vance Lowry on saxophone or banjo at the Bar Gaya, on the Rue Duphot, to absorb the music of jazz, played in a complete, integral, and pure way with a minimum of means.

In orchestration, the use of the various instruments enumerated above and the concentration of their special techniques allow for a variety of unusual expression. To form an accurate opinion of it one must of course hear a serious jazz band—made up of solid musicians who work together regularly, just like our good string quartets—that plays from orchestrations of high value, as are those of Irving Berlin. There have been mediocre jazz bands who have left erroneous and false impressions. Their balance was incorrect and their instrumental technique was poor; often the percussion was entrusted to instrumentalists without taste who, thinking that they were enriching their part, used "false" elements such as auto horns, sirens, Klaxons, etc. It is truly extraordinary how many of these odd instruments quickly lost fashion, demoted to museum pieces, even in the case of the water whistle, with its pretty sound midway between a whistle and a human voice. But listen to a serious jazz band, like that of Billy Arnold or Paul Whiteman. Nothing is left to chance; everything is balanced out with care, with proportion and equilibrium typical of the playing of a musician who knows precisely the capabilities of each instrument. Then go and hear a soirée given by Billy Arnold's band at the casinos in Cannes or Deauville. Sometimes he will have four saxophones, sometimes a violin, clarinet, trumpet, and trombone, then again an infinite variety of instrumental combinations which blend one after the other with the piano and percussion, each with its own sense, logic, sonority, and distinctive expression.

Since jazz was first heard here, it has undergone an extensive evolution. In place of its cataract of sound has come a remarkable improvement in melodiousness: this happened during the period of the "blues." This has a simple melody supported by a very clear and restrained rhythm; the percussion is hardly heard, being more and more subdued. Then the almost mechanical style of Paul Whiteman at the Palais

Royal in New York, with its steely brilliance, was supplanted by the jazz heard at the Hotel Brunswick in Boston—quiet, sensitive, almost impalpable.

The North Americans have discovered in jazz the expression of an art form that is quite their own. Their main jazz bands achieve a perfection in playing that is the equal of our symphony orchestras, such as our Conservatory orchestra, our organizations such as the Société Moderne d'Instruments à Vent, or the Capet Quartet, our most famous one.

These bands possess sonorous and rhythmic materials that are absolutely new and appropriate to them, but how do they use them? Until now they have done so only for dancing. Music written for jazz band still consists only of ragtimes, fox trots, shimmies, etc. They have erred in transcribing celebrated works—the prayer in *Tosca, Peer Gynt,* Gretchaninov's *Berceuse*—for jazz orchestra, using their melodies for dancing. This was a lapse in taste, comparable to the use of auto horns as percussion instruments, etc. These wonderful orchestras need a concert repertory. When Billy Arnold's jazz band played at Jean Wiéner's concert on 6 December 1921 at the Salle des Agriculteurs, it was entirely proper to present these admirable musicians in a "concert" setting. But they should have music other than their dance pieces; they need a chamber music written to capitalize on the sonorities of their orchestra. The influence of these American dances has led here to the "Rag-Time du Paquebot" in Erik Satie's *Parade* and George Auric's *Adieu New-York.* In such works we have a portrait of ragtime or foxtrot through the symphony orchestra [Auric's *Adieu New-York* is for piano]. In Igor Stravinsky's *Piano-Rag-Music* we have a piano piece that uses the rhythmic elements of the rag, interpreted as a concert work. Jean Wiéner, in his *Sonatine syncopée* has given us a piece of chamber music that takes its diverse styles from jazz but uses them in the form of a sonata. We have a ways to go. We still need to give jazz bands pieces of instrumental chamber music including concerted sonatas written for the instruments used in jazz.

Harmony has been the element slowest to develop, given the exclusive use of dance music in the jazz band repertory. But it is following the same course as has contemporary harmony. Successions of seventh and ninth chords, which were so astonishing in 1900, are now used commonly in the most fashionable new dances (in *Ivy* by Jones and Jimmy Johnson, for example). No doubt in years to come polytonal and atonal harmonies will be customary in the dances that follow from the shimmies of 1920. Already, we hear simultaneous major and minor forms of a common triad (as in Zez Confrey's *Kitten On the Keys*).

In the United States there is an entire series of texts on jazz—methods for trombone (showing the main glissandos to be used and how to play them), for saxophone, for clarinet (with all the new jazz techniques). In New York there is a school, the Winn School of Popular Music, that has published three methods (*How to Play Popular Music, How to Play Rag-Time, How to Play Jazz and Blues*) that are of much technical interest and show how all the special effects of this type of music can be learned in a logical and complete way. These manuals are valuable not only for technical study and performing works of jazz music, but also for learning the basics of improvisation and composing so as to give this music its special character, including échap-

pées, passing dissonance, broken chords, arpeggios, trills, embellishments, ornaments, variations, improvisations played ad libitum within the different instrumental
parts when strict rhythm cannot be altered.

In addition to mechanized music, whose machinelike precision is achieved by a
clean style and by the utterly unique performances of the American jazz orchestras,
there exists a music that comes from the same source but which has evolved in a very
different way amid the Negroes of North America. Plainly, the origins of jazz music
are to be sought among the Negroes. The primitive African element remains firmly
rooted among blacks in the United States, and here is seen the source of that formidable rhythmic power, that expressive melody, which comes from a lyricism that only
oppressed races can produce. The first pieces of Negro music to be published were
the "Negro spirituals," slave hymns of popular and very ancient origin. They have
been collected and written down by [Henry] Burleigh. The emotion contained in
these hymns is not very different from that heard in the melodies of "blues," whose
form comes from [W. C.] Handy. Listen to the *St. Louis Blues*, or *Aunt Hagar's Children's Blues*. There is the same tenderness, the same sadness, the same faith as
expressed by slaves in their spirituals when they compare their lot to that of the Jews,
captives of the Egyptians, who call with all their soul to Moses to save them (*Go
Down Moses!*).

In addition to their dance music, in which improvisation gives a life and expressivity that is only found among blacks, they use jazz in the theater in a very happy
way! There are operettas with a delightful musicality, such as *Shuffle Along* by Noble
Sissle and Eubie Blake, or *Liza* by Maceo Pinkard, in which singers, choristers, and
dancers are accompanied by a jazz orchestra. In *Liza* the orchestra is made up of a
flute, clarinet, two trumpets, trombone, percussion for one player, piano, string quartet (in which the viola is replaced by a saxophone), and string bass.

Even now among the Negroes the ethnic element is intact. In [white] American jazz, everything is done to a tee, nothing is unprepared. But among the blacks
improvisation plays a larger role, and what a formidable musical resource it is, what
power of imagination it takes to do it without fault. From the technical point of view
a greater ease is found among them. Each instrument continues along its own melodic line and improvises according to the harmonic framework that underlies the work.
We are constantly in the presence of a play of lines, often achieving a baffling complexity in which major and minor triads are used simultaneously and quarter tones
arise by blending glissandos and vibrato (achieved with the trombone slide, pronounced vibration of the valves of the trumpet, or slight shifting of the finger on the
violin string). The quarter tone has a uniquely expressive character and relates to
diatonic harmony just as does chromaticism when used in passing motions within a
diatonic scale. It has no relevance to the system of quarter tones currently used in
central Europe, which is based on a division of degrees of the twelve-tone scale and
which relates instead to atonal harmony.

In the music of the Negroes we thus depart from the purity and mundane character of music that we so often encounter in [white] American jazz. With the
Negroes the dance preserves a wild African character. In its intense and persistent

rhythms and melodies there arises a sense of tragedy and despair. In a little dance hall in New York, like the Capitol uptown on Lennox Avenue near 140th Street, it is not rare to hear a Negress sing the same melody for more than an hour, a melody often poignant and as pure in design as any beautiful classical recitative, accompanied by a jazz made from a collection of melodies constantly repeated. Its variations have the breadth of a symphony. We are far from the elegant dancing of Broadway, which we hear in Paris at the Hotel Claridge! There, we approach the very source of this music, as profound in humanity as music can be and which can stir the soul as deeply as any universally recognized masterpiece of music.

Notes

[Text: Milhaud, "L'Évolution du jazz-band et la musique des nègres d'Amérique du nord," *Le courrier musical* 25/9 (May 1923): 163–64. Reprinted in Milhaud's *Études* (Paris: Aveline, 1927) and in Milhaud's *Notes sur la musique: Essais et chroniques*, edited by Jeremy Drake (Paris: Flammarion, 1982). Translated by Bryan R. Simms. Used by permission of Madeleine Milhaud.]

1. Milhaud, *My Happy Life*, translated by Donald Evans, George Hall, and Christopher Palmer (London and New York: Marion Boyars, 1995): 110.

26

VIRGIL THOMSON

(1 8 9 6 – 1 9 8 9)

Virgil Thomson's description of jazz, made in this article for H. L. Mencken's magazine *The American Mercury*, reinforced a common understanding of the term in the early 1920s. Jazz, Thomson says, is a rhythmic style that consists of a syncopated melody against an accompaniment with regular rhythm and beat. It was music associated with dancing in bordellos and bawdy houses—a description in line with Carl Engel's slightly earlier summary: "The silly, lewd gyrations for which jazz is held responsible by some are the release of tension in a witless, neurotic stratum of society." Jazz for Thomson was limited in emotion and expressivity—"exactly analogous to the hoochie-coochie," he concludes. There is no indication that he considered jazz to be a form of musical expression more characteristic of African-Americans than of white Americans, and the word improvisation is not even mentioned.

Although Thomson's discussion of jazz may now appear limited, he was one of the first to attempt a musical analysis of the rhythmic language and other features of style in jazzlike dance music of the early 1920s. Similarly to Darius Milhaud's slightly earlier discussion of the jazz band (see essay no. 25), Thomson emphasizes the importance of new playing techniques, including glissando, vibrato, and mute effects. His reference to the "blues formula" concerns the use of blue notes, especially the lowered third scale degree, which Thomson attributes to "alternations of tonic major and minor."

Virgil Thomson's career was divided between composing and music criticism. His music represents an extreme form of the tendency that existed in America between the world wars toward a simplified, populist, and regionalist idiom. He was an extraordinarily gifted writer who had a keen ability to assess openly all types of contemporary music, showing an understanding for styles that were not always congenial to him. He was long uncomfortable with jazz as an artistic form of musical expression, although he frequently wrote about it, and his inquisitiveness led him later to a deeper understanding and appreciation of it.

Thomson's Writings: A Selective Bibliography

American Music Since 1910. New York: Holt, Rinehart and Winston, 1971.

The Art of Judging Music. New York: Alfred A. Knopf, 1948. Collection of articles from the *New York Herald Tribune*, for which Thomson was chief music critic from 1946 to 1954.

The Musical Scene. New York: Alfred A. Knopf, 1945. Articles from the *New York Herald Tribune*.

Music Reviewed, 1940–1954. New York: Random House, 1967. Articles from the *New York Herald Tribune*.

Music Right and Left. New York: Henry Holt, 1951. Articles from the *New York Herald Tribune*.

The State of Music. New York: William Morrow, 1939. Revised edition. New York: Random House, 1962.

Virgil Thomson. New York: Alfred A. Knopf, 1966.

A Virgil Thomson Reader. New York: E. P. Dutton, 1981. Collection of articles and reviews.

—⟋𝔴⟍—

JAZZ
(1924)

Jazz, in brief, is a compound of (a) the fox-trot rhythm, a four-four measure (alla breve) with a double accent, and (b) a syncopated melody over this rhythm. Neither alone will make jazz. The monotonous fox-trot rhythm, by itself, will either put you to sleep or drive you mad. And a highly syncopated line like the second subject of the Franck Symphony in D minor or the principal theme of Beethoven's third *Leonora* Overture is merely syncopation until you add to it the heavy bump-bump of the fox-trot beat. The combination is jazz. Try it on your piano. Apply the recipe to any tune you know. In case you are not satisfied with the result, play the right hand a little before the left.

The fox-trot, which appeared about 1914, is the culmination of a tendency in American dancing that has been active ever since ragtime was invented in the early years of the century. The Viennese waltz and its brother, the two-step, died about 1912. For two years following, fancy steps like the tango, the maxixe, and the hesitation, with their infinite and amazing variations, made anarchy in the ballroom. This was resolved by a return to the utmost simplicity, and the common language of legs became a sort of straight-away walk. Any man could teach his partner in ten steps his peculiar form of it, whether he called it the "castle walk," the "lame duck," or whatnot.

Soon after this primitive step became established ballroom dancing began to show the disturbance that shook all of polite society when the lid of segregation was taken off of vice and the bordello irrupted into the drawing-room. Ragging, a style of dancing with slight footwork, but with much shoulder-throwing, came home from the bawdy house bearing the mark of the earlier hoochie-coochie, a monotonous beat without accentuation. It infected the walk-steps, had a convulsion called the turkey-trot, which proved too difficult to keep up, and finally, calling itself both the one-step and the fox-trot, became national and endemic. The former name, which merely indicated a tempo, is no longer used. The tempo of the latter has been expanded to include it.

At present the fox-trot is our only common dance rhythm. Its speed varies from 66 to 108 half-notes to the minute. It will bear any amount of muscular embroidery, from the shimmy to the halt, because its rhythm is in the simplest possible terms. The Viennese waltz is practically extinct in America. What is now called a waltz is simply a three-four fox-trot, as the two-step was a four-four waltz. The rhythm of the Viennese waltz is

$$| \underline{\textbf{𝅗𝅥}} \quad 𝅘𝅥 \; |$$

or

$$| \underline{𝅘𝅥.} \quad 𝅘𝅥𝅮𝅘𝅥 \; |$$

and that of the hesitation

$$| 𝅘𝅥 \quad \underline{𝅘𝅥} \quad 𝄾 \; |$$

or

$$| 𝅘𝅥 \quad \underline{𝅘𝅥.} \quad 𝅘𝅥𝅮 |$$

There is one accent to a measure, as indicated. The two-step also had one accent:

$$| \underline{𝅘𝅥.} \quad 𝅘𝅥𝅮𝅘𝅥 \quad 𝅘𝅥 \; |$$

or

$$| \underline{𝅘𝅥.} \quad 𝅘𝅥𝅮𝅘𝅥 \; |$$

But the fox-trot has two:

$$| \underline{𝅘𝅥} \quad 𝄾 \quad \underline{𝅘𝅥} \quad 𝄾 \; |$$

and the jazz waltz has three:

$$| \underline{𝅘𝅥𝅮} 𝄾 \quad \underline{𝅘𝅥𝅮} 𝄾 \quad \underline{𝅘𝅥𝅮} 𝄾 \; |$$

The waltz, however, is not at home in jazz. After a century of Europeans, from Schubert to Ravel, had played with it, there was small possibility for further rhythmic variations. It is not comfortable now, for the true waltz-step is almost impossible to do unless the music has a flowing rhythm to tempt a flowing motion of the body.

We learned syncopation from three different teachers—the Indians, the Negroes, and our neighbors in Mexico. It had become firmly established before the Civil War. It is the characteristic twist of nearly every familiar old tune. The dance craze of the last twenty-five years has simply exaggerated it. Because the way to make a strong pulse on [beat] 3 is by tying it to 2, thus,

$$| 𝅘𝅥 \quad 𝅘𝅥\underset{\smile}{}𝅘𝅥 \quad 𝅘𝅥 \; |$$

A silent accent is the strongest of all accents. It forces the body to replace it with a motion. But a syncopated tune is not jazz unless it is supported by a monotonous, accentless rhythm underneath. Alone it may only confuse the listener. But with the rhythm definitely expressed, syncopation intensifies the anticipated beat into an imperative bodily motion. The shorter the anticipation the stronger the effect. The systematic striking of melodic notes an instant before the beat is the most powerful device of motor music yet discovered. But a fluent melody with a syncopated accompaniment is an inversion of the fundamental jazz process, and its effect is sedative.

If certain formulae of beat produce motion, probably certain motions have suggested these formulae. But I have no interest in the hen-and-egg controversy. I wish merely to show that the peculiar character of jazz is a rhythm, and that that rhythm is one which provokes jerky motions of the body. Instead of the following "normal" rhythms:

and

we have

and

and

and

—in brief, all the divisions which the masters of music-not-meant-for-dancing have used sparingly or with special antidotes, for the very reason that they make the body move instead of keeping it quiet so that the music can progress.

The instrumentation is not an essential element in jazz, as anyone knows who has heard a good performer play it on the piano. It is possible to [use] practically any number or group of instruments, because, above the rhythmic accompaniment, which also sets the harmony, it is contrapuntal rather than homophonic and does not require balanced timbres. Certain instruments and effects, however, are characteristic, especially the use of the saxophone, which, in pairs or in quartets, makes a rich and penetrating diapason, and the monotonous banjo accompaniment, giving out the ground-rhythm—a rhythm so sonorous that it would be unendurable were not its hypnotic effect turned into motor stimuli by bizarre cross-accents.

Another thing characteristic of jazz is the use of the glissando. It has long been common on the trombone. It is also possible on the clarinet and the saxophone for about a major third. A descending succession of little glissandi makes the "laughing saxophone." The Frisco whistle plays a continuous glissando; and the glissando on a plucked string, introduced from Hawaii, has been applied to every stringed instrument except the banjo. It is difficult there because of the frets and because the banjo, having no sound-box, gives a tone which, though powerful, is of short duration.

With the growth of the contrapuntal style, enforced by disparate combinations, the varieties of wind tone have been considerably extended. Passionate or startling expression has been found in all sorts of vibrati and flutter-tonguing and in the covered tones of the muted trumpet and trombone, the muted clarinet, and the trombone played through a megaphone. Most of these devices, of course, are not new. Rimsky-Korsakov knew all the tricks on the trumpet that you now hear in the dance-hall, and more. Berlioz employed the muted clarinet. Richard Strauss and Vincent d'Indy wrote for quartets of saxophones years ago. Stravinsky has even written glissandi for the horn! But the megaphone trick, which takes the blare out of the trombone and makes it sound fat and oily like a euphonium, is probably new. Certainly the use of a free-hanging mute is new, though when it takes the form of a tin can or a silk hat it is surely no addition to orchestral elegance.

In the current jazz one hears piano figures that are ingenious, counter-melodies that are far from timid, and experiments in instrumental balance that are of interest to any composer. The harmony itself is at times varied and delicate. The blues formula—subdominant modulation with alternations of tonic major and minor—is simple and effective. The chromatic (or diatonic) succession of dominant ninths so dear to Franck and Chabrier has become popular, and the mediant or sub-mediant tonality offers a pleasing relief from the more obvious dominant. The Neapolitan sixth is quite common and even the "barbershop" chord, the augmented six-five-three, or German sixth, is sometimes used in a manner that is not at all crude.

These characters of jazz are partially supported by serious music and partially contributory to it. Skillful composers on higher planes snap up quickly any novelty that the makers of jazz invent. Union musicians play one night at the movie, and the next night with the local symphony orchestra. They bring a few tricks to the latter, and they take home a great many more. Orchestral and harmonic styles in jazz are still experimental and shifting. But the essence of the thing remains the fox-trot with a monotonous rhythm underneath. That rhythm shakes but it won't flow. There is no climax. It never gets anywhere emotionally. In the symphony, it would either lose its character or wreck the structure. It is exactly analogous to the hoochie-coochie.

Notes

[Text: Thomson, "Jazz," *The American Mercury*, August 1924, 465–67. Reprinted by permission of the Virgil Thomson Foundation, Ltd., copyright owner.]

2 7

AARON COPLAND

(1 9 0 0 – 1 9 9 0)

The reader of Copland's "Jazz Structure and Influence" may well be surprised to learn what the author understood in 1927 by the term *jazz*. His perspective—shared by many writers in the early 1920s—is limited almost entirely to published popular songs and piano pieces, a genre now known as tin pan alley. Improvisational jazz, such as blues singing or New Orleans jazz, is not mentioned. The word *jazz* was applied, then as now, to many different types of American popular music, with no general agreement as to what had to be included or excluded to do justice to the term.

Copland announces that his intention in the article is to deal with the structure of jazz, which he locates not in formal archetypes but in characteristic rhythmic and metric features. Since the repertory that he considers jazz is limited to derivatives from ragtime, the rhythmic phenomena that he finds are also related to ragtime prototypes. The most distinctive feature, he concludes, is a melody that contains temporal irregularities (syncopations and asymmetrical meters) placed against an accompaniment in regular meter and rhythm. The simplest melodic irregularity, which he attributes to ragtime per se, is a dotted rhythm or a syncopation confined within a single beat. A more sophisticated phenomenon, which Copland finds characteristic of the fox-trot, is a syncopation that extends over two adjacent beats, which he interprets as an irregular subdivision of a measure into groups of two, three, and five. More sophisticated still is the use of a triple meter in the melody against the predictable duple meter in the accompaniment. Finally, in recent works such as Gershwin's *Clap Yo' Hands,* the ragtime prototype is entirely masked by an alternation between duple and triple meters in both melody and accompaniment.

Copland predicts that these rhythmic elements will exert a lasting influence on American classical music, and his own musical oeuvre offers many examples of the validity of this forecast. In fact, a subtext of his article concerns the relation of American modern music to its European counterpart. American musicians, whether popular or classical, have a genius for innovative rhythms, he asserts, and the exploitation of this skill can bring a distinctive voice to American music, making it both regional and technically advanced.

A bibliography of Copland's writings is found with essay no. 23.

—ɯ—

JAZZ STRUCTURE AND INFLUENCE
(1927)

Although jazz has been many months now in the hands of professional theorists I have seen nowhere a study of its influence upon noncommercial composers. Its structure, which interests me most as a musician, has received so little attention that it seems to have been avoided. Paul Whiteman admits this in his recent book:[1] "Comparatively little has been written in an analytical way about jazz." And when asked "What is jazz?" he says: "I have been dodging this question for years because I haven't been able to figure out an adequate answer." Speaking exactly, no one else has. In certain quarters it has been suggested that the jazz band created jazz. This is confusing color with substance. Although the jazz band is largely responsible for the present day perfection of the idiom, in the beginning it merely added a distinctive color to what already existed.

One point has been generally made and agreed upon: that the essential character of jazz is its rhythm. Yet no one has carefully analyzed even this. Virgil Thomson has wisely said: "Jazz is a certain way of sounding two rhythms at once. . . . a counterpoint of regular against irregular beats."[2] These discerning but epigrammatic investigations have been carried a little though not much farther by Don Knowlton in an article in *Harper's* (April 1926). Henry O. Osgood in his book, *So This Is Jazz*, begins by complimenting Mr. Thomson on his definition: "Jazz, in brief, is a compound of (a) the fox-trot rhythm . . . and (b) a syncopated melody over this rhythm." But a few pages later he insists: "Jazz is not to be bound by Mr. Thomson's fox-trot rhythm, and . . . it is obvious that syncopation, while a frequent characteristic of jazz, is by no means an essential factor." He concludes: "It is the spirit of the music, not the mechanics of its frame . . . that determines whether or not it is jazz."

This seems to me to be far from the truth. I had rather not let jazz pass too easily as indefinable without first inspecting its structure. There may be some connection between Mr. Osgood's attitude and that of most Americans, who believe too confidently that they can tell jazz from what isn't jazz and let it go at that. Such vagueness will do nothing toward a real understanding of it; on the other hand the very first move toward understanding requires precisely what Mr. Osgood by implication advises against, a study of the mechanics of its frame. And this can best be accomplished by considering its origin and development.

It began, I suppose, on some Negro's dull tomtom in Africa; it descended through the spirituals, some of which are as much jazz as Gershwin's newest song. Its nearer ancestor is, of course, ragtime. The rhythmic foundation of ragtime is an unchanging 1 - 2 - 3 - 4 bass in quick tempo (stressing the most obvious beats of the first and third)—just as 1 - 2 - 3 is the rhythmic foundation of the waltz. Over the ragtime bass is carried invariably one of two rhythms, sometimes both: either the dotted eighth followed by a sixteenth:

or this most ordinary syncopation:

The former of these produced the characteristic ragtime jerk which is perhaps remembered from *Everybody's Doin' It*. Ragtime is much inferior to jazz and musically uninteresting; it consists of old formulas familiar in the classics which were rediscovered one day and overworked.

Modern jazz began with the fox-trot. For this new dance the four-quarter bass was used as in ragtime but at a considerably slower pace and miraculously improved by accenting the least obvious beats, the second and fourth—1 - 2 - 3 - 4. With this was combined another rhythmic element, sometimes in the melody but by no means always there, which is generally supposed to be a kind of 1 - 2 - 3 - 4 and is always written:

This notation, however, is deceptive, as Mr. Knowlton has pointed out. His article reveals the practice followed by popular music publishers of writing extremely complex jazz compositions very simply so as to sell them more easily to the musically uneducated. He was the first to show that this jazz rhythm is in reality much subtler than in its printed form and is properly expressed thus:

Therefore it contains no syncopation; it is instead a rhythm of four quarters split into eight eighths and is arranged thus: 1 - 2 - 3 / 1 - 2 - 3 - 4 - 5, or even more precisely: 1 - 2 - 3 / 1 - 2 - 3 / 1 - 2. Put this over the four-quarter bass:

and you have the play of two independent rhythms within the space of one measure. It is the beginning, it is a molecule of jazz.

Whatever melody is subjected to this procedure comes out jazzed. This explains the widespread facile reincarnation of classic tunes as song and dance hits: It also explains Mr. Whiteman's remark: "Jazz is not as yet the thing said, it is the manner of saying it." And it should make clear to Mr. Osgood how a melody he cites, that of *I'm Always Chasing Rainbows*, can show no signs of jazz and yet be jazz. It is not the melody which determines this point, but the interplay of rhythms around, above and under it.

The next step infinitely complicated these, in fact it produced polyrhythms. In employing two rhythms within one measure jazz after all merely did something that had been done before, if we remember, for instance, the use by older composers of 3/4 against 6/8. But the next era in the jazz age—typified by the song *Stumbling*—saw independent rhythms spread over more than one measure, over a series of measures:

That is, while the conventional 4/4 bass was retained the melody was put into 3/4 time. This particular combination of rhythms was probably put to best use by [Zez] Confrey in his *Kitten on the Keys*:

Within small limits jazz had achieved a new synthesis in music. It was so difficult for ordinary ears and so exhilarating to ordinary sensibilities that the jazz composers, always intent upon their public, dared not use it for more than a few measures at a time. George Gershwin was the composer who took most advantage of the discovery made with *Stumbling*. His *Fascinating Rhythm* is rhythmically not only the most fascinating but the most original jazz song yet composed:

With the introduction of the Charleston the most tyrannical element of our popular music—the evenly rhythmed bass—was eliminated for the space of a few measures at least. The Charleston consists of the upper fox-trot rhythm: 1 - 2 - 3 /

1 - 2 - 3 - 4 - 5 used below as well as above instead of the formerly unflagging 1 - 2 - 3 - 4 bass:

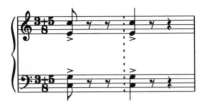

This old bondage (the unchanging bass) which has probably brought jazz more musical enemies than any other quality, has been broken in another way by Gershwin in his latest dance hit, *Clap Yo' Hands*. Instead of the 3/4 against 4/4 polyrhythm which in the brisk competition of Broadway has now become old stuff, he uses this:

That is, he varies a 4/4 rhythm with two measures of 3/4 rhythm. Critically, from the standpoint of all music, this may be counted a step backward, a return to processes already familiar—in the Russian folk song for example; but from the standpoint of jazz it means an advance through the relief it offers from the old relentless 4/4 bass. Polyrhythms are, as is known, not in themselves an innovation. They have been highly developed among primitive races and have made intermittent, momentary appearances in the works of recent European composers. They have also occurred abundantly in the English madrigals. The madrigal polyrhythms were the result of the madrigal prosody and therefore an intricate deft interknitting in which no single downbeat was too definitely stressed. In a sense, therefore, the madrigal was arhythmic rather than polyrhythmic. In fact, the madrigalists were charged by later English generations with lacking a proper sense of rhythm.

But the polyrhythms of jazz are different in quality and effect not only from those of the madrigals but from all others as well. The peculiar excitement they produce by clashing two definitely and regularly marked rhythms is unprecedented in occidental music. Its polyrhythm is the real contribution of jazz.

This has not been appreciated by modern European composers although in other ways our American popular music has to some extent influenced them. In the days of ragtime, Debussy and Stravinsky, in the days of jazz, Ravel, Milhaud, Honegger, Hindemith, Jean Wiéner exploited it as an exotic novelty. But with most of them it remained a novelty, a monotonous bass, a shining melody, a glissando on a trombone. . . . These tricks soon lost their first charm. Meanwhile, however, at least one authentic small masterpiece had been inspired in Europe by America, Darius Milhaud's *La création du monde*—little known, strangely, in this country. But according to Milhaud himself, jazz is now distinctly passé in Europe and not a young composer there is interested in it any longer.

This is not so in America, nor is it going to be. Since jazz is not exotic here but indigenous, since it is the music an American has heard as a child, it will be traceable more and more frequently in his symphonies and concertos. Possibly the chief influence of jazz will be shown in the development of the polyrhythm. This startling new synthesis has provided the American composer with an instrument he should appreciate and utilize. It should stir his imagination; he should see it freed of its present connotations. It may be the substance not only of his fox-trots and Charlestons but of his lullabies and nocturnes. He may express through it not always gaiety but love, tragedy, remorse.

Notes

[Text: Copland, "Jazz Structure and Influence," *Modern Music* 4/2 (1927): 9–14. Reprinted by permission of the League of Composers.]

[1. Paul Whiteman and Mary Margaret McBride, *Jazz* (New York: J. H. Sears, 1926).]

[2. Virgil Thomson, "The Cult of Jazz," *Vanity Fair* 23 (June 1925): 54.]

JELLY ROLL MORTON

(1 8 8 5 – 1 9 4 1)

In 1938 the New Orleans jazz composer Ferdinand ("Jelly Roll") Morton remi-
nisced about his life in an oral hstory recorded for the Archive of American Folk-
song at the Library of Congress. The archive, headed by folklorists John and
Alan Lomax, was primarily devoted to preserving folk singing, but Morton's rec-
ollections proved to be of such value to the history of jazz that Alan Lomax transcribed them in his book *Mister Jelly Roll: The Fortunes of Jelly Roll Morton, New
Orleans Creole and "Inventor of Jazz"* (1950). Even if only a part of Morton's rec-
ollections is true, he led a remarkable life. He was born in New Orleans, where
he learned to play the piano and, in the ragtime tradition, to read music and to
compose. In 1907 he left his home city and began a life of perpetual travel
throughout the United States, making his living as pianist and band leader, composer, vaudeville comedian, gambler, and pool shark.

By 1938 Morton's New Orleans style of jazz was fading into obscurity.
His compositions, based on the style and form of ragtime, and his band recordings from the 1920s seemed dated in comparison to the popular swing music
of big bands of the 1930s. In his oral history at the Library of Congress he
wished, most of all, to set the record straight about his own contribution to
music, brashly claiming that around 1902 he invented jazz.

Whether this famous claim is plausible or not depends on what Morton
meant by jazz. In "Sweet, Soft, Plenty Rhythm"—which is extracted from *Mister Jelly Roll*—he talks about the type of music at the turn of the century for
which he used this term. It was obviously related to ragtime but different in its
style of performance. Judging from Morton's recordings the differences were
mainly in rhythm and improvisation. The melody in Morton's jazz uses swinging
triplet rhythms that often press slightly ahead of the accompaniment. This is different from ragtime, in which subdivisions of the beat are normally duple or
quadruple. Morton also took improvisatory freedoms with a given melodic line,
different again from the relatively strict fidelity to the score in ragtime. In this
episode from his oral history he also alludes to other characteristics of jazz: it
was basically a music for small bands, it sometimes used asymmetical Latin
rhythms, the accompaniment was enlivened by the presence of "riffs," and cli-
maxes were formed by the frequent use of "breaks." Riffs are melodic figures,
either in a melody or in its accompaniment, made from the repetition of a short
motive over changing harmonies. A break is a sudden and brief suspension of
beat within a phrase, during which an instrument improvises a short and often
explosive phrase. Finally, Morton insists that jazz is a music of expressivity and
nuance, "sweet, soft, plenty rhythm."

Morton's Writings and Interviews: A Selective Bibliography

Jelly Roll Morton: The Library of Congress Recordings. Library of Congress Recordings RLP 90001—90012, 1957. Contains excerpts from Morton's oral history of 1938. Recording no. 3 contains the excerpt "Sweet, Soft, Plenty Rhythm."

Lomax, Alan. *Mister Jelly Roll: The Fortunes of Jelly Roll Morton, New Orleans Creole and "Inventor of Jazz."* Second edition. Berkeley: University of California Press, 1973. Contains selections from Morton's oral history of 1938 to which Lomax adds interviews with relatives and other musicians.

Morton, Jelly Roll. "I Discovered Jazz in 1902." *Downbeat*, August 1938. Reprinted in Ralph de Toledano, *Frontiers of Jazz*, second edition (New York: Frederick Ungar, 1962): 104–107.

—ɯ—

"SWEET, SOFT, PLENTY RHYTHM"
FROM *MISTER JELLY ROLL*
(1938)

. . . I might name some of the other great hot men operating around New Orleans at this period and a little later. There was Emmanuel Perez, played strictly ragtime, who was maybe the best trumpet in New Orleans till Freddie Keppard came along. John Robechaux probably had the best band in New Orleans at the time, a strictly all-reading, legitimate bunch. Before him, there was Happy Galloway. Both men had the same type seven-piece orchestra—cornet, clarinet, trombone, drums, mandolin, guitar, and bass. A guy named Payton had a band that played a very lowdown type of quadrille for the low-class dance halls. Also a lot of bad bands that we used to call "spasm" bands, played any jobs they could get in the streets. They did a lot of ad-libbing in ragtime style with different solos in succession, not in a regular routine, but just as one guy would get tired and let another musician have the lead.

None of these men made much money—maybe a dollar a night or a couple of bucks for a funeral, but still they didn't like to leave New Orleans. They used to say, "This is the best town in the world. What's the use for me to go any other place?" So the town was full of the best musicians you ever heard. Even the rags-bottles-and-bones men would advertise their trade by playing the blues on the wooden mouth-pieces of Christmas horns—yes sir, play more lowdown, dirty blues on those Kress horns than the rest of the country ever thought of.

All these people played ragtime in a hot style, but man, you can play hot all you want to, and you still won't be playing jazz. Hot means something spicy. Ragtime is a certain type of syncopation and only certain tunes can be played in that idea. But jazz is a style that can be applied to any type of tune. I started using the word in 1902 to show people the difference between jazz and ragtime.

Jazz music came from New Orleans and New Orleans was inhabited with maybe every race on the face of the globe and, of course, plenty of French people. Many of the earliest tunes in New Orleans was from French origin. I'm telling you when they started playing this little thing they would really whoop it up—everybody got hot and threw their hats away. . . .

> C'été 'n aut' can-can, payé donc,
>
> C'été 'n aut' can-can, payé donc. . . .

Then we had Spanish people there. I heard a lot of Spanish tunes and I tried to play them in correct tempo, but I personally didn't believe they were really perfected in the tempos. Now take *La Paloma,* which I transformed in New Orleans style. You leave the left hand just the same. The difference comes in the right hand—in the syncopation, which gives it an entirely different color that really changes the color from red to blue.

Now in one of my earliest tunes, *New Orleans Blues,* you can notice the "Spanish tinge." In fact, if you can't manage to put tinges of Spanish in your tunes, you will never be able to get the right seasoning, I call it, for jazz. This *New Orleans Blues* comes from around 1902. I wrote it with the help of Frank Richards, a great piano player in the ragtime style. All the bands in the city played it at that time.

Most of these ragtime guys, especially those that couldn't play very well, would have the inspiration they were doing okay if they kept increasing the tempo during a piece. I decided that was a mistake and I must have been right, because everybody grabbed my style. I thought that accurate tempo would be the right tempo for any tune. Regardless to any tempo you might set, especially if it was meant for a dance tune, you ought to end up in that same tempo. So I found that the slow tunes, especially the medium slow tunes, did more for the development of jazz than any other type, due to the fact that you could always hit a note twice in such a tune, when ordinarily you could only hit it once, which gave the music a very good flavor.

About harmony, my theory is never to discard the melody. Always have a melody going some kind of way against a background of perfect harmony with plenty of riffs—meaning figures. A riff is something that gives an orchestra a great background and is the main idea in playing jazz. No jazz piano player can really play good jazz unless they try to give an imitation of a band, that is, by providing a basis of riffs. I've seen riffs blundered up so many times it has give me heart failure, because most of these modern guys don't regard the harmony or the rules of the system of music at all. They just play anything, their main idea being to keep the bass going. They think by keeping the bass going and getting a set rhythm, they are doing the right thing, which is wrong. Of all the pianists today, I know of only one that has a tendency to be on the right track and that's Bob Zurke of the Bob Crosby Band. Far as the rest of them, all I can see is ragtime pianists in a very fine form.

Now the riff is what we call a foundation, like something that you walk on. It's standard. But without breaks and without clean breaks and without beautiful ideas in breaks, you don't even need to think about doing anything else, you haven't got a jazz band and you can't play jazz. Even if a tune haven't got a break in it, it's always necessary to arrange some kind of a spot to make a break.

A break, itself, is like a musical surprise which didn't come in until I originated the idea of jazz, as I told you. We New Orleans musicians were always looking for novelty effects to attract the public, and many of the most important things in jazz originated in some guy's crazy idea that we tried out for a laugh or just to surprise the folks.

Most people don't understand the novelty side of jazz. Vibrato—which is all right for one instrument but the worst thing that ever happened when a whole bunch of instruments use it—was nothing at the beginning but an imitation of a jackass hollering. There were many other imitations of animal sounds we used—such as the wah-wahs on trumpets and trombones. Mutes came in with King Oliver, who first just stuck bottles into his trumpet so he could play softer, but then began to use all sorts of mutes to give his instrument a different flavor. And I, myself, by accident, discovered the swats [brushes] on drums. Out in Los Angeles I had a drummer that hit his snares so loud that one night I gave him a couple of fly swatters for a gag. This drummer fell in with the joke and used them, but they worked so smooth he kept right on using them. So we have "the swats" today—a nice soft way to keep your rhythm going.

A lot of people have a wrong conception of jazz. Somehow it got into the dictionary that jazz was considered a lot of blatant noises and discordant tones, something that would be even harmful to the ears. The fact of it is that every musician in America had the wrong understanding of jazz music. I know many times that I'd be playing against different orchestras and I would notice some of the patrons get near an orchestra and put their hands over their ears. (Of course, I wouldn't permit mine to play that way.) Anyhow, I heard a funny fellow say once: "If that fellow blows any louder, he'll knock my ear drums down." Even Germany and Italy don't want this discordant type of jazz, because of the noise.

Jazz music is to be played sweet, soft, plenty rhythm. When you have your plenty rhythm with your plenty swing, it becomes beautiful. To start with, you can't make crescendos and diminuendos when one is playing triple forte. You got to be able to come down in order to go up. If a glass of water is full, you can't fill it any more; but if you have a half a glass, you have the opportunity to put more water in it. Jazz music is based on the same principles, because jazz is based on strictly music. You have the finest ideas from the greatest operas, symphonies and overtures in jazz music. There is nothing finer than jazz music because it comes from everything of the finest class music. Take the Sextet from *Lucia* [*di Lammermoor* by Donizetti] and the "Miserery" [*Miserere*] from *Il Trovatore* [by Verdi], that they used to play in the French Opera House, tunes that have always lived in my mind as the great favorites of the opera singers; I transformed a lot of those numbers into jazz time, using different little variations and ideas to masquerade the tunes.

The *Tiger Rag*, for an instance, I happened to transform from an old quadrille, which was originally in many different tempos. First there was an introduction, "Everybody get your partners!" and the people would be rushing around the hall getting their partners. After a five minute lapse of time, the next strain would be the waltz strain . . . then another strain that comes right beside the waltz strain in mazooka [mazurka] time. . . .

We had two other strains in two-four time. Then I transformed these strains into the *Tiger Rag* which I also named, from the way I made the tiger roar with my elbow. A person said once, "That sounds like a tiger hollering." I said to myself, "That's the name." All this happened back in the early days before the Dixieland Band was ever heard of.

Notes

[Text: Morton, "Sweet, Soft, Plenty Rhythm," from *Mister Jelly Roll: The Fortunes of Jelly Roll Morton, New Orleans Creole and "Inventor of Jazz"*, by Alan Lomax. © 1950, 1978 by Alan Lomax. Used by permission of Dutton Signet, a division of Penguin Books USA Inc.]

29

GUNTHER SCHULLER

(B .   1 9 2 5)

Gunther Schuller's essay "The Future of Form in Jazz" shows the pervasive emphasis on form that characterized musical thinking of the 1950s. Jazz, says Schuller, should be concerned with a strict and integrated form, comparable to serialized music of the same time. His emphasis on the need for strict form in jazz suggests that composed jazz could in the future supersede improvised jazz, which would make it susceptible to the same systematic structure that was then apparent in totally serialized classical compositions.

For these ideas Schuller was plainly indebted to a conception of music shared by serialists such as Pierre Boulez in Europe and Milton Babbitt in America. Like Boulez (see his "Schoenberg Is Dead," essay no. 14) Schuller criticizes Schoenberg for the futility of applying tonal forms outside of a tonal context, and he points, as did Boulez, to Webern as the source of a more advanced formal model for the future. Schuller does not suggest that twelve-tone procedures per se should be applied to jazz, but that some comparable system could integrate the various elements of a jazz composition. He points approvingly to the system advanced by George Russell, called by Russell the "Lydian Concept of Tonal Organization," as an example of an integrated and systematic compositional approach.

Schuller concludes his article by asserting the similarity between jazz and classical music. The "spontaneous recreating" of classical masterpieces, he says, is close to the art of jazz improvisation. When this article was written in 1957 Schuller was composing music that merged classical, modernist styles with jazz media and limited opportunities for improvisation, a genre that he called "third stream." This mixed idiom held the promise of a distinctively American development; indeed a similar amalgamation was attempted in 1957 by Milton Babbitt in a totally serialized work for jazz band, *All Set,* although the jazz element in this composition is not so pronounced as in Schuller's third stream pieces.

With the appearance in 1957 of this essay on jazz, Gunther Schuller opened another door in his remarkable career in music. At the time, he was known mainly as a prodigious French horn virtuoso—principal hornist in the orchestra of the Metropolitan Opera since the age of only nineteen—and as the composer of orchestral music that used aspects of jazz in an otherwise modernist idiom. Now he became a jazz critic and historian, speaking authoritatively on its form and on its future prospects and directions. He was later the author of two important books on jazz history.

Schuller's Writings: A Selective Bibliography

Musings: The Musical Worlds of Gunther Schuller. New York: Oxford University Press, 1986. A collection of essays.

The History of Jazz. Two volumes (*Early Jazz* and *The Swing Era*). New York: Oxford University Press, 1968, 1989.

—⟋⟍—

THE FUTURE OF FORM IN JAZZ

(1957)

If there is one aspect of present-day modern jazz that differentiates it from the jazz of even five years ago, it is its preoccupation with new musical forms. Jazz today, with its greatly enriched language, seems to feel the need for organization at a more extended level. Few musicians seem to find complete satisfaction in the procedure so prevalent even a few years ago of wedging a group of generally unrelated "blowing" solos and several choruses of "fours" between an opening and closing theme.

At a time, therefore, when one hears and reads terms such as "extended form" and "free form" almost every day, and because there seems to be very little agreement as to what is meant by these expressions, it might be interesting to examine these new tendencies, to see where they may be leading modern jazz, and to investigate what role composition is beginning to play in a music whose greatest contribution has been a renaissance of the art of improvisation.

I suppose the question will be raised: Why new or extended forms? Why not continue with the same conventions and forms we associate with the main tradition of jazz? Obviously an art form which is to remain a legitimate expression of its times must grow and develop. As jazz becomes more and more a music to be *listened* to, it will automatically reach out for more complex ideas, a wider range of expression. Obviously, too, more complex harmonies and techniques require more complex musical forms to support the increased load of this superstructure. The long-playing record, moreover, has emancipated jazz from its previous three-minute limitation, and the *forming* of tonal material on a larger scale has thus automatically become a main concern of the younger generation.

It would be dangerous, however, if the jazz musician were to be satisfied with complacently reaching over into the classical field and there borrowing forms upon which to *graft* his music. The well-known classical forms—such as sonata or fugue, for instance—arose out of and were directly related to specific existing conditions, musical as well as social: and their effectiveness in most cases has been greatly diminished to the extent that these conditions have changed.

For example, the sonata form, originally based upon the dominant-tonic relationship which governed diatonic music, obviously no longer applies to an atonal work. This has been amply proven by the discrepancy between musical material and form in many Schoenberg works, and by the progress made in this respect by Anton Webern and the young generation of composers following in his footsteps. It has become increasingly clear that "form" need not be a confining mold into which the tonal materials are poured, but rather that the forming process can be *directly* related to the musical material employed in a specific instance. In other words, form evolves *out* of the material itself and is not imposed upon it. We must learn to think of form as a verb rather than a noun.

Experience, moreover, has shown us that the borrowing of a baroque form such as the fugue—the most widely used non-jazz form at the moment—very rarely produces the happiest results. Even when successful, it is certainly not the ultimate solution to the problem of evolving new forms in jazz, mainly because jazz is a player's art, and the old classical and baroque forms are definitely related to the art of composing (Bach's ability to improvise complete fugues notwithstanding). Used in jazz these classic forms can, at best, produce only specific and limited results, but cannot open the way to a new musical order. Jazz, it seems to me, is strong and rich enough to find within its own domain forms much more indigenous to its own essential nature.

The idea of extending or enlarging musical form is not a new one in jazz. By the middle thirties Duke Ellington, the masterly precursor of so many innovations in common use today, had already made two attempts to break beyond the confines of the ten-inch disk with his *Creole Rhapsody* of 1931 and the twelve-minute *Reminiscing in Tempo*. The latter work, written in 1935, took up four ten-inch sides, but the Columbia label blithely continued to call it a "fox-trot." Its length, its advanced harmonic changes, its unusual asymmetrically coupled fourteen- and ten-bar phrases aroused angry reactions and cries of "arty," "pretentious" and "not jazz." In retrospect we find that it is a poem of quiet melancholy, evoking that special nostalgia which so consistently distinguishes early Ellington from most of his contemporaries; and we see that it was simply trying to do two things: (1) to break away from the conventional phrase patterns based upon multiples of four measures (in *Creole Rhapsody* he had already experimented with a sixteen-bar phrase made up of a pattern of 5 plus 5 plus 4 plus 2); (2) to organize his musical material in a slightly more complex form, at the same time integrating solos within that form so that the entire work would produce a unified whole. The least ambitious but perhaps the most inspired of his large-scale works, *Reminiscing in Tempo*, opened up a new vista on the jazz horizon.

And yet Ellington—in those days always years ahead of his colleagues—was to wait a decade to see his early experiments emulated by other musicians. Perhaps the intense commercialism of the swing era with its emphasis on polish (and too often slickness) led jazz temporarily in other directions; or maybe it was simply that jazz had reached a period of consolidation and gestation. Be that as it may, a new style began to crystallize in the early forties under the influence of Parker and Gillespie, a style which already embodied in an embryonic stage the considerable strides jazz has made in the last fifteen years.

It is impossible within the limits of this discussion to examine all the achievements that have led jazz to its present status. The genius of Charlie Parker, the important contributions made by the Miles Davis Capitol recordings, and the success of the Modern Jazz Quartet in popularizing a musical concept that combines classical organization with conventional jazz traditions—all these have already become a matter of history and require no further emphasis here.

More recently, serious contributions to the freeing of form have been made by an ever-increasing number of musicians. Among them (without attempting a complete listing) are Teddy Charles (although he says most of what he and Hall Overton are doing is not jazz), Buddy Collette, Giuffre, [Gigi] Gryce, [John] La Porta, John Lewis, [Teo] Macero, [Charles] Mingus, the Phil Nimmons group in Toronto, George Russell, the Sandole brothers, Tony Scott, and many others.

A closer look, however, at some outstanding representative examples may help to give a clearer idea of what solutions in the search for new forms have been found.

One of the most interesting uses of form has been developed by Charlie Mingus with what he calls "extended form." I think some of the confusion regarding this term arises from the fact that "extended form" can mean simply *that*—extending form in a general way—but also can mean a more specific idea as envisioned by Mingus. For him it means taking one part of a chord pattern, perhaps only one measure, and extending it indefinitely by repetition until the soloist or the "composer" feels that the development of the piece requires moving on to another idea. Actually, this procedure does not represent a new form as such, since it is simply a stretching or magnifying of a standard pattern. Its liberating possibilities, however, are considerable, as exemplified by Mingus's finest efforts in this direction, *Pithecanthropus erectus* and *Love Chant* (Atlantic 12-inch LP 1237).

Jimmy Giuffre made a giant step forward with his *Tangents in Jazz*, the full implications of which may not be assimilated for years. Aside from his remarkable musical gift, his concern for clarity and logic, his economical means and direct approach indicate that Giuffre is already one of the most influential innovators in present-day jazz. Excellent examples of his concern for formal clarity, with actually extremely simple means, are his written pieces like *Side Pipers*, *Sheepherder* and the moving *Down Home* with its Ellingtonish mood of quiet intensity (Atlantic 12-inch LP 1238).

Down Home makes me think of another earlier masterpiece with the same combination of formal perfection and mature musical sensitivity, namely John Lewis's *Django* (Prestige).

What can be done in terms of integrating musical substance with form is also beautifully illustrated by recent recordings of André Hodeir in France. In two albums, not released as yet in this country, Hodeir not only incorporates some of the most recent compositional techniques of European twelve-tone writing, but also indicates through them ways in which original forms can be derived from the very core of a musical idea.

Suffice it to cite one especially felicitous example, *On a Blues*. Beneath an evenly sustained tenor solo of some length there appears, at first imperceptibly, a riff, which gradually increases dynamically and orchestrationally until it has overpowered and absorbed the improvised solo. The riff, moreover, is not simply repeated in its original form, but undergoes a gradual transformation, at first by means of changing registers, then by inversion, still later by increasingly complex harmonization, and finally through a kind of harmonic and rhythmic condensation of the original riff into a new shape. This building line of intensity, both dynamically and structurally gives the piece a unique driving force and makes it swing beautifully.

Another remarkable instance of total musical organization (without sacrificing the essential vitality and spirit of jazz) is George Russell's *Lydian M-1* (Atlantic 12-inch LP 1229), a swinging piece that moves with relentless drive and "quiet fury," to quote Teddy Charles. In a way which is rare in jazz, the entire piece grows tonally and formalistically out of a nucleus of thematic material which in turn is based on a principle which the composer calls the "Lydian Concept of Tonal Organization."

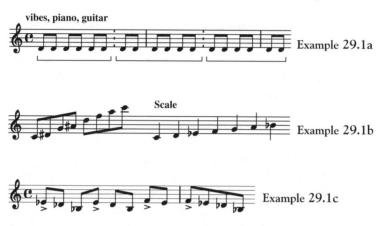

vibes, piano, guitar

Example 29.1a

Scale

Example 29.1b

Example 29.1c

An eighth-note figure of considerable length dominates the opening, and from this, as we shall see, emanates almost all that is to follow. This figure (Example 29.1a) consists at first of a single repeated note divided into a 3/4 pattern (against an underlying 4/4 rhythm set up by the drums), then breaks out into an ascending arpeggio-like pattern (Example 29.1b) which sounds all the notes of the modal scale that determines the tonality of the work. As the thematic line continues, it descends gradually via a series of asymmetrically grouped rhythmic patterns (constantly shifting combinations of 3/8 and 2/8, Example 29.1c) to its original starting point, but now grouped in a 3/2 pattern. (The emphasis on ternary rhythms is obvious.) This pattern extended over sixteen measures provides a sort of running commentary to chordal aggregates in the "horns," again derived from the thematic material by combining vertically (harmonically) what had previously been stated horizontally (melodically). Four bars of the original repeated-note figure (Example 29.1a) provide a bridge to a sort of second aspect of the main theme, this time characterized by a blue-note motive (Example 29.2a) which, however, still relates back to the original underlying modal scale.

Example 29.2a

Example 29.2b

During the course of the composition, unity is achieved through reference to this reservoir of material: a 3/2 pattern by the rhythm section contrasts vividly with a trumpet solo in quarter-note triples; or chordal accompaniments (Example 29.2b) retain the modality of the opening by being derived through transposition almost entirely from the blue-note motive (Example 29.2a); a recurring chord progression that frames the three improvised solos is based on the modal scale (Example 29.1b); and so on.

Above all, the overall form of the piece is a direct natural product of its own tonal material, giving the whole a feeling of rightness and completeness that marks the work of art.

Now this high degree of integration—which should appeal to anyone admiring order and logic—is considered by many jazz musicians to be too inhibiting. They claim it limits their "freedom of expression" and they consider such music outside the realm of jazz. There is violent disagreement on this point—not without reason. It is a difficult point, usually beclouded by subjectivism and the intrusion of the ego, and it needs to be discussed.

The assumption that restrictions upon intuitive creativity (such as improvisation) are inhibiting is, I think, not tenable, as is demonstrated by all successful art. A great masterpiece, for example, grows out of the interacting stimulus of the constant friction between freedom and constraint, between emotion and intellect.

Charlie Parker seems to have known this. But he also sensed that his work would have been stimulated to even greater heights by the freedom inherent in a context more complex. The chord patterns of his day began to bore him; he said he knew every way they could be played. Many of his solos were so loaded—even overloaded—with musical complexities and razor-sharp subtleties that the implications of a more complex overall structural level seem incontrovertible. That he did not live to realize the implications of his own style is one of the tragedies of recent music history.

In this connection, there is another point that needs to be aired. It is very much in vogue these days for jazz musicians to "put down" the classical or "legit" way of playing. They scorn the playing of written music (and therefore also composing) and exalt improvisation beyond all reasonable justification.

This is a delicate subject since it touches the very core of a musician's personality, and his reasons for being a musician. The subject thus always arouses a defensive and subjective reaction—on either side. I think, however, certain *objective* facts can be stated regarding this controversy which may help set things right.

Many jazz musicians claim that the classical musician's playing lacks spontaneity, that it has become dulled by repetition and by the very act of reproducing music rather than by creating it. Only those musicians who have actually played in a first-rate symphony or opera orchestra under an inspired conductor can know to what height of collective spontaneity an orchestra can rise. After fifteen years of playing in such organizations, I can personally attest to this most positively. Admittedly it *is* rare, since it depends on many factors. But it does occur, and, I think, with more or less the same degree of frequency with which it occurs in jazz.

Listening to several sets on an average night by an average group at Birdland or at an all-night private session will bear this out. How often does a group *really* swing or *really* communicate at an artistic level? (After all, getting "knocked-out" by the beat of an average rhythm section is not yet communication at a very high level. I may respond to it—and I generally do—but that does not by itself make what I'm hearing great music.)

Moreover, is the batting average of a quartet playing *How High the Moon* for the umpteenth time any higher than a symphony orchestra doing its annual performance of the Beethoven *Eroica*? I humbly suggest that the average jazz musician is not in a position to answer that question since he has seldom, if ever, been to a symphony concert, and even more rarely has he caught one of those inspired performances. Furthermore, the Parkers, Gillespies, and Lester Youngs exist in the classical world too, only their names are Lipatti, Szigeti, and Gieseking, and *they are indeed just as rare*. Obviously, I do not mean musicians who can improvise like those first three, but soloists who are as highly trained and sensitive in their job of *spontaneously recreating* a masterpiece as those jazz-greats are in creation.

The illusion of spontaneous recreation is a factual possibility, as we all know from great acting performances in the theatre. At its highest level, it is an art as rare and as fine as improvisation at *its* highest level—no better, no worse; just different. If recreating another man's music authentically and illuminatingly were all that easy, then every jazz trumpet player could play the trumpet part from *The Rite of Spring*. Obviously what needs to be reiterated is that both ways of playing are highly specialized and require a different combination of skills.

Improvisation is the heart of jazz and I, for one, will always be happy to wait for that five percent which constitutes inspired improvising, but is the average jazz musician prepared to look for that five percent in classical music?

As for the purists who feel that the pieces under discussion here—and all those works that seem to be gravitating toward classical or composed music—do not qualify as jazz, one can only say that a music as vital and far-reaching as jazz will develop and deepen in an ever-widening circle of alternating penetration and absorption, of giving and taking.

Actually it matters little what this music is called; the important thing is that it is created and that it represents the thoughts and ways of life of its times. Let the academicians worry about what to label it. Seen in this light, the future of this music—jazz or not—is an exciting one. And a fascinating one, because exactly what shape this future will take will not become entirely clear until the next Charlie Parker arrives on the scene.

Notes

[Text: Schuller, "The Future of Form in Jazz," *Saturday Review*, 40 (12 January 1957): 62–68. Reprinted by permission of Gunther Schuller.]

DUKE ELLINGTON

(1 8 9 9 – 1 9 7 4)

In this short survey called "Jazz for Young People," Duke Ellington asserts that the history of the idiom is primarily a history of individuals—performers who developed the musical ideas of their forebears with such originality as to influence the next generation, forming an ever-evolving network of style. For this reason jazz cannot be any single phenomenon, instead, it is an intermingled composite of regional idioms and constantly evolving forms and practices. To learn about jazz, observers cannot rely on generalities or look for any single line of development. They must study the music of the individuals who have participated in its far-flung history.

The musicians named by Ellington as central to his own development are primarily ragtime pianists who worked in New York, including James P. Johnson, Luckey Roberts, and Willie "The Lion" Smith. In fact Ellington points to the East as one of the distinctive cradles of jazz in the early twentieth century, rejecting the idea that any single region, such as New Orleans, was its sole birthplace. The contribution of the East Coast musicians, he says, was found in their discipline and formal training.

Duke Ellington, one of the greatest composers of jazz and probably its most renowned individual figure, rarely wrote on music, although his ideas were often recorded through interviews. Toward the end of his life he put down his memoirs in a book titled *Music Is My Mistress*. In addition to autobiographical information, this collection provides a series of vignettes concerning the many jazz musicians whom he knew. He also includes the article that is reprinted here, which had originally appeared under the title "Listening to Jazz" in *Boy's Life* in May 1972.

Ellington's Writings: A Selective Bibliography

Music Is My Mistress. Garden City: Doubleday, 1973. Ellington's main literary work.

The Duke Ellington Reader. Edited by Mark Tucker. New York and Oxford: Oxford University Press, 1993. An anthology of 101 essays by and about Ellington. This is the most convenient source for Ellington's own short writings, which appeared in numerous European and American journals beginning in the 1930s. "The Duke Steps Out" (1931), "Duke Says Swing Is Stagnant" (1939), "Where Is Jazz Going" (1962), and "Reminiscing in Tempo" (1964) are especially recommended, although the editor of the volume cautions that Ellington may have collaborated with editors or other authors on some of them.

—⟋⟋⟍—

"JAZZ FOR YOUNG PEOPLE"
FROM *MUSIC IS MY MISTRESS*
(1972)

The story of jazz is a long list of great names, rather like those lists of kings and queens and presidents in history books. Divided up by instruments instead of countries, you can easily trace how the crown was passed down—and sometimes usurped. On trumpet, for example, the order might run something like this: Buddy Bolden, Joe Oliver, Louis Armstrong, Bix Beiderbecke, Cootie Williams, Roy Eldridge, Ray Nance, Dizzy Gillespie, Clark Terry, Clifford Brown, Miles Davis. . . . Similar sequences of highly influential musicians, each with popular imitators, can be made for all the other instruments.

To listen to jazz without any knowledge of its history is to miss much of its charm. The first "king" we have any knowledge of was Buddy Bolden, a powerful trumpet man who could be heard right across the Mississippi in New Orleans. When he was ready to begin playing in a dance hall or club, he would tune up, stick his trumpet out the window, and "call his children home."

There are many other colorful legends about the early days in New Orleans, where the name "jazz" was first given to a new kind of music around the turn of the century. It was an animated music with a strong African pulse beneath what often sounded like a caricature of a military band. Much of its development, in fact, came about through the playing of small Negro—or Black, if you prefer—bands in street parades, especially at Mardi Gras time, the instruments commonly in use being cornet (or trumpet), trombone, clarinet, bass, and drums. These bands were accompanied by what was known as the "second line," a group of supporters who danced attendance on them before, behind, and on the sidewalks alongside. Pomp and circumstance were not what these people wanted, and to increase their enjoyment musicians "ragged" or "jazzed up" the music, introducing humorous effects and improvising on the melodies. Sometimes, too, these bands would take part in funeral processions, and on the way to the cemetery they would play slow, solemn dirges, but coming back they would pick up the tempo and try to blow away sadness with lively versions of the same dirges and other familiar songs. Such customs still survive in New Orleans, and you can see how from the beginning there was a close relationship between jazz and dancing, or physical movement, and that is why the same musicians were soon in demand to play in dance halls.

Many fine musicians came out of New Orleans, some of the best and most famous being "King" Joe Oliver and his protégé, Louis Armstrong, both trumpet players; the clarinetists Sidney Bechet, Jimmie Noone, Johnny Dodds, Barney Bigard, and Omer Simeon; Kid Ory, the trombonist; Jelly Roll Morton, the pianist; Wellman Braud and Pops Foster, the bass players; and the drummers, Zutty Singleton, Paul Barbarin and Baby Dodds. Many of them, like Fate Marable, the bandleader and pianist, played on the Mississippi riverboats, and it was not long before they and their music started to influence other musicians in such cities as Memphis, St. Louis, Chicago, Kansas City, Los Angeles, Washington, D.C., Boston, and New York. Not all the New Orleans musicians, I must point out, were black. For example, the Original Dixieland Jazz Band, led by cornetist Nick La Rocca, was a white band and one of the first to introduce the New Orleans or Dixieland idiom to New York and Europe. But the maximum impact came when Louis Armstrong joined Joe Oliver in Chicago, a subject to which we will return.

Before ever it reached New Orleans, the original African element had made itself felt in the West Indies, and from there it branched off in two directions. In one case, it went to the Latin-American countries, where it picked up Spanish and Portuguese influences that resulted in a distinctive Afro-Latin music. The heritage of African drums survived strongly, and a more complex use of percussion instruments—conga drums, bongos, and timbales—is a striking characteristic of this music even today. African rhythms have always been considered the most sophisticated.

The African impulse was also influential on the East Coast of the United States, where a more disciplined music resulted because more of the musicians there had the benefit of formal schooling, and even conservatory training. This was in contrast with the experience of most of the early New Orleans musicians, who played by ear. They tended to emphasize the instruments of the brass band, whereas on the East Coast the string instruments, and particularly pianos, had a more significant place. As a young man in Washington, D.C., I was impressed by many fine local pianists, as well as by men like James P. Johnson and Luckey Roberts when they came visiting from New York. In those days, player pianos were extremely popular, and one of my major inspirations was a piano roll of "Carolina Shout" by Johnson. I also tried to copy the spectacular manner in which Luckey Roberts lifted his hands high above the keyboard as he played. Later, when I went to New York, I was enchanted by another pianist, Willie "The Lion" Smith, whose striking personality and individual style influenced me very much. My first real encounter with the New Orleans idiom came when I heard Sidney Bechet in my hometown, and I have never forgotten the power and imagination with which he played.

The different strains fused to form what was soon known throughout the world as jazz. The New Orleans men dominated the scene in Chicago during the '20s, and there they inspired such well-known white musicians as Bix Beiderbecke and Muggsy Spanier, both cornet players; the clarinetists Benny Goodman, Frank Teschemacher, and Mezz Mezzrow; Bud Freeman, the tenor saxophonist; and the drummers Dave Tough, George Wettling, and Gene Krupa. But a major development came when they and the East Coast musicians got together in New York. The "westerners," as we thought of them, brought their own favorite numbers like "King Porter Stomp," "Muskrat Ramble," "Tiger Rag," and "Sugar Foot Strut," and they also interpreted the blues with a sincere, earthy kind of feeling.

Now the blues are basic to all jazz, and although they are often thought of as sad, they are in fact performed with every variety of expression. Their relative simplicity has been a great factor in their lasting popularity. In its essential form, a blues consists of twelve bars divided into three sections of four bars each. When sung, the words of the first section are usually repeated in the second, while the third offers a wry comment on the first two, or completes their meaning. The words may deal with hard times, bad luck, disastrous floods, hunger, or—most often—unhappy love affairs, but there is usually an underlying vein of humor, optimism, or defiance in them. "I may be down," they say, "but I won't be down always." For a long time the blues existed in the minds, mouths, and fingers of those who performed them, and they were seldom written down until a trumpet player named W. C. Handy collected some of the most popular and published them under titles that became world-famous, such as *St. Louis Blues, Memphis Blues, Beale Street Blues,* and *Yellow Dog Blues.*

There have been many great blues performers. In the early days, some of the most influential were Ma Rainey, Blind Lemon Jefferson, Bessie Smith, Leroy Carr, Robert Johnson, and Big Bill Broonzy. Today you can hear the same tradition maintained by Muddy Waters, Memphis Slim, John Lee Hooker, B. B. King, Joe Turner, T-Bone Walker, and Eddie Vinson. The realism and simplicity in what they sing are qualities different from those found in popular, sentimental ballads. Oddly enough, the tribute paid them, and the use made of them, by British groups like the Rolling Stones and the Beatles was much responsible for a revival of interest in this country during the '60s.

The blues were worldly songs, but the gospel songs and spirituals of the Black churches were also an important element from the beginning, for the way they were sung, with soulfulness and great enthusiasm, made an unforgettable impression on most jazz musicians when they were young. If you compare records by Bessie Smith and the great gospel singer Mahalia Jackson, you will see that despite the difference in *what* they sang, there is a similarity in the *way* they sang, and that there is a joint relationship with early forms of jazz expression. The fervor and warmth of gospel music were often translated as directly as possible by jazz musicians, and for a long time the adjective "hot" was used in praise of their improvised solos and tonal qualities.

When the folky character of the blues, the fervor of the gospel songs, the rhythmic attack of the New Orleans musicians, and the more sophisticated approach of the East Coast players all came together in New York, jazz was provided with a new springboard. It was also transformed by the genius of Louis Armstrong, who influenced almost every trumpet player of his own and the following generations. He had tremendous gifts and a likable personality that won him friends everywhere. His imagination was matched by his technical ability, and he played high notes on his horn such as had not been heard before. And it was not only trumpet players who tried to imitate his phrasing, but trombonists, saxophonists, and clarinetists, too. In Chicago, he teamed up with a young man from Pittsburgh named Earl Hines, who developed an unusual style on the piano that was the counterpart of his trumpet playing. This piano style also became widely influential.

Before that, however, Armstrong had been to New York to play with Fletcher Henderson, who had one of the best dance bands of the period. It was bigger than the usual New Orleans group, and because it had more instruments written arrangements were necessary. There were three trumpets, a trombone, and three saxophones, and it was not possible for all these men to memorize or merely improvise their different parts as was done in New Orleans. So Henderson and his chief arranger, Don Redman, both schooled musicians, *wrote* the music for the band to play, leaving gaps or choruses for improvisation. The rhythmic effect created by Armstrong in his solo choruses was stirring—an extra lift above and beyond the basic beat—and this sort of thing was what became known as "swinging." Soon the whole band caught on to his way of phrasing and began to swing together. In 1932, I wrote a song which became quite famous as the expression of a sentiment which prevailed among jazz musicians at that time. It was called *It Don't Mean a Thing If It Ain't Got That Swing.*

Henderson's, more than any other, was the band that introduced what became known as the "swing era." When I first formed a big band in New York, his was the one I wanted mine to sound like. In those days, before electrical amplification, big bands were essential in big ballrooms, and singers had to use megaphones. Ballrooms were very important in the jazz story, and so was the inspiration we derived from the people who danced in them, but not all the bands who worked in them played jazz in the strictest sense of the word. Generally speaking, the Black bands led the way, and besides Henderson's there were soon many others that were popular, such as McKinney's Cotton Pickers, Chick Webb's, Charlie Johnson's, Don Redman's, Earl Hines's, Luis Russell's, Bennie Moten's, Claude Hopkins's, Alphonso Trent's, Zack Whyte's, Jimmie Lunceford's, and ours. Among the first white bands to get the message were Jean Goldkette's, Ben Pollack's, Paul Tremaine's, and the Casa Loma Orchestra.

As bands of this kind grew in popularity, demands for their services increased. Paul Whiteman, who was credited with having "made a lady out of jazz," hired the best musicians he could get from all over the country and played what was called "symphonic" jazz. This music was more elaborate and designed for concert performance. In vaudeville theatres and the bigger nightclubs, bands were also required to play music that was more complex, colorful, and showy than was normally required in dance halls. This was the case at Connie's Inn in New York where Don Redman played, and at the Cotton Club where we played, and at the Grand Terrace in Chicago where Earl Hines played. During one period at the Cotton Club, much attention was paid to acts with an African setting, and to accompany these we developed what was termed "jungle style" jazz. (As a student of Negro history I had, in any case, a natural inclination in this direction.) Its most striking characteristic was the use of mutes—often the plumber's everyday rubber plunger—by Bubber Miley on trumpet and Joe "Tricky Sam" Nanton on trombone. They founded a tradition we have maintained ever since. This kind of theatrical experience, and the demands it made upon us, was both educative and enriching, and it brought about a further broadening of the music's scope. We, too, began to think in terms of concert and theatre, and when I went to Europe for the first time in 1933 1 found I was expected to give a concert in one of the largest cinemas in the world, before an audience almost entirely composed of musicians!

Big bands continued to grow in public favor through the '30s, until at the height of the swing era theirs was the most popular form of music in the country. Besides those I mentioned earlier, Count Basie had formed a band in Kansas City that exerted a great influence with its uncompromising emphasis on swinging. There were now also white bands led by such talented instrumentalists as Tommy and Jimmy Dorsey, and the clarinetists Benny Goodman, Artie Shaw, and Woody Herman. Goodman, using Fletcher Henderson's arrangements and playing an exciting clarinet style, was the most successful of all. Out of all these bands, too, rose famous singers like Ella Fitzgerald, Billie Holiday, Sarah Vaughan, Peggy Lee, Frank Sinatra, Billy Eckstine, and Jimmy Rushing.

The foundation of jazz as we know it today had by now been thoroughly laid. What was built upon it was the work of great innovators. I must emphasize that jazz was and is a highly competitive form of music, and many of the ideas that transformed it were first heard in what were called "cutting contests" or "jam sessions," where the musicians tried to learn from and outdo one another. The rise of the big bands did not mean the end of small groups, for they were always to be heard in the smaller clubs and in those places where musicians played "after hours," very late at night. There you might find James P. Johnson, Fats Waller, and The Lion competing with one another. Or several trumpet players, or saxophonists, or clarinetists. Ideas were exchanged, and newcomers learned from those with more experience. Certain innovators, like the great virtuoso of the piano, Art Tatum, remained virtually inimitable, but they were a constant source of inspiration.

By this time, jazz had become very much identified with the saxophone, and jazz musicians found new ways to express themselves on it. Out of Fletcher Henderson's band came Coleman Hawkins, whose big tone on the tenor saxophone remained the model for the profession until Lester Young appeared with Count Basie's band during 1936. Young's approach and spare tone were quite different, and they were copied by, among many others, Stan Getz, who later did so much to popularize *bossa nova*, a Brazilian form which set "cool" jazz to samba rhythm. Years later, John Coltrane came to the fore in turn with a searching style that was all his own. On alto saxophone, similarly, there was Johnny Hodges, who played in our band and was widely imitated until Charlie Parker came along with his bop style in the '40s.

Bop was regarded by many people as a revolution against the values of the previous era. At first hearing, it sounded very difficult and complicated. Parker and Dizzy Gillespie, the trumpet player, seemed to be playing many notes very fast, and the drummer and pianist accompanying them were no longer content with providing a steady, regular beat. Because of the speed of execution, the old tonal values were sacrificed (it was no longer possible to play with the former expressive vibrato), and the new music had a shrill, cooler sound. Soon it was fashionable to play "cool" rather than "hot."

Since that time there have been new category labels for several different varieties of jazz, but each has primarily been created and dominated by the distinct tonal personality of a gifted individual. The fascination of jazz as a music lies in the performer's freedom of expression, so that the listener is always asking himself, "Where do we go from here?"

Although his background seemed to give the black musician the edge, because environment is intensely important as a shaping factor, jazz was so contagious that many white musicians were infected by it and grew close to the black soul. Names that come to mind are Bunny Berigan, Jack Teagarden, Dave Tough, Jess Stacy, Nat Pierce, and Mezz Mezzrow. On the other hand, there were black musicians who were impressed by white standards of playing, acquired comparable techniques, and retired from the competitive arena into the comparative safety of the television, movie, and recording studios.

Today, jazz is an international music that is played everywhere in the world on almost every conceivable instrument. It is a music of such extraordinary variety that it is most consistently recognizable by its rhythmic vitality. But just imagine the dilemma you could find yourself in with a creature newly arrived from outer space.

"Young man," he asks, "will you please let me hear some jazz?"

"I'll be glad to, sir," you say hospitably, turning to your record player. "Listen to these."

Now what or whose music would you play? That of Louis Armstrong, King Oliver, Dizzy Gillespie, Miles Davis, Jack Teagarden, J. J. Johnson, The Lion, Earl Hines, Art Tatum, Dave Brubeck, Bill Evans, Johnny Hodges, Char!ie Parker, Ornette Coleman, Coleman Hawkins, Lester Young, John Coltrane, Sidney Bechet, Buster Bailey, Benny Goodman, Charlie Christian, Django Reinhardt, Kenny Burrell, Fletcher Henderson, Count Basie, Stan Kenton, Buddy Rich, Woody Herman, the Modern Jazz Quartet, or . . . ?

As I said at the beginning, the story of jazz is a long list of great names. In its different phases, different instruments have enjoyed a vogue with the public—piano, trumpet, clarinet, tenor saxophone, flute, organ, and guitar have all had their day in the sun, and drums and drum solos are *always* popular. Or if you choose to examine jazz state by state, or city by city, you will find that great musicians were born in all of them. For example, W. C. Handy, Nat Cole, Dinah Washington, Cootie Williams, Urbie Green, Dud and Paul Bascomb, Erskine Hawkins, Teddy Hill, and Avery Parrish all came from Alabama. Texas, that big state, gave us Lips Page, Tyree Glenn, Teddy Wilson, Buddy Tate, Herschel Evans, Sammy Price, Budd and Keg Johnson, Arnett Cobb, Ornette Coleman, Ray McKinley, Harold Land, Eddie Vinson, Herb Ellis, T-Bone Walker, Jack and Charlie Teagarden, and so many more.

St. Louis is a city that should be famous for more than the blues, because so many fine musicians came from there, such as Jimmy Blanton, Wendell Marshall, Clark Terry, Shorty Baker, Louis Metcalf, Milt and Ted Buckner, Gene Sedric, Pee Wee Russell, and the arrangers Oliver Nelson and Ernie Wilkins.

New Orleans, Chicago, New York, and—this may surprise you—Philadelphia would need separate pages here to list all the famous musicians they have given the world. So would countries like England and France.

The Jersey Crescent is an unusual and outstanding territory for our kind of music. For example: Willie "The Lion" Smith made his professional debut in Newark; Sarah Vaughan, the Divine One, was born in the same city; Count Basie is from Red Bank; Sonny Greer, the Sweet Singing Drummer, is from Long Branch; James P. Johnson was born in New Brunswick; Donald Lambert, The Lamb, was from

Princeton; Sam Woodyard is from Elizabeth; Slam Stewart is from Englewood; Cozy Cole is from East Orange; Joya Sherrill is from Bayonne; Buddy De Franco and Butch Ballard are from Camden; Charlie Persip, Tony Scott, and Bobby Tucker are all three from Morristown; Nelson Riddle is from Oradell; Bill Evans is from Plainfield; Joe Benjamin and Chris Columbus are from Atlantic City; and in the wake of the same romantic soul wave, Newark gave us Ike Quebec, Wayne Shorter, Babs Gonzales, Bobby Plater, Al Haig, and so many more. When Billy Strayhorn joined us, it was at the Adams Theatre in Newark!

Our concert with Henry Lewis, the great conductor of symphony and opera, and the New Jersey State Symphony, was one of my truly enchanting musical adventures. I remember, too, that New Jersey has big supporters like Bill Cook and Bill Franklin, patrons like Rose Stewart and the Fourteen Pals and Patrons, and that Mayor Kenneth Gibson of Newark acclaims both the music and us, the purveyors.

And I remember further back, to the old days in Harlem, and how, just when you were getting acclimatized and feeling yourself more or less acceptable and equal to exposure before the low, hip circle, one of the older Big Boys on the corner would explode your illusions. "Gather round, kids," he would say, lowering the hipper boom, "and let me tell you what time it is!" Then he would relate a spicy little inside episode on how it used to be across the Hudson River, in Newark.

Newark remains today a sort of peripheral spread for the Jersey Crescent, which contains the homes and springboards of so many great musicians. And don't ever forget that Francis Albert Sinatra is from Hoboken! In fact, I wonder how the greatest metropolis in the world would manage, or what it would do, without the splendid auto roads and turnpike in New Jersey to serve as a red carpet entrance way.

Notes

[Text: Ellington, "Jazz for Young People," 415–23 in *Music Is My Mistress* (Garden City: Doubleday, 1973). © 1973 by Duke Ellington, Inc. Used by permission of Doubleday, a division of Bantam Doubleday Dell Publishing Group, Inc.]

INDEX